Capitalists in Spite of Themselves

Capitalists in Spite of Themselves

*Elite Conflict and Economic Transitions
in Early Modern Europe*

RICHARD LACHMANN

New York   Oxford

Oxford University Press

2000

Oxford University Press

Oxford   New York
Athens   Auckland   Bangkok   Bogotá   Buenos Aires   Calcutta
Cape Town   Chennai   Dar es Salaam   Delhi   Florence   Hong Kong   Istanbul
Karachi   Kuala Lumpur   Madrid   Melbourne   Mexico City   Mumbai
Nairobi   Paris   São Paulo   Singapore   Taipei   Tokyo   Toronto   Warsaw

and associated companies in
Berlin   Ibadan

Published by Oxford University Press, Inc.
198 Madison Avenue, New York, New York 10016

Oxford is a registered trademark of Oxford University Press.

Library of Congress Cataloging-in-Publication Data
Lachmann, Richard.
   Capitalists in spite of themselves : elite conflict and economic
transitions in early modern Europe / Richard Lachmann.
      p.   cm.
   Includes bibliographical references and index.
   ISBN 0–19–507568–4
     1. Capitalism—Europe—History.   2. Europe—Economic conditions.
3. Elite (Social sciences)—Europe—History.   4. Social conflict—
Europe—History.   I. Title.
HC240.L253   1999
330.12'2'094—DC21   98–37405

9 8 7 6 5 4 3 2 1
Printed in the United States of America
on acid-free paper

To my mother,

LOTTE BECKER LACHMANN,

and the memory of my father,

KARL EDUARD LACHMANN

Acknowledgments

THIS BOOK HAS BEEN A LONG TIME in preparation. Over the years, many teachers, colleagues, and students provided assistance and advice in a variety of ways. Well before I made specific plans for this book I was given direction and guidance in thinking about historical sociology in general, and the development of capitalism in early modern Europe in particular, by my teachers at Princeton and Harvard, Gilbert Rozman, Marion Levy Jr., Theda Skocpol, Harrison White, John Padgett, George Homans, Ron Breiger, and Gosta Esping-Anderson. Theda Skocpol, John Padgett, and especially Harrison White have continued to offer advice and incisive readings of my work even after they and I left Harvard.

Colleagues at the University of Wisconsin at Madison and the State University of New York at Albany provided useful comments on chapter drafts or earlier, article-length versions of my arguments. At Madison, Erik Olin Wright, Ivan Szelenyi, Gerald Marwell, Ron Aminzade, Pam Oliver, Ann Orloff, Wolfgang Streck, and Roberto Franzosi combined friendship and advice and so provided relief from the narrow sociological orthodoxy of Wisconsin. At Albany, Steven Seidman, John Logan, and Ron Jacobs made suggestions that have guided me in revisions of various chapters in this book.

Students at Wisconsin and Albany have provided suitably critical audiences for the histories and theories I advanced in colloquia and seminars. Their questions and objections prodded me to rethink and rewrite. I want to give special acknowledgment to two wonderful graduate assistants. Stephen Petterson spent a year researching Renaissance Florence and helped me write the first draft of Chapter Three. While the final version is quite distant from what Steve and I wrote back then, his work provided a cornerstone for my subsequent thinking and writing about Italian city-states. Julia Adams co-authored an article, "Absolutism's Antinomies," which focused my thinking on the development of the ancien régime French state. Julia also helped me begin my research on the Netherlands; her own work on that country has guided my thinking. Julia commented on several chapters and has been a great friend over two decades.

I have never been shy about asking for advice, although I often have been stubborn about following it. Therefore, I must take full responsibility for any errors and shortcomings in this book, despite the advice of so many distinguished scholars. I want to thank the following historians and sociologists, whom I met in various venues or who generously responded to my written requests, for their helpful bibliographic and critical comments: Charles Tilly, Immanuel Wallerstein, Michael Mann, Eric Hobsbawm, Robert Brenner, Dominique Julia, Michel Vovelle, William Beik, David Parker, James B. Collins, Domenico Sella, Michael Kimmel, Edgar Kiser, Rebecca Jean Emigh, Mark Gould, Greg Hooks, Mary Fulbrook, and Rosemary Hopcroft.

An earlier version of part of the introductory chapter was previously published as "Class Formation without Class Struggle," in *American Sociological Review* 55 (1990): 398–414. Portions of chapter 4 previously appeared in my articles "Elite Conflict and State Formation in 16th- and 17th-Century England and France," *American Sociological Review* 54 (1989): 141–62, and, co-authored by Julia Adams, "Absolutism's Antinomies: Class Formation, State Fiscal Structures, and the Origins of the French Revolution," *Political Power and Social Theory* 7 (1988): 135–75. A few pages of chapter 6 are drawn from my previous book, *From Manor to Market: Structural Change in England, 1536–1640* (Madison: University of Wisconsin Press, 1987). A part of chapter 7 was previously published as "State, Church, and the Distablishment of Magic," in *The Production of English Renaissance Culture*, edited by David Lee Miller et al. (Ithaca: Cornell University Press, 1994).

My wife, Lyn Miller-Lachmann, came to my aid whenever I encountered computer disasters. Her confidence that I would actually finish this book sustained me. My children, Derrick and Madeleine, diverted my attention and slowed my progress, for which I am grateful. Finally, my late father, Karl Eduard Lachmann, and my mother, Lotte Becker Lachmann, fostered my intellectual development in more ways than I can recount. I dedicate this book to them.

Albany, New York
August 1998   R. L.

Contents

Capitalists in Spite of Themselves

I

Something Happened

SOMETHING HAPPENED IN WESTERN EUROPE in the fifteenth through eighteenth centuries. Sociology's founders believed the task for their discipline
was to define that something and to explain why it happened when and where it did.
Karl Marx, Max Weber, and Emile Durkheim each dedicated their intellectual lives
to that project. Over the past century sociologists and scholars in related fields have
differed, and have defined themselves, in their identification of the salient features of
the European transformation.[1]

Europeans changed intellectually and spiritually, as well as in the material conditions of their lives. First from within Roman Catholicism, then as Protestants, a
growing corps of thinkers developed new understandings of the natural world and of
the human body and mind as well. New knowledge first appeared in the guise of the
rediscovery of old classics. The Renaissance began with republications and com-
mentaries on Greek and Latin manuscripts that had been "lost" in monastic and aristocratic libraries. The intellectual awakening in Christian Europe also drew upon the
robust libraries and scholarly communities of the interwoven Muslim and Jewish
societies in the Middle East, northern Africa, and Spain.

The pace of intellectual discovery quickened as the invention of printing with
moveable type allowed individuals and institutional libraries to accumulate works
by both classical and contemporary authors. "The advent of printing completely transformed the conditions under which texts were produced, distributed and consumed.
. . . It arrested textual corruption, fixed texts more permanently, and enabled them to
accumulate at an accelerated rate. It made possible new forms of cross-cultural inter-
change and systematic large-scale data collection" (Eisenstein 1969, p. 24).

Discoveries, in part spurred by rereadings of classical texts, ranged from the profound to the mundane. Copernicus, Kepler, and Galileo transformed European conceptions of the heavenly bodies. Their systematic observations of the night sky led
them to formulate a heliocentric model of the solar system in place of the church-
approved geocentric model. Significantly, Copernicus, who sent his findings in let-
ters and manuscripts to a select audience, was tolerated and even encouraged by the

high clerics with whom he corresponded. Galileo evoked the wrath of the church when he published theories similar to those of Copernicus in books available to all buyers (Mandrou 1979, pp. 32–40).

Most books addressed less lofty subjects. A great wave of agricultural innovation began in the fifteenth century. Farmers developed improved seed stocks, new crops, and more efficient rotations and invented irrigation and drainage techniques. Each innovation became widely known, within decades of its successful implementation, to readers of pamphlets and popular journals published in various languages throughout Western Europe. Then, as now, pornography became the "killer app" of the new technology. A plurality of books dealt with pornographic subjects. Yet, pornographic works also addressed—sometimes directly, sometimes obliquely—political controversies. Philosophes challenged royal, aristocratic, and clerical privileges directly with intellectual and sociological arguments; pornographers undermined social order with ridicule and through repeated fantasies of alternative elective affinities.[2] More and more people were able to read the newly plentiful books, newspapers, and periodicals. Literacy increased from under a tenth of the medieval population to more than a third of the adults in seventeenth-century England and the Netherlands, and perhaps a quarter in seventeenth-century France.

Literary, philosophical, religious, scientific, and political treatises combined to subvert acceptance of the prevailing social order. The possibility of progress made existing social relations seem like fetters. Carlo Ginzberg (1976) traces the transmutation, in literary and popular writings, of the medieval clerical maxim "Do not seek to know high things" into the Dutch Calvinist motto "Dare to be wise." The medieval church sought to prevent common folk from trying to analyze God's creation and his plans for the afterworld. Clerics and lay officials combined to condemn efforts to understand or to question the social order created by kings and aristocrats. Religious skepticism and political dissent developed in conjunction with scientific and technological inquiry.

Europeans daringly strove to know high things in various realms. The development of perspective in painting in the fourteenth century gave artists and viewers the sense that they were seeing a deeper and truer reality than ever before. "Viewers [of such paintings] were suddenly confronted with a completely plausible image of the mystic Terrestrial Paradise, where they could physically sense God's primal light, breathe in his heavenly atmosphere, and touch the Font of the Four Rivers in which our First Parents bathed" (Edgerton 1985, p. 21). Human bodies were painted with realism and detail. (Painters were aided by new and more accurate anatomical textbooks, drawn by physicians who autopsied bodies in contravention of church doctrine.) Viewers gained a new respect for each person's humanity that appeared to be derived from divine form, although artists' and viewers' images of God, Jesus, and angels of course were based on knowledge of the human body. Some artists began to incorporate Galileo's discoveries in their paintings, depicting the shooting stars and craters on the moon that they had read about in Galileo's teatises or in church denunciations of the astronomer (Reeves 1997).

Some Europeans expressed their skepticism toward church institutions by seeking to harness natural and supernatural forces themselves. Magic, astrology, and alchemy all flourished during the Renaissance, and especially in the post-Reformation era. "The magical desire for power had created an intellectual environment favourable to experiment and induction; it marked a break with the characteristic medieval attitude of contemplative resignation" (Thomas 1971, p. 643).

Openness toward experimentation spread from magic to science. Newton maintained a lifelong interest in alchemy even as he developed his theory of gravity and became, simultaneously with Leibniz, the discoverer of calculus. New, precise scientific instruments and scientific societies provided the means for carrying out and disseminating the results of experiments in physics, chemistry, and physiology. Natural species and the systems of the human body were identified and classified. Most significantly, the seventeenth century was the era in which the foundations of modern mathematics were laid down. In addition to calculus, analytic geometry was formalized by Descartes and Fermat. Fermat and Pascal established the theories of probability. These mathematical discoveries added to Europeans' senses that the universe operated under laws discoverable and calculable by humankind.

Public health improvements virtually eliminated the incidence of plague in England by the late seventeenth century. Similar improvements were achieved elsewhere in northwestern Europe in the eighteenth century. But while public health reduced the incidence of disease, once people got sick physicians were of virtually no help. Progress in medicine was minimal until the end of the eighteenth century in large part because physicians sustained their belief in the Galenic theory of humors throughout the early modern period. The first vaccine, for smallpox, was developed in 1796.

The doubling of agricultural productivity in much of Western Europe between the thirteenth and eighteenth centuries and the introductions of new foodstuffs did reduce hunger, famine, and the diseases and death that followed in their wake. Life expectancy, however, remained low and infant mortality hardly declined at all until the nineteenth century. In England in 1541, life expectancy at birth was slightly under thirty-four years. In 1696, it had risen by less than five months to slightly above thirty-four years. Life expectancy rose above forty years only in the 1830s. (Wrigley and Schofield 1981, pp. 528–29). Life spans were equally short in ancien régime France and in the rest of Europe as well (Dupaquier 1979).

Agricultural and public health innovations were accompanied by advances in engineering, manufacture, the military hardware of death, and shipbuilding and navigation. New fire-fighting techniques reduced the dangers of death and destruction from massive fires in the seventeenth and eighteenth centuries. When European city dwellers watched fire brigades with wagons and hoses battle fires, they gained a sense that social forces could control the natural world, just as in earlier centuries church appeals for charity toward victims of fire reminded laymen of the fragility of their lives and homes and of the power of arbitrary fate (Thomas 1971, pp. 647–56).

European bronze guns first matched, and then by the late fifteenth century exceeded, the firepower of the Chinese guns from which they were adapted. With the development of iron guns in the sixteenth century, European armies and navies could deploy unprecedentedly powerful artillery. The new guns transformed continental warfare. The military advantage shifted from nobles holed up in fortified castles to states with the resources to field armies and to provision them with the artillery that could batter nobles and their fortresses into submission.

Rapid advances in shipbuilding techniques in the late Middle Ages and the development of full-rigging in the fifteenth century allowed Europeans to take their new arms to Asia, Africa, and the Americas for conquest and then to transport home the fruits of military and commercial domination. "The gunned ship developed by Atlantic Europe in the course of the fourteenth and fifteenth centuries was the contrivance that made possible the European saga. . . . When the sailing vessels of Atlantic Europe arrived, hardly anything could resist them" (Cippola 1965, p. 137).

European minds were stretched by the mere consciousness of new worlds populated by peoples of different customs and colors. Travelers drew ever more accurate and detailed maps and their accounts of journeys to other continents were printed in a myriad books and newspapers. European purses were stretched by the spices, foodstuffs, treasure, and manufacturers brought home from all parts of the world. Vast new fortunes were made by explorers, colonizers, and merchants in Asia, Africa, and the Americas.

Greater agricultural output allowed a large fraction of the population to engage in nonfarm occupations, while wealth from trade sustained urban workers in new and expanding occupations. The urban population of Europe almost quadrupled between 1500 and 1800, while the percentage of Europeans living in cities doubled from 5 percent to 10 percent. In 1800, England, the Netherlands, and Belgium each had more than a fifth of their populations living in cities.

European cities were transformed from the isolated islands of the medieval era into regional, national, and eventually international centers of commerce and government. The largest European cities in the fourteenth and fifteenth centuries were commercial entrepôts; those cities served as intermediaries between the vastly richer and more sophisticated centers of the Middle East and Asia and the rural aristocracies, provincial cities, and clergies of medieval Europe. The great cities of the sixteenth and later centuries were administrative as well as commercial centers. Urbanites were transformed from glorified haberdashers into the rulers of large territorial states. With the European conquest of the Americas, and much of Asia and Africa, city dwellers handled and profited from the surpluses extracted from peasants, laborers, and slaves on every continent inhabited by humans.

European cities became centers of a mass consumer culture. In a precursor to the mass production of the Industrial Revolution, urban workshops and networks of rural home producers created standardized nonluxury goods intended for a broad, middle-class market. English and Dutch commercial farmers, tradesmen, and professionals formed the first mass rural market for manufactured goods. The number and range of manufactured products found in urban and rural homes grew enormously in the seventeenth and eighteenth centuries, creating a taste for the vaster profusion of goods that working- as well as middle-class consumers would purchase in the nineteenth and twentieth centuries.

The wealth from international and internal domination and from rising agricultural productivity in the European core was invested in the institutions that still mark the modern world: states and firms. Tribute and taxes financed states, and commercial profits were invested in state offices and debts. State officials used the resources under their command to increase the number of people and the extent of territory under their control. Europe, which in 1490 was "divided into something like 500 states, would-be states, statelets, and statelike organizations," was by 1990 "divided into a mere 25 to 28 states" (Tilly 1990, pp. 42–43). At the same time, state officials collectively appropriated a growing share of their subjects' wealth and presumed to regulate their subjects' behavior ever more closely.

State officials and clerics vied with one another to impose uniform standards of action and belief upon their subjects. First the Reformation and Counter-Reformation sought to stamp out unofficial and local religious practices that could pose challenges to the orthodoxies of each. European churches had always demanded formal allegiance, regular attendance, and monetary payments. After the Reformation, Catholic and Protestant churches became increasing ambitious and adept at monitoring the beliefs of their parishioners and at policing laymen's behaviors outside of religious services.

Lay officials also made more extensive and intrusive claims upon the minds and bodies of their subjects.[3] Aristocrats were induced by kings to compete for state offices and honors. Localized customs and particularistic legal systems were gradually subordinated to provincial and then national judicial bodies. Kings knocked down noble castles and disbanded magnate armies. (Medieval city-states had done the same to the urban fortresses of aristocratic clans.) Dueling was suppressed. Knights were integrated into armies that adopted new technologies and modes of discipline that made it impossible for noblemen to sustain feudal chivalry and fighting techniques.

Antiaristocratic offensives on the part of city-state and royal governments were paralleled by popular challenges to elite rule. Old and new systems of domination were challenged by experiments in self-government. Renaissance philosophers began to propose new constitutions. City-states in Italy and in the German Hanse broke free from reigning sovereigns and attempted self-rule with governments elected through limited franchises. Those cities offered a direct and powerful challenge to the divine right of kings, however narrow the voting populace.

The English Revolution took the challenge to monarchy, aristocracy, and clergy to new heights. For eleven years, a major European nation was governed by an elected Parliament and by a popular army with elected officers. During part of that period, radical groups that proposed to abolish private property and that argued that each man could face God on his own without clerical intermediaries commanded wide followings and vied to shape English society.

Popular rebellions inspired governments to devise new methods for controlling common citizens. In supposedly decentralized England, Poor Laws regulated the residence and work lives of a large fraction of the citizenry. Instances of premarital sex and illegitimacy were detected and punished. The French created a national police force during the last century of the ancien régime. That innovation was copied by other continental monarchies. Police created networks of informers, tracked subjects in vast files, and enjoyed significant successes in uncovering and punishing religious and political dissent.

State and clerical pretensions depended on systems for policing subjects scattered over wide territories. While we cannot describe police and other agencies as bureaucratic, the new networks of often venal and patrimonial officials were effective enough to make subjects hear and respond to, if not accept, central ideologies. Coordination was aided by developing transportation systems. Newly built roads and canals eased travel over short and long distances. Public and private shipping networks made the transportation of people, goods, and news cheaper and faster. These infrastructural and organizational improvements were instituted first in the Netherlands and England during the seventeenth century, and in parts of France in the following decades.

Advances in knowledge and in the projection and organization of power coincided with the advent of capitalism. Manorial lands, immobilized by the overlapping use and income rights of peasant cultivators, aristocrats, clergies, and monarchs, became private property that could be improved and used according to the calculus of a single investor. As land was freed of peasant rights, peasants were proletarianized. A majority of English peasants lost their farms and became wage laborers in the sixteenth and seventeenth centuries. More than three-quarters of French farm families became dependent upon wage labor for their subsistence by 1700.

Grain yields doubled in most of northwestern Europe in the three centuries following the Reformation. The quality of agricultural produce increased as well, with manifold increases in the output of meat, wine, dairy products, vegetables and fruits, and crops with industrial uses. Peasants, regardless of their land-tenure arrangements, and laborers ended up with none of the increased wealth their agricultural work yielded from the land. Indeed, agricultural and industrial wages declined or stagnated throughout those three centuries. Consumers also did not benefit since food prices rose during those centuries as well.

Landowners and, in France, government officials made off with all the benefits of increased agricultural productivity. Landowners benefited as well from the conversion of medieval use rights into private property, which generated a greater income stream than had seigneurial and clerical dues, and which could be sold or used as collateral for other investments. While much of the income and assets that accumulated in landowners' and officeholders' hands was wasted on conspicuous consumption or European warfare, a significant share was invested productively. Land was improved. Rural and urban industries, albeit on a small scale, were organized. Some tax revenues were invested in domestic infrastructures, mainly roads and canals. State military forces were employed in conquering foreign colonies and trade routes, which had perhaps the most significant effect on later capitalist development of any state activity.

England, the Netherlands, part of France, and isolated places elsewhere in eighteenth-century Western Europe were capitalist by any definition of that term. All the conditions necessary for the Industrial Revolution, which began in England at the end of the eighteenth century, after the period covered in this book, were present. Land and other forces of production were held as private property. Most laborers were proletarianized. States guaranteed property rights, regulated labor and markets, and sought to secure foreign trading privileges for favored citizens and firms.

Many things, then, happened in Europe between the fifteenth and eighteenth centuries. The intellectual, political, and economic developments that transformed Europe in those centuries have been described in rich detail by numerous historians. There is no need for yet another descriptive book on the "origins of the modern world." The causes of those changes, however, still are a subject of debate.

Many scholars think of causality in terms of a master process that, as it developed, transformed the rest of society. Since there is no consensus over which cause deserves priority, much of the debate consists of assertions shouted past one another:

All these changes were a Renaissance, an intellectual awakening from the deep sleep of the Dark Ages. Medieval society was transformed because a new class gained control of economic and political resources and used them to further its interests. The modern world was formed by the Weberian rise of rational action in an array of spheres—economic (capitalism), political (bureaucratic states), scientific and medical (the experimental method)—and in the systematic development and theorization of knowledge in the arts, theology, and history. The changes were primarily increases in the demographic or political scale of societies that then created a critical mass that transformed the qualities of social relations. Class conflict tore apart the fetters of feudal society, freeing capitalists to create new forms of domination. The rise of a world system was the master transformation that then stuck the peoples of the world into positions that determined their political and economic experiences.

Scholars offer another array of theories when they seek to identify the motivations that led early modern Europeans to transform their social worlds.[4] For Weber, the unprecedented practice of rational action in sixteenth-century Europe derived from arational fears provoked by new Protestant conceptions of God and salvation. Modernization theory sees the competition for material goods, scientific achievement, national power and prestige, and bureaucratic office (perhaps motivated by a vulgarized notion of the Protestant ethic or stemming from a desire to keep up with the ever more modern Joneses) as propelling any and all historical developments. Other strains of historical sociology concentrate their attentions on the motivations of particular groups of actors, seeing those as the master causal forces of historical change. Thus, scholars of state formation see self-interested state elites employing technological advances (especially in the military realm) and overcoming impediments to bureaucratic development to center resources and authority within nation-states. Self-described "rational choice" theorists see states, other organizations, and especially capitalist markets as the fulfillment of self-interested individuals who have learned how to maximize their desired ends. Some Marxists see capitalists' pursuit of surplus value as the engine of social transformation.

If social change is to be explained in terms of motivation, then it becomes necessary either to show how and why the motivation arose just before the transformation of social action or to demonstrate how effective action once was blocked and then became unblocked, allowing the motivation to affect social reality. Weber adopts the former approach, using the Protestant Reformation as the causal switch that sent human behavior down the track of rational action. Thus, his model of capitalist origins has logical coherence, even though it is at odds with the historical evidence. The other models take the latter course, pointing to impediments to state formation, rational action, or capitalist social relations as the reason eternal human desires for power, prestige, material plenty, or mastery over nature did not yield nation-states and capitalist markets before the sixteenth century.

I have written this book because I found the descriptions of those impediments to action and the analyses of how they were overcome unconvincing. They lack the specificity to explain differences across and within the countries of Europe and often merely assert that impediments were removed without identifying the actors or processes that accomplished such social changes. The true bases of historical comparison are obscured when scholars assume that all Protestants shared a single understanding of the path to salvation, that the "bourgeois" victors of feudal conflicts pursued the same capitalist interests, or that the various inhabitants of "state" organizations sought to aggrandize a common interest.

I follow much recent work among sociologists, economists, and others and assume that individuals are rational and that when they combine with other similarly interested individuals and act within organizations or markets as elites and classes that they collectively retain a rational orientation. As I hope to demonstrate, the Reformation did not usher in an era of rational action. Medieval Europeans were rational as well.

Assuming or showing rationality on the part of historical agents does not explain much. Opportunities for effective action were rare in the times and places under study here. Most of the time, historical actors could have reached the same decisions and achieved the same ends had they merely followed custom rather than engaging in rational calculation. Rarely and briefly, opportunities for changing one's situation for the better emerged. Rational action was essential to taking advantage of those opportunities, and historical actors in those circumstances invariably were rational enough to seize the day.

Once rational actors saw their opportunities and took them, they set in train series of consequences that could not have been foreseen. Thus, the ultimate effects of rational actions were as often to the detriment of their instigators as to their benefit. Such differences of outcomes never can be explained by differences in degrees of rationality; they are explained instead by the specific structural contexts within which rational actors effect history. As I demonstrate these assertions in this book, I highlight the limits of rational choice theory as an explanation for differences in social relations and action across time and place.

We must begin by asking: Who in medieval Europe was able to act in new ways? Then we can take the next analytic steps and ask: How did those medieval Europeans act to transform the overall structure of social relations, and how were new possibilities for action opened by those transformations? This book, then, is concerned with identifying and explaining chains of cause and effect. Instead of a master lever of change or an essentialist unfolding of a state system or of capitalism, we find a highly contingent development of various polities and economies. While people were agents of change, they did not intend to create the social arrangements that emerged. Medieval social actors sought to sustain or improve their positions. Individuals and groups effected change to solve their own problems that they defined within the actually existing contexts of their medieval and early modern societies. All long-term changes were inadvertent. As I show in this book, the agents of change were capitalists in spite of themselves.

Elites and Classes as Agents of History

Not all people are equally able to effect change. Most people in most times are located at points within the social structure where they cannot fundamentally challenge their relations to other social actors. Structural change can be predicted and analyzed only by locating the agents of change in relation to other actors who, however indirectly or inadvertently, create a strategic opening by their own actions within the same total structural setting. Our task is to identify the chains of causality through which actors in one location transformed social structure in ways that created further strategic opportunities for other actors at other sites. This book seeks to find the beginnings of such "chains of opportunity"[5] within medieval social structure and to trace the chains of action that created capitalist social relations.

My fundamental finding is that the chains of contingent change began with elites, not classes or individuals. Elite conflict propelled and directed each era of transformation. If we want to understand why capitalism developed first at a particular moment in certain parts of Europe, and if we want to understand the differences among European economies and polities, we must begin by tracing the differences in the structure of relations among elites, and between elites and classes, in the city-states, empires, and states of medieval and early modern Europe.

An elite can be defined as a group of rulers with the capacity to appropriate resources from nonelites and who inhabit a distinct organizational apparatus.[6] An elite "in itself" is defined by the characteristics of the organizational apparatus it inhabits.[7] Only some elites, however, are able to protect and extend their autonomy and power by altering to their advantage relations with rival elites and with the producing classes who are the object of their appropriations. Social change is effected by elites acting "for themselves."

A society is ruled by a single elite if, and only if, (1) all resources taken from the producing class(es) are appropriated through a unified organization; (2) no putative elite is able to construct a rival organization of appropriation; and (3) individual members or groups within the elite cannot disrupt the existing organization of rule by withdrawing their support for the remaining members of an elite. Multiple elites come into existence when a group of actors (either from within the old elite or from nonelite positions) develops the capacity to extract resources from nonelites in such a way that other elites must tolerate them to preserve their own access to nonelite resources.

Elites, according to this definition, are similar to ruling classes in that both live by exploiting producing classes. Elites differ from ruling classes, however, in two significant ways: First, while in Marx's theoretical framework the fundamental interest of the ruling class is to reproduce its exploitative relation to the producing class, in the elite conflict model this interest is complemented by an equally vital interest in preserving the capacity to extend its organizational reach against rival elites. In other words, when a single elite rules, its interests can be analyzed in Marx's terms since their only opponent is the producing class. When multiple elites rule, their interests are directed against challenges from competing elites as well as from subordinate classes.

Second, each elite's capacity to pursue its interests derives primarily from the structure of relations among the various coexisting elites and only secondarily from the interclass relations of production. (Again, if a single elite is not constrained by rival elites then, as Marx would predict, its capacities and interests are directed solely against the subordinate classes.)

An elite first enhances its capacity to pursue its interests by subordinating part or all of a rival elite's organizational apparatus within its own, a process I term elite conflict. Success in elite conflict is measured by whether the amalgamating elite's means of appropriating resources are rendered less vulnerable. If the expanding elite is able to fend off challenges from rival elites, it can use its enhanced organizational capacities to affect the relations of production, enhance its appropriation of resources from producers, and reduce the prospects for resistance by the producing class.

All elites must appropriate resources from nonelites if they are to persevere. Their interest in doing so is shaped primarily by class forces, that is, by the relations of production. However, the capacity of each elite to realize its interests is determined primarily by the structure of interelite relations. Elite conflict is the primary threat to elite capacities. Yet, the interests each elite seeks to defend are grounded in its relations with the producing classes.

If an elite's organizational base is distinguished by its relation to production, then that elite can also be defined as a class fraction. A static analysis of an elite's or class fraction's relations with the producing class or of its efforts to defend itself against a rival elite cannot adjudicate between Marxist and elite conflict theories since both focus upon the organization of extraction by an elite that was also a class fraction. Historical study is necessary to test the two models. A case in which elite and class relations shift in response to changes in relations of production would confirm the advantage of Marxist over elitist theory. Indeed, Marxist theory would claim that multiple elites usually are class fractions. They can ultimately be recognized and their interests and capacities predicted from their relation to production. Marx, in *The Eighteenth Brumaire* ([1852] 1963), makes such an argument for the interests of class fractions while tracing the ways in which fractional capacities were determined by organizational and ideological factors not reducible to class terms.

My elite conflict theory acknowledges that some elites are class fractions. However, except for instances when a single elite rules and a class analysis is sufficient, class fractions share their rule with elites that are not distinguishable by their relations to production. When a class fraction competes with nonclass elites, the fraction gains or loses class capacity *after* a shift in the structure of relations among elites. For example, the historical discussion of early modern England in chapters 4 and 6 specifies the greater power of the elite conflict model over a Marxist model to predict shifts in the interests and capacities of the gentry class fraction. The gentry was able to transform agrarian class relations only *after* elite conflict had removed the capacity of the clergy, which was not a class fraction, to regulate relations of production.

To determine which elite or class fraction will prevail, one must first examine the total structure of relations among elites. Changes in the organizational power of elites are reflected in changes in each elite's control over the organization of production. Both the elite conflict and Marx's models posit a relational sense of capacity—capacity is exercised at the level of production and at a level of institutions removed from production. The elite conflict model generates a dynamic of conflict and change that differs from the Marxist model by placing the primary cause at the elite level rather than at the level of class relations.

Marx's theoretical framework derives its elegance from the assumption that the beneficiaries of a mode of production are also its creators and enforcers, and that possibilities for agency are defined by the structure of economic relations. In other words, Marx contends that both class interest and class capacity are determined by relations of production. However, he contends that further development in the forces of production is required before the exploited class can transform the relations of production in its own interests.

For Marx, changes in the forces of production render problematic the ruling class's capacity to reproduce favorable relations of production. At the same time, the weakening of the ruling class's control over production aids the exploited class in its efforts to recast the relations of production in its own interest. The rising new class may exercise its growing capacities at an organizational or ideological level. However, the real interest of a class is in winning and reproducing domination over the means of production.[8]

Marx's temporal sequence assumes that change in the forces and relations of production precedes change in the interests and capacities of each class. Since historical change is continuous at all levels, the sequence is difficult to discern. Only by studying epochal transformations such as the transition from feudalism to capitalism, or from capitalism to socialism, can one see the true logic emerge.

Elite conflict theory suggests a causal sequence of conflict and structural change different from Marx. Classes at the point of production have less room for agency than do elites because classes are doubly constrained—first, as Marx indicates, by the slow change in the forces of production and the resulting balance of class forces; second, by the capacities of multiple elites to embed their autonomy in their organizational means for extracting resources from the productive classes. As a result, the producing classes are divided and their interests shaped by the ways in which groups of producers and facets of production are incorporated within different elite organizations of appropriation.

Opportunities for agency by subordinate classes are altered primarily by changes in the structure of elite relations. When elites are numerous, the producing classes will be divided and less capable of mounting struggles for their own interests. Lack of pressure from producers frees elites to challenge one another without endangering their control over nonelites. Elite conflicts, by disrupting ties between elites and fractions of the producing classes, increase opportunities for class agency by allowing producers to merge interests and capacities previously lodged in separate elite-imposed organizations of production. As elite conflict reorders a once-stable structure of multiple elites and consolidates formerly autonomous elites, new opportunities for alliances among nonelites are created. When producers are capable of acting as a class, elites are forced to compromise their disputes if they are to fend off class challenges. The capacities of the producing classes are most severely constricted when multiple elites combine, through compromise or conflict, into a single unified elite. A single unified elite has the greatest opportunity to transform the relations of production in ways that will sustain and intensify its exploitation of the producing classes.

Elite conflict occurs when an elite attempts to undermine another elite's capacity to extract resources from nonelites. Such an effort can assume a variety of forms, for example, the mere subordination of one elite to another, with no effect on the structure of relations among other elites or the relations of production. If only two elites exist and one absorbs the other, the outcome would have a profound effect upon class relations because the single elite would be constrained only by the capacities of the subordinate class. If more than one elite remains, then the consequences of conflict can be determined only by analyzing the resulting interaction of elite and class structures.

Most often, an elite enjoys only partial success in its attack on the other—for example, the weaker elite may offer a portion of what it appropriates from the producing classes in return for a degree of autonomy in relation to the stronger elite. This sort of compromise may weaken the links between the primary appropriators of resources within the weakened elite and the secondary receivers of revenues who reached the agreement with the rival elite. Under such conditions, the primary appropriators may constitute themselves as an elite separate from its nominal leaders, either alone, in alliance with, or under pressure from a third elite.

Splits within an elite due to internal conflicts or pressures or inducements from rival elites raise the question of how to determine the boundaries of an elite. Are all beneficiaries of an organization members of the same elite, or are some merely employees of the elite? Agents are included in an elite if they are essential to the operation of the elite's organizational apparatus and if they can leave and create their own apparatus. If only the former condition holds, they are merely "middle class" employees of the organization, able to demand privileges by withholding their services or their goodwill but still dependent upon the genuine elite. No actor can remain in an elite if he is not essential to it. At issue is how disruptive an individual or group's departure would be to an elite, and how forming a new elite or augmenting an existing elite would affect overall elite relations as well as the strength of the remaining members of the old elite.

Whether members of an organization are necessary to an elite or are capable of establishing their own organizational apparatus cannot be determined from the portion of a surplus retained by actors along the path appropriated resources flow. Instead, since elites are defined in terms of power, actors should be defined as part of an elite only if they could sustain the appropriation of resources without other agents along the path.

There is no way of deducing who is indispensable to an organization of appropriation, and it is on this point that the differences between Marxist and elite conflict theory become apparent. For Marx, classes are defined by the mode of production, and class fractions are created in the development of the forces of production. Elite conflict theory reverses that causality be contending that a system of production is determined by the capacities of elites to organize a system of appropriation, although at times an elite's organization of appropriation will correspond to and determine the structure of production.

Elite theory concurs with Marxist theory in viewing capacities and interests as relational rather than as absolute. However, the organizational capacities of elites and their abilities to fend off or to subordinate rival elites can change without prior changes in production. This is true even for elites that are class fractions. Elite strength is determined by the structure of relations among elites. Openings for an elite to augment its power are found in the interstices of interelite relations. Indeed, it is often impossible to identify the outcomes of elite conflicts from the existing relations of production. Thus, a production-based analysis of class fractions would not necessarily allow one to predict the dimensions and results of elite conflict. However, power gained from elite conflict is transitory unless embedded within the relations of production.

An elite theory of history is essentially pessimistic about the possibilities for class conflict to transform class relations. One reason for that pessimism is suggested by Marx's own dialectic. In each era of transition, except for the transition to socialism, the new ruling class is not one of the antagonistic classes involved in the struggles that Marx found to be endemic to the old social order. As a result, Marx needs to posit some mechanism for change in the forces of production that can reorder the relations of production, giving rise to a new class with capacities and interests different from the two old antagonistic classes.

There are empirical difficulties with Marx's method. Since most conflict is between the two old classes, it is hard to identify the footprints of the new class in the events of transformation. One solution to Marx's conundrum is to contend that the transforming agent is not initially a class in itself or for itself. Instead, it develops as a by-product, a structural accretion of the struggles among the old classes. Indeed, the increasing concern by Marxists and non-Marxists alike with feudal and capitalist states comes from a realization that states are products of existing social actors and are the sites were new social relations and interests can be formed.

The elite conflict model suggests a logic that can explain the long-running immobility of classes within existing modes of production and predict when and why new class interests are formed. If the ruling agents in a society have divergent interests, if they are simultaneously part of a class and members of distinct elites, then it becomes possible to explain why the capacities of the ruling and subordinate classes develop at different rates. Under this model, the subordinate producing class is constrained by the relations of production and by the various organizational apparatuses of multiple elites. At the same time, ruling class agency is limited by the dual interests of maintaining class power and autonomy against rival elites.

My model shows that different opportunities for agency can be found within the structures of elite and class relations. The latter are constrained by elite and class forces, while it is possible for elite relations to be altered without immediately affecting class relations. The elite conflict model of historical change builds upon the lack of symmetry and the temporal lag between change in elite and class relations. Class constraints upon elites are less immediate and less total than elite constraints on class agency.

Marx and his successors are unable to explain why conflicts between the same classes yield different outcomes, at different times, even when the position of the subordinate class in the relations of production remains unchanged. Elite conflict theory addresses this problem by recognizing that elites are defined by their capacities to prevent changes in the relations of production that could undermine their autonomy. The subordinate class, in contrast, is unable to resist maneuvers among elites that augment the powers of one elite at the expense of another. This incapacity is central to the producing class's subordination. It is part of the essence of the elites' collective rule over nonelites, and it is why changes in class relations must await changes in elite relations.

The consequences of elite conflicts for class relations are indirect. Elite conflicts increase the capacities of one or another class by reducing divisions within that class. When conflicts eliminate elite divisions, the surviving elite gains leverage over the producing class because that elite no longer has to restrain action out of consideration for the capacities of a rival elite. The capacity of the subordinate class is increased when fractions within that class, once tied to different elite organizations, are able to make common cause against a newly amalgamated elite.

My elite conflict theory does not yield a general proposition about the identity of the actors who gain capacity from elite consolidation. That is the task for the historical studies in the following chapters. I use my elite conflict theory in this book as a method for tracing the chains of contingent change that gave rise to capitalism. I begin with an inductive notion of agency and structure. I initially define agency solely in terms of its effect upon structure. Thus, classes, fractions, or elites exist only to the extent to which they have an observable effect upon specific structures such as production organizations or political institutions. I have formulated an elite conflict model because I find that the historical evidence for early modern Europe supports arguments for the efficacy of elites and classes, however those groups are defined within specific historical contexts.

Structures can be viewed as artifacts of past chains of agency. Rather than claim that structures have a logic of development, I show that the evolution of structures reflects the continuing limitations that actors', and especially elites', agencies place upon one another. The structures I identify through historical analysis can be used to define the long-range effects of social interactions and to deduce the limits upon actors and their actions.

My approach does not reflect pessimism over the project of comparative historical sociology. Comparative analysis is possible because the opportunities for agency are generally quite constricted. As a result, structural change is slow and amenable to analysis and comparative generalization. We must be careful, however, about how we theorize history and avoid the temptation to reify agents' limitations in the logic of structures. That is why this book advances an elite conflict theory of the middle range even as it tests and rejects various Marxist and Weberian metatheoretical approaches.

Plan of the Book

This book engages the fundamental issues and debates of European transition and of sociology, first by reanalyzing social structure in Western Europe before the transformation, and then by showing how the reordering of feudal elements created new capitalist classes and states and privileged the carriers of more rational ideologies and practices. Each portion of my argument engages a somewhat different subset of the varied debates on the European transition. For that reason, I do not undertake a comprehensive review and critique of the literature on transition. Instead, I allow my position in those debates to emerge as I build my argument step by step through the chapters of this book. The set of questions that guide the historical analysis in each chapter are formed in response to the inadequacies of previous research. Many of my more specific critiques are confined to endnotes.[10]

My previous efforts to address the shortcomings in the various Marxist and Weberian contributions to those debates (see Lachmann 1987) led me to identify three elites, rather than a unified aristocratic class, as the critical agents in feudal England, and to trace the ways in which conflict among those elites was the primary, and conflict with peasants the secondary, determinant of the forms of private property, wage labor, and of the state that emerged in the century between the Henrician Reformation and the English Revolution.

I extend my earlier argument in this volume. Chapter 2 probes the limits of elite and class conflict in England and France in the centuries before and after the Black Death. Because medieval England and France were not centralized states, I need to devote much attention to differences among English counties and French provinces, as well as to variations on the manorial level. The comparative analysis of medieval social structure shows the ways in which differences in the number and types of elites, and therefore in their relations, affected feudal production. The comparisons in this chapter also serve to identify the actual causal roles of demographic, ecological, technological, and ideological changes in the limited political and economic transformations of rural Europe during the Renaissance.

Chapter 3 goes beyond my initial focus upon the predominant agrarian sector to identify the place of cities and of larger political units in the Renaissance world. Italian city-states in general, and Florence in particular, are compared with London, Paris, Madrid, and Papal Rome on one hand, and the cities of the Netherlands and the Hanseatic League on the other hand, to identify the sources of urban autonomy and show how trans-European alliances and wars allowed certain elites to achieve hegemony within their local bases and to draw profits from commerce and politics to their capitals.

Chapters 2 and 3 also lay the groundwork for this book's confrontation with Weber's model for the origins and development of capitalism. Chapter 2 challenges Weber's depiction of feudalism as a "chronic condition" of conflict that was unable to yield significant change without the external intervention of urban merchants and ultimately of the Protestant ethic. Chapter 3 maps the limits of Renaissance urban capitalism and shows why conflicts among urban elites and classes resulted in a "refeudalization" of each city-state's polity and economy.

The stalemate of urban elites, shown in chapter 3, explains why cities did not lead Europe. The next step in my argument, and in the actual historical development of Europe, requires a return to the conflicts among the backward rural aristocracies who are the subject of chapter 2. Chapter 4 investigates the effects of the Reformation upon elite relations and conflicts in England and France. The Reformation emerges, in my analysis, as more a structural than an ideological shock to the system of Renaissance Europe.

Elite relations were reordered in fundamentally different ways in England and France. I explore those differences in Chapter 4, contrasting the "horizontal absolutism" that developed in Tudor and Stuart England with the "vertical absolutism" of France in the same era. The different absolutisms shaped the capacities of local elites to challenge the crown in the English Civil War and in the French Frondes and molded the organizations that elites used to control peasants and regulate agrarian production.

The Italian cases of chapter 3 are augmented by analyses of Spanish and Dutch elite conflicts in chapter 5. These cases allow me to examine the role of trade and imperialism in the transformation of European polities and economies. Chapter 5 addresses the question, raised by Fernand Braudel ([1979] 1984) and Immanuel Wallerstein (1974) in somewhat different ways, of why hegemony over the European economy passed from Italian cities to the Netherlands and then to Britain. Chapter 3 analyzes Italian decline through the internal dynamics of elite conflict and consolidation within each city-state. Chapter 5 explains the backwardness spawned by Spanish imperialism and the rise and stagnation of Dutch mercantile power in terms of the social structures created by elite conflicts within the particular Spanish and Dutch polities. Elite conflicts prevented the development of a nation state in early modern Italy, and in Spain and the Netherlands resulted in states whose forms stymied competition in the European economy. By comparing the effects of surviving feudal elites upon emergent state forms, it is possible to show why the Renaissance social system did not give way to capitalist classes and states throughout Western Europe.

The discussion of "failed" transitions and "weak" states is followed by a return to the core comparison of England and France. In chapter 6, I study the consequences of elite consolidation within and without the state upon agrarian class relations to explain the differences in English and French economic development. I begin by comparing the ways in which English and French landlords responded to the threats that were posed to their seigneurial incomes and powers by the elite conflicts analyzed in chapter 4. I then turn from elite to class conflicts. I inventory the range of peasant responses to the challenges posed to their long-standing rights by landlords and other elites. I explain how previous elite and class conflicts affected the strength of peasant communities and peasants' abilities to resist or to shape the agrarian relations of production that emerged in the seventeenth century. I conclude by explaining how the different British and French agrarian regimes shaped economic development in subsequent centuries. Chapter 6 completes my alternative explanation of capitalist social relations as artifacts of chains of elite and class conflicts.

Chapter 7 reconsiders Weber's Protestant ethic thesis and the later work of his elaborators and critics. Just as the continuing stalemate of feudal elites limited rationality in Renaissance Florence, so did the demise of feudal social relations open opportunities for champions of rational action among the elite and of intensified discipline for the masses. This chapter situates the Reformation Protestant and Counter-Reformation Catholic carriers of new ideologies within the structures of postfeudal England and France. I explain why some clerics and others advocated new practices, and I account for their varying success in transforming elite and popular beliefs and practices in terms of the advocates' links to elite sponsors differently located in English and French social structures. The analysis of elite structure makes it possible to understand how interests were expressed in ideas and to see how actors were motivated to transform social relations, often with consequences they could not anticipate and that evoked new ideologies to understand and new practices to move the world they had created.

Chapter 8 draws out the implications of the substantive analysis in the other chapters for the study of social change in general and of the transition to capitalism in particular. I offer suggestions about how the processes of state and class formation must be reconceptualized in the light of the general primacy of elite over class conflict. I discuss how the study of elite conflict can explain the development of revolutions—both those led by elites and those led by the emerging bourgeois and proletarian classes of the eighteenth century.

2

Feudal Dynamics

MAX WEBER BELIEVED THAT FEUDAL POLITICS was about how "the individual holders of fiefs and benefices and the other possessors of appropriated powers exercised their authority," how "these holders of privileges consociate[d] with one another for the purposes of concrete action," and how "this system of alliances, which was unavoidable because of the resulting inelasticity, . . . developed into a chronic condition" ([1922] 1978, p. 1086). Weber's principal interest in feudalism was to compare its structural and ideological rigidity with the dynamic of post-Reformation capitalism. Because of his pessimism about the possibilities for transformative action within feudal societies, Weber and his followers (with the significant exception of state-centered theorists whose work is considered in later chapters) did not attempt to identify the parameters and directions of feudal development.

Scholarship on feudal change has developed within two principal traditions. One focuses upon the growth of cities and long-distance trade. That scholarly tendency is addressed in chapter 3.[1] The other examines the relationship between demographic cycles and changes in systems of land tenure and agrarian production. Debate within this discipline has generally been between non-Marxists who identify demographics as the independent variable and Marxists who view class struggle as the mediating force between population and relations of production.

This chapter uses the debates among Marxist students of feudal demography and with non-Marxist scholars to clarify the parameters of structural change possible at the level of production in England and France from the eleventh through the fifteenth centuries. I show that neither demographic nor class conflict dynamics, or a combination of the two, is sufficient to explain the different developments of agrarian class relations on regional or national levels in the two countries. Demographic and class analyses must be grounded within a study of the multiple elites that governed agrarian society in feudal England and France. My notion of elites, as described in chapter 1, is derived in part from Weber's conception of feudalism as a condition of conflict among monarchs and holders of fiefs and benefices. In this and the following chapters, however, I show that such elite conflict did not always remain a chronic condition; in England and France elite conflict resulted in the emergence of new structures that, even before the psychological effects of Protestantism took hold, could be analyzed as capitalist.

Dobb's Marxist Version of the Transition

The objects of feudal power were land and peasants. Landlords sought to seize from one another both land and the rights to exploit peasants. They sought also to improve their collective and individual capacities to profit from the peasants under their control. Landlord capacities varied by location and changed over time. The Black Death of 1348, to most historians, is the great divide in the history of feudal agrarian economies. Thereafter, the peasants of most of Eastern Europe were reenserfed while most English and French tenants won greater degrees of autonomy from their manor lords. Students of feudalism have sought to explain the divergent results of the common European demographic decline.

Maurice Dobb (1947) initiated modern Marxist scholarship on this point by noting that the low margin of surplus in feudal economies meant that lords' efforts to squeeze peasants in moments of crisis were bound to be counterproductive. Feudal lords of the twelfth and early thirteenth centuries, who ruled in an era of rising population, the "morselization" of peasant holdings, and an absolute decline in per capita agricultural production, deepened a demographic collapse through their efforts to sustain the level of surplus they extracted from their peasants.[2]

Lords were limited in their responses to the labor shortages created by the Black Death. "The reaction of the nobility to this situation was not at all a uniform one; and it is on the difference in this reaction in different areas of Europe that a large part of the difference in the economic history of the ensuing centuries depends (Dobb 1947, pp. 50–51). Dobb argues that all feudal lords wanted to reenserf their tenants to insure a supply of labor to work the demesne, the lords' own farms. In that way, lords would receive a share of agricultural production, even if the decline in population meant that peasants no longer would bid against one another for the opportunity to pay ever higher rents on plots rented from lords.

Dobb points out that serfdom, like all other systems of forced labor, required extensive supervision to ensure that laborers worked hard enough to produce a surplus in addition to their own subsistence needs. The low level of agricultural productivity in feudal times made it unprofitable in many places for lords to invest in the military and administrative forces necessary to detain and supervise peasant laborers. Dobb argues that serfdom was financially feasible only in those areas where there was a high land-to-population ratio and where greater inputs of labor would not raise the productivity of land (1947, pp. 50–60). The former condition allowed lords to grant subsistence farms to serfs (thereby leaving to peasants the problem of their subsistence) while still retaining vast demesnes to produce grain that the lords could use or sell for their own needs. The latter condition obviated the need for much supervision: If land was only minimally productive regardless of the level of labor input, then highly motivated or intensively supervised labor would get no more out of poor quality land than would unmotivated and poorly supervised serfs. Both conditions were met only in Eastern Europe, and thus peasants were reenserfed only in those areas.

Implicit in Dobb's logic, for he does not analyze the dynamics of agrarian class relations under feudalism, is the conclusion that landlords in Western Europe did not impose serfdom because they could not make it pay. Instead, they commuted labor dues and rented out the demesne, thereby reducing administrative costs and insuring rising rents when population began to recover in the later half of the fifteenth century (1947, pp. 60–70).[3]

Dobb correctly points out that "it must not, however, be assumed that the mere fact of a change from labour-services to money-payments or a transition to leases of the demesne represented a release of the cultivator from servile obligations and the substitution of a free contractual relationship between him and the owner of the soil" (1947, p. 63). In Western Europe, the postplague transition to cash rents created what Dobb calls the "petty mode of production" (p. 85). Within that mode, agricultural and handicraft production were transformed most radically by those producers who were both excluded from aristocratic and guild privileges and free from feudal restrictions on the employment of their labor and their property. Producers' abilities to accumulate capital and to transform the petty mode of production into genuine capitalism were limited, however, by unfair competition from guilds and mercantile monopolies and from lords who continued to collect rent under the protection of the feudal state. Thus, the failure by Western European lords to reenserf peasants, which gave rise to the petty mode of production, was a necessary but by no means sufficient condition for the development of capitalism. Opportunities for producers to profit from exploiting a growing proletariat (as opposed to guilds profiting from market monopolies or petty producers profiting from self-exploitation) awaited the destruction of guild and aristocratic power in the English Revolution, which allowed "England . . . to accelerate enormously the growth of industrial capital in the next half-century—a growth surpassing that of other countries which as yet lacked any similar political upheaval" (p. 176).

Dobb's analysis of the transition from feudalism to capitalism suffers from a major flaw: He is unable to explain why there was a two-century lag from the abolition of servile labor after the Black Death to the development of private property in land and the proletarianization of a plurality of peasants in the century following the Henrician Reformation (Lachmann 1987, p. 17). Nor is Dobb able to explain why similar petty modes of production and similar late feudal political systems produced a bourgeois revolution in England a century and a half earlier than in France.

The shortcomings in Dobb's work have been addressed by three groups of scholars. The tendency of one group, which includes both Marxists and non-Marxists, has been to concur with Weber that feudalism is stagnant but to identify an urban sector external to feudalism as the locus of transformation. Their view, as expressed by Sweezy ([1950] 1976) in his critique of Dobb and by later scholars, is addressed in chapter 3 where I probe the limits of urban capitalism. A second group accepts the basic outlines of Dobb's history but then turns away from the level of production to look at the development of "ruling class self-organization" or at state formation in order to explain why policies and organizations favorable to the reproduction of the aristocracy were transformed into ones favorable to the development of a bourgeoisie and to capitalist forms of production. This argument, developed in different ways by Marxists such as Robert Brenner and by state-centered theorists, is engaged throughout the later chapters of this book. The shortcomings of those models cannot be made clear, however, until we understand the dynamics of feudalism at the level of production and connect those dynamics to the actions of aristocrats and rulers at the levels of national and international politics. To reach such an understanding, and to make clear the connections between local and European history, we must first address the critique that the third group has mounted against the Marxist version of the transition first elaborated by Dobb. This critique has been developed primarily by non-Marxist demographic historians.

Materialist Constraints on Capitalist Behavior

In the very long-run, from, say, the thirteenth to the late nineteenth century, almost all of France followed England in a transition from feudal to capitalist agriculture. Today, at the turn of the twenty-first century, it appears that all of Europe is about to arrive at the organization of agricultural production first reached in England and the Netherlands in the late sixteenth century. From that perspective, the rest of this chapter, and indeed this entire book, can be seen as a debate over quibbles.

The very long-run is the focus of the scholars reviewed in this section. They deny that there was a revolutionary break in agrarian social relations in sixteenth-century England (or indeed at any other time and place) and argue that, instead, capitalist agriculture developed gradually over a number of centuries, albeit at differing velocities, and perhaps along different paths, until each region of Western Europe reached a common end point by the nineteenth century.

Many of these historians contend that feudal land-tenure arrangements began to weaken even before the Black Death.[4] By the third quarter of the thirteenth century, Kathleen Biddick (1987, p. 279) argues, "lords had mostly ceased such intervention [in peasant land tenure arrangements] and left the fragile exoskeleton of customary holdings to bear the weight of the land market." [5] Not only do Biddick and the other historians making this argument believe that the market allocation of land is inherently more efficient than feudal systems of land control, but they imply that their understanding of the advantages to be gained from market organizations matches that of thirteenth-century landlords and peasants. In attributing market rationality to thirteenth-century agriculturalists, these historians differ from the theorists discussed in chapter 3 in that they do not assume an urban sector is the sole source of rational economic action; instead, they look to rural landlords as the primary capitalist actors in Western Europe.

This "finding" of early capitalism should raise two questions in readers' minds: First, if capitalism is so much more rational than feudalism, and some agriculturalists supposedly recognized this in the thirteenth century, then why were most European landlords and peasants blind to this wonderful new organization of production for so long? Second, why did those far-sighted early agrarian capitalists not realize the same drastic increases in production and income as the English and Dutch commercial farmers of the sixteenth century?

The scholars reviewed in this section do not answer, or even pose, the first question. They address the second by offering models, often only implicitly, to explain why agrarian actors were unable to act upon their rational understandings, or why their rationality was directed in ways that undermined the collectivity's chance to maximize the outputs of their material and human resources. This section reviews the various sorts of explanations for regional and national differences in the rate of agrarian economic development from the thirteenth century on. The focus on temporal and geographic variation provides the best method for adjudicating among explanations that highlight different causal factors in the transition to capitalism.

The Demographic Constraints
upon Economic Development

The most popular approach among French historians, and important to the work of English and other European scholars as well, is what Brenner (1976, p. 33) has labeled the "Malthusian model."[6] Associated with M. M. Postan and Emmanuel Le Roy Ladurie, this model sees a general long-term tendency toward the rational use of land and labor. These scholars associate modern, capitalist agriculture with heavy capital investment in technology to "improve" land, to increase the yield of crops, and to improve the efficiency of labor. Scholars in this tradition seek to identify the factors that retarded or advanced the modernization of agriculture in feudal Europe.

The population increase in the centuries leading up to the Black Death tended to retard agricultural improvement by directing new inputs of labor and capital to increasingly marginal lands. Peasants used communal solidarity, and legal rights guarded by the crown, to ensure that they could keep the bulk of land, and of agricultural production, to feed their own multiplying families, thereby choking off new investment in agriculture (Bois [1976] 1984, pp. 187–200; Fourquin [1970] 1976, pp. 130–15; Neveux 1975, pp. 35–39). The fall in the rate, if not in the absolute volume, of feudal rents, diminished the resources available to lords for productive investment as well (Bois 1984, pp. 215–25).

The demographic collapse of the mid-fourteenth century opened the opportunity for renewed investment in land.[7] French lords "imposed on the peasants . . . 'extra-economic' pressure . . . [and] made plans similar to those that, in other circumstances, had produced or were to produce the first or second serfdom" (Le Roy Ladurie [1977] 1987, p. 65). Peasant revolts, however, disrupted those plans, while crown lawyers limited the power of seigneurs over peasants and instead strengthened peasant communities to insure their ability to collect taxes for the state (Le Roy Ladurie [1977] 1987, pp 65–66; Neveux 1975, pp. 63–68; Nabholz 1944, pp. 533–36)).

Stymied in their efforts to coerce greater rents out of peasants, landlords granted long-term or permanent leases in return for large "fines," payable at the start of the contract (Neveux 1975, pp. 138–40). In time, inflation rendered rents on such leases trivial, resulting in the de facto transfer of much land from aristocrats to the common holders of leases. Differentiation among peasant families led to the concentration of much land under such leaseholds in the hands of an elite of commercial farmers (Le Roy Ladurie [1977] 1987, pp. 135–75).

Le Roy Ladurie and his colleagues are outstanding in explaining the effects of various peasant systems of inheritance upon the concentration of land in different regions of France.[8] But they do not account for why landlords in some regions rented lands to tenant farmers, while elsewhere they established metayage (share-cropping) arrangements, nor why landlords shifted between one and the other system in yet other provinces (Le Roy Ladurie (1977) 1987, pp. 78–81).

The lacunae in the histories of Le Roy Ladurie and his colleagues leave them unable to explain why commercial farmers gained control of land only in northern France, and not before the late seventeenth century.[9] They imply that it took three or four centuries for inflation to erode the value of seigneurial rents and for peasants to lose their leaseholds through generational division and renewed demographic calamity (Le Roy Ladurie [1977] 1987, pp. 329–48). French historians seem to take patriotic pride in pointing out that yields on small commercial farms run by resident proprietors in northern France approached or perhaps exceeded those on the larger farms run by managers for rentier capitalists in England (Bois 1984, p. 404 and passim.; Le Roy Ladurie 1975, pp. 1412–13; see also Leon 1970). They do not explain, however, why a relatively rapid and national transformation in English agriculture was repeated more slowly and only regionally in France.

Regional Ecologies

Jack Goldstone (1988) argues that ecology— that is, differences in soil types and the sorts of agricultures they can support—is the factor that must be added to demographic analyses to explain the regional differences obscured by national comparisons of England and France. For Goldstone, "the question of why post-1650 England was more productive than France dissolves into two intra-national regional questions: Why were northern, eastern, and far western English counties more productive than the traditional heartland of English arable agriculture? And why were southern and central French departments less productive than northern and eastern France?" (p. 291). Further, Goldstone asks, why did the open field regions of midland England and northern France have similar agricultural systems until 1650 but diverge after then?

Goldstone answers those questions by comparing the types of soil in the different regions of England and France. He argues that the heavy soil areas of midland England and northeastern France were the most productive sorts of lands with the agricultural methods available before 1650. Since those lands were the most valuable they were the most intensively farmed, and the most intensively regulated through the archetypal medieval open-field arable and common pasture system. Within those regions, Goldstone believes that production and class relations were governed by the basic Malthusian parameters of European history outlined by Postan, Le Roy Ladurie, and the others.

When population rose,[10] the rich soil and access to common pasture allowed peasant families to support themselves even on "morcellized" holdings subdivided through inheritance. By contrast, peasants on the poorer lands in south and west France and on the fringes of England were unable to support themselves on subdivided holdings, and as food prices and taxes rose while wages fell they were forced into bankruptcy. In France, these peasants often rebelled against state taxes, but over the long-term peasants on poor lands in both countries were dispossessed, and property was concentrated in the hands of rich peasants, bourgeois, and gentry or noble landowners.

Goldstone's image of mitigated Malthusian cycles on fertile land and concentration of property on poor lands (the latter in response to population pressures as well) depends on his ability to assert that class conflict did not result in any sudden or significant shifts in peasants' abilities to adjust to increasing population and prices in rich farming regions or cause the financial problems of tenants on poor lands in the same 1500–1650 era. Goldstone does so by pointing to the relative lack of enclosure in England in this period,[11] and by contending that the principal beneficiaries of a slow process of land concentration were rich peasants and bourgeois investors, not gentry or aristocrats.

The key change in English and French agriculture, and, Goldstone contends, the source of England's economic advantage over France, came with the invention of new techniques of cultivation after 1650. The new techniques were suitable for the light-soil regions of northern and western England, but not for the poor lands of southern and western France. As a result, development in the once similarly poor pastoral regions of England and France diverged after 1650.

The new techniques allowed light-soil regions of England to produce grain at cheaper prices than the traditional midland arable areas. The comparative advantage for midland areas shifted to pasture, supplying a market fueled by increasing mass consumption of meat in the post-1650 period of stable population and rising incomes (at least in urban areas). In that happy era of rising wages and falling commodity prices, small English farmers willingly sold their land to commercial farmers. In contrast, poor regions of France could not adjust to new markets; no one wanted to buy those lands and peasants remained in the countryside, occasionally erupting into rebellion when squeezed by falling wages and commodity prices and by rising taxes. Only in northeastern France did landowners buy out poor farmers and profit from their continuing monopoly on supplies for grain markets in Paris.

Goldstone's regional ecological analysis allows him to explain shifts in farm strategies from arable to pasture in the heavy-soil midlands, and from pasture to arable in light-soil England, and to show why successful commercialization was concentrated in northeastern France. His model has the advantages of elegance and of attention to agricultural technology and market strategies over the more ad hoc and theoretically cluttered discussions by the historians reviewed above who mix demographic and class forces in constantly varying amounts. Goldstone, however, is selective in the transformations he recognizes and is unable to explain why the gentry and large commercial farmers got rich, while so many peasants were dispossessed and impoverished in the sixteenth and subsequent centuries, even though the new agricultural techniques raised productivity on farms large and small (Allen 1992, pp. 191–231).

Specifically, Goldstone ignores the question at the heart of Marxist discussions of demographic cycles: Why were peasants bankrupted in the downward phase of population and prices after 1650 but not in the even more drastic demographic decline following the Black Death? Goldstone suggests that farmers in ecologically favorable areas wanted to sell out after 1650, since they could get good prices for their land and enter urban trades, an option clearly not open to peasants after 1348. However, the differences, of a more developed land market and greater urban sector in the seventeenth- as opposed to the fourteenth-century demographic crises, beg other questions: Why, if agricultural prices were depressed, would commercial farmers and capitalist investors want to buy land and pay for enclosures and improvements? If the agricultural sector instead was booming after 1650, why did peasants not hold onto their land, especially since Goldstone does not claim that the new techniques benefited from economies of scale?

I address these questions in chapter 6, but raise them here to show that Goldstone's effort to portray England and France as similarly stagnant—rising and falling within long-standing demographic confines—until their poorer regions diverged after 1650 does not resolve the problems of the demographic historians noted in the previous section. Regional ecology does matter; Goldstone's discussion of them, and the work of numerous students of "field systems" and farming techniques not cited in Goldstone's work, must be part of any comparative analysis. However, ecology is not the master variable capable of explaining all significant temporal and geographic divergences. More vitally, Goldstone's model cannot account for the crucial differences within and across ecological zones, which are traced in the latter part of this chapter, or for the emergence of capitalist organizations of agriculture in parts of England before 1650.

Rational Feudalism

Another explanation for the supposed longevity of common field systems in Western Europe, despite the demise of serfdom in the fourteenth century, is the claim that it was the most efficient system of farming under two conditions that prevailed until the seventeenth or later centuries. Stefano Fenoaltea (1988) argues that there were great ecological variations on manors, as well as across regions. Some pieces of land were more appropriate for intensive farming, while others were better suited for less labor-intensive crops, or for pasture. The best moments for planting or harvesting different pieces of arable land on a manor could be spread over several weeks.

If peasants had held compact farms, each confined to a particular ecological zone of the estate, then some peasants would have had only poor land, not worthy of the expenditure of labor available within their family units, while others would have had not enough family members to work their high quality land adequately. Further, compact farms would have needed to be sown or harvested all at once. Under such a system, a peasant community either would have made inefficient use of the whole manor's land or would have incurred the high supervision costs of using hired labor to assist one another at their appropriate planting and harvest times and to transfer surplus labor power from families with poor lands to families with high quality lands and inadequate labor supplies for appropriately intensive cultivation.[12] Thus "systematic diversification" through common field strips minimized "labor-market transaction costs and [maximized] the productivity of village labor as a whole" (Fenoaltea 1988, p. 192).

The transaction costs incurred by peasants in collectively managing a common field system, once such a system was established,[13] remained low as long as all the peasants on the manor believed (accurately) that such a division of land could maximize their collective incomes. That belief was shattered when and where "market access and technical innovation" (p. 192) opened the possibility for some peasants to realize greater incomes outside the manorial system than within.[14] Only then did peasants seek to exit from collective management of land. They were able to do so through disruptive tactics, raising the transaction costs of maintaining the open field system so high that the collectivity of peasants, even the majority of those who did not initially gain from private landownership and production for the market, were forced to end the open field system. Thus, Fenoaltea claims, a stable and long-lived manorial system was altered only when and where markets penetrated formerly self-sufficient rural areas.

Fenoaltea's rational choice analysis is based upon a formal model of manorial open field systems, one that achieves its elegance by stripping away much of the historical reality of European feudalism. Among other details missing from his article are landlords and class conflict.[15] He assumes a rough equality and consensus among manor tenants, when in fact there has always been stratification among peasants, and at times direct conflict between groups of tenants with different types of land rights.[16] Peasants sustained land and labor markets, even as common field systems persisted. The manorial system was not an unchanging structure, dependent upon unchanging ecological conditions, demographic cycles, or a continuing lack of access to markets. Instead, peasants incurred the transaction costs for both manorial and market systems simultaneously because each was a partial response to particular demands and opportunities.

Elites and Agrarian Class Relations in England and France, 1100–1450

The remainder of this chapter constructs a multifactorial model of shifts in agrarian social relations in England and France. Before turning to that task, however, it is important to be clear about the extent to which land tenures shifted in the two countries between the thirteenth and sixteenth centuries. This section has four parts. The first part specifies such shifts over time and across regions for France. The next two parts explain those temporal and regional variations. The fourth part examines the causes of English variations. The final section of this chapter specifies the limits of feudal agrarian change, thereby preparing the ground for an explanation in subsequent chapters of the lag between the end of serfdom and the development of capitalism.

The Temporality and Geography of Shifts in Agrarian Social Relations in France, 1100–1450

Agrarian social relations assumed many different forms in the centuries prior to the Black Death. In France, the manors of each province were characterized by the form or combination of forms of dues that peasants paid in cash or in labor to the lord of the manor. Of course, peasants also owed obligations to the church, to overlords and

TABLE 2.1. Changes in Peasant Labor Dues in France, 1100–1347

Dues Became Heavier in . . .	Dues Remained Stable in . . .	Dues Commuted to Cash Dues in . . .	Dues Commuted for Rich Peasants Only in . . .
Béarn	Auvergne	Brittany	Guyenne[1]
Burgundy	Bourbonnais	Comtat Venaissin	Île-de-France
Champagne	Bresse	Guyenne[1]	
Dauphiné	Nivernais	Languedoc	
Lyonnais	Normandy	Orléans	
Navarre		Picardy[2]	
Picardy[2]		Poitou	
Soissonnais		Provence	

Sources:
Auvergene: Goubert 1969–73, 1:74–75.
Béarn, Navarre: Lot and Fawtier 1957, pp. 185–207.
Bourbonnais, Nivernais, Orléans: Canon.
Bresse: Nabholz.
Brittany: Nabholz 1944, pp. 528–32; Fourquin.
Burgundy, Champagne, and Île-de-France: Fourquin 1976, pp. 130–33, 176–78; Brenner 1976, p. 39; Canon 1977, pp. 19–20.
Comtat Venaissin, Dauphiné: Giordanengo.
Guyenne: Neveux 1975, pp. 36–38; Fourquin.
Languedoc: Fourquin.
Lyonnais: Brenner, Canon.
Normandy: Bois 1984.
Picardy: Neveux.
Poitou: Le Roy Ladurie 1987, pp. 56–60; Nabholz
Provence: Neveux; Nabholz; Giordanengo 1988.
Soissonnais: Fourquin; Brenner.

Notes:
1. On some manors in Guyenne, all peasants owed labor dues, while on others obligations were based on peasants' wealth, as in the Île-de-France.
2. Picardy is the only province in which peasants on some manors owed labor dues while peasants on other manors paid cash dues. Although obligations varied across manors, on each manor all peasants shared the same type of obligation.

to the monarch, and with those obligations came further restrictions on freedom as well as protections of their tenures.

The sort of obligations French peasants owed to their manor lords in the centuries before the Black Death are best classified by province (see Table 2.1).[17] In most provinces, the peasants on each manor either all paid dues in cash or all performed labor in the lord's demesne in return for the right to till, and keep the produce of, their own pieces of land. In some provinces lords were able to demand increasingly heavy labor dues as peasant population and demand for land rose during the thirteenth and early fourteenth centuries, in contrast to provinces where dues remained fixed. Finally, the Île-de-France region surrounding Paris and parts of Guyenne fall into a separate category. In those two provinces only poorer and landless peasants were obligated to perform labor dues; wealthier peasants had been able to convert their obligations to cash dues. In preplague France, the Île-de-France and parts of Guyenne

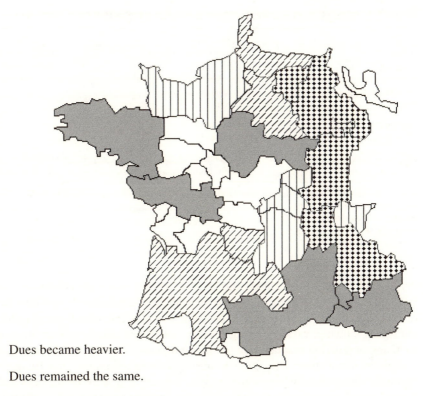

□□□ Dues became heavier.

▥ Dues remained the same.

▨ Dues were commuted to cash.

▨ Mixed outcomes (Île-de-France, Guyenne, and Picardy).

FIGURE 2.1. Changes in Peasant Labor Dues in France, 1100–1347. *Source:* See table 2.1.

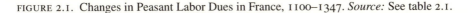

were unique in having differences in the amount of peasant wealth translate into differences in the kind of obligation to landlords.

The provinces in which labor dues were commuted to cash rents are located in the south and west of France but also include the provinces of Orleans, Île-de-France, and Picardy, which contained some of the richest farmland in France (see map 2.1).[18] The mix of ecological zones in which labor dues were commuted suggests that Goldstone's focus upon soil types would not be helpful in explaining land tenure relations in this era.[19]

Le Roy Ladurie's focus on population, as mediated through inheritance practices, also fails to predict the particular set of provinces in which labor dues were commuted. He points to Languedoc and Normandy as exemplars of the tendency for peasant communities to deal with rising population by subdividing tenancies. Since labor dues were assessed on land rather than on individuals, the subdivision of land also

TABLE 2.2. Changes in Peasant Labor Dues in France, 1348–1450

Labor Dues in . . .	Labor Dues Commuted to Cash Dues in . . .	Cash Dues for Rich, Labor Dues for Poor Tenants in . . .
Postplague Brittany ⟵———————	Preplague Britanny	
Preplague Normandy ———————⟶	Postplague Normandy	
	Postplague Île-de-France ⟵———————	Preplague Île-de-France

Sources: See sources for table 2.1 for provinces in which peasant obligations did not change after the Black Death.
Île-de-France: Neveux 1975, pp. 123–38.
Brittany: Goubert 1969–73, 1:74–75.
Normandy: Bois 1984.

divided fixed labor dues among the several families that split a previously unified holding. Subdivision therefore reduced the amount of time a family spent on the lord's demesne, allowing the time saved to be applied to more intensive farming on the peasant family's own plots. As a result, Le Roy Ladurie associates morcellation, caused by rising population mediated by partible inheritance, in the preplague period with continuing labor dues. He contrasts that with areas of unitary inheritance, citing Provence and Poitou, where some tenants accumulated large holdings, which they farmed with hired laborers from families that had lost their tenancies, and paid cash dues for, since it would have been impractical to deliver the required labor dues on such large holdings (Le Roy Ladurie 1987, pp. 56–60). Le Roy Ladurie's model correctly predicts the switch to cash dues in Provence and Poitou; but he is unable to explain why labor dues also were commuted to cash in Languedoc a province with morcellized holdings.

Finally, a rational choice model, which sees market opportunities as the primary solvent of common fields and labor dues, is unable to explain why labor dues were strengthened in regions closest to medieval trading cities, and why labor dues were commuted to cash in isolated as well as coastal provinces.

The difficulties with the demographic, ecological, and rational market approaches intensify when we turn to the postplague period. Only three provinces exhibited significant changes in land tenure arrangements during the century following the Black Death. In Normandy labor dues were changed to cash dues, in the Île-de-France labor dues were commuted for the poorer peasants still under that obligation, and in Brittany labor dues were reimposed (see table 2.2).

Only in Normandy and the Île-de-France did previously servile tenants gain freedom from labor obligations as predicted by the demographic model and, for that matter, by the class-based analyses of Dobb and Brenner. In Brittany the return to labor dues resembles the pattern of Eastern Europe, although Breton tenants were not subjected to restrictions on their freedom as severe as those on serfs east of the Elbe.

Multiple Elites and the Dynamics
of French Social Relations

The evidence displayed in tables 2.1 and 2.2 leaves us with a set of questions: Why was there so much change in tenant obligations before the Black Death, and so little after? Why was there so much variation among French provinces in both periods, and in particular why did Brittany alone revert to labor dues after the Black Death?

An answer to these questions must begin with the observation that manor lords were not the only regulators of manorial social relations, nor were they the exclusive recipients of a share of peasant production. Manor lords shared power with rival elites in medieval France, most notably with kings, the great magnates who commanded armies of their own, and the clergy.

France, in the centuries before and after the Black Death, was a site of heightened elite conflict. Formerly independent provincial rulers, corporate bodies of hereditary nobles, and autonomous manor lords came under the control of more powerful military forces and were incorporated to varying degrees within the growing political unit headed by the French monarch. Shifts in relations among lay elites affected the linkages between laity and the transnational organization of Roman Catholic clergy.

Conflicts among nobility and with clergy cannot be reduced to struggles over the means of production, nor were their timing and outcomes determined by shifts in class relations of production. In the tenth century, only the Île-de-France, as its name suggests, was under the direct control of the French monarch. The eastern part of France—what later became the provinces of Champagne, Burgundy, Bresse, Dauphiné, and Provence—was divided into duchies headed by magnates who viewed themselves, and had the power to act, as little monarchs in their own rights (Duby 1978, p. 108; Lot and Fawtier 1957,).[20] Brittany and much of western and southern France were territories in which rival magnates struggled to control increasingly fragmented corporate bodies of nobles. In many regions the clergy were the most powerful and cohesive elite, exercising a decisive influence in lay elite conflicts and over peasant land tenure arrangements. Much of central and northern France was nominally within the crown's authority; however, control was limited mainly to the right (only at times enforceable) to demand military and financial aid from nobles during time of war.

Each French province fell into one of five patterns of elite structures. Each of these patterns molded agrarian class relations, either locking peasants into one form of exploitation or creating conditions of elite unity or conflict that intensified or weakened the collective capacity of elites to exploit peasants. Only Brittany shifted from one pattern to another in the centuries under consideration here. In all other French provinces the structures of elite relations remained the same in the two centuries prior to and in the century after the Black Death (see table 2.3).

The *Magnate-dominated feudal system* was the most common system in the border areas of eastern and southwestern France where the monarch as yet had little or no influence. In these independent entities autonomous seigneurs were unified into a collective body—most often an estate—under the control of a duke or count. A set of forces combined to forge seigneurs into a unified elite. First, the threat of attack from armies under the control of kings or magnates from outside France gave seigneurs in these border regions an especially strong interest in subordinating themselves to an

TABLE 2.3. Elite Structure and Agrarian Class Relations in France, 1100–1450

Provincial Elite Structures	Dues Became Heavier in . . .	Dues Remained Stable in . . .	Dues Commuted to Cash Dues in . . .	Dues Commuted for Rich Peasants Only in . . .
Magnate-dominated feudal system	Béarn Burgundy Champagne Dauphiné Lyonnais Navarre Soissonnais			
Feudal system without magnate		Auvergne Bourbonnais Bresse Nivernais Normandy		
New feudalism		Brittany		
Magnate struggle	Picardy		Brittany Comtat Venaissin Normandy Orléans Picardy Poitou Provence	Guyenne
Magnate-clergy alliance			Languedoc	
Royal power			Île-de-France	Île-de-France

Sources: Same as for tables 2.1 and 2.2; also Major 1980, pp. 1–204; Lot and Fawtier 1957.

overlord in return for military protection. Second, lay lords were able to use their unity to weaken the clergy, increasing magnates' and seigneurs' share of peasant dues at the expense of the church. Third, once the process of noble political amalgamation was under way, holdout seigneurs found it increasingly difficult to resist the legal and military authority of the magnate and his agents.

Brittany was one of just two provinces in which elite relations were transformed in the decades following the Black Death. And only in that independent region was there a resolution of elite conflict in the fourteenth century. Available sources do not indicate whether the economic crisis of the fourteenth century played a role in the resolution of the 1341–65 Breton secession war. A demographic explanation would have to explain first why the war was able to continue for seventeen years after the onset of the Black Death. The effects of the resolution of magnate conflict, however, are quite clear. The establishment of a cohesive magnate-dominated feudal system led to the imposition of labor dues on Breton peasants, the only such instance of restrictions on peasant freedoms and of an increase in burdens in postplague France.

The *feudal system without magnate* prevailed in three central provinces, Bresse in the east, and in Normandy until the disruptions of the Black Death and the Hundred Years' War (1337–1436). Seigneurial unity in these provinces was based in a collective estate that was not dominated by a magnate. Seigneurs were freed from the fiscal and military obligations imposed upon their counterparts in areas dominated by a duke or count. In the absence of a magnate, however, the clergy remained a strong rival elite, with a capacity for collective mobilization and for administering a court system to protect its interests on manors alongside those of the lay lords.

Magnate struggle, which divided seigneurs while the clergy remained united, was the condition of many provinces throughout the medieval period. Indeed, in all these provinces (with the exception of Brittany) magnate conflict was resolved only when the rival factions were incorporated within the absolutist state in the sixteenth and subsequent centuries. Seigneurs in these provinces were drawn into factions in the hopes of gaining office and estate if their leader prevailed, and in the fear of being overwhelmed if they remained outside of a faction. In a state of factional conflict, the clergy were able to retain and in some instances expand their authority and property.

Magnate-clergy alliance against seigneurs was the unique condition of elite conflict in Languedoc. There, in the twelfth century, a count allied with the powerful clergy to weaken the seigneurs, increasing clerical tithe and countal tax revenues at the expense of dues for lay manor lords (Given 1990).

Royal power was dominant only in the Île-de-France. The crown had an interest in preserving peasants' abilities to pay taxes and realized that interest by guaranteeing peasant land rights. As a result, manor lords were weakened in their efforts to dominate tenants and enforce labor dues. The crown also controlled the clergy and siphoned off much of its revenues in this region.

The clear correlations between particular elite structures and provincial differences in peasant obligations, presented in table 2.3, could not be predicted from demographic cycles, landlord-peasant conflict, or geographic differences. The attention to elite structures allows us to answer the questions posed at the outset of this section. Peasant obligations underwent so much change in the period before the Black Death, and so little in the following century, because elite conflict was far more intense in France during the twelfth and thirteen centuries than in the fourteenth and fifteenth centuries.

During the centuries leading up to the Black Death formerly autonomous and locally based seigneurs in some provinces were amalgamated within centralized feudal structures under the direction of a duke or count, or through a collective body without leadership from a single magnate. In other provinces, a single overlord failed to emerge and manor lords were drawn into rival factions. The outcomes of such elite conflicts and amalgamations determined manor lords' capacities to take advantage of rising population and increase labor obligations in the ways described by both Marxists and non-Marxist demographic historians.

Only in provinces where seigneurs were brought under the direction of a single magnate did landlords have the political power to force peasants to perform heavier labor dues, and to prevent the separate clerical elite from intervening in class relations on lay manors to pursue their own agenda of guarding peasant interests to secure tithe rights (Mousnier 1979, pp. 494–528; Blet 1959, 1:88–99). Where lay lords united, but without the centralized authority and military force provided by magnate rule, they were unable to fend off clerical interference on lay manors and therefore could only preserve, but not extend, existing labor dues.

The transition to cash dues, in full or for rich peasants only, occurred in those provinces where the centralization of feudal power spawned warring factions rather than a unified magnate government. The complex situation in Picardy, where factions enjoyed undisputed authority over some areas, even as other parts of the province were open to continuing dispute, explains why labor dues could be strengthened against peasants in some parts of the province, while elsewhere peasants took advantage of elite conflict to win freedom.

Languedoc is the exceptional case that proves the importance of elite conflict as the primary determinant of a transition from labor to cash dues in preplague France. Conflict in Languedoc was not factional. It engaged an emerging magnate allied with clergy on one hand and a weakening corps of lay manor lords on the other. The primacy of elite over class conflict is evidenced by the Languedocean count and clergy's willingness to enhance peasant rights, even at the cost of reducing revenues on their own manors, in order to weaken their landlord rivals (Fliche 1957, pp. 71–99).

Finally, the Île-de-France represents another type of elite division. There the French king and his retainers were able to weaken and subordinate both clergy and lay landlords. The efforts to weaken rival judicial systems and institutions for agrarian surplus extraction liberated peasants from labor obligations, although royal taxes began their long upward climb even as cash rents stagnated and fell after the Black Death (Fourquin 1976, pp. 176–78).

Despite the general level of peasant communal solidarity and power which Brenner (1976; 1982) claims to find throughout France, the differences across provinces argue that the level of elite conflict and the resulting variations in elite structures account for at least the differences in the capacity of the "feudal ruling class" in each province. The above comparative analysis suggests that differences in elite structures also affected the unity and capacities of the peasant class as well. Peasant abilities to fend off seigneurial demands depended, in part, upon legal protections from clerical courts, as evidenced in the contrast between stable labor dues in provinces where the clergy was strong and rising labor dues in those magnate-dominated provinces where clerical power had been reduced.

The Limits of Agrarian Change in France before 1450

The three cases of shifts in French agrarian class relations after the Black Death serve to identify the parameters of change in France in the late fourteenth and fifteenth centuries. In the Île-de-France, the continuing capacity of the king to undermine the authority of lay manor lords led to the freeing of poorer peasants from labor dues. The general freeing of all Norman peasants from labor dues in the postplague era cannot be explained by demographic factors, even mediated through class forces as Bois ([1976] 1984) attempts to do. Bois makes the error of generalizing from the single case of Normandy, the only province in which a stable elite structure was riven by conflict in the century following the Black Death. As a result, Bois mistakenly assumes that Norman peasants' gains were due to their favorable demographic position after the Black Death, when peasants in other provinces, whose scarce labor was of similar value to manor lords in those places, were not able to escape from existing labor dues. Those other peasants remained under the control of unified feudal elites, while only Norman peasants were able to take advantage of new peasant conflicts to win their freedom.

Bois and Le Roy Ladurie (1987) and his followers do make the additional argument that the Hundred Years' War contributed to the decline of population and thereby added to the demographic and economic advantage of surviving peasants in those zones most affected by war. Normandy, however, sustained only average damage from the war (Canon 1977, p. 9).

The Hundred Years' War had a unique effect on Norman class relations, not because the English invaders killed an especially large number of peasants or because they wrought great devastation on the Norman countryside, but because they in Normandy, and in parts of Guyenne, had the strongest presence and in those regions they most disrupted the organizational cohesion of native French elites (Canon 1977, pp. 14–15).

At the other extreme, only in Brittany were elite conflicts resolved with the only postplague creation of a new system of magnate-directed feudal cohesion. Thus, only in Brittany were landlords able to "solve" the demographic crisis by imposing new labor burdens on their tenants.

The paucity of change in agrarian class relations in England and France in the two centuries following the Black Death is explained by the stability of elite structures in the two countries. Thus, we need to ask why there was so little change in elite structure if we want to understand why such a large fraction of French peasants continued to owe labor dues in those centuries. The rigidity of elite relations may explain why the transition to cash dues did not in itself lead to agrarian capitalism, as Le Roy Ladurie and others at times suggest.

The limits upon elite structural change in the fourteenth and fifteenth centuries are clarified in chapter 3, where I examine the limited effects of urban polities and economies on national and provincial elite relations and upon agrarian class relations, and in chapter 4, where I identify how and why elites were reorganized within "states" in the sixteenth and seventeenth centuries. To lay the groundwork, this chapter examines elite and class relations in England, providing the basis for a conclusion comparing the relative salience of elite, class, and demographic forces in the making of agrarian social relations in feudal England and France.

Class Dynamics in England, 1250–1450

English medieval elite and class structure, thanks in large part to the Norman invaders of 1066, was much more uniform and therefore is easier to analyze than that of France, whose provincial differences were deepened in some part by the same Norman rulers[21]. The English monarchs of the preplague era, unlike their French counterparts, played a critical role in shaping agrarian class relations at the local level. In each English county, the crown had been able to endow its armed retainers with "freehold," land that the retainers could farm or to lease without owing any labor dues to the lord on whose manor the freehold was situated. Thus, in each English county there were two strata of tenants: a privileged group of freeholders who did not owe labor dues and who paid only nominal cash dues to the manor lord, and a much larger strata of "villeins" who were required to perform labor dues on the manor lord's demense (Postan 1972, p. 82; Kosminsky 1956, pp. 68–151).

Superficially, the preplague division between freeholders and villeins on English manors resembles the pattern in the Île-de-France and Guyenne (see table 2.1) where richer peasants paid cash rents while poorer peasants owed labor dues. The English system of tenant stratification differed from that in the two French provinces, however, in two crucial respects. First, English freehold and villein status were not directly linked to wealth; instead they were attributes of individuals and of the tenements they occupied and inherited over generations. Indeed, many individuals had inherited and therefore held both freehold and villein lands and thereby combined in their persons the obligations and privileges of both sorts of positions (Razi 1981, pp. 3–15; Kosminsky 1956, pp. 197–255; Dyer 1980, pp. 105–7).[22]

Second, freehold tenancies enjoyed uniform common law protections throughout England, enforceable in royal courts. The lack of a national system of royal justice in preplague France resulted in different systems of tenant law and custom, and therefore of tenant rights and obligations, across provinces and indeed localities. In England, the same diversity held for villeins, whose rights were determined by the custom of the manor on which they held land. For freeholders, however, the protection of royal justice provided a uniform counterweight to the particular capacities of manor lords and proved critical in the shifts in agrarian class relations after the Black Death.

The Black Death created a crisis for English seigneurs similar to that in France. The decline in the number of peasants affected seigneurial revenues in two sorts of ways. First, the deaths of villeins and of famuli (villeins who performed labor dues but did not hold tenements of their own)[23] reduced the amount of labor available to work the lord's demesne. That loss was most severe on the mainly smaller, often clerical, manors with high demesne-to-villein ratios.[24] Second, lords on all manors were challenged by peasants' willingness to abandon tenements with the heaviest cash and labor dues and move to other manors whose lords were willing to rent vacant tenements at lower rents or offered reduced labor obligations.[25]

Many landlords sought to enforce preexisting labor obligations by preventing peasants from leaving their home manors. The Statute of Labourers, passed by Parliament in 1349, empowered the justices of the peace in each county to appoint commissioners of labor to enforce labor dues and to return fleeing villeins and famuli to their home manors (Putnam 1908, pp. 13–26). English villeins, like their counterparts in France and elsewhere in Europe, resisted restrictions on their mobility (Fryde and Fryde 1991). English peasants were unusually fortunate, however, in that virtually all villeins and famuli were able to abandon labor dues after the Black Death. The Statute of Labourers was an almost total failure in restricting peasant mobility across manors (Farmer 1991).

The uniformity of peasant success throughout England argues against the importance of regional ecology in this period.[26] Peasants' improvement of their terms of tenancy appears to support a demographic supply and demand model; however, as Brenner argues and as I discuss above, the "neo-Malthusian" model cannot explain why English peasants were almost unique among Europeans in attaining freedom from labor dues on all manors within the country.

Brenner's model lumps together English and French peasants as successful avoiders of reenserfment. He does not recognize that while almost all English peasants were able to shed labor dues, French peasants in most provinces saw no improvement in tenant conditions during the postplague era as labor dues continued albeit without becoming more severe. Brenner's emphasis on the strength of English peasant communities fails to account for the weaker effect of similar resistance by French peasants. Clearly, the supposed equally sufficient strength of English and French peasant communities cannot explain the commutation of labor dues in England, the Île-de-France, and Normandy as well as the maintenance of labor dues that fell short of serfdom in the rest of France.

Just as differences in the postplague fate of French peasants turned on the varying elite structures of each province, so divisions among English elites were the key factor in the failure of the Statute of Labourers. Small lay landlords and almost all clerical lords—who relied upon peasant demesne labor to grow the food needed to supply monasteries—were most eager to enforce the statute as the means of retaining villeins and famuli. Lay lords of large manors with relatively small demesnes gained more from leasing vacant lands, albeit at lowered rents, than from enforcing labor dues on the demesne. All were affected, however, by the drop in population, and resulting 30 percent drop in grain prices (Abel 1980, p. 46)[27], which reduced the value of demesne commodities for sale in markets. Only on manors that fed many clerics or less wealthy lords, for whom free demesne food was a significant factor in their family budget, was the retention of villein and famuli labor a top priority (DuBoulay 1966, 1970; Dyer 1980, pp. 118–57; Hatcher 1970, pp. 148–73; Hilton 1947, p. 105).

Differences among English landlords over how to respond to the loss of peasant labor after the Black Death were not forced to a resolution by the sorts of rigid elite political structures that prevailed in most provinces of postplague France. In England, each of the three principal elites—the king and his immediate retainers, lay landlords, and the clergy—had the organizational means to guard their interests at both the national and the manorial level. The English monarch's main interest in the peasantry was in securing financial aid from freeholders to whom earlier kings had granted fiefs in return for military service. As a result, royal judges actively protected freeholders' rights against lay and clerical manor lords (Taylor 1950, pp. 219–58; Kerridge 1969, pp. 19–23, 32–35).

Royal support for freeholders provided indirect assistance to villeins. After the Black Death, freeholders came to have an interest in allying with villeins to eliminate labor dues. For wealthy peasants, the path to greater prosperity lay in leasing more land, to be farmed by family members and, at times, by other peasants paid in wages. The opportunity for profit would have been lost if each new leaseholding meant further labor dues to the lord on the demesne. Thus, it was to the advantage of freeholders to rent new lands for cheap cash, rather than with scarce labor. Further, land for expansion had to come largely from the demesne, once the tenant lands left vacant by deaths in the plague had been redistributed. All groups of peasants could unite in their refusal to participate in the manorial court and in their preference to lease the demesne for cash and to commute labor dues to cash dues (Hilton 1975, pp. 54–73; Hatcher 1970, pp. 225–35; Dyer 1980, pp. 264–69). The organization of freeholders and villeins through a common village organization allowed them to take advantage of royal support for freeholders and divisions among elites to successfully resist landlords' efforts to retain labor dues and the elevated rents of the preplague era (Razi 1981, pp. 12–16, 27–36; Dyer 1980, pp. 264–69).

The other elite division that helped peasants escape labor dues after the Black Death was that between lay manor lords and the clergy. Clerics were the main supporters and beneficiaries of the Statute of Labourers. However, they and the small lay landlords who looked to the statute for aid were dependent for enforcement upon the county commissions of the peace, which were controlled by magnates and other large lay landlords who had little reason to enforce, and often a strong reason to undermine, the statute. As a result, the statute was rarely enforced. Records of fines collected for the three years beginning with 1352 show total receipts of £.7,747. That compares with a total royal subsidy of £.114,767 collected for the same three years (Putnam 1908, p. 321; DuBoulay 1966, pp. 287–88). The meager total of fines collected is a demonstration of the weakness of efforts to punish tenants fleeing obligations and seeking wages above the legal maximum.

Even after they escaped from labor dues, villeins and famuli remained manorial tenants and were still subject to the protections and to some of the other obligations of manorial custom. In the first two centuries after the Black Death, copyholders (villeins and famuli assumed the status of copyholder once they were relieved of labor dues) rented most of their land under terms that did not vary in response to market conditions (Bean 1991, pp. 573–76; Raftis 1964, pp. 183–204; 1957, pp. 251–301; Harvey 1965, pp. 135–40; Hatcher 1970, pp. 102–21; Howell 1983, pp. 42–57). Copyhold tenancies were like villein tenancies in that both were protected from arbitrary cancellation or from increases in rents or in the "fines" paid by heirs to renew their predecessors' leases (Kerridge 1969, pp. 35–45; Gray 1963, pp. 4–12). Copyholders' rights were protected by the manorial court and by clerical courts as well (Kerridge 1969, pp. 35–45; Gray 1963, pp. 4–12; DuBoulay 1966, pp. 297–312; Houlbrooke 1979, pp. 7–20; Hill 1963, pp. 84–92).

During the first century after the Black Death, copyholders gained no financial advantage from leasing their tenements under the protection of the manorial court rather than merely renting land under short-term leases. Only when population, and grain and land prices, rose in the late fifteenth and sixteenth centuries did the advantage of copyhold over mere leasehold become apparent (Abel 1980, p. 125; DuBoulay 1965). Then, in the late sixteenth and the seventeenth century, the specific language used in registering copyholds in the manor rolls "came to be of considerable significance . . . when a strict reading of the language of the copy allowed lords to deny and attempt to alter the prescriptive rights of their tenants" (Hoyle 1990, p. 7).

The existence of copyhold status for more than two centuries raises the questions I posed in the discussion of Dobb's work at the outset of this chapter: Why did the demise of labor dues not lead directly to the development of private property in land and the proletarianization of labor? Neither later Marxist analyses nor the various non-Marxist studies of population, regional ecology, or feudal production explain the continuing viability of manorial social relations.

Despite the variety of legal terms used to record the transformation of villein tenures into copyholds (and the variations in the durability of such tenures in the sixteenth and subsequent centuries), all parties to the new arrangements created in the century following the Black Death believed they were granting or receiving perpetual rights to hold and will tenements to heirs at fixed cash rents and fines. Peasants struggled not only to escape labor dues but to receive copyholds instead of leaseholds (Razi 1981, pp. 12–16, 27–36). Many manor lords— large and small, lay and clerical, and even the bailiffs of manors held by the crown—tried to avoid granting such favorable leases to their tenants (DuBoulay 1964; 1966, pp. 218–37; Dyer 1980, pp. 118–49; Hatcher 1970, pp. 102–21; Raftis 1964, pp. 183–204).

Peasant class unity and elite divisions combined to preserve manorial organizations of agrarian production in the two centuries following the Black Death and to preserve them on terms most favorable to peasants. As mentioned above, freeholders shared with villeins an interest in ensuring that they too could rent vacant lands for cash rents rather than be forced to invest their limited labor time on the demesne in return for larger family farms. As a result, all peasants were united in demanding conversion to cash dues. Further, all peasants were wary of taking on leases that depended on the lord's good will to maintain stable rents.

Peasant unity was not enough in itself to win such favorable terms of tenure.[28] As the comparison of French provinces makes clear, the further condition of elite divisions were necessary to secure gains for peasants. The same constellation of elite forces that undermined the Statute of Labourers also ensured that vacant land was rented in copyhold. The two nationally directed elites—the crown and the clergy—aided peasants in their struggles against locally based manor lords. Royal assize judges and clerical court judges, following the directions of the king and bishops more interested in preserving a nationwide base of tax and tithe payers than in maximizing income on their own manors, upheld peasants' rights to lease land as copyhold even against the bailiffs of royal estates and against clerical manor lords (Gray 1963, pp. 34–49; Blanchard 1971, pp. 16–22; Hill 1963, pp. 84–92; Houlbrooke 1979, pp. 7–20). Clerical court judges, by linking copyholders' land tenure rights to their tithe obligations, forged an alliance between the majority of peasants and clerical benefice holders, even at the expense of clerical and lay manor lords (Raftis 1964, pp. 198–204; DuBoulay 1965, pp. 443–55).

The crown's assize judges played relatively little role in directly protecting copyholder land tenure in the fifteenth century (Gray 1963, pp. 23–24). Few peasants had the resources to afford a case before the king's judges; by contrast, clerical courts were easily accessible and affordable to most copyholders. The crown's real contributions to peasant land rights came when it repeatedly upheld clerical judges' jurisdiction over disputes between peasants and manor lords. The crown had a double interest in maintaining the clergy's power in land-tenure cases; the crown tapped clerical tithe revenues for state income, and kings regarded an independent peasantry as the prime source of tax revenues (Scarisbrick 1960, pp. 41–54; DuBoulay 1966, pp. 92–113) and therefore wanted to preserve the clergy's legal capacity to protect peasants as a counterweight to manor lords.

The Persistence of Manorial Structures in England and France

This chapter's study of the transformation of agrarian class relations in the centuries before and after the Black Death allows us to draw some conclusions about the limits of change in medieval England and France. In both countries all shifts in peasant status were between different sorts of tenancies on manors. Peasants did not escape, nor were they expelled from, their residence on manors. In the centuries after the plague, they continued to derive their (at times shifting) rights and obligations from their status as tenants on manors. Virtually no peasants were proletarianized in England and France before the sixteenth century. Virtually no landlord in either country succeeded in transforming the nondemesne land on their manors into private property that could be managed, rented, or sold as the lord pleased. Indeed, the above discussion demonstrates that the trend was in the opposite direction, with many landlords forced to convert demesne into peasant tenements.

The balance of class forces cannot explain both the persistence of manorial class relations and the variations of land tenure arrangements within that archetypal feudal organization. Instead, elite structure is the crucial explanatory variable. Where elites were in active and unresolved conflict, peasants gained freedom from labor obligations and rights to secure tenure and stable rents, regardless of the demographic, economic, or ecological conditions. Where elite conflicts had been resolved, peasants were subjected to new or intensified labor dues.

The crucial difference between England and France was in the level of elite organization. In France, elites were organized, with the clergy as the main exception, at the provincial level. In England, crown and clergy exercised national and decisive influence over lay lords, who were organized within counties. No national elite, in this era before absolutist states, was able to achieve elite hegemony within an entire nation. What the English crown and clergy were able to do with their national organizations was to prevent the hegemony of lay landlords within counties. As a result, the pattern of many French provinces, in which lay landlords were united under the rule of a magnate or within a collective estate, was not duplicated in English counties.

Two stable patterns, each of which lasted for two centuries, were created in post-plague England and France. In most French provinces, lay elites were able to limit interventions by rival elites from within and without the province and to use their provincial hegemony to hold peasants to labor obligations. In England, and in Brittany, Comtat Venaissin, Normandy, Orléans, Picardy, Poitou, Provence, and Guyenne, magnate conflict—between lay lords and the clergy in those French provinces, and between lay lords and a coalition of clergy and crown in England—ensured that peasants escaped labor dues and retained secure tenure over their lands. In the Île-de-France kings used their power to prevent lay landlord hegemony and to guard peasant freedom as a counterweight to the aristocracy and as an alternate source of tax revenue. In Languedoc, a magnate-clergy alliance pursued a similar strategy of weakening manor lords and strengthening peasant communities.

The transition to agrarian capitalism awaited further transformations of elite structure. In the following chapters, I examine the possible sources of change in feudal polities. Chapter 3 looks to cities—both independent city-states and autonomous cities within nations—as sites of political formations that challenged agrarian elites but in the end did not generate capitalist social relations. Then Chapters 4–6 study different types of states in formation—imperial Spain, the corporate coalition that became the Dutch Republic, and the contrasting absolutisms of England and France—to identify the latter two as the particular forms that both undermined feudal polities and generated new elite structures that were ultimately conducive of capitalism.

A Brief Note on the Asiatic Mode of Production

Sociologists and historians who study non-European societies almost all agree that it is long past time to finally bury Marx's least useful notion, the Asiatic mode of production.[29] Marx's holds that large-scale despotic states in Asia used coercion to appropriate labor directly. The Asiatic mode of production, in Marx's formulation, differed from European feudalism in that corvée labor was organized by centralized institutions, whereas serfs and tenant labor dues were used locally by manor lords. Different ruling classes were supported by each labor system, Marx argues. Although landlords were numerous and prosperous in Asia as well as in Europe, in Asia, military and bureaucratic corps were the main beneficiaries of forced labor, whereas in Europe lords reaped most of the surplus.

Marx had little to say about the dynamics of class conflict and social change in Asia. Indeed, scholars of non-European societies find the Asiatic mode of production such an unhelpful concept precisely because it inhibits analysis of the actual dynamics of social change in societies labeled "Asiatic" by Marx and Marxists. At the same time, students of Asian history have had a hard time going beyond their richly empirical and nuanced historical accounts to generate a new theoretical framework that could allow for comparisons across Asian societies and with Europe.[30]

The analysis of Asian transitions has become stuck in a rut because scholars have tried to infer trajectories of social change from typologies of agrarian production and surplus extraction viewed in isolation from the broader structures of elite and class relations.[31] Weberians have even less to contribute to our understanding of Asian historical development than do the Marxists. Weberians take an essentialist approach, arguing that Asian worldviews and social practices lacked certain crucial features present in Europe and Japan. As a result, they claim, Asian societies aside from Japan never developed as European societies did.[32] Weberians fail to explain the different dynamics of Asian societies and instead content themselves with descriptions of stagnant cultures.

The analysis of elites in this chapter suggests that the crucial characteristic of any European or Asian society is the total structure of elite and class relations rather than the dominant form of surplus extraction at a single historical moment or any complex of cultural practices. Change occurs in the interstices of elite and class relations. We will not find the point of transformative change by comparing modes of production or "rent-collecting" and "tax-collecting" societies (Berktay 1987), or by contrasting empires, kingdoms, and tribal systems. Instead, what matters is the complex of organizations of production and extraction or, to use Bertay's terminology, the mix of rent and taxes and the relations among rent- and tax-collecting elites. Structure matters, in Asia as well as in Europe, as the context within which opportunities for elite and class agency are opened or foreclosed.

If elite structure can best explain the persistence of European feudalism before the sixteenth century, then a similar model can address the persistence of noncapitalist modes of production in Asia and the unique development of agrarian capitalism in Japan beginning in the seventeenth century. We need to ask whether the complex of elite and class relations created openings for transformative conflicts in each country, or city or locale, at particular historical moments. Contingent change happened in

Asia as well as in Europe and all other societies. We need to find the structural points where elites and classes had agency. This book endeavors to do that for Western Europe. In so doing, we can construct a theoretical and methodological framework for future studies of Asia that will be able to explain and compare the particular historical developments of each society.

3

The Limits
of Urban Capitalism

CITIES WERE THE STARS OF medieval and Renaissance Europe. In contrast to the political stasis and virtual autarky of rural areas depicted in the previous chapter, urban areas were sites of rapid demographic change, the nodes of international trading and production networks, and the stages upon which elites and classes became agents of historical change, inventing new and challenging old political arrangements.

During the twelfth through fourteenth centuries cities throughout Europe achieved de facto autonomy and some, especially in northern Italy, gained formal independence from the kingdoms, principalities, and dukedoms by which they were surrounded. Autonomous cities and city-states secured their freedoms through military and financial means. City governments exploited the industry within their walls and the trade that passed through their territories by levying taxes, duties, and loans upon their residents and visitors. (Cities, especially in Italy, also collected tribute from rural areas under their control.) As the budgets of the greatest cities came to exceed those of the largest kingdoms in Europe, those cities became able to field armies that rivaled and often overwhelmed the military forces controlled by kings and aristocrats. Smaller and less wealthy cities bought more limited freedoms from their overlords.

Cities achieved international as well as regional power. Cities formed transnational leagues and coalitions; some cities began to conquer others, becoming the capitals of largely urban empires. Those great cities controlled the key European trade routes, further increasing their citizens' wealth and the income of their governments. The richest urban citizens loaned money to kings and popes, using their control over the main stores of liquid capital in Europe to make demands on kings and eventually to dominate the papacy.

Urban centers achieved levels of population and industry not seen in Europe since the fall of Rome. While innovations in techniques of production and in the conduct of business were few, growth in the quantity of economic activity combined with the reintegration of Europe into Asian and Middle Eastern trade networks to give the appearance of a new quality of economic behavior.

An urban-centered social order appeared to emerge in Europe in the century leading up to the Black Death. Cities seemed poised to become hegemonic on the Western half of the continent as urban places began to recover demographically and economically in the fifteenth century. Under that social system in formation, cities were becoming the exploiters of rural Europe. While aristocrats were the immediate extractors of wealth from peasant producers, nobles and kings in turn surrendered much of their wealth to urban entrepreneurs through usurious loans and overpriced manufactured goods, and at times through military subjugation. Italian, and later specifically Medician, control of a strengthening papacy funneled clerical tithe and land revenues from throughout Western Europe to Italy, and especially to Rome and Florence.

The outlines of a political system in which noncontiguous territories were linked through the domination of a single city or a league of cities became apparent on parts of the continent. Backward Europe was connected to the more advanced regions of Asia and the Middle East through a few great cities; access to the technological innovations, products, and wealth of the rest of the world was controlled by those cities with the connections, military power, and capital to dominate transcontinental trade.

The developing hegemony of urban Europe was lost in the sixteenth century. Most cities were forced to surrender their independence or lost much of their autonomy. The great cities of Italy lost control over trade routes, the papacy, and even much of Italian territory to newly powerful nation-states. Nation-states triumphed because their armies and their abilities to raise revenues came to vastly overwhelm those of cities in the sixteenth century. Even industry began to move out of cities during that century, which became the era of emergence for rural "proto-industry." The population of Italian city-states stagnated or declined during the sixteenth century, even as Europe's overall population and its urban population rose significantly; for the first time, the capitals of nation states displaced the city-states as the most populous in Europe.

Weber and His Critics

Historians and sociologists have devoted much effort to highlighting the aspects of urban life that could explain the rise and prosperity of autonomous cities in the medieval era. Henri Pirenne, Paul Sweezy, and Fernand Braudel exemplify scholars from otherwise quite different perspectives who equate urbanism with capitalist development. Of the three, only Braudel even acknowledges, though he does not explain, the abrupt declines of autonomous cities in the sixteenth century. Other scholars, such as Frederic C. Lane, Charles Tilly, and the students of proto-industry, point to the self-evident (to them) advantages of nation-states and rural industry over city-states and urban merchants yet are not able to articulate why urban politicians and producers were able to thrive, despite their supposed disadvantages, until the sixteenth century.

Max Weber is alone in advancing a single model to explain both the early advantages and subsequent disadvantages of city-based merchants. However, despite the superior logical coherence of his argument, scholars from the other two approaches have successfully undermined the historical foundations of Weber's writings on cities. This review of Weber and his critics makes clear the need for a new analysis of European city-states, and how my elite conflict model can fill that bill. Subsequent sections of this chapter illustrate the value of my approach for medieval and Renaissance Florence.

The City as Capitalism

Weber's writings often are associated, mistakenly as I argue,[1] with a line of scholars who identify autonomous cities as the fonts of capitalism. Pirenne (1925) views cities as islands of economic and political freedom within feudal society, and therefore as the only places in medieval Europe where entrepreneurs could pursue profit away from the structural restrictions of lords and the inhibitions of backward rural customs. Over centuries, the dynamics of urban capitalism came to dominate the entire continent in Pirenne's view, subverting aristocratic rule and transforming subsistence agricultural economies.

Pirenne's writings have influenced Marxists as well as non-Marxists. Sweezy's critique ([1950] 1976) of Dobb echoes Pirenne's pessimistic view of the possibilities for structural change and economic development within the rural sector of feudal Europe. Braudel, the most influential contemporary historian of medieval and Renaissance European economic development, is so confident that capitalism *tout court* existed in medieval cities that he abruptly dismisses Weber's Protestant ethic thesis.

> For Max Weber, capitalism in the modern sense of the word was no more and no less than a creation of Protestantism or, to be more accurate, of Puritanism.
>
> All historians have opposed this tenuous theory, although they have not managed to be rid of it once and for all. Yet it is clearly false. The northern countries took over the place that earlier had so long and so brilliantly been occupied by the old capitalist centers of the Mediterranean. They invented nothing, either in technology or in business management. (1977, pp. 65–66)

Braudel's critique of Weber exemplifies the most common complaint leveled against both the social psychological approach to the origins of capitalism, exemplified in *The Protestant Ethic and the Spirit of Capitalism,* and the sort of structural model, emphasizing classes, elites, and state formation, that I present in this book. Braudel contends that capitalism, in both the Weberian and the Marxist sense, existed in the city-states of Renaissance Italy and was practiced as well by the Italians' northern rivals who were based in the towns of the Hanseatic league and in the urban centers of the Low Countries. What Marx, Weber, and their successors describe as the beginnings of capitalism in sixteenth-century England was no more than a "shift . . . from the Mediterranean to the North Sea represent[ing] the victory of a new region over an old one. It also represented a vast change of scale" (p. 67). For Braudel ([1979] 1984), the rise of England (and of the Netherlands) was a major transformation within an already existent European capitalist system.

Braudel, who both anticipates and borrows from Immanuel Wallerstein's world system model, raises an argument that must be addressed.[2] His work is given weight, not only by his own historical erudition and the sophistication of his theoretical model, but also by the preponderant tendency among historians to characterize urban merchants of Renaissance Europe as capitalists. This debate is, in part, one of definition. Since some scholars define capitalism in terms of characteristics that were present in Renaissance cities, while other authors view practices or relations that originated in the sixteenth or later centuries as essential to capitalism, everyone can win this debate by highlighting cases that conform to his or her favored definition. Braudel however, in arguing that his studies of Renaissance cities reveal capitalism as defined by Marx and Weber, is making an even broader claim.[3] That claim is incorrect; despite Braudel's assertions, Marx's and Weber's definitions of capitalism do differ in crucial respects from the descriptions of Renaissance Europe offered by Braudel and like-minded historians.

Braudel offers an essentialist view of capitalism: "I have argued that capitalism has been potentially visible since the dawn of history, and that it has developed and perpetuated itself down the ages. . . . Throughout even this formidable transformation [the Industrial Revolution] capitalism remained essentially true to itself" ([1979] 1984, pp. 620, 621). By contrast, Marx, Weber, and the model I develop in this book give emphasis to the varied and disjunctive nature of the development of state and classes, of capitalist structures, relations, and practices across Europe from the fourteenth through the eighteenth century.[4]

Disjunctures are especially evident in the histories of urban centers in the medieval and Renaissance eras. During the thirteenth century, hundreds of Italian cities, dozens of German and Swiss cities, as well as some French cities and scattered cities elsewhere won autonomy from aristocratic rule (Blockmans 1978, Burke 1986, Friedrichs 1981). Over the following five hundred years virtually all those cities came under the control of nobles or states, with some cities losing and gaining their freedom a number of times over centuries, decades, years, and even months. Economically, as Braudel recognizes, villages and towns were transformed into centers of commerce and industry and at times just as quickly abandoned for new and more promising economic enters. The demographic fluctuations of European urban centers track their political and economic turns of fate.

Shifts in economic fortune and demographic centrality are depicted, by Braudel, as part of the dynamic of capitalism.[5] Unfortunately, description is not a substitute for causation. Braudel and like-minded historians are unable to identify a set of factors that could account for the rise and fall of urban centers. All the accounts of "capitalism" among Renaissance urban merchants have not provided an answer to the crucial question of why did the first great commercial cities of late medieval Europe not become the centers of subsequent capitalist development?

Braudel ([1979] 1984) tries to finesse that question by enumerating the requisites for economic leadership at each stage in the development of the European "world economy." His history offers vivid descriptions of the successive loss of economic leadership by Italian city-states, to Antwerp, and the subsequent passing of hegemony to Genoa, Amsterdam, and then London. When Braudel moves from description to explanation, however, his account is ad hoc rather than systematic and thereby becomes less satisfying. His lack of attention to the internal political dynamics of urban centers leaves him unable to explain why existing capitals of European trade could not preempt challenges from rival cities by adapting to the new requirements for control over production and exchange in the European world system.[6]

Weber's City: "Politically Oriented Capitalism"

Intuitively, one would expect that advantages of greater capital accumulations and control over existing trade networks should have given the already functioning economic centers of Renaissance Italy and the Low Countries advantages over putative rivals. That those cities lost their edges suggests a need to systematically study the structures of social relations within those cities, as well as (and in interaction with) shifts in the political and economic relations among units in the European "world economy." Weber addressed the shift in European economic hegemony by labeling Renaissance Italian economies "politically oriented capitalism," as opposed to the "economically oriented capitalism" of Puritan nations.[7] Weber argues that Renaissance Italian businessmen were well suited to realizing opportunities for profit in feudal Europe by their political orientation toward profit. However, that orientation rendered the Medici and their ilk incapable of adapting to compete in the new economic climate created by economically oriented Protestant businessmen in the sixteenth and subsequent centuries.

"Politically oriented events and processes which open up these profit opportunities exploited by political capitalism are irrational from an economic point of view— that is, from the point of view of orientation to market advantages and thus to the consumption needs of budgetary units" (Weber 1978, p. 166). The contingency of economic activities on political processes introduces arbitrary, hence unpredictable and incalculable elements into a capitalist's decisions. This, for Weber, was the principal factor in the Italians' loss of competitive advantage to northern, Protestant Europeans. Weber suggests that had the politically oriented Italians been able to adopt an economic orientation they would have been able to compete successfully with Protestant businessmen. In his view, however, businessmen's orientations are quite rigid and fixed. New structural conditions created the different, economic orientation in other, non-Italian capitalists.

Weber saw the replacement of patrimonial states, which "check the development of capitalism by creating vested interests in the maintenance of existing sources of fees and contributions" by bureaucratic states "conducting the collection of the taxes (but no other economic activity) through its own staff, . . . [which] provide the optimal environment for a rational market-oriented capitalism" (1978, p, 199) as a necessary precondition for the development of rational capitalism.[8] Although Weber's distinctions between patrimonial and bureaucratic states and between politically and economically oriented capitalism are idealized,[9] they call needed attention to the political aspect of the sixteenth-century disjuncture in European economic development.

Braudel may be correct that psychological factors are not necessary to account for the shift in economic hegemony in sixteenth-century Europe. However, a challenge to Weber's social psychology must posit some causal relation between shifts in forms of economic domination on one hand and in forms of political power on the other hand and must identify the mechanisms through which economy and polity affected one another.

Nation-States and the Decline of Cities

The rise of nation-states coincided with the decline of autonomous city-states as military powers and later as the leading centers of production and trade. Frederic Lane (1958; 1979) defines city-states and nation-states as organizations that collect taxes to meet the expenses of policing and maintaining a monopoly on force within a territory. The more efficiently a state can provide those services, the greater the profit the state can retain from its tax revenues. In Lane's view, the political history of Europe from A.D. 700 to 1700 is based on the "changing relation of violence-using enterprises to the amount and distribution of surplus" (1958, p. 412). Thus, the greater efficiency of nation-states ensured their triumph over both city-states and autonomous rural lords.

Charles Tilly deepens Lane's model. Tilly traces the consolidation of political units in Europe from "500 states, would-be states, statelets, and statelike organizations" in 1490 to "a mere 25 to 28 states" in 1990 (1990, pp. 42–43). He identifies varying mixtures of capital and coercion located at particular sites in Europe and describes how political actors' access to those two resources determined the sorts of states they erected.

City-states, in Tilly's view, were rich in capital but were unable to appropriate significant coercive resources except by purchasing mercenary armies. City-states were doomed by two changes in the sixteenth century. First, Atlantic trade and associated production grew while "Mediterranean city-states' . . . own waterways were limited by Muslin powers" (1990, p. 190). Second, as states controlling larger populations developed the means to extract capital and coercion from broad territories, even if at a fraction of the rate of city states, their vastly greater size gave them the means to outspend and overpower city states. Such resources became critical as "war expanded in scale and cost" (p. 190). For Tilly, the heyday of city states lasted only until large states began to coalesce and to organize mechanisms for taxation and for fielding national armies.[10]

I evaluate Lane and Tilly's models of state formation more fully in chapter 4. For now, however, even if we allow that Tilly has fully explained how the availability of capital and coercion shaped the development of state structures, his model cannot explain why capital and coercion were organized in national units rather than in the networks of noncontiguous cities and territories that were developing in medieval and Renaissance Europe.

From the vantage point of the present, or of the nineteenth century, we can recognize the ways in which contiguous territories, and populations molded into a shared sense of nationality, help states in the tasks of collecting taxes, drafting armies, and defending borders. However, the states that triumphed militarily and economically over the city-states in the sixteenth century often were not contiguous or ethnically and linguistically homogeneous. Indeed, the most successful sixteenth-century states fought wars for the purpose of seizing noncontiguous territories and bringing foreign peoples under their rule. The advantages of mature, nineteenth-century nation-states cannot be used anachronistically to explain why rural-based aristocrats came to dominate urban-based merchants in the sixteenth century rather than the reverse.

Before we turn to state formation, the topic of chapter 4, we must answer two counterfactual questions: Why did the great cities of medieval and Renaissance Europe not become the economic and political centers of subsequent capitalist development and state formation? Why were the elites of the city-states overwhelmed in the sixteenth and subsequent centuries by rival rural elites that were able to consolidate vast rural territories and to dominate the cities in their midst?

To answer those questions, one must explain the decline of city-states as well as the rise of nation-states. Weber attempted to do that. But his model, as Braudel and other scholars of Renaissance Italy demonstrate, exaggerates the differences in outlook and action between medieval and post-Reformation Europeans. Weber's argument also mistakenly suggests that individuals, firms, and perhaps societies are either politically or economically oriented and because of their fixed orientations are psychologically unable to switch between or combine political and economic rationalities, depending upon circumstances. In fact, individuals' political and economic plans usually were tailored to the specific and limited structural openings available in any particular time and place. Opportunities for profit were accessed through the organizational structures of city-states and nation-states, structures that, as Tilly's oeuvre demonstrates, were themselves the products of long histories of formation and of collective action.

Toward a Structural Model of the Rise and Demise of City-States

This chapter posits a structural model of the interaction between economy and polity in Renaissance Florence and tests it against Weber's theory of the limits of politically oriented capitalism within patrimonial city-states. I begin with an overview of shifts in the demographic rankings of European cities in order to trace and time the decline of autonomous commercial cities in comparison with the rise of capitals of nation-states. The body of this chapter addresses the dynamics of urban capitalism through an extended case study of Florence. I chose Florence because it was the archetypal Italian city-state in its periodic dominance of international exchange and luxury manufacture in medieval Europe, and because it continued to play a major role in Italian and European politics and trade throughout the Renaissance. As such, Florence's history can be studied to explain movement back and forth from the apex to a secondary, though still central, position in the political economy of medieval and Renaissance Europe.[11]

Florence is uniquely important among Renaissance cities because Medici control of the papacy provided the basis for an alternative system of agrarian surplus extraction in which urban elites would have dominated subordinate rural aristocracies. Florence's decline ended that possible path of historical development. Churches instead became defined in increasingly national terms as they were subordinated to lay nobilities that were organizing along national lines.

It is vital to specify the limits to political and economic autonomy possible for Florence, and for the other leading Renaissance cities that I discuss in less depth and in comparison with Florence, in order to explain why the development of trade, production, and political power shifted from city-states ruled by oligarchies to nation-states ruled by classes. This chapter approaches that problem by looking at Florence and other city-states, not just as temporary leaders of an evolving world system or as sites of an inadequate capitalist spirit, but also as social formations with dynamics that evoked certain behaviors on the part of social actors whose interests were defined and whose capacities were limited by the local and global settings within which they were embedded. Determining the causal priority of social psychological, world systemic, military-technological, and internal structural factors in the relative decline of Renaissance urban capitalism is a necessary prior step to explaining why states, and not just cities, world systems, or the minds of individuals, were the sites necessary for the formation of capitalist classes and for the practice of capitalist social relations. This chapter concludes with observations on the limits of economic action within city-states, laying the groundwork for the focus of the following chapters on state and class formation in the sixteenth through eighteenth centuries.[12]

Demographic Measures of Urban Power, 1300–1700

Historical demographers use population as the best proxy for the wealth of medieval and Renaissance cities. Gains and losses of population are used to track the rise and fall of leading economic and political centers of those eras. The proportion of a region's population that is urban, and the number of levels of urban places and markets, stand as measures for the influence of cities and of urbanization upon the political economies of rural hinterlands.[13]

By those measures, Europe underwent two distinct phases of urbanization in the centuries before the Industrial Revolution. From the eleventh century until the Black Death, the proportion of Europeans (excluding Russia) who lived in places of five thousand or more rose from perhaps 9.5 percent to 10.5 percent. That percentage increase was magnified by the doubling of total European population in those centuries, thereby more than doubling the number of cities with populations measured at above ten thousand (Bairoch 1988, pp. 136–37). Total population, both urban and rural, fell drastically after the Black Death, while the level of urbanization fell slightly and the number of cities stagnated.

General recovery from the Black Death preceded a renewal of "urban growth [that] began slowly in the first half of the sixteenth century . . . quickened its pace dramatically in the century from 1550 to 1650, and then decelerated, reaching a low point in the first half of the eighteenth century" (De Vries 1984, p. 39).[14]

Data for all of Europe mask critical differences in urban growth across regions and countries in each era. In 1300, northern Italy was the most urbanized part of Europe, with between a fifth and a quarter of the populations in the regions of Milan, Venice, and Florence living in towns. The recently Muslim region of Cordoba was next in urbanization (17 percent), followed by the Belgian territory centered on Ghent (14 percent), and Aragon (14 percent). The region headed by Montpellier (11 percent) was the only other part of Europe with more than 8 percent of its population in towns (Russell 1972, p. 235).

By 1500, Belgium had become the most urbanized region of Europe, with a percentage of city dwellers approximately four times the average of Europe excluding Russia.[15] The Netherlands followed with about triple the average, and northern Italy was slightly less urbanized. Spain was at the European average, and all other countries were less urbanized.

Two hundred years later, the Netherlands had become the leading urban nation of Europe at four times the average. Belgium and northern Italy, which had stagnated and perhaps fallen in their levels of urbanization while the continent increased overall, were at two and one-half and one and one-half times the European average, respectively. Northern Italy's level of urbanization in 1700 was virtually identical to that of England and Portugal. Spain and France were at, and all other countries well below, the European mean.

The above figures trace the shift from "south to north" in European urbanization in the period 1450–1550, which Braudel has called the "first" sixteenth century (quoted in Wallerstein 1974–89, 1:68). During the "second" sixteenth century (1550–1640) the Netherlands displaced Belgium, while London was about to enter the exponential part of its growth to world dominance.

The picture of a movement of urban hegemony from Italy to Belgium, the Netherlands, and ultimately England, painted by the broad brush of national-level data, misses the timing and location of the most vital elements in Renaissance urbanization for two reasons. First, national-level classifications are anachronistic for most Renaissance cities that either were the dominant elements in independent subnational political units (the city-states) or shared sovereignty over their regions with weak monarchs and nobles and often secured political strength and access to trade through membership in transnational networks (such as the Hanseatic League cities). The political and economic fates of such autonomous cities (which comprised almost all the major European cities until the sixteenth century) had little to do with the future nation-states within which they were located. Indeed, the second problem with national-level data—its conflation of rising and falling cities within national or regional averages—reflects the weak role of national polities and economies in the fates of Renaissance cities.

The dominant role of independent city-states in the urban sector of Renaissance Europe is revealed by their populations. A comparison of the populations of Christian European cities with populations greater than fifty thousand in the years 1300 and 1500 shows the dominance of commercial centers over administrative capitals in that era (see table 3.1).[16]

The first date, 1320, is the peak of urbanization prior to the demographic crisis that culminated in the Black Death. Of the eleven leading cities, seven are commercial cities that controlled little territory beyond their walls. The dominance of Italy is revealed in the concentration of six of the seven commercial cities there (the other is in present-day Belgium). In addition, Palermo was a trading center as well as the capital of Sicily, which had recently seceded from the kingdom of Naples. Just two of the leading cities were capitals of extensive political units; London's population was a product at least as much of its role as a port and commercial center as of its status as the seat of a growing state. Only Paris, the capital of what already was emerging as the most populous political unit in Western Europe, qualified as a true administrative center.[17]

TABLE 3.1. Cities with Populations Greater
than 50,000 in Christian Europe, 1320–1500

1320	1500
Commercial Cities	
Venice 100,000	Venice 115,000
Florence 96,000	Milan 89,000
Milan 75,000	Florence 70,000
Bologna 65,000	Genoa 62,000
Genoa 60,000	Bologna 55,000
Siena 52,000	Ghent 80,000
Ghent 56,000	Bruges 60,000
Capital/Port Cities	
London 60,000	Naples 114,000
Palermo 50,000	Lisbon 55,000
	London 50,000
Capital Cities	
Paris 80,000	Paris 185,000
	Moscow 80,000
	Prague 70,000
Reconquered Cities	
Cordoba 60,000	Granada 70,000

Sources: For 1320, Russell 1972; for 1500, Chandler 1987,
p. 19.

The picture in 1500, just before the second phase of European urban growth, is indicative of the growing prominence of political capitals as centers of urban resources. There are still seven commercial cities with populations greater than fifty thousand. The beginnings of a shift from Italy to the Low Countries are illustrated by the replacement of Italian Siena by Belgian Bruges on this list. More remarkable are the addition of four political capitals to the list. Two—Lisbon and Naples—also were shipping centers. Paris had become by a significant margin the greatest European city. Prague and Moscow joined the list almost exclusively by attracting population to governmental centers.

The populations of medieval commercial and governmental centers proved highly unstable over the following centuries, fluctuating relatively and absolutely as cities gained and lost hegemony over trade routes and political domains. Eighteen cities placed one or more times among the largest ten in Europe in the years 1320, 1500, 1600, and 1700 (see table 3.2).[18]

The northern Italian commercial city-states, which held six of the top ten slots in 1300, declined to four slots by 1500, and to two in 1600 and 1700. So overwhelming was the concentration of economic power, and of urbanization, in northern Italy during the preplague era, that not only were the lead cities of three regions—Venice,

TABLE 3.2. Population and Rank of the Ten Largest Cities in Christian Europe, 1320–1700

	Year			
	1320	1500	1600	1700
Commercial Cities				
Venice	100,000 (1)	115,000 (2)	151,000 (4)	144,000 (6)
Florence	96,000 (2)	70,000 (7)	65,000 (14)	68,000 (18)
Milan	75,000 (4)	89,000 (4)	107,000 (7)	113,000 (10)
Bologna	65,000 (5)	55,000 (12)	62,000 (18)	63,000 (22)
Genoa	60,000 (6)	62,000 (9)	65,000 (14)	67,000 (19)
Ghent	56,000 (8)	80,000 (5)	31,000 (40)	49,000 (32)
Siena	52,000 (9)	22,000 (37)	>20,000 (<100)	>20,000 (<100)
Seville	40,000 (14)	46,000 (16)	126,000 (5)	80,000 (13)
Bruges	30,000 (25)	60,000 (10)	25,000 (57)	35,000 (50)
Capital/Port Cities				
London	60,000 (6)	50,000 (13)	187,000 (3)	550,000 (1)
Palermo	50,000 (10)	39,000 (18)	105,000 (8)	124,000 (8)
Naples	25,000 (34)	114,000 (3)	224,000 (2)	207,000 (4)
Lisbon	20,000 (44)	55,000 (12)	100,000 (10)	188,000 (5)
Amsterdam	>1,000 (>100)	10,000 (>100)	48,000 (30)	210,000 (3)
Capital Cities				
Paris	80,000 (3)	185,000 (1)	245,000 (1)	530,000 (2)
Prague	30,000 (24)	70,000 (7)	110,000 (6)	48,000 (33)
Rome	25,000 (38)	38,000 (20)	102,000 (9)	138,000 (7)
Moscow	22,000 (41)	80,000 (5)	80,000 (11)	114,000 (9)

Sources: For 1320, Russell 1972; for 1500–1700, Chandler 1987, pp. 19–21.

Note: The rankings for 1320 are derived from the population figures Russell gives for the twenty regions located in Europe. For reasons I note in the text, I have excluded Granada and Cordoba from the 1320 and 1500 lists and do not figure them into the rankings of city sizes. The figure for Moscow in the 1320 column is for 1337, nine years after it became the Russian capital. For the 1320 size rankings I add in the five Russian cities with populations greater than 20,000 listed by Chandler.

Florence, and Milan—at the apex of European cities, but also the second cities of those regions—Bologna, Siena, and Genoa—were in the top ten as well. By 1500, however, the second cities had lost population both relatively and absolutely. Genoa, which gained a high measure of economic autonomy from Milan, was a partial exception to this trend. During the sixteenth century, only Venice and Milan among the city-states recorded significant population gains, with just Venice outpacing the overall European increase in urbanization.

The sixteenth century was the last era of prominence for any of the Italian city-states. Even within Italy, they were rivaled by the political capitals of Rome and Palermo.[19] In the whole of Europe, the sixteenth and seventeenth centuries marked the moment of arrival for the great capital cities. London joined Paris as the greatest cities of Europe. With populations more than two and one-half times that of Amsterdam, the third city of 1700, the capitals of the two emerging great political and economic

TABLE 3.3. Population Changes in Florence and Cities of over 100,000, 1600–1700

City	Population 1600	Population 1700	Change 1600–1700 (%)
Capitals of Major Powers			
Amsterdam	48,000	210,000	+338
Vienna	30,000	105,000	+250
London	187,000	550,000	+194
Paris	245,000	530,000	+116
Capitals of Lesser Powers			
Lisbon	100,000	188,000	+88
Moscow	80,000	114,000	+43
Rome	102,000	138,000	+35
Madrid	80,000	105,000	+31
Italian Cities			
Palermo	105,000	124,000	+18
Milan	107,000	113,000	+6
Florence	65,000	68,000	+5
Venice	151,000	144,000	−5
Naples	224,000	207,000	−8
Cities Subordinated to New Capitals			
Seville	126,000	80,000	−37
Prague	110,000	48,000	−56

Source: For population data, Chandler 1987, pp. 20–21.

powers enjoyed demographic margins over the next cities larger than any European leading cities since Constantinople and Rome were imperial capitals.

Cities' virtual total loss of autonomy in the seventeenth century and their powerful dependence upon the national political units within which they were situated is reflected in demographic changes (see table 3.3). Among cities with populations of over 100,000 in either 1600 or 1700, the greatest population increases were among the capitals of major political and military powers. Lesser, but still substantial growth was recorded in the capitals of lesser or declining powers. The Italian cities, which were capitals only of themselves or of small regions, grew hardly at all or declined in population. Finally, cities that were incorporated within states in which they were not capitals suffered catastrophic declines. Seville is emblematic of this. Once Madrid was named the capital of a major nation state (even one soon to stagnate and then decline) in 1561, it grew from a village to a major city within four decades and then switched population levels and demographic rankings with Seville, once the leading and a strongly autonomous city of Spain.

The most outstanding feature of European urbanization before the Industrial Revolution, as depicted in the three tables above, is its fragility. Cities and urban networks gained and lost relative advantages within one or two centuries. Florence, Genoa, Milan, and Venice all became major commercial centers in the late thirteenth century. Milan and Florence declined to secondary positions in the 1340s. Genoa was the leading Italian power until its defeat by Venice in 1379. Venice then became Europe's leading commercial city until the end of the fifteenth century, with Florence posing a significant challenge in banking and manufacture from the 1420s until the end of the century.

Italy was rivaled by two other commercial centers in the century leading up to the Black Death. The towns of the Champagne fairs competed with Italian cities until they lost special status after 1285 and were replaced by Lyons (Abu-Lughod 1989, pp. 51–77). More important were the Belgian cities of Bruges and Ghent, which alternated in their dominance of northern European trade and textile manufacture from the late thirteenth century until Venice usurped their commercial networks in the 1370s. Both cities' manufacturing enterprises and populations went into sharp absolute declines in the late fifteenth century. Antwerp was the leading commercial city of Europe from the beginning of the sixteenth century until it was overtaken by a resurgent Genoa in the 1550s. The heyday of autonomous city-states was finally ended with Amsterdam's arrival in the 1620s as the first European national capital to become for a time the leading capitalist city of the world.[20]

The Bases of Urban Autonomy

Cities won urban autonomy when their merchant elites possessed and were able to mobilize resources sufficient to take advantage of divisions among feudal lords and monarchs. Where urban merchants lacked resources or, more commonly, were unable to mobilize the resources they did possess, city dwellers lost the opportunity to profit from conflict among aristocrats. Absent exploitable divisions, however, no level of urban wealth was sufficient to gain a high degree of autonomy.

Obstacles to Urban Autonomy: England, France, and Germany

In a comparison of levels of autonomy among cities of Western Europe, English cities stand at one end of a continuum (see fig.3.1). As I demonstrate in chapter 2, English elites had a relatively low degree of transformative conflict in the feudal era. English towns, therefore, had almost no opportunities to exploit divisions among feudal elites. Regardless of the level of wealth of English urban dwellers, their towns never were

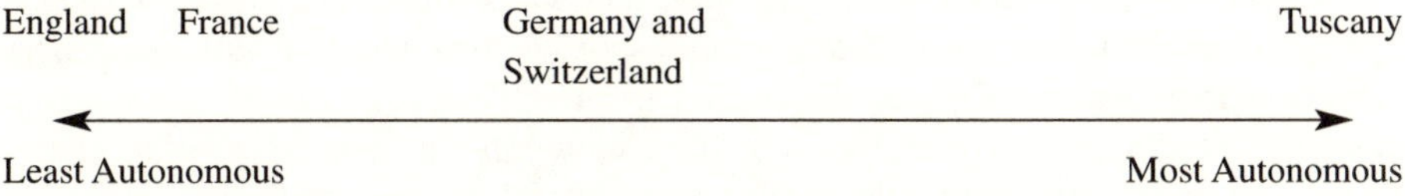

England	France	Germany and Switzerland		Tuscany

← ——————————————————————————————→

Least Autonomous　　　　　　　　　　　　　　　　　　　　Most Autonomous

FIGURE 3.1. Urban Autonomy in Medieval and Renaissance Western Europe

able to raise their own armed forces or to gain more than nominal representation in Parliament.

The political weakness of Enlgish towns placed them at a disadvantage in economic affairs. English monarchs granted many of their most lucrative concessions to foreigners rather than to merchants from English towns. Florentine and Sienese merchants were among the beneficiaries of English merchants' lack of leverage over their crown. The Italians, beginning in 1220, won the rights to be the only foreign merchants resident in England and were given exclusive license to buy high quality English wool (de Roover 1963, p. 71). As a result of those concessions, Italian and not English merchants gained control over the luxury trade in woolens (p. 71).

French towns enjoyed a measure of autonomy in those provinces where and in those eras when elites were divided by conflicts among provincial magnates and with aggrandizing monarchs. Janet Abu-Lughod locates the heyday of the Champagne fair towns during the century when the counts of Champagne battled to maintain their independence against the French crown and the papacy. The counts of Champagne were in the weakest position of the three elites and offered the best terms to local and foreign merchants. The four Champagne fair towns became the centers of trade and of cloth manufacture in France, and came to be inhabited by a substantial number of proletarianized laborers (Abu-Lughod 1989, pp. 55–67).[21]

Once feudal elite conflict was resolved with the incorporation of Champagne into the kingdom of France in 1285, the fair towns lost their autonomy. Despite their wealth, the Champagne merchants lost their privileges (Abu-Lughod 1989, pp. 55–67). The French crown made Lyons the new center of trade and manufacture for the kingdom without offering merchants there the same liberal concessions they had been able to win when Champagne was a terrain of elite conflict. Indeed, Florentines, with their ties to "the Papacy and its alliance with the Angevin royal houses of Florence and Naples," rather than the politically emasculated French merchants, became the recipients of favorable trade concessions and opportunities to loan funds to the French crown (Larner 1980, p. 44; see also Goldthwaite 1980, pp. 34–35, 39; 1987, pp. 16–17; Partner 1972, p. 267).

Cities in what became Germany and Switzerland occupy a middle ground in the subordination-independence continuum. Those cities took advantage of the conflicts between local aristocrats, the Holy Roman emperor, and the pope and bishops (who sometimes worked at cross-purposes to their de jure superior) "to enhance their own power by playing off the interests of one great dynasty against another" (Friedrichs 1981, p. 113). Cities that were administrative centers of the Holy Roman Empire or episcopal seats or the capitals of great aristocratic domains "attracted large settlements of merchants and craftsmen [who] beginning in the twelfth century . . . began to form communes, associations of citizens committed to securing a greater degree of self-government from their municipal overlords" (p. 114).[22]

Urban communes in the future Germany and Switzerland at first won privileges by subordinating themselves to autonomous bishops who protected the urban dwellers from lay nobles or by mortgaging the city to a great noble dynasty, thereby exchanging annual tribute payments for protection and trade monopolies within the noble's territory. A city could win a higher degree of autonomy if the commune leaders were able to induce the Holy Roman emperor to grant their city imperial status. Such status allowed communes to govern themselves and their cities with less interference by and obligation to ecclesiastical or noble overlords. The emperor could grant and enforce imperial rights only when and where he had the power to compel nobles and bishops to adhere to his edicts.

Imperial power reached a peak in the late thirteenth and fourteenth centuries. During that era, many cities became self-governing (although at times to raise money the emperor would mortgage cities to nobles, once again limiting urban autonomy until the commune could buy out the mortgage from the noble). Cities sought to preserve their autonomy by forming leagues that could coordinate military, economic, and diplomatic pressure against nobles who sought to reassert control over urban centers. The Hanseatic League, the Swabian League of south German cities, the Rhenish city league, and smaller leagues of south German cities all reached peaks of influence in the fourteenth century. Cities were forced to withdraw from the Hansa, and that league shrank in size, as nobles regained control over cities within their territories, starting in the fifteenth century. The other leagues also suffered military defeats and collapsed or were reorganized on smaller scales during the 1400s.

The dwindling number of German cities that remained autonomous into the seventeenth century were the ones located in areas where the emperor was strongest in relation to regional aristocratic dynasties. Ultimately, urban autonomy in Germany and Switzerland was far more a function of the relative power of emperor and nobles than it was determined by the level of resources of the cities themselves. Contrary to Tilly's argument (1990, pp. 131–33), German cities, despite their control of long-distance trade and relatively high concentrations of capital, had little bargaining power against aristocrats. Only when aristocrats and the emperor were divided were cities able to use their capital to win autonomy. When the emperor or an aristocrat had unchallenged control over a region, or when they cooperated to extort money from urban merchants, the cities within that territory were forced to accept the terms of government dictated by their ruler.

The Devolution of Power and Urban Autonomy in Tuscany

Carolingian hegemony over northern Italy collapsed following the death of King Louis II in 875. Over the following three hundred years, French and Burgundian kings and German emperors fought each other for authority over the Italian kingdom and then for its disintegrating parts. They also struggled with the pope to control the parallel ecclesiastical government and its extensive domains. The conflicts among kings, emperors, and popes were fought mainly through Italian proxies. The rival pretenders to Italian rule each enlisted allies by delegating authority and lands to powerful local families who would then have an interest in fighting for their patrons' claims as a way of guarding the powers and properties they had been granted by their sponsor.

Tuscany was the region of Italy in which the balance of power among king, emperor, and pope was contested most intensely and for the longest period. As a result, Tuscan nobles—both urban and rural—were best positioned to play their competing overlords against one another and win more permanent and secure land rights and official autonomy than elsewhere in Italy. Power devolved in Tuscany upon corporate bodies of nobles and untitled families living within cities.

The process of political devolution began under the Carolingians as those rulers sought to blunt challenges from marquises, who were the dominant economic and military powers in the countryside, and by the pope and his rival ecclesiastical government. The Carolingian kings moved to create a network of aristocrats loyal to the crown by naming members of old noble families in the cities as bishops. The appointments, which were nonhereditary, rewarded the loyalty of the king's allies and weakened papal control over clerical offices. The bishops who ruled the cities then served as a countervailing force to the great rural nobles (Hyde 1973, p. 44; Wickham 1981, pp. 56–57).

The rivals for the Italian crown continued the Carolingian methods of divide and rule after 875. However, with royal power itself divided and contested, a welter of new families gained estates and offices during the tenth century. This process resulted in a rapid formation of new urban and rural elites. "Very few of the important aristocratic families of 1000 had been important a century before" (Wickham 1981, p. 181). When rural marquises moved to restrict the authority of appointed bishops to ecclesiastical affairs, German emperors promoted the interests of previously minor urban counts as a check on the ambitions of the rural marquises. As a result, Florence and other Tuscan cities were ruled mostly by counts during the tenth and eleventh centuries (Wickham 1981, pp. 184–85; Schevill 1961, pp. 32–36).

The marquises, bishops, and counts, who all took advantage of the conflicts between emperors, kings, and popes to gain new powers, also were endangered when military defeats removed their sponsors from the sections of northern Italy in which they resided. To guard against disruptions of support from above, Tuscan aristocrats attempted to create their own cadres of supporters who could supplement or substitute for the military and political support provided by their often weak or absent imperial, royal, and papal sponsors. Aristocrats enlisted allies by enfeoffing their estates, that is, granting a portion of their lands and income rights to supporters in return for military aid (Hyde 1973, pp. 44; Luzzatto 1961, pp. 41–42).

Several centuries of progressive enfeoffment divided up the great noble and clerical estates, converting them from feudal manors into the separate estates of a new strata of lesser nobles (Jones 1968, pp. 206–14). Bishops gave away church properties to their relatives and allies. The church's share of land in all of Italy declined from 31 percent in the ninth century to 16 percent in 1200 (Herlihy 1961, p. 86; see also Cipolla 1947).

Many members of the new strata of nobles, created as a result of the enfeoffment and alienation of noble and clerical estates, migrated to cities in the eleventh century (Hyde 1973, p. 106). These new nobles, who as individual families lacked the power to control urban political or ecclesiastical offices, organized themselves into communes. Those collective urban bodies successfully played the pretenders to the Italian throne and the Pope against one another, just as marquises, counts and bishops had done before them.

A resurgent papacy's attempts to reassert the right to appoint bishops was the source of the principal great power conflicts in northern Italy during the late tenth and eleventh centuries. As long as the German emperor remained the dominant power in northern Italy, and retained control over the appointment of bishops, the pope was unable to regain authority over the church. During the late tenth century and through the eleventh century, reformist popes spent much of the treasure and income still controlled by the church to repurchase lands that could be used to support a newly celibate and reformed clergy (Herlihy 1957). Those expenditures were part of a larger effort by the papacy to regain appointment power over the bishops.[23] "The general struggle which ensued, rather misleadingly called the Investiture Contest, divided the old regime against itself, the imperialist nobility against the allies of the reformers, imperialist bishops against the supporters of the reformers" (Hyde 1973, p. 49).

The schism between the German emperors and the papacy created strategic opportunities for noble newcomers to challenge the old aristocracy's control over city governments and over the bishoprics. The militarily weakened emperors of the eleventh century were forced to recognize the autonomy of Florence and the other urban communes in order to prevent the new urban nobles from allying with the pope (Pullan 1972, pp. 22–23, 86; Schevill 1961, pp. 60–61). The potential for an alliance between urban notables and the papacy was based on their shared interest in removing the bishops and counts appointed by the emperor. Urban elites were unable to establish autonomous communes as long as the emperor's appointees held power in the cities. The reforming popes needed to remove bishops beholden to the emperor if they were to recover control over the income and patronage attached to the bishops' offices and use those assets as patronage to recruit allies in their contest with the emperor. The emperor forestalled such an alliance, even in Florence, which strongly supported papal reforms, by ceding much of the bishops' and counts' authority to the urban communes (Hyde 1973, pp. 49–50).

Tuscan urban autonomy in general, and Florentine autonomy in particular, was not achieved because the nobles who flocked to cities and organized themselves collectively there possessed particularly large concentrations of capital, or of coercive forces. Indeed, the new nobles of eleventh-century Florence held merely the shards of much greater concentrations of land, income rights, and authority that had been thrown to them by kings, emperors, popes, and great magnates who alienated portions of their estates and offices to enlist allies in their great power and regional conflicts. Tuscan urban autonomy was built in the interstices of long-stalemated conflicts between the most powerful feudal elites in Western Europe.

The Uniqueness of Florence

The new ruling aristocracy of eleventh-century Florence was a feudal elite with a crucial difference.[24] It was, to a degree, like the aristocracies described in chapter 2, drawing income, power, and status from their lordships (though of lesser power and scope than those of the older aristocracies) on their enfeoffed estates. At the same time, the new nobles were part of a collective body (the communes of Florence and other northern Italian cities) quite unlike the aristocratic corporate institutions elsewhere in Europe. Lacking a monarch, like the ones to whom other European nobles were forced to defer or against whom they could unite to extract concessions, the communes of northern Italy were consumed by conflicts among clans, factions, and parties.

The new elite that came to power in the eleventh century and dominated the commune during the twelfth century molded Florentine society, politics, and urban geography in its own rural and feudal image. When rural noble clans migrated to cities they brought their poor relatives with them, building large family compounds that became urban neighborhoods inhabited by a single extended family (Heers 1977, pp. 17–34; Padgett and Ansell 1993, p. 1289). The extended families provided the clan leaders with an armed retinue that allowed them to demand a share of the commune's governing offices.

Florentine communal politics in the eleventh century was clan politics. Aristocratic clans were large. Up to one-tenth of the rural population of eleventh-century Tuscany was noble (i.e., members of such extended families), even though most were landless and not much better off than the average nonaristocrat (Heers 1977, pp. 1–34). Clans enlarged by absorbing other noble families through marriage and by accepting weaker and poorer noble families into the clan's urban compound in return for political and military allegiance to the aristocratic *consorzeria* (consortia of mutual assistance among aristocrats) (Waley 1969, pp. 170–79; Martines 1979, pp. 34–38).

The aristocratic *consorzeria* of Florence amalgamated, during the twelfth century, into two shifting alliances: the Guelfs and the Ghibellines. The Ghibellines professed loyalty to the German emperor and his claims over Italy, while the Guelfs tied themselves to the alliance between the pope and the French crown that sought to secure Angevin rule over southern Italy (Waley 1969, pp. 200–204). "Medieval factions were driven by local neighborhood antagonisms at their root, even when they aggregated under broader, pope-versus-emperor banners" (Padgett and Ansell 1993, p. 1295). Florentine clans could and did shift from one party to the other when doing so yielded offices or other rewards within the city's polity (Waley 1969, p. 207; the fecklessness and opportunism of Florentine aristocrats becomes obvious in the detailed descriptions of politics in Hyde 1973 and Martines 1979).

The new nobles looked above and below for allies in their struggles with rival factions. The long-standing nature of the stalemate among the great powers in northern Italy had the dual effect of preserving urban autonomy and of ensuring that factional conflicts would not be decided, except during brief interludes of foreign occupation, by the intervention of a single dominant power from above. The lack of closure from above, unique in Western Europe in that era, allowed and encouraged urban nobles to rely upon nonaristocratic allies in communal politics. Northern Italy's central position in European commerce expanded the number of potential allies and the resources they could bring to factional conflicts.

Florentine aristocrats transformed their city's polity, and ultimately undermined their own rule, through their strategy of mimicking the earlier royal and imperial efforts to gain leverage by reaching down[25] to secure allies through grants of limited sovereignty. The aristocrats looked to the merchant elite for financial and political assistance. To secure the aid of rich commoners, the aristocrats had to admit them into the government of the commune. Just as communes of aristocrats had played their stalemated superiors against one another to win grants of autonomy that rendered all royal, imperial, and papal claims to sovereignty over Florence merely symbolic, so did the nonaristocrats empowered by noble factions expand their constitutional role in the commune. During the thirteenth century this new elite, the so-called patricians, gained dominance of communal government and then moved to revoke the aristo-crats' feudal rights in the *contado* (countryside) and to ban nobles from communal government.

The following part of this chapter traces the devolution of power from the aris-tocracy to the patricians, the consolidation of the patricians into an oligarchic elite, and the subsequent rise of the Medici and their party. The narrative history of elite con-flict and of popular challenges to oligarchic rule provides a basis for considering the questions with which I introduce this chapter. I explore how the unique political struc-ture of Renaissance Florence created particular advantages for Florentine merchants in their accumulation of capital and in their efforts to gain leverage over political ac-tors outside the city during the twelfth through fifteenth centuries. I then discuss how the social structure that became fixed under Medici rule limited the capacities of Flo-rentine businessmen to adapt to new economic opportunities and challenges in the six-teenth century. At the end of this chapter I suggest ways in which the Florentine case can be generalized to explain the transfer of political and economic leadership from elites located in city-states to ones in nation-states during the sixteenth century.

Political Conflict and Structural Change in Florence, 1100–1737

A succession of elites vied for political and social hegemony over the autonomous Florentine commune. Once Florence had attained virtually unchallenged independ-ence from emperors and kings in the eleventh century, the outcomes of elite conflicts were determined mainly by the structure of elite and class relations within the com-mune rather than by the interventions of great powers.

This section provides a narrative political history of Florence to illuminate, and explain the structural dynamics behind, the succession of power among the various elites that, alone or in coalitions and with or without the *popolo* (guildsmen), ruled Florence (see figure 3.2). I begin with the issue of elite and class formation. I iden-tify the economic bases, within the Florentine commune and beyond, for the rise of the oligarchs and their nemeses the "new men" and the *popolo* during the twelfth and thirteenth centuries. I then examine the thirteenth-century culmination of politi-cal devolution in the permanent displacement, by nonaristocratic patricians, of the en-feoffed nobles who had won autonomy for the commune from the great powers and had seized urban and church offices from older aristocracies. The patricians enriched themselves and undermined the bases for an aristocratic revival by bringing the lands and offices once held by nobles families under the control of communal government, thereby ensuring that the benefits of feudal rights would flow to the new patrician rulers of the commune. I go on to explain how the patricians were able to consolidate themselves as an oligarchy and thereby prevent the further devolution of power onto the new men or the *popolo*. I conclude this political history of Florence with an ac-count of the rise of the Medici and an anatomy of their rule, which continued, with few interruptions, until 1737. By exploring the effects of Medici hegemony upon the Florentine polity and elite and class structure, I lay the groundwork for the discussion in the concluding sections of the limits of Florentine enterprise.

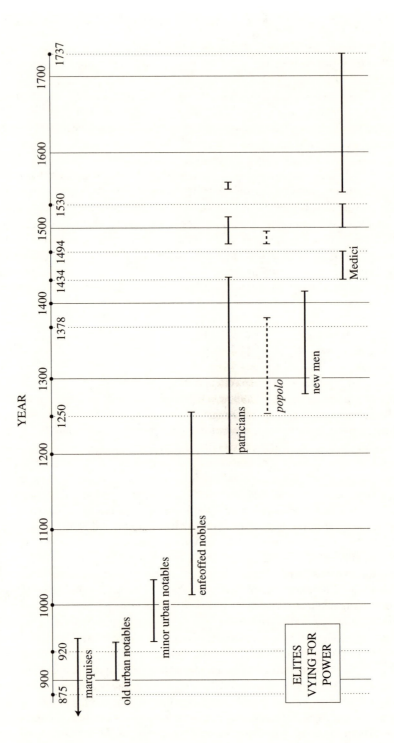

YEAR

875
920
900
marquises
old urban notables
minor urban notables
enfeoffed nobles
1000
1100
1200
1250
patricians
1300
1378
popolo
new men
1400
1434 1494
Medici
1500
1530
1737
1600
1700

ELITES
VYING FOR
POWER

Elite and Class Formation during the Twelfth and Thirteenth Centuries

The same geopolitical stalemate that allowed Florentine and other Italian nobles to achieve autonomy for themselves and their cities also created openings for entrepreneurs to capture trade routes, to engage in banking, and to sell luxury manufactures throughout Europe. The Crusades disrupted Byzantine and Arab control of Mediterranean trade routes. However, Venetian and Genoese merchants were the primary beneficiaries of the emerging Roman Catholic European hegemony in the Mediterranean, with the two cities vying for dominance of the most profitable trade routes throughout the twelfth and thirteenth centuries (Abu-Lughod 1989, pp. 102–34; Luzzatto 1961, pp. 47–55, 86–90).

Florentine merchants were relegated, by their city's inability to compete with Venice and Genoa for military hegemony of the Mediterranean, to the less lucrative wool trade. As a result, Florentines' commercial practices and trade networks became quite different from those of their Venetian, Genoese, and Pisan counterparts. Florentine traders were forced to create a network of branch offices in England, France, and Flanders (and in the Spanish and North African wool-producing centers as well), for the purpose of buying wool and transporting it home. In contrast to the merchants of coastal Italian cities, who formed temporary syndicates for each journey eastward, the Florentines had ongoing partnerships with members situated in key cities along the trade routes of Western Europe (Renouard 1941, pp. 106–17; 1949, pp. 69–72).[26]

The unique Florentine business structure, created because merchants of that city were at a relative disadvantage to rivals from militarily more powerful cities, gave Florentines a particular advantage in vying for the opportunity to extend loans to popes during the Crusades. Popes relied upon their French, Flemish, and English allies to finance the Crusades by agreeing to turn over to the papacy a share of clerical tithes and other church revenues that kings or bishops of those countries otherwise would have kept for themselves (Renouard 1941, pp. 167–69). Popes needed bankers who could advance the funds they were due to receive from the various national churches in return for the right to "farm" tithes (i.e., for the bankers to collect for themselves the clerical revenues promised the pope) as repayment of the loans. Venetian and

FIGURE 3.2. The Succession of Ruling Elites in Florence, 875–1737. The solid lines denote the eras in which an elite controlled the Florentine government. Where lines overlap, rule was contested with the particular elites either sharing or alternating power. The broken line for the *popolo* indicates the period during which the minor guilds mounted periodic revolutionary challenges to the ruling elites or enjoyed brief periods of significant participation in the commune's government. Such periods were confined to the thirteenth and fourteenth centuries, except for the brief revival of popular power during Savonarola's rule, 1494–98. Old urban notables were appointed as bishops by Carolingian kings. Minor urban notables were elevated to titles of count by the German emperors. Enfeoffed nobles migrated from the countryside to the cities with their clans. Patricians were the non-aristocrats from the leading guilds. They became the ruling oligarchy in the thirteenth century and lost power to the Medici in 1498, eventually coalescing under Soderini from 1502 to 1512. The oligarchy returned to power during the second Medici exile from power, 1527–30.

Genoese merchants had their liquid assets tied up in ship syndicates that had seemed the most lucrative possible investments. Further, there was no ongoing association of merchants in those cities, or in any other Italian city besides Florence, capable of mobilizing a sufficient store of capital to meet papal needs to pay the immediate costs of the Crusades. And only the Florentines had an existent network of branch offices in the countries from which the clerical revenues were to be collected to service the papal loans (Renouard 1941, pp. 87–94, 106–17). As a result, beginning in 1254, and continuing with only brief interruptions through the following three hundred years, Florentine bankers gained a virtual monopoly on papal loans and in managing the papacy's financial relations with the Catholic Churches of Western Europe (Renouard 1941; Housley 1982, pp. 232–38; Holmes 1986, pp. 36–43).[27]

Florentines used their control over papal finance to become the principal bankers to the English and French monarchs and to strengthen their domination of wool, and later of silk, trade, and production. Florentine bankers quickly extended their financial services for the pope to cover the entire "Guelf" alliance, a coalition comprised of the pope, the English and French monarchs, the French monarch's candidate for king of Sicily, and pro-Guelf allies elsewhere in Tuscany. During the 1260s Florentine bankers extended credit to the English and French kings, assisting first the former and then the latter in paying for an army to conquer Sicily (Fryde and Fryde 1965, p. 454).

The bankers' political bets paid off in 1266. Charles of Anjou defeated his German rival and took the throne of Sicily. His armies then turned north, defeating the Ghibelline governments in Florence and Siena, restoring the exiled Florentine Guelf bankers to power in their hometown (Pullan 1972, pp. 28–45). The pope aided his Florentine financiers during the Ghibelline interregnum of 1260–66 by imposing an interdict on Florence. The seventeen principal Florentine bankers who controlled papal finances left the city for the duration of the interdict, "thus depriving Florence of the wealth and employment their firms provided" (Trexler 1974, pp. 22–23). Throughout those six years the exiled Florentines maintained their papal concessions, even as their properties in the city were confiscated and their towers razed by the Ghibellines (Waley 1969, pp. 200–207).

Florentines' skill and luck in bankrolling the winners in European great power conflicts paid rich dividends by creating the political conditions for an entrepreneurial synergy among the Florentines' various lines of business. The first fruits of the Florentines' political connections came from Sicily. A few Florentine firms—the Bardi, Peruzzi, and Acciaiuoli in particular—became the bankers to Charles of Anjou. "For the Florentines, the loans simply lubricated a more extensive commercial network that was the real source of profits and the real attraction of trade in the south" (Abulafia 1981, p. 381). Florentines became the sole exporters of Sicilian agricultural goods to the rest of Italy and beyond. Sicilians, in turn, became the first great foreign market for Florentine woolens (Abulafia 1981, pp. 381–88; Brucker 1969, pp. 52–54).

Florence's first great manufacturing industry, high quality woolens, was a byproduct of Florentine bankers' ties to the English crown. The English crown gained initial access to Tuscan bankers in 1254 when the pope asked Henry III to conquer Sicily in his behalf. The English crown's unprecedented appetite for cash to finance wars in Sicily and the Low Countries and against France proved too much for the Riccardi of Lucca (who went bankrupt), for the Frescobaldi of Florence, and Antonio Pessagno of Genoa. Finally, a partnership of the Bardi and Peruzzi of Florence provided loans in sufficient volume to sustain the English crown's war ambitions from 1312 until the de facto bankruptcy of the English crown in 1341 (Fryde and Fryde 1965, pp. 451–61; Kaeuper 1988, pp. 43–55; Prestwich 1979).

The Frescobaldi and the Bardi-Peruzzi syndicate both demanded and received monopoly control over the export of English wool, which was the highest quality in Europe, as partial payment for loans extended to the crown (Goldthwaite 1980, p. 42; Prestwich 1979). The bankers directed wool exports to their hometown, building a Florentine wool industry at the expense of the older centers of trade at the Champagne fairs and of manufacture in Flemish towns. The English crown's periodic embargoes on wool exports to France and the Low Countries in revenge for those territories' opposition to English military ventures pushed French and Flemish wool merchants and weavers to leave home in search of work. The bankers' control over English wool attracted the skilled weavers to work in Florence (Hoshino 1983, pp. 184–86, 200–204).

Florentines became the sole exporters of the highest quality English wool by the 1320s. English wool was manufactured, along with cheaper and lower quality wool from Spain and western Africa, into cloth and finished products that the Florentines sold throughout Europe and even exported to Asia through Genoa and Venice (Hoshino 1983, pp. 184–86, 200–204). "By plugging into the papal financial network at its center, major firms were able to build an extensive system of branch operations all over Europe," allowing Florentines to sell their draperies in all the European markets where the pope had political influence and a financial presence (Goldthwaite 1980, p. 35).

The Florentine woolen industry was the largest manufacturing industry in Italy in the early fourteenth century (Luzzato 1961, pp. 97–98). In 1300 there were three hundred Florentine cloth workshops, producing one hundred thousand woolen clothes a year with a total value of 750,000 gold florins. By 1330 there were two hundred shops, producing eighty thousand pieces of generally higher quality than earlier, thereby raising the total annual product to 1.2 million florins (p. 106).

Florence's central role in banking, trade, and wool production throughout Western Europe was reflected in rapid population growth during the thirteenth and early fourteenth centuries. Florence, which had a quarter of Milan's population and a fifth of Venice's in 1200, surpassed Milan and almost equaled Venice by 1320 (Chandler 1987, pp. 111, 115, 123; Russell 1972). Much of this growth was due to the migration to Florence of skilled craftsmen who joined the twenty-one recognized guilds and of far more numerous laborers who assisted guildsmen in their workshops or supported themselves through casual labor.

The Bases for Challenges to Aristocratic Power

The nonaristocratic population of thirteenth- and fourteenth-century Florence can be grouped into three strata: (1) the nonaristocratic guild elite (the patricians), (2) ordinary guild members, and (3) wage laborers who were employed and exploited by guildsmen (the *popolo di Dio*). The size of all three groups grew until the Black Death of 1348. During those centuries differences in wealth, status, and political power between the elite and ordinary guild members became ever greater, and the portion of the elite with true power in the commune narrowed into a small oligarchy. At the same

time, guildsmen allied to strengthen their authority over the *popolo di Dio* and to extract concessions from the ruling aristocracy.

Two developments external to Florence were necessary, though not sufficient, for
the rise of guild power and the formation of a nonaristocratic elite at the expense of
the city's noble rulers during the thirteenth century. One external factor, discussed
above, was the opening of the European economy that created the conditions for the
expansion in numbers and wealth of guildsmen. The other external factor was the
abrupt lessening of great power conflicts and interventions in Tuscany. The German
Emperor's hold on Tuscany was broken when he was defeated by Charles of Anjou
in 1266. Charles, in turn, lost control of Tuscany when an uprising threatened his control over Sicily in 1282, forcing him to direct his forces to the south. Once German
and French forces had withdrawn from Tuscany and the threat of external conquest
had disappeared, guildsmen no longer had to defer their demand for power to what
had been "the most urgent issue faced by the Italian cities, . . . the preservation of their
independence against imperial authority, a task best entrusted to the aristocracies"
(Najemy 1982, p. 4; see also Holmes 1986, pp. 3–43).

Wealthy and geopolitically secure urban merchants achieved political power
only when and where ruling aristocracies were riven by factional conflicts. Milanese
guildsmen were the pioneers in taking advantage of aristocratic divisions, winning a
growing measure of power in the eleventh century. Factionalized aristocracies lost
power to nonaristocratic commune governments in Milan, Lucca, Pisa, Genoa, and
Siena as well as a number of lesser cities during the twelfth and thirteenth centuries
(Previté-Orton 1964, pp. 218–24; Martines 1979, pp. 34–44). Guilds became the institutions through which non-nobles in the city-states of northern Italy could invest
a part of their capital in mercenary armies and ally their armed forces with one party
or the other in return for recognition, through the commune, of the guilds' rights to
regulate themselves and to participate in the government of their city (Hyde 1973,
chap. 4; Najemy 1979; Waley 1969, pp. 182–88).

Aristocracies retained a measure of power in most cities and remained in positions to take advantage of thirteenth-century divisions within the nonaristocratic
polities of many communes (Waley 1969, pp. 221–30; Martines 1979, pp. 22–61).
Thus, aristocracies lost and regained power in many Italian city-states in tandem with
the intensification and resolution of factional conflicts within the aristocratic and
communal camps contending for authority (Martines 1979). Communal governments
fell even as the wealthy merchants who advanced and benefited from such regimes
continued to grow wealthy from trade and manufacture.

Florence and Venice are unusual among Italian cities in the finality with which
the aristocracy was driven from power in the former city and in the Venetian aristocracy's long-term immunity from challenge. Venice offers a clear contrast to Florence.
Venice had been able to insulate itself from imperial and papal threats (in part because
it had been attached to the Byzantine empire) in the tenth century, far earlier than Florence. Protected from great power interference, the Venetian aristocracy was able to
establish a unified hierarchy and self-perpetuating government without the sort of factionalism characteristic of Florence during subsequent centuries (Lane 1973, pp. 91–
114; McNeil 1974, pp. 59–60). The unitary Venetian government was able to channel
the fruits of trade into the hands of the existing aristocracy because the state controlled
the merchant fleets. The ruling aristocracy benefited from the state fleets in two ways.

First, much of the profit from trade was skimmed off by the state and used to pay the salaries of aristocrats who supported themselves through salaried offices (McNeil 1974, pp. 59–60). Second, the Muda system of renting cargo space on state galleys to all citizens fostered mercantile competition and kept private enterprises small (pp. 60–64), preventing merchants from cornering markets, realizing windfall profits, and building mercantile fortunes that could rival the land-based wealth of the old Venetian aristocracy. Thus, the Venetian aristocracy was unique among Italian aristocracies in retaining the unity to control their city-state's polity and, through the state, dominance over the economy, blocking economic and social as well as political challenges from below until the late fourteenth century.[28]

Florentine patricians used the guilds to organize themselves to take advantage of clan and party divisions among urban aristocrats in the thirteenth century. In so doing, patricians moved the guilds beyond their limited twelfth-century role as instruments for occupational groups to regulate their own spheres of economic activity. In the thirteenth century, guilds became the key institutions for nonaristocrats to define their status and to participate in Florentine politics. Twenty-one guilds (seven "major" and fourteen "minor") received official recognition from the Florentine commune in the thirteenth century. "The guild community thus included more than a third of the adult males of" Florence in 1300 (Najemy 1979, p. 60).

A patrician elite, drawn from the richest members of the five leading guilds moved to differentiate themselves from the mass of guildsmen in the fourteenth century. This elite was drawn together by the twin desires to achieve social distance from poorer guildsmen and to monopolize political power within Florence. The patricians cemented their loyalty to one another through a web of marital, business, and patronage ties. They established a parallel organization, the Mercanzia, that operated alongside and in competition with the guilds. "Although the Mercanzia was itself a corporation, it was never integrated into the guild federation. In fact, it was later used by the oligarchs as an instrument for imposing electoral and political controls over the guilds themselves" (Najemy 1982, p. 11).

The Mercanzia was the initial, and only formal institutional, basis for patricians to differentiate themselves from fellow guild members. During the fourteenth century, however, an oligarchic elite within the Mercanzia distinguished itself from their less socially eminent and politically powerful colleagues. The oligarchs especially disdained the "new men," who often were as wealthy as the oligarchs and shared their contempt for ordinary guildsmen but had achieved their riches and began to vie for power only after the oligarchs already had attained hegemony in Florence. (The Medici were patricians who enjoyed a measure of support from the new men that other oligarchs never achieved or sought.) The new men alternated between opportunistic alliances with the *popolo* to displace the oligarchs and obsequious yet largely unsuccessful efforts to gain entry into the oligarchy through marriage, business alliances, and office holding.

The Triumph of the Patricians and the Collectivization of Feudal Rights

Florentine governmental institutions were transformed time and again in the period 1250–1400. Historians trace (and debate the relative importance of) mobilizations by the different strata of Florentine society and their external allies to change the personnel and the constitutional form of the commune's polity.[29] I do not rehearse the historians' debates nor do I recount each shift in regime. More useful, for answering the questions posed by the Florentine case for this chapter, is to identify the combinations of elite and class conflict that effected the four great changes in the distribution of governmental power in the commune during this period: (1) the elimination of the aristocracy from any formal role in governance by the end of the thirteenth century, (2) the subordination of the *contado* in general, and of aristocrats' feudal holdings in particular, to the fiscal and legal control of city government, (3) the periodic rise and final demise of *popolo* (both guild and mass) participation in politics, and (4) the consolidation of a narrow oligarchy as the rulers of the commune by 1400, under the guise of broad-based though substantively meaningless participation in government by new men and guildsmen. I discuss the first two developments in this, and the latter two in the next, section.

The comparison of Florence with Venice in the previous section makes clear that factional divisions among Florentine aristocrats were necessary to allow guildsmen to take advantage of their new-found wealth and the lull in great power rivalries in northern Italy during the later half of the thirteenth century. At each moment of extreme conflict between aristocratic factions, always marked by violence and sometimes by the intervention and dictatorship of foreign forces, guildsmen gained a measure of participation in government. When in power, guild officials moved to dismantle the fortified urban towers of the great clans, confiscate their property, and ban aristocrats from public office (Larner 1980, pp. 119–25; Becker 1967, pp. 65–86; Brucker 1977, pp. 39–44).

From the first half of the thirteenth century through the Primo Popolo regime of 1250–60 and to the rule of the papal-imposed government of "the Fourteen" of 1280–12, aristocrats alternated between periods of fratricidal conflict culminating in *popolo* participation in government and the exile, banning, and expropriation of the losing aristocratic faction's property, with years when aristocrats managed to reach truces in their battles and unite to resume control of government. In those latter periods, most aristocrats managed to reverse their bans on political activity, return from exile, and regain some of their property (though they usually could not rebuild their fortresses). However, the aristocracy was progressively weakened and the leading guilds strengthened, politically and financially, during those decades of internecine warfare by clans and parties. Aristocrats permanently lost control of Florentine government in 1282–83. In 1282, the leaders of the major guilds formed a priorate (the Signoria) to rule alongside the aristocratic body of the Fourteen. The following year the Fourteen lost all real power and the Signoria became the ruling body of Florence, holding de facto power until the 1434 triumph of the Medici and de jure power as long as Florence remained a republic (Brucker 1977, pp. 3–44; Martines 1979, p. 58; Najemy 1982, pp. 17–19).

The patricians took advantage of widespread antiaristocratic mobilization and militant support from members of all guilds to secure control of government, through the Signoria, for the richest members of the top guilds. During the first ten years of the Signoria (1282–92), half of all priors were members of the Calimala and Cambio (cloth merchants and bankers) guilds, two-thirds were from those two guilds and the

Giudici e Notai (lawyers and notaries), and more than 90 percent from six of the top seven guilds (Najemy 1982, pp. 29–30).

Patricians, ordinary guildsmen, and the *popolo di Dio,* despite their struggles to control the Signoria, agreed upon and fought for the political and financial emasculation and social rejection of the aristocracy. From 1282 until the creation of a different social ideology under the Medici, the commune suppressed urban and rural festivals created by feudal nobles and replaced them with civic, although (pace Weber) not disenchanted, festivals that honored the commune itself. Guilds rather than aristocratic titles were regarded as the sources of honor (Trexler 1980, pp. xxi–xxii, 216–63 and passim). Aristocrats ceased to play a role in commune government, except for those families with the wealth, and resultant marriage or business connections to ruling patrician families, to buy permission to renounce their titles and regain political rights (Becker 1968a, pp. 209–10).

Popular governments, both before and after the 1282 institution of the Signoria, sought to solve the commune's fiscal crises, which were precipitated by the costs of periodic wars, by expropriating aristocrats' urban properties and taxing their rural seigneuries (Becker 1966, pp. 16–17). Beginning with the "first priorate" of 1282–92, the Florentine commune indirectly appropriated feudal lordships by limiting to fixed and increasingly nominal amounts the labor dues and rents, in cash and in kind, to which manor lords were entitled. As peasant obligations fell, they were replaced by taxes assessed by and payable to the commune itself (Jones 1968, pp 212–14; Jones 1966; de la Roncière 1968). The *contado*'s contribution to commune revenues rose from almost nothing prior to 1250 to half by 1400 (Becker 1968b, p. 131).[30]

The patricians who came to power in the late twelfth century were a new elite, distinct from the Florentine aristocracy whom they displaced. Patricians differed from the aristocrats in the organizational mechanisms through which they appropriated resources and came together to vie for political power. Tuscan aristocrats, like aristocrats of England and France, appropriated resources through fiefs. The authority and income rights of the fief accrued directly to noble families, not through any corporate body of which they were members.[31] When Tuscan nobles entered into strategic alliances with other lords, they did so to preserve or extend the autonomy and organizational integrity of their fiefs against challenges from rival elites or peasants. Participation in aristocratic coalitions did not, in thirteenth-century Europe, force aristocrats to cede their sovereignty to the alliances of which they were a part, a reality demonstrated by Tuscan aristocrats' frequent defections from one party to another.

Thirteenth-century Florentine patricians, by contrast, had neither social identity nor political power separate from their memberships in guilds and the Mercanzia. Although patricians appropriated resources through family firms and partnerships, they were able to invest their assets profitably only by virtue of their institutional bases in guild, Mercanzia, and later Signoria. The great extent to which patricians were empowered by their memberships in commune organizations, in contrast to aristocrats' independent identities, which allowed them to flit from party to party, is evidenced by the commune's use of exile as the ultimate sanction.[32]

Aristocrats and patricians' different organizational bases in the Florentine economy and polity clearly mark them as distinct elites. Their class identity is a more complex issue. Over the long term, from the thirteenth through the sixteenth century, members of the two elites increasingly shared interests in the two principal Florentine industries: banking and cloth production and trade. Although the earliest and most of the wealthiest participants in those industries were nonaristocrats, they were joined through marriage and business partnerships by older aristocratic families (Martines 1963, pp. 18–84; Jones 1965; Kent 1978, pp. 136–85). Merchants, rentiers, and officials, and people who combined all three bases of income, increasingly were found in both elites.

Patricians held relatively little land during the centuries of their assent to power, purchasing large rural estates in imitation of the nobility mainly in the sixteenth century and after (Litchfield 1986, pp. 215–32). However, whether they profited from agriculture indirectly as the officials of a state that received most of the agrarian surplus through taxes in the fourteenth and fifteenth centuries or directly as the new aristocracy in formation in the sixteenth and subsequent centuries, the patricians always were rentiers, differing from their aristocratic predecessors only in the organizational means through which they extracted resources from the peasant class. Aristocratic landlords, patrician state officials, and Medician landlords all were part of the feudal ruling class in Marx's sense of the term: They all used extra-economic means, whether taxes or rents, to extract a surplus from peasants. All these elites did so without transforming the process of agricultural production in rural Tuscany.[33]

The two elites were closest to being two different classes during the twelfth and thirteenth centuries: In that period, aristocrats mainly were landlords; patricians mainly merchants and manufacturers. Yet neither qualitative nor quantitative differences in the class characters of aristocrats and patricians determined the latter's political triumph over the former. Instead, the nature of each elite's organizational apparatus and the position of each elite in the complex of social relations within and beyond Florence determined the outcomes of their conflicts. Similarly, the "aristocratization" of the patricians under oligarchic and Medici rule had mainly political causes. I address those causes in the following sections and conclude this chapter by discussing the consequences of rearistocratization for the position of Florence and its elites in the larger political economy of Europe.

The End of Devolution and the Subjugation of the New Men and the *Popolo*

The patricians of the Mercanzia had used their fellow guild members in the twelfth and thirteenth centuries to remove the aristocracy from commune government and to tax and control nobles' rural properties. The patricians then turned on their guild brethren after 1283 and succeeded, by 1400, in constituting themselves as an oligarchy and limiting, to a nominal and virtually meaningless level, popular participation in commune government.

Patricians were able to limit their factionalism, and thereby reduce the incentive for any of their number to gain leverage over rivals by devolving power to lower-class allies, for two reasons: First, the organizational bases of the patricians' power (and terrains of conflict) were the collectively governed commune and guild institutions. Unlike an aristocrat's fief, which could be subinfeudated without permission from other lords, the communal Signoria, the Mercanzia, and the guilds could admit new participants only with majority permission. The controlling coterie of the Priorate and the guilds was able to block efforts by minority factions to reach down and open the institutions to new allies. Second, the group directly below the patricians in thirteenth-century Florence were the guildsmen who needed the help of the patrician-governed commune to control the *popolo di Dio,* the proletarians whom guildsmen directly exploited for their livelihood. Mass mobilization was an immediate threat to the guildsmen.

The patricians were challenged in five major episodes during the fourteenth century in their quest to restrict popular participation in the commune and to establish oligarchic rule over Florence.[34] The unusual combination of external and internal forces needed to create the opportunities for those five challenges, and the ease with which those challenges were turned aside once the unusual conditions dissipated, demonstrate the patricians' strategic advantages over their rivals. The first three challenges were due to temporary interventions, or the threat of invasion, by foreign powers to install themselves or their Florentine lackeys in power.[35] Once the foreign threat was removed, restoring the long-term stalemate and lack of involvement by foreign powers in Tuscany, elective government was restored in Florence.

The other two disruptions of stable patrician rule were caused by a combination of factors. In 1340 the Bardi, a leading patrician family prominent in politics and banking, joined a conspiracy of magnates to overthrow the government. The Bardi were motivated by the impending default of English King Edward III on loans extended by the Bardi and other Florentine financiers. The Bardi hoped to use their control of the commune to bail themselves out financially. The coup failed, yet, combined with the wave of bankruptcies sparked by Edward's default in 1342, it led "magnates eager to regain political influence, . . . bankers hoping to salvage their fortunes, and . . . artisans impoverished by the business depression" to appeal to Walter of Brienne, Duke of Athens, to become signore for life in September 1342 (Brucker 1962, p. 7). The split among the patricians, induced by foreign financial crisis, had reopened opportunities for political action by magnates and the lower guilds.

The patricians returned to power the next year by allying with members of the lower guilds who provided the manpower to overthrow Walter in July 1343 and to defeat the magnates and their retainers in street battles. The magnates once again were excluded from politics. The patricians, however, were forced to share control of the Signoria with members of the lower guilds who had been decisive in defeating Walter, the Bardi, and their magnate allies (Brucker 1962, pp. 6–9). The conflicts of the 1340s demonstrated that patrician divisions created the only openings for magnate and lower-guild political action. Once the patricians reunited, they managed to progressively exclude the guilds from substantive political power, finally using the occasion of the Black Death to purge lower guildsmen from the scrutiny lists (Brucker 1977, pp. 39–44).[36]

Patricians again divided into factions, headed by the Albizzi and the Ricci families, in the 1360s. The Albizzi were pro-Guelf and drew support from most of the wealthiest and most politically powerful oligarchs. Their support for papal foreign policy was motivated by the desire for ecclesiastical office (Brucker 1962, pp. 229–30). Indeed, in 1371, the Ricci were won over to their enemies' side by the promise and delivery of high clerical offices (p. 249).

The Ricci were typical of the oligarchy as a whole in the fears and incentives that drove their foreign and local allegiances. "The most concrete factor in the perpetuation and intensification of partisan conflict would seem to be the depressed economic situation in Florence. . . . In the 1370's the scene was particularly bleak: a depression in the cloth industry, a rising bankruptcy rate, a visitation of the plague in 1374 followed by a famine, and the heavy burdens and losses occasioned by the papal war. These conditions moved thoughtful men . . . to consider the decline of their family fortunes and to regard the future with grave apprehension. Since the possession of political influence was a vital bulwark of social and economic status, men fought desperately for this prize," especially the oligarchs of the Guelf party (Brucker 1962, p. 392).

The antioligarch faction, first headed by the Ricci and then by several anti-Guelf patricians and dominated by "new men," gained control over the government because the absence of unity among the patricians allowed the minority of nonpatricians chosen for scrutiny to determine the balance of power in the Signoria and affect public policy.[37] This shift led to the banning of most oligarchs from office, and to Florence's abandonment of the Guelf alliance to side with other Tuscan communes in their struggle for autonomy from a resurgent papacy in the War of the "Eight Saints" from 1375 to 1378.

The war against the papacy, like all wars of that era, forced a drastic increase in governmental expenditures and in debt and taxes to meet the costs of war. The War of the Eight Saints "required outlays of 2.5 million florins—some eight times the total annual revenue collected by the commune from all principal imposts" (Becker 1968, p. 188). Much of the burden was borne by the aristocracy, both directly through taxes on wealth and indirectly through seizures of ecclesiastical properties from which the oligarchs had profited and through taxes on the *contado*. (pp. 189–91). At the same time, the patricians and new men who came to power in the anti-Guelf regime were the principal profiteers from speculation in the increasing state debt issued by the Monte.

The pope sought to place further pressure on Florence with an interdict, forbidding residents of the papal territories and its allies from doing business with Florentines, except for those Guelfs who went into exile. Not all the pope's allies joined the interdict, and, ironically, the Florentines who suffered the greatest financial losses from the interdict were Guelfs and other patricians who did business directly with the pope rather than the anti-Guelf new men, many of whom had business connections to France, Venice and elsewhere in Tuscany where the interdict was not upheld (Trexler 1974, pp. 43–101).

Factional conflict reached a climax in 1378 when the oligarchs of the Guelf party combined with some of the old aristocrats in an attempt to force Florence to sue for peace. The Guelf attacks on the regime and its supporters failed, sparking an armed uprising by both guild members and the *popolo di Dio,* who, on June 22, 1378, systematically burned the homes of the leading Guelfs. The popular uprising broke the Guelf party as an autonomous force with an institutional presence in Florentine government. A new scrutiny was held in August in which nominees from the seven major guilds were joined by candidates submitted by the fourteen minor guilds, and three newly recognized guilds of the *popolo di Dio,* including a twenty-fourth guild for the truly proletarianized workers, the Ciompi. The Ciompi's success was short-lived; in September the Ciompi guild was dissolved and its representatives removed from the

Signoria and the scrutiny lists. Nevertheless, nonoligarch members of major guilds aided by minor guildsmen continued to dominate the Florentine government until the patricians reunited and regained control of the scrutiny and the Signoria in 1382 (Najemy 1982, pp. 231–62).

The Ciompi Revolt appears, to Marxist eyes, "remarkably modern[;] . . . there were strikes, secret meetings, the beginning of working men's associations. Food riots were rare. . . . Instead of arising out of dire material scarcity, the riots arose against the backdrop of sharply rising wages." The revolt was about state power and the organization of wool production (Cohn 1980, p. 205 and passim). Brucker counters: "The disorders of 1378 were not initiated by the Ciompi; they were instigated and directed by a faction within the regime. The first manifestations of violence involved guildsmen, not the disenfranchised cloth workers. As in the 1340's, lower-class participation in revolution occurred only after the ruling group had precipitated the crisis: in 1342, by establishing a dictatorship, in 1378, by indulging in irresponsible partisan tactics" (1962, pp. 388–89).

Brucker is correct that elite factionalism created an opening for proletarian action. Cohn has justification for describing the 1378 Ciompi as proletarian revolutionaries in their organization and tactics, if not in their "moderate legislative demands, . . . their attachment to communal institutions, and, above all, their very gradual transformation into a radical political force" (Brucker 1962, p. 389). Ultimately, the debate over the class character of the Ciompi during a few weeks in 1378 is as static and barren as the debate over the class identities of aristocrats and patricians in 1300. Again, the interesting and apt questions are about the dynamic of class formation and conflict. Why did the heyday of "proletarian" action in Florence last for only a few days? Why did the *popolo di Dio* cease to be a significant actor in Florentine politics only months after the victory of Ciompi?

Brucker's and Cohn's works suggest remarkably similar answers to those questions. Both of them argue that the Ciompi frightened the patricians, acting as a permanent brake upon excessive factionalism and insuring a closing of elite ranks against any of their number who sought advancement through an alliance with the lower guilds, or even with nonpatrician members of the upper guilds.[38] However "advanced" in organization and consciousness the *popolo di Dio* may have been, it could act politically only if and when the patricians were beset by factionalism and guildsmen initiated and encouraged protests by their workers.

The patricians institutionalized the lessons they learned from the Ciompi Revolt. Capitalizing on the major guilds' fears of political and workshop action by minor guilds and the Ciompi, the patricians enlisted the *maggiori* in the political emasculation of the *minori*. "No restrictions of any sort whatsoever were placed on the nomination of candidates; . . . [T]he significance of this open approach to nominations was that it deprived the guilds of the right they had gained in 1378 to determine the eligibility of candidates and thereby to influence the size and composition of the political class" (Najemy 1982, pp. 269–70).

Effective control over the scrutiny and over the decisions of the Signoria itself became ever more concentrated in the hands of an oligarchy of patricians. The average number of "new men" [(i.e., of wealthy and not-so-wealthy guildsmen who were not from patrician families with members who had served on the Signoria prior to

1343)] on the nine-man Signoria fell from 3.3 seats in the period 1382–87 to 0.7 seats between 1401 and 1407. The number of seats held by "leading" families rose from 2.2 in the former period to 4.4 in the latter (Najemy 1982, p. 296). Forty-four families dominated the Signoria with four or more priors each from 1382 to 1399 (p. 298) and an even heavier presence in the era 1400–1434 (Brucker 1977, pp. 264–71; Stephens 1983, pp. 8–23). These families were the survivors of the patrician elite that had come to power in the wake of the aristocracy's banishment from power in 1283. One hundred and forty-six families held Signoria posts ten or more times in the period 1282–1399. Those families constituted 11 percent of the families ever to have members sit as priors, yet held 49 percent of the total seats in that period. Only eleven of those families made their first appearance after 1328; the last such family in 1354 (Najemy 1982, pp. 320–27).

Most of the newcomers (236 of 275, or 86 percent) to the Signoria in the two decades following the Ciompi served only a single two-month term on that body. The brief, two-month terms made it impossible for newcomers to the Signoria (i.e., priors who were the first from their families to ever hold that office) to affect policy. Old families, making repeated appearances, and having positions in an ongoing network of power, controlled policy collectively whether in or out of office.[39] The open nomination process meant that newcomers neither were selected by nor represent the guilds. The newcomers had merely won "a giant political lottery. . . . [They] were "politically isolated and dependent. . . . [Their] extremely fragmented patterns of office holding made organized opposition nearly impossible" (Najemy 1982, p. 299).

The Rise of the Medici

The oligarchs established two permanent innovations in the governance of the Florentine commune and in relations among elites and classes. First, the major guilds were relegated to a subordinate position in the polity from which they never emerged. As institutions they ceased to play a role in the actual selection of men to serve in high government office. The guilds did retain control over the organization of work, with the capacity to prevent the *popolo di Dio* from ever again organizing themselves.[40] Second, the oligarchs' system of scrutiny provided a mechanism for a small cabal to control the government while providing the illusion of broad participation in public office.

The main remaining obstacle to permanent oligarch hegemony was the disjunction between political power and wealth.[41] During the decades of oligarch rule, families outside the political inner circle made great fortunes that outstripped those of most of the oligarchs (Brucker 1977, pp. 270–71; Padgett and Ansell 1993, pp. 1314–16). The oligarchs could neither prevent the accumulation of new fortunes nor seize the wealth of old or new families for themselves. The main avenues to wealth in fourteenth- and early fifteenth-century Florence—banking and commerce—were largely unregulated by the commune, nor could they be accessed through state office (Goldthwaite 1980, pp. 29–66).[42]

The Medici's independent relationship with the Roman papacy was emblematic of the commune's lack of control over its citizens' economic activities. The commune's government doggedly supported, through diplomacy and with funds and troops, the efforts by Roman popes to regain undivided control over the church. However, the Medici engaged in their own efforts to control the selection of popes and gained a virtual monopoly over papal finances and the rewards of that position, without having to defer to Signoria policies or to share the fruits of their successes with the commune (Holmes 1986; Partner 1968).

The gap between power and wealth became crucial when Florence yet again went to war, first against Milan (1423–28) and then against Lucca (1429–33). The wars led to a disruption of Florentine trade and of rural production that in turn caused a decline in receipts from ordinary indirect taxes and other levies on the *contado* (Mohlo 1971, pp. 54, 61). The commune was forced to rely upon forced loans (*prestanze* and *catasti*) to meet the widening gap between declining ordinary revenues and rising extraordinary war expenses. "From the beginning of 1428 until the end of 1433 . . . the citizens of Florence were asked to pay 153 5/6 catasti. Since each catasto assessed at the rate of 0.5% . . . on net capitalization, . . . it follows that over a period of six years the city undertook to collect in taxes 76% of the total net capitalization available in the city [or] according to the calculations of the communal officials . . . taxes amounting to approximately 180% of [taxpayers'] income" (p. 92). "This set off a frantic scramble, among everyone, to escape ruinous tax assessment" (Padgett and Ansell 1993, p. 1305).

Oligarchs sought to use their control of government to shift the burden of taxes from the mainly fixed and easily assessed assets they held to the often hidden business assets of the new men. Since business assets were hard to determine, assessment became a matter of political, and eventually armed, might (Padgett and Ansell 1993, pp. 1305–6; Mohlo 1971, pp. 113–82; Brucker 1977, pp. 472–500). The previous unwillingness of oligarchs, especially poorer oligarchs (Martines 1963, pp. 18–84), to dilute their power by sharing it with rich new men was reinforced by their need to find targets for war-tax assessments.

The war-induced fiscal crisis, and the underlying split between politically powerful oligarchs and politically impotent rich new men, created an opening for the Medici. Padgett and Ansell (1993) use block models of marriage and business ties to explain how the Medici, who had been in the Ricci faction before the Ciompi and thus were ostracized by the ultimately successful oligarchs from the Albizzi faction, used marriage ties with patricians outside the oligarchy and business ties with new men to draw together families that had been isolated and excluded from power by the oligarchic regime. When new men appealed to their Medici business partners for help against oligarch tax assessments they "triggered Medici self-consciousness of themselves as a political party. . . . Oligarchs [by their exclusionary marriage practices and political system] funneled new men's support to [the Medici] and then cut off any possibility of equivocating response" (p. 1306). When the Albizzi and other oligarchs attempted to use force to seize power from the Signoria, which Medici allies dominated because of the luck of the September 1434 draw from scrutiny bags, Medici allies and many neutrals took to the streets. The coup attempt failed and the Albizzi and their allies were banned from office and exiled (Kent 1978, pp. 289–351; Padgett and Ansell 1993, pp. 1309–10; Hale 1977, pp. 22–24).

Medici Rule and the Politicization (and Refeudalization) of Everything

The Medici rise to power marked, with the exception of two interludes (1494–1512 and 1527–30) of Medici exile, the end of patrician factionalism. The Medici were able to make membership in the oligarchy, and access to opportunities for accumulating wealth, dependent upon favor from their single family because their victory over the oligarchs, and the subsequent election of a pro-Florentine pope,[43] allowed them to combine three formerly distinct elite organizations—the Florentine government, the papacy, and the Medici bank—under the control of a single family-directed party. The revenues that the bank received, primarily from servicing papal finances and from extending loans to the papacy and to Florence, were used to subsidize Medici political allies in Florence. As the Medici extended their control over the papal administration, they were able to reward political allies, in Florence and in Rome, with lucrative church offices (Stephens 1983, pp. 124–64; Bullard 1980, pp. 24–44).

The Medici allies of 1434 constituted the initial oligarchy of the new regime, which was gradually supplemented by some old aristocrats who assumed commoner status to enter Florentine politics and by new men whose wealth from commerce and Florentine or papal office holding in the service of the Medici enabled them to rise into the oligarchy (Litchfield 1986, pp. 24–28; Hale 1977, pp. 35–39; Najemy 1982, pp. 306–7, 320–23, 327–31; Stephens 1983, pp. 16–23). Guild and popular participation in government was limited to a nominal level (except during the two interregnums of non-Medici government) by the Medici's continued use of the electoral system developed by the oligarchs.

The importance of the papacy, and of papal patronage and revenues, for Medici hegemony are demonstrated by the circumstances under which the long (1434–1737) Medici rule over Florence was twice broken and reconstituted.[44] Both Medici exiles (in 1494 and 1527) were brought on by papal defeat or threat of attack against the pope by a great power with which the Medici were not allied.[45] The Medici returned to power (in 1512 and 1530) when a great power, allied with the Medici-dominated papacy, gained military hegemony in Tuscany and forced the commune to accept the return of its first family.[46] The Medici hold over the papal administration was sustained, in turn, by the use of wealth garnered through the Medici bank, and by the Medici's ability to mobilize Florentine diplomatic and military support for papal aims and to direct financial subsidies from commune to Curia (Bullard 1980, pp. 119–50; Hale 1977).

Even while in exile, the Medici employed papal patronage to retain ties to Florentine patricians and insure their acquiescence if not their enthusiasm for a Medician return to power (Butters 1985, pp. 187–225; Bullard 1980, pp. 119–50). The Medici's continued hold on oligarch families during exile, and confidence in those families' loyalty upon their return, is exemplified by the fact that 26 of the 55 members of the first Balia established to reassert Medici control over the government upon their return from exile in 1512 had been members of the anti-Medici Soderini government in the previous four years (Butters 1985, p. 188).

Under the duchy, opportunities for wealth became ever more dependent upon access to Florentine and papal offices under Medici control. It is in this sense that the

Florentine polity and economy were "refeudalized." The structural innovations of the Florentine commune that had marked the devolution of power from *contado* to city and from aristocracy to an elite of urban merchants were reversed as the Medici pursued sources of income for themselves and their allies unencumbered by effective opposition because rival elites and classes were unable to crack the Medici's triple base of power in duchy, papacy, and bank.

Taxes and duties collected in Florence and its territories were assigned to specific offices that were then granted to Medici allies or in return for loans to the state (Litchfield 1986, pp. 141–90; Bullard 1980, pp. 151–72). State and clerical offices, while not formally venal, remained in the hands of a single family unless it lost favor with the Medici (a rare occurrence) or the state moved to repay the loans for which the office had been granted (a virtual impossibility for the heavily indebted duchy). The value of high office rose dramatically during the sixteenth century. Adding the official and private components of officials' compensation, Litchfield (1986, pp. 194, 358–61) estimates that income from the top offices filled by Medici allies rose 240–260 percent between 1551 and 1736, after accounting for inflation, while magistracies filled by men from older families barely kept up with inflation in those centuries.

The tax structure and the nature of relations between city and *contado,* which had been established under the republic, were transformed by the Medici to generate the revenues needed to reward their allies and sustain the political machine that controlled the ducal and papal organizations. The *contado*'s political subordination to the city, and its economic exploitation as a source of cheap food and heavy taxes, were undermined by grants of fiefdoms with judicial powers and immunities from taxes to Medici allies (Litchfield 1986, pp. 35–40, 116–25). As the countryside became reinfeudated, tax revenues from the *contado* fell relatively if not absolutely, and were replaced by heavier taxes on those lands not given over as fiefs to Medici allies and on "captive" towns such as Pisa and Pistoia. Customs on goods traveling into and out of the city walls, which fell on landlords selling grain from their estates in Florence, were largely replaced by indirect salt and notary taxes, which fell on urban guildsmen, the *popolo di Dio,* and peasants (pp. 99–100). Florentine regulation of grain prices had been for centuries, along with taxes on the *contado,* the mark of guildsmen's ability to force politically weakened aristocrats and their peasants to subsidize urban interests. In the later half of the sixteenth century, as Medici allies became rural landlords, prices were allowed to rise, transforming urban consumers into subsidizers of rural estates and rising land prices (pp. 244–61).

The hegemony of the Medici party over the Florentine polity and economy, and its use of feudal controls over offices and land to preserve and subsidize its rule, was represented in the literal rearistocratization of the Florentine ruling elite under the duchy. Family "was elevated to a much more idealistic realm as men began to intellectualize their sense of lineage into a concept of nobility, dignity, wealth, status or any other such nebulous ideal which they wished to attribute to their particular family tradition" (Goldthwaite 1968, p. 270; see also Berner 1971; Cochrane 1965).

The leading families of Florence followed the example of the Medici dukes and accepted noble patents from the Medici themselves or attempted to resurrect ancient titles supposedly granted to their ancestors (Burke 1972, p. 245). "The advantages of titles were chiefly political; they secured [and acknowledged] one a permanent place at the ducal court" (Litchfield 1986, p. 36). Of the 426 families whose members had served most frequently as priors in the fifteenth century (discounting those families that became extinct), half had been ennobled by 1600 and virtually all by 1700 (p. 35).

Through spending on palaces in a great building boom in the late sixteenth century, and a concurrent escalation in the formerly stable and modest level of dowries (Litchfield 1986, pp. 41–45), on artworks (especially self- and family portraits), and on a mannered life punctuated with lavish entertainments, Florentines became preoccupied with the "presentation of self" (Burke 1986, pp. 132–67). The social life of the Florentine ruling elite in the seventeenth century reflected their immunity from challenge by rival elites and classes and their inability to exploit structural openings for profit beyond those afforded by existing offices and fiefs.

The Economic Limits of the Florentine Polity

This extended analysis of the interactions of elite and class conflicts upon the structure of the Florentine polity prepares the way for an explanation of the sources and limits of Florentine economic growth. Favorable conditions external to Florence were necessary for the development of urban autonomy, the rise of new elites, and the prosperity of the principal industries (cloth and banking) located in the city. However, those conditions were present in the environs of other European cities and did not yield similar economic developments. Further, Florence enjoyed the same external conditions that aided the rise of its industries as it did during the irreversible decline of those industries during the sixteenth century. Florentines largely surrendered continuing opportunities to profit from rational economic action in the sixteenth century in favor of making money through office and land holding in ways similar to the practices of rural aristocracies whose status the former merchants of Florence sought to ape.

Florentines of the thirteenth through fifteenth centuries made money in the interstices of feudal Europe. Their business practices, most notably the development of double-entry bookkeeping (deRoover 1963; Cohen 1980), were the epitome of what Weber labels "rational technique." However, opportunities for rational economic action, which were virtually nonexistent in most of Europe during those centuries, were only partially and episodically present for Florentine bankers and cloth merchants.

Florentine bankers and merchants were more prosperous over longer periods than their counterparts in most other European cities because of favorable conditions external to the city. First among those factors was the long-standing stalemate of great powers in northern Italy, which gave Florentines the freedom to enter into business arrangements with popes, kings, wool and silk suppliers, and customers throughout Europe without having to surrender their autonomy and most of their profits to the single kings or aristocrats who ruled most cities and who quickly came to dominate the briefly autonomous cities of Champagne and Germany examined earlier in this chapter.

The second "favorable" factor was Florence's military weakness, which kept its merchants from dominating Mediterranean trade in the manner of the Venetians or the Genoese. Florentines' inability to call upon a strong military force from their own city or from a great power ally forced them into what appeared to be the less profitable wool and silk trades and into efforts to curry business from a papacy whom other Italians disdained in favor of the more profitable Mediterranean trade routes they won in defiance of the pope's foreign policies. The industries into which thirteenth-century Florentines were shunted proved over the following centuries to be more durable than Mediterranean trade, which was disrupted by Turkish military power in the fifteenth century and finally was eclipsed with the rise of the Atlantic trade in the sixteenth century. Meanwhile, the wool, silk, and banking industries thrived, although increasingly outside the Florentine duchy. The remainder of this chapter is concerned first with the reasons for the decline of wool, silk, and banking as specifically Florentine industries and then with the shift of Florentine capital and efforts into the *monte,* offices, and land.

The Rise and Demise of Florentine Wool and Silk Industries

The wool and silk industries were the sectors in which possibilities for economically oriented capitalism (Weber 1978, p. 165), if not rational economic action (pp. 69–74), were strongest and most enduring. The Florentines had used their politically won monopoly over the export of English wool to draw skilled French and Flemish weavers to Florence and to dominate the market for luxury woolens in the thirteenth century. However, the English crown's default on loans to the Bardi and Peruzzi in 1342 and unsuccessful Florentine efforts to claim English royal revenues and offices as repayment on the debt led to a break in the Florentine-English alliance. The English crown stopped wool exports to Florence, alternately selling wool elsewhere in return for new loans and restricting exports in an effort to stimulate a domestic cloth industry (Fryde and Fryde 1965, pp. 461–63). Florentine access to alternative sources of wool was limited by the rise of Turkish power in the eastern Mediterranean (Luzzato 1961, pp. 137–41). Florentine production of luxury woolens declined from eighty thousand pieces in 1330 (p. 106) to twenty-five thousand pieces by 1378 (Lopez and Miskimin 1962, p. 419).

Once they lost their politically derived monopoly over English wool, Florentine merchants sought to change guild work rules and cut wages in order to compete economically in the markets for lower-priced cloth made from the cheaper wool and cotton to which they still had access (Luzzato 1961, pp. 159–61; Mazzaoui 1981, pp. 70, 121–24). Lower guildsmen reacted to this threat to their incomes by allying with magnates to support the installation of Walter of Brienne in 1342 (Brucker 1962, p. 7). As I discuss above, the patricians returned to power the next year by compromising their own differences and by making temporary political and continuing economic concessions to the members of the lower guilds in order to enlist their support in overthrowing Walter and his magnate allies. Florentine wool merchants were unable to make the transition from monopoly luxury to competitive discount production because their position in the Florentine polity (which had given them privileged access to English wool and had created their industry in the first place) was threatened by magnate rivals whose defeat depended upon the merchants' and other patricians' ability to buy the support or at least the neutrality of the mass of guild members.[47]

Following Weber, one could describe the cloth merchants' sacrifice (through an alliance with lower guildmen) of potential economic advantage (in lower-price cloth markets) in favor of the social prestige and political power of public office as politically oriented capitalism. Such a description implies, however, that the merchants would have made a different choice had they been possessed of an economic rather than political orientation. Whether an alternative path was open to cloth merchants is highly doubtful. Even if the merchants had subordinated themselves politically to Walter and the oligarchs in return for that regime's support for an attack on guild privileges, it is unclear whether such an alliance could have overcome the street forces of the remaining patricians and guildsmen. Nor would the oligarchs have been certain to accept such a deal. The benefits for nonmerchant oligarchs and their regime in fostering a competitive low-cost cloth industry were speculative, while the threat of rebellion from the guilds was real.

Ascriptions of orientations are clouded further by the fact that many cloth merchants of the Calimala were engaged, either through their own investments or through family ties of blood and marriage, in multiple lines of business (Goldthwaite 1968, p. 236). Cloth merchants and their kin also were investors in banks and ships, traders of grain and other commodities, officeholders and clerics (Becker 1959; 1967, pp. 89–96; Abulafia 1981).

Cloth merchants could not break with the other patricians, sacrificing the interests of bankers, traders, and officeholders for the benefit of new modes of woolen and cotton production, because the cloth merchants themselves and through their families *were* the bankers, traders, and officeholders.[48] The cloth merchants of the Calimala were embedded in mid-fourteenth-century Florence in a system of extended families, joint ventures, and political alliances that severely limited opportunities for political or economic agency, regardless of their rationality or psychological orientation. A chain of contingencies had placed Florentine cloth merchants in a position to dominate the European market for luxury cloths. When another chain of events destroyed that monopoly, the merchants remained fixed in a web of alliances and ventures that forced them to sacrifice opportunities in one industry to the preservation of their, their families', and their allies' interests in the political rule that guaranteed the greater sum of all their other sources of profit.

The concentration of skilled weavers and other craftsmen in Florence, and Florentine bankers' continuing domination of European trade networks through their alliance with the papacy, allowed for the development of a new luxury industry in silks in the late fourteenth century (Luzzato 1961, p. 142). Florentines dominated the European silk market for the next two centuries because of their superior workmanship and the high quality of silk they used (Mazzaoui 1981, pp. 132–33). The high profit margins from this luxury trade allowed (and the demand for quality products from wealthy buyers required) that Florentine silk merchants employ well-paid and skilled guild workers. Florentine silk merchants overcame the problems of supply that plagued their predecessors in the wool trade by encouraging landlords throughout Italy to increase the portion of their estates devoted to mulberry and silkworm production (Aymard 1982, p. 152).[49]

Like the wool industry in the fourteenth century, the Florentine silk industry went into decline during the seventeenth century although for different reasons.[50] Where the wool crisis had begun on the supply side, silk was challenged by a transformation of demand. Aristocrats' capacities to buy expensive silks eroded in the long-lasting depression that marked the crisis of the seventeenth century. Florentine merchants could not produce cheap silks within their city-state because they continued to be confined by guild rules (Mazzaoui 1981, pp. 138–51; Cipolla 1974; Sella 1974). Again, the merchants' weak political position prevented them from translating their understanding of what the market required into effective rational economic action. The Medici so dominated Florentine politics that they could ignore merchants' pleas for aid; yet the Medici still feared arousing the mass of guildsmen and the *popolo di Dio* by cutting wages for silk workers (Litchfield 1986, pp. 233–44). Nonguild silk production was blocked by the Medici state even in rural areas it controlled (Belfanti 1993, pp. 266–67).[51]

From the seventeenth century on, growth in the European textile industry was confined to the production of lower quality French-made silks and woolens from England and Holland (Mazzei 1979, p. 202).[52] Italian guildsmen almost entirely and rural Italians largely were excluded from those sectors of textile production. However, some Italian bankers and merchants were active in financing and selling the products of foreign proto-industry. The structural factors that impeded nonguild production in most Italian polities did not block Italian investors from pursuing maximum profits outside their homelands.[53]

Seventeenth-century Italian participants in foreign textile production and trade differed from their predecessors in two crucial aspects. First, these Italians generally did not hold the diverse portfolios of the Calimala elite of previous centuries. The wealthiest Florentines, the Medici and their ennobled allies, placed their capital where it earned the greatest returns, in land, public debt, offices, and luxury production (Litchfield 1986, pp. 206–13).[54] The Florentines who invested in foreign textile production were those who were excluded from more lucrative Florentine investments because of their relative lack of political power. Exclusion from investment opportunities at home made it easier for Florentine businessmen abroad to make the second critical change of the seventeenth century. As nation-states became stronger, they imposed growing restrictions on foreigners. Some Florentines, such as those resident in Cracow, in response "married the daughters of the local bourgeoisie, obtained citizenship and even achieved public office" (Mazzei 1979, p. 205). Florentine cloth merchants had an orientation toward profit; however, they were able to engage in rational economic action only outside their city-state and often by assuming French, Spanish, Neapolitan, or Polish citizenship (Litchfield 1986, p. 41; see also Luzzato 1961, p. 161).

Papal and Royal Finance: From Banking to Office

Florentine bankers were innovators in rational economic technique. When the Florentines were locked out of the most lucrative Mediterranean trade routes because of their weak military position, they had turned to the less profitable wool trade and built an unprecedented network of branch offices throughout Europe. That network gave Florentines the technical means necessary to act as papal bankers, and their inability to contest for Mediterranean hegemony eliminated the main source of potential geopolitical conflict with the papacy. Florentines developed a host of techniques for facilitating trade and the transfer of money through their branch office system (deRoover 1963, pp. 77–107; Goldthwaite 1980, p. 47): This was their great contribution to the creation of rational techniques of investment and exchange.[55]

Remember, though, that the Florentines became innovators in spite of themselves. They took to papal banking and continental exchange as a second-best option because they were frozen out of the more lucrative long-distance trade routes dominated by the Venetians and the Genoese. Florentine bankers of the thirteenth and fourteenth centuries realized enormous, windfall profits from initially small capital investments, yet also they were exposed to sudden bankruptcy when the popes and monarchs who bestowed banking concessions decided to transfer their business to new allies or when the governments to which the bankers had extended loans themselves became bankrupt.

In its heyday, in the half century leading up to 1340, banking for the pope and for the English and Sicilian monarchs was by far the most profitable venture in Florence and probably in Europe. While wool merchants averaged a return on capital of 12 percent in the 1330s and bank depositors received from 6 to 10 percent interest,[56] the profit from foreign loans and foreign exchange services for the pope and monarchs ranged up to 33 percent. Investors in the Peruzzi, Bardi, and Alberti banks realized returns of 15 to 20 percent each year from 1300 until the collapse of those banks in the 1330s and 1340s (Renouard 1949, pp. 141–42).

The Bardi and Peruzzi took on numerous partners and sought to attract ever more depositors in order to generate the enormous amount of capital the English and Sicilian monarchs wished to borrow. In 1318 the Bardi listed 875,638 florins on their books in capital and deposits. Almost all of that total, and of the Peruzzi bank's funds, were on loan to the kings of England and Sicily (Renouard 1949, p. 124). Bank partners received extraordinarily high returns on their investments because they leveraged their own funds with their depositors' money. Conversely, when the English crown defaulted on its loans, the bank partners were virtually wiped out. In 1335, investors in the Peruzzi bank received only 15.5 percent of their invested capital at liquidation (Renouard 1949, p. 144). The wider default by the English crown in 1342 brought down the Bardi bank. The Bardi lost at least 594,176 florins in loans and unpaid interest due from the English king (Cipolla 1982, p. 6), wiping out all of its partners' capital and most of the money in depositors' accounts and causing a chain of bankruptcies among those businessmen as well as numerous cloth merchants who no longer could buy English wool from the bankers on credit. Even the commune government was forced to partially suspend payment on its debt in 1345 because of a decline in tax revenues caused by the wave of bankruptcies (Cipolla 1982, pp. 7–12).

Florentine banking revived in the fifteenth century as the Medici family gained influence and then control over the papacy. Organizationally, the Medici bank was even more of a political entity and less of a business enterprise than its Bardi and Peruzzi predecessors. The Medici had virtually no partners or depositors and provided almost all of their bank's limited capital themselves. In 1420 the bank's capital was only 27,570 florins (deRoover 1963, p. 50). Of its 1451 capital of 72,000 florins, "54,000 florins came from the Medici themselves" (Goldthwaite 1987, p. 16).

Control, as well as majority ownership, was held by a single line of fathers and sons, beginning with Giovanni di Bicci in 1397 and continuing with his son Cosimo

TABLE 3.4. Medici Bank Profits and the Papacy, 1397–1494

	Years		
Profits	1397–1420	1420–35	1435–51
% return on total bank capital	31%	44%	37%
% return in Rome branch	86%	110%	—
% return from all other branches	17%	20%	—
Average profit p.a. in Rome branch (in florins)	3,443 fl.	7,800 fl.	5,532 fl.
% of total Medici profit from Rome branch	55%	65%	34%

Source: All figures are calculated from data in de Roover 1963.

Note: The Medici and their partners periodically recapitalized the bank, and return on capital is based on the bank's capitalization at the start of each period. Thus, the period 1397–1420 is calculated from the bank's 1402 capitalization of 20,000 florins, of which 4,000 was invested in the Rome branch. In 1420, the bank was recapitalized with 27,570 florins, of which 7,000 florins were invested in the Rome branch: Those totals are used to calculate the returns in the period 1420–35. In 1441 the bank again was recapitalized with 44,000 florins. The Rome bank no longer had any capital attached to it, and a return for the Rome branch can not be given for the last period. The percentage of profits from the Rome branch is calculated only in terms of Medici profits from banking given by de Roover.

di Medici, his grandson Piero, and his great-grandson Lorenzo. (Two years after Lorenzo's death in 1492 the bank, under Lorenzo's son Piero, was closed when the Medici were exiled from Florence.) Few cousins were involved in the bank either as investors or as employees (Goldthwaite 1987, pp. 7–13).

The Medici bank could prosper with hardly more than the family patriarch's own funds as capital because the firm's profits came mainly from its control over papal finances rather than as a creditor. DeRoover (1963) provides data on the capital and profitability of the Medici bank from 1397 through 1351. Those data are summarized in table 3.4.

During the Medici bank's first four decades (1397–1435) 55 to 65 percent of the profits came from the Rome branch. Returns on the capital invested in that branch approached and then exceeded 100 percent per annum. Profits from all the other bank branches combined ranged from 17 to 20 percent. Even those profits compare favorably with the 14 percent that was the usual "commercial rate of interest in the fifteenth century" (deRoover 1963, p. 121), or with the Medici's 12 percent return on capital invested in the wool and silk manufacture in the period 1435–51.[57]

The Medici's extraordinary returns from the Rome office were more purely political than even the windfall profits enjoyed by the Bardi and Peruzzi before their downfalls. Unlike the earlier Florentine financiers, the Medici did not have to risk much capital to reap huge profits from managing the finances of their papal allies. Nor did the Medici have to create and sustain a large corps of bank officials to manage papal finances. In 1402 the Medici bank employed seventeen staff members, whose salaries totaled 1,053 florins that year or 17 percent of the average annual bank profits for the period 1397–1420 (deRoover 1963, p. 44). In 1460, the Medici bank employed fifty-seven staff members, only six of whom worked in the Roman Curia (p. 95).[58]

The Medici's business with the papacy supported the rest of the bank organizationally as well as financially. During the first half of the fifteenth century, the Medici established branch offices in ten cities (up from the initial three), using corespondents who had handled papal finances on behalf of the bank to invest papal profits in loans to monarchs and businesses in the major cities of Western Europe (de Roover 1963, pp. 53–76).

The Medici bank was dissolved in 1494 upon the family's exile from Florence. However, several branches had been closed over the past three decades because of lack of profitability, and the bank as a whole was losing money in its last decade. De Roover (1963, pp. 358–75) attributes the decline of the Medici bank to a combination of: (1) the incompetence and inattention of the Medici who succeeded Cosimo as head of the bank after his death in 1464 and (2) declining profitability due to a general depression at the end of the fifteenth century that affected most Italian banks, notably the Florentine Pazzi bank, whose collapse occasioned the Pazzi Conspiracy of 1478.[59]

Neither of the factors cited by deRoover can explain the loss of the Medici financial mainstay, the papal concessions that alone could have insured the bank's profitability even under the otherwise adverse conditions of the late fifteenth century. The Medici lost their access to papal favor, and the assets of the Rome branch were impounded in 1478 when Pope Sixtus IV turned against the Medici and their Florentine government. The Medici eventually recovered some of their Roman assets; but that branch never again was profitable (Hale 1977, pp. 66–72; deRoover 1963, p. 221).[60] Medici wealth from outside of Florence came from papal favor. The withdrawal of papal favor spelled the doom of the Medici bank.

The Medici regained their financial ties to Rome, however, with the election of Cardinal Giovanni de Medici as Pope Leo X in 1513.[61] During their pontificates the Medici acted in large part through their in-law and ally Filippo Strozzi, who served as the depositor general to the pope and as depositor for the Florentine Signoria. Strozzi used his control over the principal financial offices in Florence and in Rome to become the wealthiest man in Italy. He made his fortune collecting commissions on all papal financial transactions and by making side deals on supplies for papal and Florentine military and civilian endeavors (Bullard 1980, pp. 103–18).

The Medici, following their return to power in 1530, used their control over Florence to generate funds to subsidize papal military expenses. Strozzi, as treasurer to both Florence and the papacy, facilitated the transfer of funds. Thus, during the sixteenth century the Medician connection to Rome became a burden rather than a benefit to the Florentine economy and balance of payments (Bullard 1980, pp. 119–50).

After the death of the Medici pope Clement VII in 1534, enemies of the Medici audited Strozzi's Roman accounts and the new pope, Paul III, refused to honor many of the papacy's debts to Strozzi. Strozzi sought to ally with the anti-Medician forces in Rome in order to regain his position as papal treasurer and to insure repayment of his loans to the pontificate. Strozzi was executed in Florence in 1538 in retaliation for his betrayal of the Medici (Bullard 1980, pp. 151–78).

Strozzi's career illustrates the extent to which bankers were dependent upon political favor, rather than the ability to raise capital, for profit. Strozzi made his great fortune as the intermediary between two political entities. When his Medici patrons temporarily lost control of the papacy, it was he and not the Medici whose investments were imperiled. By using Strozzi as a proxy rather than reestablishing their own bank in the sixteenth century, the Medici still were able to benefit financially from political power without having to expose their own capital to the vicissitudes of Italian politics. And so it was Strozzi and not the Medici whose fortune, and life, were lost during the cold war between Florence and the papacy under Paul III.

Following Strozzi's downfall, international and papal banking never again became a source of great profit for Florentines. Popes, in the following decades and centuries, distributed financial concessions to bankers in various cities in an effort to build ties to all Italian factions and thereby achieve a measure of autonomy for the church (Goldthwaite 1968, p. 238; Luzzato 1961, p. 144).[62]

Genoa was the only other Italian city-state to become a dominant banking center; its heyday lasted from 1557 to 1627. Genoese success, like that of the Florentines before them, depended upon two conditions: first, a network of offices in the key locales of Spain and the Low countries (which had been created by the Genoese to exploit trade opportunities in those European locales to which they had access), and second, a political alliance (in Genoa's case with the government of Castile, which needed to convert American silver into gold to pay its troops in the Low Countries). Genoese bankers prospered as long as those two conditions prevailed, although they were forced to share their profits with other Italian bankers who had access to gold coins and were willing to trade them for silver. Once the Spanish lost control of the Netherlands, Genoa fell into obscurity as a banking center and Amsterdam (as I show in chapter 4) became for a time the new center of European finance (Braudel 1972, pp. 500–508; Bergier 1979).[63]

Banking in Europe from the thirteenth to the eighteenth century was concerned mainly with raising loans for rulers and popes and servicing their fiscal administrations. As such, political influence mattered far more than technical skill or even access to capital. Indeed, bankers without political access, like the Florentines of the late sixteenth and seventeenth centuries, invested with bankers who were politically favored, like the Genoese at the Spanish court. Florentines, to be sure, had been innovators in the establishment of systems of branch offices to facilitate the transfer of money across Europe and initially had gained favored positions with popes and English kings because of those skills. Other Italians, however, and then bankers from elsewhere in Europe copied Florentine techniques and added refinements of their own.

Florentine bankers never had a distinctly political or economic orientation. Instead, they adopted whatever strategy yielded the highest return on their capital. By the 1530s, Florentines no longer had opportunities to make windfall profits as financiers to foreign governments. Some Florentines continued to involve themselves in commercial banking, but most increasingly invested their capital at home, in the *monte* (shares in the city-state's debt), in offices, and in feudal estates.

The Feudalization of Capital: *Monte,* Office, Land

Florentines were stymied in their ability to invest in commercial expansion at home by the limited market for luxury textiles and by guild restrictions on low-cost mass production. The long decline of Florentine influence over popes and kings (and of papal influence over kings and national churches), a decline marked by bankrupting conflicts between Florentine financiers and the rulers to whom they extended credit, limited the opportunities for large profits outside the city-state. However, just as opportunities for international enterprise of both an economic and a political nature were being foreclosed, the stabilization of Florence's position in European geopolitics and the end of political devolution gave patricians new opportunities to appropriate income within their city-state. These investments were, for the most part, passively held. Owners derived income from the *monte,* from offices, and from land through their individual and collective political power as much as from their investment of capital.

The Florentine *monte* was modeled on the Venetian Monte Veechio, which, when it was established in 1262, was the first sustained instance in European history of a marketable state debt (Lane 1973, p. 150). The *montes* of Venice, Florence, and other Italian city-states were a significant contribution to the development of rational economic technique and a precursor to the later Dutch and English development of negotiable state bonds. From founding of the *monte* in 1343 through Florence's incorporation into the Hapsburg empire in 1737, holders of *monte* debt had the right to sell their shares. Since the state almost never attempted to repay principal, *monte* investors could recover their capital only through the market. The value of *monte* shares fluctuated widely in reaction to the government's varying capacity to meet its ever-rising interest costs.

State debt holders can be separated into two classes. A privileged clique composed of the principal supporters of whatever party controlled the commune and, after 1513, of the Medici and their allies was given the opportunity to finance military and other governmental costs in return for *monte* shares with a face value several times the amount they had advanced (Mohlo 1971, pp. 136–37, 180–12). In that way, these investors earned interest payments of 20 to 40 percent, and "the loans seem to have amortized quite rapidly with the income from forced levies. Moreover, since these very bankers were the men selected to be on the committee in charge of administering public funds, their loans were in effect fully secured" (Goldthwaite 1987, p. 27). These politically privileged elites of Monte investors were the epitome of Weber's politically oriented capitalists who made windfall profits from extraordinary transactions with political bodies: "Opportunities to invest in the floating debt . . . were sporadic and temporary. . . . In short, the government did not loom large in the strategy of a bank [or wealthy investor] to maximize profits, however attractive bankers found the occasional opportunity for investing in state debt" (Goldthwaite 1987, p. 27)

The second, and much larger, group of *monte* investors was made up of politically weaker citizens who became bondholders by virtue of their obligation to pay periodic *prestanza* (forced loans) in lieu of a wealth tax (the *estimo*). As *monte* debt expanded from 500,000 florins in 1345 to 8 million florins by 1450, *monte* shares became a major part of wealthy Florentines' assets. By 1380, 5,000 Florentines, or one-twelfth of the adult population, was invested in the *monte. Monte* shares were used for dowries, linking the reproduction of the propertied class to the city-state's geopolitical fortunes (Becker 1968a, pp. 152–59).

During the years in the fourteenth century when the state was solvent, *monte* shares purchased through *prestanza* paid 10 to 15 percent, while commercial enterprises averaged 8 to 10 percent and land 5 to 7 percent per annum (Molho 1971, p. 65; Jones 1966, pp. 413–29). The higher return on the *monte* compensated for the greater risk and periodic suspensions of interest payments (Molho 1971, pp. 66–73).

The vast growth of the *monte* reflected the Florentine city-state's inability to meet the extraordinary expenses of war with ordinary revenues, or even to repay war debts with budget surpluses during peacetime. Permanent, war-induced debts were a feature of almost all the other city-states of Italy and indeed of virtually all states in the medieval and subsequent eras. What is noteworthy, however, is the increasing eagerness of almost all Florentine payers of *prestanza* to hold the shares they were issued for their forced loans and of wealthy Florentines to invest in voluntary *montes,* such as that for dowries.

Three principal factors contributed to the movement of wealth into passive investments such as the *monte*, offices, and land. First was the declining return and increasing risk of investments in cloth manufacture and banking. As noted above, Florentines were increasingly limited in their prospects for manufacturing profits within their city-state and for banking profits abroad. Second was political stabilization within Florence under the oligarchy and then the Medici which widened opportunities for political insiders to realize windfalls from speculating in *monte* shares, which increased the ruling elite's income from office.

The third factor that contributed to the attractiveness of *monte* debt was the relatively cautious foreign policy of the Medici. The Medici recognized, especially after their return to power in 1530, the limited role of the city-state in the geopolitics of Europe and stabilized their government's relations with the papacy and other European powers, allowing a diminution of military expenditures (Spini 1979; Diaz 1978, pp. 96–97). *Monte* payments became more secure as a result (Goldthwaite 1987, p. 24), and state debt became, along with land, the favored investment of wealthy citizens (Litchfield 1986, pp. 203–32). The decline in Florentine war-making and therefore in extraordinary military expenses was reflected in state debt levels. The *monte* debt, which had expanded from 500,000 florins in 1345 to 8 million florins in 1450 rose at a much slower rate to 14 million scudi, the equivalent of 13 million florins, in 1737 when Florence was incorporated into the Hapsburg Empire (Litchfield 1986, pp. xiii, 103).[64]

The *monte* was the institutional embodiment of patrician rule over the Florentine city-state. Interest charges on the *monte* were financed from taxes on the *contado* and on urban consumers (Litchfield 1986, pp. 99–100). *Monte* interest generally was not financed from new *monte* shares. The *monte* was not a pyramid scheme. Instead, the level of commune debt increased in periodic spurts to meet extraordinary war expenses (Becker 1968a, pp. 151–200; Mohlo 1971). The *monte* was a rational, increasingly regular, economic investment because of the political stability of patrician and Medici rule in Florence in the fifteenth through seventeenth centuries.

Profits from offices, like those from the *monte*, became safer and more predictable after the Medici established their rule over Florence. During the fourteenth and earlier centuries, the winners of factional struggles used their control over Florentine government to enrich themselves and their supporters. Gains from offices were windfalls that could not be anticipated or regularized over the long term.

Many offices became de facto venal under Medici rule. Officials were allowed to name their successors. Since the state did not collect a fee in return for that right, officials themselves profited by selling the positions they occupied to their successors. The Medici rewarded supporters by creating lucrative offices that the allies could then keep or sell to raise funds (Litchfield 1986, pp. 177–81). The duchy increased the value and price of offices by allowing incumbents to enforce regulations and collect fees in addition to their official salaries. As discussed above, incomes from top offices filled by Medici allies rose 240 to 260 percent between 1551 and 1736 (pp. 194, 358–61).

Office holding remained a political form of profit, transferring income from the mass of consumer and peasant taxpayers to the ruling elite of Florence, and new offices were windfalls to political supporters of the Medici.[65] For purchasers and heirs of offices, government positions were an economically rational investment with a stable return on capital and the assurance that ownership of an office could be willed to an heir or sold. Increases in income from office were granted by the Medici for political reasons and should be considered windfalls in the same sense as the original grant of an office.

Land became the favorite investment for Florentine patricians and for the elites of other city-states, especially the Venetians (Woolf 1968), in the sixteenth and seventeenth centuries. Litchfield (1986) calculates that the value of urban Florentines' agricultural land holdings increased 165 percent from 1534 to 1695 and stabilized thereafter (p. 219). Land held by Florentines in the *contado* and beyond was increasingly concentrated in the hands of a few wealthy families at the expense of lesser Florentines who were compelled by falling incomes and by increases in the cost of living and in dowry costs to sell their smaller holdings to the richest patricians (pp. 215–32).

Florentines and other Italian businessmen bought land for a combination of political, social, and economic reasons. Florentine patricians bought fiefs newly created by the Medici dukes; wealthy commoners from elsewhere in Italy were customers for the even more numerous ennobling estates created by the Duchy of Milan, the kingdom of Naples, and by various minor political entities (Litchfield 1986, pp. 35–36). Such titles conferred social prestige upon their purchasers and guaranteed certain political privileges in the rearistocratized city-states of Italy.

Grain prices in Italy tripled from 1500 until they stabilized in the 1620s (Abel 1980, pp. 304–5), spurring a rise in land values and rents that peaked several decades later throughout Europe (Abel 1980, pp. 128–30, 147–53, 161–64; Litchfield 1986, p. 225). Land, therefore, seemed to be a good investment for all buyers in the sixteenth and early seventeenth century, and a relative bargain to the wealthiest families that still held liquid capital for investment in the subsequent decades.

As they and their patrician allies bought land in the *contado* (Diaz 1978, pp. 101–2), the Medici dukes changed Florentine state policy on taxes to benefit landlords at the expense of urban consumers. Beginning in the fourteenth century, Florence had exploited the conquered territories through heavy taxes on the land holdings of nobles and clerics (Epstein 1991; Becker 1966). By the early 1400s, the countryside contributed half of Florence's ordinary revenues (Becker 1968b, p. 130).[66] In 1534, however, Florence froze land assessments; they were not revised until the 1830s. The high inflation of the sixteenth century reduced the land tax burden in the *contado* to a nominal level (Litchfield 1986, pp. 215–16). By 1550 direct tax revenues from territories outside the city of Florence itself had fallen to 20 percent of the government's annual ordinary revenues. They rose to 27 percent of ordinary revenues in the 1730s because taxes on captive towns such as Pisa and Pistoia had increased; land taxes from the *contado* continued to fall. Lost revenues were made up by indirect taxes that fell on the mass of urban and rural consumers (Litchfield 1986, pp. 99–100).

Government food policy remained relatively constant from the mid-fourteenth century until the end of the Medici duchy in 1737. Throughout those centuries the communal and ducal governments imposed price controls on agricultural commodities and forced subject territories to sell food stuffs in Florence, often at below market prices (Herlihy 1967, pp. 156–60; Litchfield 1986, pp. 244–61). Despite such controls, food prices did rise from the 1570s through the 1650s in Tuscany as well as in the rest of Europe (Litchfield 1986, p. 247; Abel 1980, pp. 117, 150, 158).

The transfer of land from rural nobles to Florentine merchants, and then the concentration of agrarian holdings in the hands of the wealthiest patricians-turned-nobles had little effect upon the organization of agricultural production. Nor did the rise in land values and the decades of high commodity prices in the late sixteenth and early seventeenth centuries spur much technological innovation or capital investment in agriculture. Historians of the Florentine *contado,* and of rural Italy in general, concur in drawing a picture of rural life little changed through the late Middle Ages and Renaissance.[67]

Control over land and lordships shifted rapidly and frequently among elites from the ninth through the sixteenth century. At the same time relations between landlords and peasants changed in certain respects while remaining within the confines of a feudal structure. Recall that from the ninth through the fourteenth century monarchs, popes, nobles, and clerics had enfeoffed their estates in order to recruit and reward allies. As agrarian lordships and regional political power devolved into the hands of nonaristocratic elites, and as the communes ruled by those elites conquered the countryside, seigneurial powers were undermined throughout Tuscany and in much of northern and central Italy during the eleventh through thirteenth centuries. Serfdom and labor dues were converted into cash rents on enfeoffed estates, demesnes were rented out, and the lords of small estates were either not granted or could not enforce the juridical powers previously enjoyed by overlords (Jones 1966, pp. 402–9; 1968, pp. 205–14).

Florence and the other city-states restricted and appropriated for themselves the rights of great and lesser lords in the *contados.* The communes prevented lords from raising their tenants' rents, which then were rendered nominal by the inflation of the twelfth and thirteenth centuries (Jones 1968, pp. 205–14). Most peasants did not benefit from communal controls on landlords. The main beneficiaries were urban merchants who either were themselves the "tenants" on enfeoffed estates or who gained de facto control of peasant farms when peasant holders were unable to repay loans extended by the merchants.

Merchant, and later ennobled, landlords rarely established commercial farms on their land holdings. Instead, they divided their holdings (which often were patchworks of small farms intermingled with the holdings of other landlords) into *poderi,* farms let to peasant families in a sharecropping arrangement. A minority of peasant families emerged from the Middle Ages as the de facto owners of their own farms; more often peasants augmented their own lands, which were too small to support a family, with *poderi.* The poorest peasants, with no land of their own and little or no access to *poderi,* worked as wage laborers on the farms of landlords or rich peasants (Jones 1968, pp. 227–37).[68]

Landlords, for the most part, were content to collect and market their share of peasant production while neither intervening in the process of production nor investing capital in improvements on the land. Innovation and investment were limited for four main reasons: First, Florentine landlords were absentee. They "hardly ever visited their estates, except in the few weeks of *villeggiatura* of the late summer, or when younger sons were forced into rural exile to seek places of temporary lodging" (Litchfield 1986, p. 224). Instead, Florentine landlords spent most of their time in the city, tending to their far more important and lucrative urban political and business affairs. Since landlords were otherwise occupied, they could not devote the attention necessary to ensuring that capital inputs would be used efficiently. Landlords did hire estate agents called *fattori*, who collected rents and crop shares for patricians (p. 222). There is no evidence that *fattori* had either the skills or the motivation necessary to make them effective "improving" managers of Tuscan farms. Landlords could have tried to raise *fattori* salaries high enough to provide the motivation, but that would have cost much of the farm profits on a speculative effort to improve yields.[69]

Second, "investment in agriculture formed a specific aspect of Florentine business activities. Agricultural holdings diversified Florentines' investment portfolios: Profits were lower in agriculture but more secure" (Emigh 1997, p. 433; see also Litchfield 1986, pp. 215–36; Dowd 1961, pp. 158–59; Woolf 1968). Landowners realized a profit of 3 to 5 percent on their holdings in the seventeenth century (Romano 1964, p. 43). Often that was a return on a "political" windfall rather than a cash investment. Many Florentines initially acquired land as gifts from political patrons or as a by-product of their city's military conquests, as did the urban patricians of the other city-states. Later purchasers valued land and revived or newly minted aristocratic titles as resources for political power and social prestige, not as high-yielding investments.

Third, city governments imposed restrictions upon landlords that made most investments in improving land uneconomical. Price controls and forced sales, combined with aggressive purchases of grain from abroad, kept down the returns from sales on foodstuffs from the *contado*. Indeed, the main form of investment in land—the clearing of new lands rather than the improvement of existing lands—occurred mainly in the sixteenth and early seventeenth centuries, during the period of unusual increases in food and land prices (Litchfield 1986, pp. 255–56; McArdle 1978). Most of the "investment" required to clear land was labor, and peasants provided that labor free in return for the right to sharecrop on wastelands they had cleared (McArdle 1978; Aymard 1982, pp. 158–60).

Finally, the sharecropping system, with short (often one-year) contracts, itself reduced incentives for both landlords and tenants to improve farms. Landlords would not invest in improvements to boost output when half or more of the output went to the sharecroppers rather than the investing landlord. Tenants would not invest capital along with their labor to improve lands that they held only for short leases. Furthermore, few peasants accumulated the capital needed to become commercial farmers themselves, nor were nonpeasant investors willing to invest in land leases and improvements as did commercial farmers of the type found in England in the seventeenth and subsequent centuries. Sharecropping peasants were constantly in debt; "even in good years, the burden of his debt acted to keep *mezzadro* [the sharecropper] from having access to market, which was reserved to landowners, and therefore from having any access to any form of accumulation of capital or of the means of production (Aymard 1982, p. 160).

There was some investment in new crops, above all the mulberry vital for silk production. Again, the sharecropping system limited returns, and hence incentives, for such investments. Lombardy's exceptional investment in new crops highlights the rarity with which structural factors inhibiting investment were overcome. The main incentive for investment in Lombardy was an unusual provision in "the agrarian law of Lombardy [that] provided that if the landlord at the termination of the rent contract had not completely reimbursed the renter for the expenses of improvement made in his tenure, he was obliged to re-rent the same land to the same renter at the same rent until the aforesaid reimbursement was made. When the businessmen of the time rented the lands of the church and invested substantially in capital improvements, they knew that the church would never be able to reimburse them, and that after many improvements, they would be able to take control of the land itself, for a token amount" (Cipolla quoted in Dowd 1961, p. 154). This unusual legal provision made it pay for Lombard investors to initiate mulberry cultivation and other new crops. Lombard commercial farmers provided for the silk industry of Florence as well as of Milan; absent the legal opportunity to use investment in improvements to gain land, Florentine merchant-landlords had little incentive to improve lands that (unlike their Lombard counterparts) they already controlled (Dowd 1961; Litchfield 1986, McArdle 1978).

Even in Lombardy, "changes in technique, apart from improvements in irrigation facilities, were not undertaken" (Dowd 1961, p. 152). Production of new crops was initiated or expanded only when the silk industry, or the incomes of urban residents who consumed luxury foods, expanded as well. The depression of the seventeenth century resulted in a halt in agricultural investment and cutbacks in new crops. Sharecroppers throughout the Renaissance used their portion of the increased output from new lands not to increase their standard of living or for investment but to expand the sizes of their families (Litchfield 1986, pp. 254–56).

Italian landlords gained and lost income as control of land shifted among elites through essentially political processes. Peasants came to be exploited through sharecropping rather than labor dues; however, neither system created room for innovation or investment in new techniques of production. The profitability of land for landlords as a class was determined by the political relationship between city and country, and by local and continental prices for grain that responded to demographic factors. As the ruling elites of Florence, Milan, Genoa, and other city-states added land to their investment portfolios and seigneurial titles to their political and social status, the policies of their governments gave more favorable tax and market treatment to landlords at the expense of urban consumers.[70] Land reflected as it buttressed the increasingly passive economic orientation of patricians secure in their political control of a duchy that guarded income from *monte* shares, offices, and rural estates. Income from such sources waxed and waned with the political power of families and elites.

The Logic of Refeudalization in City-States

We now can answer the questions posed at the outset of this chapter: Why did the great cities of medieval and Renaissance Europe not become the economic and political centers of subsequent capitalist development and state formation? Why were the elites of the city-states overwhelmed in the sixteenth and subsequent centuries by rival rural elites that were able to consolidate vast rural territories and to dominate the cities in their midst?

The short answer to those questions is that the same set of circumstances that made it possible for urban elites to gain political autonomy and to grab commercial advantages also locked those elites into institutional arrangements that limited later opportunities for maneuver. Great power competition and the stalemate among feudal elites, such as kings, the pope, nobles, and clerics, allowed nonaristocratic urban elites to play feudal rivals against one another and win a measure of urban autonomy. Elite stalemate persisted unusually long in northern and central Italy and therefore political devolution was most far-reaching there. Urban oligarchies, which were nonaristocratic in almost all Italian cities, with the notable exception of Venice, gained full autonomy within their cities from monarchs and rural aristocrats by the fourteenth century. Then and in later centuries the urban oligarchs took further advantage of the lack of aristocratic hegemony by conquering and exploiting the countrysides surrounding their cities.

Great power stalemate did not simply create an opening for urban autonomy; it set in train a process of political devolution as elites "reached down" to recruit allies from below.[71] As lesser elites, and eventually privileged strata of the guilds, gained a measure of power, they engaged one another in conflict for control of commune government. It was that conflict, largely internal to each city-state, that determined the political institutions, economic opportunities, and limits upon further structural change for each city-state.

Commerce thrived in the "free air" of autonomous cities. Political self-aggrandizement and foreign adventurism thrived as well among the elites of Italian and other European autonomous cities. Urban elites of the Renaissance cannot be divided neatly between backward, politically oriented aristocrats and rational, economically oriented bourgeois. Again and again in this chapter, we see classes, elites, occupational groups, families, and individuals simultaneously pursuing both political and economic sources of profit. These Renaissance actors were polymorphous in their pursuit of profit and power. None appears to have been restrained by a political orientation when opportunities for economically oriented capitalism appeared in the wool trade, silkworm cultivation and production, commercial banking, or financial speculation.

Florentine and other urban elites were restrained by the political arrangements that they constructed in their struggles for power. The very openings in Italian and European great power politics that gave urban elites their political autonomy and economic opportunity also encouraged Florentine patricians and their counterparts in Venice, Genoa, and Milan to institute oligarchies and then to refeudalize their polities and economies as the best way of preserving power and maximizing wealth.

The opportunities for effective action in Renaissance Italian cities were different from those available to the rural aristocrats in sixteenth- and seventeenth-century England and France who are the subject of the next chapter. Almost always when Florentine patricians gained control over land, offices, industries, and markets they did so by creating institutional arrangements that inhibited "continuous buying and selling on the market . . . [or the reinvestment of profits and other capital] in continuous production of goods," in Weber's formulation (1978, p. 164). Florentine business-men instead were encouraged to preserve guild restrictions, trade monopolies, and rigid, limited, and politically manipulated markets, not only because those were more profitable than a purer capitalism might have been in the economically back-ward and poor Europe of the Renaissance, but also because rich Florentines de-pended upon political power for the preservation of their wealth and for any access to commercial opportunities. Florentines therefore made rational decisions, certainly in the light of their political situation within the commune and probably as well in the context of the European economy of the Renaissance, to forsake "real" capital-ism in favor of investment in politically protected bonds, offices, estates, and foreign concessions.

Decisions that were rational in the short and middle-term had long-term conse-quences that were destructive of the economic and political positions of Florentine and other Italian urban elites. The dynamics of elite conflict examined in this chapter explain why rational strategies had such deleterious consequences. Florentine patri-cians were locked into mutually reinforcing networks of finance and trade that de-pended upon papal favor and expanding luxury markets. As long as those conditions held, profits from such politically protected enterprises were greater than other pos-sible investments. Combined with the gains from offices, land, and the *monte*, Flo-rence's particular mode of manufacture and trade generated wealth that justified the oligarchy's, and later the Medician aristocracy's, costly concessions to guilds and expenditures for winning allies and building prestige at home and abroad.

Similarly rational decisions were made by the ruling elites of Venice, Genoa, and other Italian city-states. Venice's and Genoa's concentration upon military control of Mediterranean trade routes and the building of massive shipping industries best ex-ploited the opportunities open to the elites of those city-states. The ruling aristocracy and oligarchy of those cities had to make accommodations with other elites and reach a class compromise with at least the major guilds in order to mobilize the resources needed to pursue their sensible geopolitical and commercial strategies. The political and economic institutions and relations of production created out of those compromises prevented the rulers of Venice and Genoa from adopting new strategies in later cen-turies. For the Venetian aristocracy, their lack of room for maneuver meant that they and their city were relegated to the status of tourist attraction by the seventeenth cen-tury. Genoa's polity and economy allowed its rulers to take advantage of the unusual opportunities opened by Spanish imperialism and New World silver in the sixteenth century. Similarly, Milan's triumph over the church in Lombardy created unusual in-centives and opportunities for agricultural investment and innovation. However, those opportunities lasted only as long as the luxury silk industry prospered and while the Spanish crown needed to convert New World silver into gold coins for its Low Coun-try armies.

This chapter explains why opportunities for agency opened to different degrees in Renaissance French, German, and Italian cities. It also shows how geopolitical stale-mates and local elite conflicts combined to define and delimit the opportunities for ra-tional economic action in Renaissance Italy. The particular openings for political and economic agency determined structures of power, production, and exchange that pre-cluded further amalgamations of capital and coercion that might have allowed cities to become the nodes of a continental system of political consolidation and economic development. The stalemate of urban elites explains only why cities did not lead Europe; that further development took place at all and was led by previously backward rural aristocracies is due to the dynamic of conflict among those elites and is the subject of the following chapters.

4

State Formation
England and France

S OMETHING BEGAN TO HAPPEN in the sixteenth century in the most unlikely places. Rural aristocrats, who previously had defined their interests
in terms of particularistic corporate and local privileges, were drawn into nationwide
networks. As those networks became institutionalized, aristocrats, once locally oriented, began holding office in nation-states and developing new, broad class interests
as the beneficiaries of capitalist relations of production.

Historians offer us good and increasingly detailed descriptions of the ways in
which aristocrats came to assume nationalistic and economically grounded identities.
However, the causes of changes in aristocratic identity and behavior remain a subject
of dispute. As the discussion of Florence in chapter 3 shows, the "free air" of cities
was not a sufficient source of universalistic values. Urban elites held different interests
and were embedded within different networks than their rural rivals; Florentine and
other urban oligarchs therefore never transcended local interests and eventually became rearistocratized to protect their privileges.

International trade made some elites rich but did not necessarily spur capitalism
or help to build strong states. A comparison of the countries analyzed in this and the
next chapter demonstrate that trade and colonialism could buttress local privileges and
retard state formation (as it did in Portugal, Spain, and to a degree the Netherlands)
or be largely irrelevant to class and state formation until well after those states were
formed and capitalists and proletarians were locked into class conflict (as in England
and France).

Warfare existed both before and after the formation of the first nation-states. The
work of Charles Tilly and others allows us to trace how increases in the scale, technology, and cost of military competition marginalized and eliminated weak sovereigns
until the hundreds of overlapping political units in Europe were reduced to a few
dozen. Neither Tillyesque analyses of the intensification of coercion within and among
nations nor historians' more descriptive studies of war and diplomacy are able to explain why competition among elites began to organize itself along national lines in the

sixteenth century. This chapter finds the first cause of state formation in the national-ization of elite conflicts and social relations.

Max Weber, as I note in previous chapters, saw competition among feudal elites as a "chronic condition" and looked to the external shock of the Reformation to create a new psychology that spawned new interests and new forms of behavior. Karl Marx and Marxists are of two minds, as demonstrated in the debate over the meaning of Marx's famous discussion, in volume 3 of *Capital,* of "two roads" of transition from feudalism to capitalism. Marx was unsure whether merchants alone could transform production through the growing demands of trade, or whether "producers" (whoever they were) had to institute capitalist relations of production first in order to destroy feudal autarky and create markets that in turn would spur more capitalist production. This argument between trade and class struggle as the engine of change has been carried on most notably by Paul Sweezy and Immanuel Wallerstein on the trade side and Maurice Dobb, Eric Hobsbawm, Perry Anderson, and Robert Brenner on the class side.[1] Both positions remain inconclusive: we never learn exactly how trade spurs cap-italism rather than slavery, feudalism, sharecropping, and other modes of production that were and remain highly compatible with markets and trade. Marxists who see class struggle as the prime mover of capitalism have yet to explain how and why feudal class conflicts took a new turn in the sixteenth century and how the new parameters of conflict generated capitalist relations of production.

I propose a new solution to the old problem of origins in this and the following chapters. As readers might guess, I present elite, not class, conflict as the prime mover in state formation and capitalist development. Specifically, I agree with Weber in see-ing the Protestant Reformation as the turning point in the history of European feu-dalism, but not for the social-psychological reasons he posits. Rather, the Reforma-tion was decisive because it opened a new cleavage in elite interests, transformed elite capacities, and thereby shaped the course of state and class formation in Europe in the sixteenth and seventeenth centuries.

Chapter 2 concludes with an analysis of the limits of agrarian change in medieval England and France. The persistence of multiple elites limited the capacity of any in-dividual elite to either abolish peasant land tenure or impose serfdom. Instead, land-lords extracted cash or labor dues, with the patterns of exploitation varying across regions and over time in response to the fixed or changing structures of elite relations in each French province and in England. The "chronic conditions" of conflict among multiple elites and of feudal relations of production were affected by the Reformation, which opened new strategic opportunities for elite conflicts in England and France. I begin this chapter by enumerating the ways in which each elite in France and England attempted to exploit the opportunities created by religious division. I then trace the concatenation of tactical moves by multiple elites into the political transformations that created two quite different national states in the two countries.

Reformation and Elite Divisions in England and France

The Reformation disrupted existing alliances among aristocrats and with urban no-tables and clerics in both England and France. Initially, the Reformation did not alter the social psychologies of individuals. As this and the following chapters make clear, political transformations preceded and determined changes in economic behavior and relations of production in both countries, contrary to Weber.[2] New social networks among coreligionists did form by the end of the sixteenth century, linking together land-lords and urban notables across counties and provinces. Eventually, such ideologically-based ties affected the lines of political alliance in both Britain and France. However, the Reformation created political opportunities for kings before it did for regional magnates or locally based landlords. Kings benefited first because their ties across counties and provinces, however weak, were sturdier and more numerous than those of regional magnates or great merchants, not to mention local landlords or provincial bourgeois.

The English and French monarchs both tried to exploit religious conflicts among their subjects to divide rivals and to win new clients. The kings also took advantage of the Protestant challenge to win concessions from the pope and from the Catholic hierarchies within their countries. The strategies each monarch adopted reflected his existing structural positions with respect to rival elites. The results of those strategies were determined by the overall structure of elites in the two countries.

Three Theories of Absolutism

The notion of the Reformation as a strategic "break" that disrupted the chronic con-dition of frequent yet structurally ineffective elite and class conflict is at odds with the dominant paradigms in the study of absolutism as well as with Weber's understand-ing of the Reformation. I reserve my critique of Weber's Protestant ethic thesis for chapter 7 but must relate my analysis of elite conflict to previous work on absolutism and state formation at the outset of this chapter.

Each model of absolutism is able to point to evidence that accords with its de-scriptive definition of the early modern state. The relative merits of competing theo-ries of state formation can be evaluated along two dimensions. The first dimension is how each theory explains the nature and timing of each state's divergence from the others and especially from the polities of the medieval era. The second is how each model predicts the lines of alliance and the outcomes of antistate rebellions. For En-gland and France, a successful theory must explain the divergent outcomes of the French Frondes of 1648–53 in which the crown defeated aristocratic rebels and the English Revolution and Civil War of 1640–49.

Students of absolutism agree that the English and French states increased their military power, legal authority, and revenues in the sixteenth and seventeenth centuries. Three general hypotheses have been offered for how power and resources were centralized, and whether absolutist monarchies were formed at the behest or at the expense of feudal aristocracies. One theory argues that peasant challenges to feudal exploitation forced the nobility to reorganize their coercive power within organs of a centralized state. Thus, absolutism served nobles by affording them greater security and a larger share of peasant production than they would have gained through localized struggles. A second theory claims that a rising bourgeoisie attained economic parity with the nobility during the sixteenth century. During the unusual and transitory balance and stalemate between two putative ruling classes, state managers achieved a relative autonomy over both parties. Their autonomy eroded as soon as the bourgeoisie gained sufficient power to defeat the nobility and subordinate the state to its exclusive interest. A third theory proposes that state power and autonomy are cumulative and self-generating. As self-serving state elites gain revenues, they invest those resources in armies and bureaucracies that are then deployed to capture territory and extract further revenues from "citizens." This constitutes the process of nation formation.

Behind theories that view the absolutist state as representative of the nobility, relatively autonomous, or progressively autonomous, notions are introduced to explain when and how state officials and classes engage in efficacious action. This section probes those often implicit notions and generates hypotheses and identifies the sorts of evidence that supports or undermines each theory.

Perry Anderson represents the first view: "One of the basic axioms of historical materialism [is] that the secular struggle between classes is ultimately resolved at the *political*—not at the economic or cultural—level of society" (1974, p. 11). He argues that during feudalism the nobility and peasantry were politically efficacious to the extent that they were able to strengthen or weaken the state. Anderson conceives the state as a complex of legal-coercive institutions that guarded feudal property relations.

Anderson traces the development of the absolutist state to the feudal crisis that followed the Black Death. Absolutism was the response of the aristocracy to this crisis, "a redeployed and recharged apparatus of feudal domination designed to clamp the peasant masses back into their traditional social position. . . . The result was a displacement of political-legal coercion upwards towards a centralized, militarized summit—the Absolutist state. Diluted at village level, it became concentrated at 'national' level" (1974, pp. 18–19).

Anderson gives primary emphasis to class struggles between nobles and peasants. In the formation of absolutist states, he regards as relatively unimportant the conflicts among aristocratic factions, even though he acknowledges that, "for many individual nobles," absolutism "signified indignity or ruin, against which they rebelled" (1974, p. 47). However, "no feudal ruling class could afford to jettison the advances achieved by Absolutism, which were the expression of profound historical necessities working themselves out right across the continent, without jeopardizing its own existence; none, in fact, ever was wholly or mainly won to the cause of revolt" (p. 54). As a result, regionally and factionally based rebellions, such as the Frondes in France, failed less because of the military or fiscal capacities of the absolutist monarchy and more because most aristocrats had no choice but to remain loyal to absolutist monarchies upon whom they depended for the power and legal legitimacy necessary to extract resources from peasants. Absolutist states' aristocratic character is further indicated by their relations with the rising class of bourgeois. Anderson sees "a potential *field of compatibility* . . . between the nature and programme of the Absolutist State and the operations of mercantile and manufacturing capital" (p. 41), with both state and capital growing and profiting from the monetization of taxes and rents, the sale of state offices, and the establishment of protected monopolies domestically and of colonial ventures abroad. Nevertheless, in his view, the bourgeoisie always remained subordinate to the nobility in the policies of absolutist states.

To support Anderson's thesis, there should be no evidence that the bourgeoisie played a critical role in the antiabsolutist rebellions as long as the bourgeoisie was subordinate to the aristocracy. And as long as the aristocracy remains the dominant class, absolutist monarchies should have been invulnerable to challenge from any source. Thus, Anderson contends that the Frondes failed because the aristocracy was unwilling, and the peasantry and bourgeoisie were unable, to overthrow absolutism. The unique success of the English Civil War among seventeenth-century antistate rebellions is a sign that "a commercialized gentry, a capitalist city, a commoner arti-sanate and yeomanry" developed precociously and gained strength to challenge and defeat an aristocratic state (1974, p. 142). To support that contention, Anderson needs to demonstrate that the interests of the new bourgeois class in England differed from those of disgruntled elements of the old aristocracy who had headed previous rebellions, and he needs to explain how that new bourgeoisie developed within the confines of a feudal system.

Other Marxists are less convinced about the aristocratic character of absolutism. Frederick Engels, in *The Origin of the Family, Private Property, and the State*, differentiates "the feudal state, [which] was the organ of the nobility for holding down the peasant serfs and bondsmen" from "the absolute monarchy, . . . which balanced the nobility and bourgeoisie against one another" ([1884] 1972, p. 231). Marx, in *The German Ideology,* found "the independence of the State . . . in those countries where the estates have not yet completely developed into classes [and] . . . in which no section of the population can achieve dominance over the others" ([1846] 1970, p. 80). For Marx and Engels, the absolutist state was not the instrument of noble class rule, as Anderson asserts, but an artifact of the nobility's loss of hegemony. Marx and Engels believed that the growing power of the new bourgeoisie, rather than heightened challenges from the peasantry, allowed monarchs to recast feudal states once controlled by nobles into instruments of absolutist rule increasingly staffed by bourgeois purchasers of offices sold by the crown. Marx and Engels view absolutist states as only relatively autonomous, because once the bourgeoisie achieved control over production, the state was quickly subordinated to capitalist class interests, regardless of the organizational capacities and resources accumulated by the state elite during the transitional era.[3]

The third set of theories views autonomous state elites as the crucial agents of social change and argues that their actions explain the parallel formation of European absolutist states and bourgeois classes. Charles Tilly (1985) compares European monarchs with Mafia chieftains who use their military might to threaten war on peoples and territories unless they pay "protection" in the form of taxes. War within and between nations enhances states' revenue-collecting capacities, which in turn provide the revenues to support ever-larger military forces. Michael Mann (1980, 1986) advances a similar argument for England. The elites that command the military and taxation organizations of the state are self-interested.[4]

Tilly and Mann view state-building as a process: As state elites build their mutually reinforcing fiscal-administrative and military coercive capacities, the growing corps of state officials augment their power and their share of the national income at the expense of nobles and peasants alike. Tilly and Mann see the bourgeoisie as an inadvertent by-product of state formation. State taxation concentrated resources at a national level, creating (mainly through military procurement) the initial markets for capitalist enterprises. More important for Tilly is the effect of state tax demands upon the French agrarian economy. Rising taxes increased peasants' need for cash, forcing them into markets to sell a growing portion of their produce and often their labor. When peasants could not realize enough cash, they fell into debt, eventually losing their land in bankruptcy sales to the bourgeoisie. By dispossessing the peasantry, the state was indirectly responsible for freeing the land for capital and for the concomitant genesis of a labor market (Tilly 1981, pp. 202–6).

The expansion of the state also altered the nature of class mobilization and political conflict. Monarchs used their vast resources to "create a large class of officials and financiers who served their own advantage by helping to pay the expense of the state" (Tilly 1986, p. 132). As monarchs enticed and compelled nobles, urban merchants, and new bourgeois to tie their personal fortunes to the state's fate, the long-standing alliance of regional magnates and peasants was broken. The crown's victory in the Frondes demonstrated, in Tilly's view, that the nobility had more interest in guarding state revenues than in protecting special privileges for their provincial subordinates.

Tilly argues that changes in the actors and issues involved in conflicts within France are the best indicators of the extent and consequences of state formation. State officials and taxpayers replaced lords and peasants as the principal antagonists in rural conflicts. Rebellions and lesser forms of resistance were increasingly directed against state demands for taxes, provisions, or men for armies rather than against landlords' requirements for rents or feudal labor dues (Tilly 1986, pp. 119–61). Tilly's model would be further supported by evidence that the aristocracy and bourgeoisie were not cohesive. He argues that they divided into two camps. One camp held offices, monopolies, contracts, and other sinecures and therefore supported the state. The other camp were the nobles and merchants who opposed absolutism because they did not benefit from it.

Several scholars have tried to apply a state-centered approach to the development of English absolutism. Mann (1980, 1986) interprets as evidence of state formation the increases in the crown's revenues and the growing number of nobles and bourgeois who benefited from state favors. He does not claim that the state played a major role in the development of English capitalism. This would be difficult to sustain, since agrarian and merchant capitalism developed faster in England than in France. Instead, Mann (1980, p. 203) views the English state as almost exclusively an international military actor that did not create a bourgeoisie but merely "pushed classes toward a national form of organization." He consigns state actors and social classes to two different military and economic spheres, arguing that they interacted only when the former hindered the latter with tax demands or aided capitalists in their conquest of foreign markets. As a result, Mann is unable to find grounds for the 1640 revolution against the monarchy. Indeed Mann (1980, 1986) completely passes over the Revolution and Civil War in his studies of English state development.[5]

English historians H. R. Trevor-Roper (1965) and Lawrence Stone (1970) explain the English Civil War as a conflict between a "court" composed of self-interested state officials and the "country" that was forced to bear the increasing burden of taxes. They argue that the division between court and country does not correspond to the sorts of class divisions highlighted by Marxist analyses. Instead, the common feature among the proroyalist factions was an interest in government offices or patronage. Although the parliamentary side of the Civil War suffered from class and regional differences, it was united against court demands. These historians differ from Tilly and Mann in regarding the Civil War and Frondes as rebellions against the unusual demands and corruption of "Renaissance states." Trevor-Roper (1965, pp. 88–94) contends that, regardless of the outcomes of the mid-seventeenth-century rebellions, both the victorious French kings and the reconstituted English monarchy adopted mercantilist policies that were less burdensome on their subjects and eventually spurred economic development.[6]

Horizontal and Vertical Absolutism

Existing theories are unable to address the politics of antiabsolutist revolutions because of the way they conceptualize state formation. All three perspectives conflate two different forms of absolutism—horizontal and vertical. Horizontal absolutism is distinguished by the crown's ability to subordinate its two principal rivals at the national level—great nobles, referred to by historians as magnates, who fielded their own independent armed forces and subordinated lesser landlords, and clerics organized into a national church. Thus, horizontal absolutism existed where the crown exercised a monopoly over armed force and dominated the national church. Historians' descriptions of English absolutism as it developed in the sixteenth and seventeenth centuries fit this model. While in England the Roman Catholic Church was subordinated in a Protestant Reformation, other monarchs achieved horizontal control over their churches while remaining Catholic (e.g., in the Austrian Empire and Poland) at the same time as some Protestant monarchs lost control over the reformed churches of their nations (e.g., Württemberg).[7] Another variation in horizontal absolutism is the relationship of national assemblies to the crown. In countries (primarily in Eastern Europe) where national assemblies remained congresses of aristocrats and clerics, horizontal absolutism led to the subordination of those assemblies to the crown. In England, however, as I show below, the crown purged most clerics and many magnates from Parliament. Parliament therefore shifted from being an assembly of men with national power to a congress representing local interests, which, as they found common bases of unity, became a new opposition to English horizontal absolutism.

The second form of absolutism resulted from monarchs' inabilities to eliminate rival magnates or to dominate the national church. As a second-best strategy, rulers formed direct ties to locally based officials and corporate bodies, and hence the term *vertical absolutism*. In time, the successful construction of vertical absolutism created corps of officeholders who rivaled clerics, magnates, and their retainers in their access to revenues and in their control over judicial and military organizations. The crown's aristocratic rivals then sought to exploit the power and profits of vertical absolutism, seeking to purchase or to be appointed to high venal offices. Thus, strong vertical absolutism yielded a measure of horizontal absolutism as well, as formerly independent magnates and clerics became officeholders themselves. I describe this general form and French absolutism in particular as vertical, rather than as a combination of vertical and horizontal, to emphasize the different starting points and developmental trajectories of the two forms and to highlight contrasts in the ties between magnates and the crown, and between magnates and lesser landlords and officehold-ers, in societies marked by the two forms of absolutism.

My thesis is that monarchs' abilities to pursue strategies that fostered vertical or horizontal absolutism depended on the structure of relations existing among the elites in both countries. All three perspectives tend to examine the aristocracy as a class and to confine their debates to questions about the interests of the aristocracy as a whole and its relationship to rival peasant and bourgeois classes and to the state. They thus obscure the conflicts within the feudal ruling class and the ways in which those con-flicts became embedded in the horizontal and vertical forms of absolutism. As a re-sult, the theorists are unable to account for the divisions among aristocrats into loyal and rebellious factions during the Civil War and in the Frondes. Moreover, previous efforts to track alignments among classes and state officials have paid insufficient attention to the complexes of alliances and conflicts in seventeenth-century England and France. I seek to remedy those shortcomings as I contrast French vertical and English horizontal absolutism in this chapter.

Taking Advantage of the Reformation

Elites throughout Catholic Europe sought to respond to the dangers and opportuni-ties created by the Reformation. Each elite's strategy was determined by its position within the overall structure of European elites more than by the relative or absolute strength of its organizational capacities.

The clergy was the elite with the most to lose from the Reformation. The French Catholic Church had been far more vulnerable to lay control than the English Church in the medieval era and therefore appeared to be in a weaker position at the outset of the sixteenth century. French nobles controlled appointments to most ecclesiastical offices and used that control to claim much of the church's tithe income. Such con-trol was usually exercised independently of the crown, as French magnates negotiated directly with the papacy to gain official approval for their candidates for archbishop and bishop. Many French bishoprics remained in the hands of single families for centuries, with incumbents retiring in favor of related successors. Bishops in turn used lesser church offices to reward their noble families' political clients (Salmon 1975, pp. 80–13; Shennan 1969, pp. 16–19).

The French Catholic Church lost judicial powers as it surrendered control over its offices and finances. The crown endorsed legal ruses that parlements devised to en-croach upon the authority of ecclesiastical judges to regulate manorial land tenure and familial relations (Blet 1959, pp. 88–99). The medieval French Church did not play a significant role in the regulation of peasant land tenure in many provinces, as the ty-pology of elite structures and agrarian class relations in France discussed in chapter 2 shows.

English clerics were far more successful than their French counterparts at main-taining the independence and fiscal integrity of their offices in the centuries leading up to the Reformation. The degree of papal control over the English Catholic Church was reflected in the international character of the church hierarchy; popes appointed foreign churchmen to English bishoprics into the fifteenth century and English church-men made careers abroad. Some English benefices were held by French churches until the mid-fifteenth century (Swanson 1989, pp. 7–11). To the extent that the pope lost control over church offices and benefices in England it was to the king, not to lay lords. Benefices did not fall under the permanent control of noble families; rather, English kings shifted bishoprics among aristocratic factions as part of the overall royal strategy of balancing magnate parties at the national level (pp. 64–74, 103–22).

English kings guarded the institutional autonomy of the church from lay predations because the crown wanted to appropriate clerical revenues for itself. Indeed, until the Reformation, the English crown was virtually the only secular beneficiary of English church wealth (Swanson 1989, pp. 64–74, 103–22), in contrast to France where the aristocracy gained control of benefices and other church assets at the expense of both the papacy and the monarchy (Bergin 1982; Cloulas 1958). English kings guarded the church's secular authority from challenges by laymen so that the crown could continue to use the clergy as royal officials and as tax collectors to supplement and counterbalance the unpaid laymen who filled offices within the counties. Clerics also formed the largest bloc under royal control in Parliament, especially in the House of Lords, where churchmen were close to a majority until the Reformation (Swanson 1989, pp. 103–22).

Royal judges limited the power of clerical courts in the fifteenth century, but only to the extent necessary to allow the crown to appropriate church properties and income rights (Swanson 1989, pp. 140–90). As a result, English clerical judges retained the independence to protect the church's fiscal interest against encroachments by laymen, even when that required intervention into landlord-peasant disputes over land tenure, as I point out in the discussion of the aftermath of the Black Death in chapter 2 (Hill 1963, pp. 84–92; Houlbrooke 1979, pp. 7–20).

The consequences of the Reformation for the Catholic Churches of England and France and for the divergent courses of absolutism in the two kingdoms can be derived, not from an inventory of each church's or monarch's capacities taken singly, but from the outcomes of alliances and conflicts within which they deployed those capacities. The incongruence between the strategic accomplishments and capacities of groups is demonstrated by the contrasting outcomes of the Reformation in England and France. The more autonomous national church of England lost most of its assets and authority in the Dissolution of Monasteries, while the French clergy preserved its administrative and fiscal organization. English historians from all perspectives view the Reformation as key to the subsequent development of English absolutism and sharply differentiate that nation's political landscape from France's. Yet, theorists of the three perspectives give the clergy and the Reformation (or its nonoccurrence in France) little weight. In this section I offer an explanation of why the English and not the French clerical elite was subordinated to the monarchy and then traces the consequences of the divergent church fates on the strategic opportunities open to both monarchs. I then evaluate the three theories of absolutism against my elite-focused model for their abilities to explain the patterns of conflict and alliance.

The strength of the English Church's institutional autonomy represented weakness for the clergy's position in English politics. Since lay landlords lacked influence over clerical appointments and were opposed by ecclesiastical courts in land tenure conflicts, they had no interest in preserving church authority and assets. In contrast, French nobles, who controlled clerical appointments and revenues of church offices, wanted to preserve the formal autonomy of the Catholic Church from royal appropriation. Of the 129 men appointed as bishops during the reign of King François I (1514–47), 93 were nobles of the sword who held land and headed military companies independent of the crown. The majority of bishoprics were kept within nobles' families, and incumbent bishops enjoyed the de facto right to name successors (Salmon 1975, pp. 8–83). Consequently, when kings submitted their fiscal and legal demands to national assemblies of bishops, clerics enjoyed sufficiently strong ties to provincial nobles to resist royal threats to their interests (Blet 1959). Clerical subordination to their aristocratic kin saved clerical property from being expropriated by the crown.

The English Church's autonomy from county landlords created a situation in which the monarchy needed to control only a few dozen clerics at the top of the hierarchy. The hierarchical character of the church, the absence of ties between lower-level clerics and lay landlords, and Henry VIII's dominance of the bishops enabled him to gain parliamentary ratification for the transfer of revenues and assets from the clerical hierarchy to the crown. Through the Dissolution, the monarch assumed rights to the third of all English manors that had been held by the monasteries. Combining his pre-Reformation landholdings with the assessed value of the monastic manors, Henry VIII was to receive two hundred thousand pounds a year. This would have been enough to guarantee the crown's fiscal independence from the aristocracy and Parliament in peacetime while giving the crown the resources necessary to build a royal bureaucracy (Hill 1963, pp. 3–5).

Henry VIII's successful appropriation of the former English Catholic Church's assets and infrastructure opened the possibility of building "horizontal absolutism," that is, of achieving national level hegemony at the expense of magnates as well as the once-autonomous clerical hierarchy. Henry and his successors were drawn into an alliance with nonmagnate lay landlords—the gentry—in order to secure and expand their national level domination of church and state. In so doing, English monarchs set in train a transformation of polities and economies on the local as well as the national level.

The failure of successive French monarchs to appropriate the bulk of clerical offices and assets, which remained under the control of lay families, precluded the possibility of building a strong, English-style absolutism. At the same time, the inability of the French crown to actually control the national church allowed magnates, lesser aristocrats, and urban notables to politicize their religious differences, creating rival Catholic and Huguenot (Protestant) coalitions. Religious factionalism created an opening for French kings to "reach down"[8] and win allies within provinces once closed to royal interference by cohesive magnate organizations. Reaching down to create overlapping and competing corps of venal officeholders, all beholden to the king, became the French crown's only feasible strategy of self-aggrandizement, creating a second-best "horizontal absolutism."

England

Guarding the Gains of the Reformation

The Henrician Reformation sparked limited internal rebellion at the same time that it undermined royal control over both Parliament and county government. The crown

TABLE 4.1. Revenue and Expenditure for War under Henry VII and Henry VIII

Revenue and Expenditures	Henry VII (1491–1500)	Henry VIII (1539–47)
Received from fifteenth and tenth	136,700	180,000
Received from subsidy	30,000	478,200
Total parliamentary lay tax revenue received	166,700	658,200
Total war expenditures	107,600	2,134,000
Lay tax revenues as % of war expenditures	155%	31%

Sources: For war expenditures, Dietz 1964, introduction; for tax revenues, Schofield 1963, pp. 360–61, 415–16. All figures are in pounds.

used properties seized in the Dissolution of the Monasteries to insure lay elite support for the Reformation against clerical and popular opposition. Henry VIII also sold monastic lands, treasure, and benefices to pay for the wars he initiated beginning in 1539. He was unable to raise taxes sufficiently to meet the cost of war because the elimination of most clerics from Parliament during the Reformation removed the group of members most subservient to the crown (Hill 1963, pp. ix–xi). A comparison of revenues received and monies spent on war during the reigns of Henry VII and Henry VIII illustrates the abrupt decline in the crown's ability to make Parliament approve taxes sufficient to pay for foreign wars (see table 4.1). Henry VII was able to more than pay for his major war from 1491 to 1500 with parliamentary lay taxes totaling more than one and one-half times the total military expenditures in those years. In contrast, Henry VIII raised under one-third of his war costs from taxes.

The fiscal shortfall was made up in part from rents received from seized monastic manors and from the clerical subsidy, a tax imposed by the crown on tithes that diverted the payments once made by the clergy to the pope. The difference between the costs of war and the revenues of the crown was bridged traditionally with loans. But London financiers were unwilling to make loans for interest when they could use their capital to buy monastic lands from the crown. Thus, more than a quarter of the cost of war—more than that borne by English lay taxpayers—was met by selling monastic lands (see table 4.2).[9]

The dismissal of many clerics in the Dissolution, and the suspicion under which so many others were held by Henry VIII after the Reformation and especially after the Pilgrimage of Grace (a peasant protest against the Dissolution of the Monasteries in 1536 that was supported by some clerics),[10] made the crown dependent upon lay rather than clerical officials to a greater extent than ever before. Lay administrators of former monastic estates and assessors of clerical properties for sale took advantage of their offices to engage in self-dealing.

The Valor Ecclesiasticus, a survey of monastic wealth conducted in 1535 by commissions headed by bishops who were subject to royal removal and thus eager to show their loyalty, revealed a total monastic gross income of £160,000 a year (Savine 1909, pp. 76–100). That total included income from agricultural estates as well as "spiritual income," which mainly was tithe rights. All such property, tithe rights as well as estates, typically was sold for "twenty years' rent"—twenty times the income produced each

TABLE 4.2. Sources of Extraordinary Revenues Received by Henry VIII, 1535–47

Sources	Amount (£)	% of Total
Parliamentary lay taxes	737,500	25.9
Clerical taxes	712,200	25.0
Monastic treasures	79,500	2.8
Income from seized monastic estates	525,100	18.5
Sales of former monastic lands	789,400	27.8
Total	2,843,700	100.0

Sources: For Parliamentary lay taxes, Schofield 1963, pp. 360–61, 415–16; for all other revenues, Dietz 1964, pp. 137–43.

Note: Amounts in pounds are rounded to nearest £100. Parliamentary lay taxes include total receipts for the fifteenth and tenths and for ubsidies. Clerical taxes include total receipts for clerical subsidies, first fruits and tenths, and fines. Monastic treasures are the total value of gold, silver plate, and jewels delievered to the Jewel House of the King. The last two amounts are the total received by the Court of Augmentations; the Court itself distinguished amounts received as income from former monastic estates and revenues from sales of such properties.

year (Habakkuk 1958). Thus, monastic lands had a potential sale value of £3.2 million.[11] In addition, the king's jewel house received £79,500 of valuables from dissolved monasteries (Woodward 1966, p. 125); the actual value of monastic treasures, and therefore the amount skimmed off by lay liquidators of those treasures, is unknown and unknowable since even gentlemen thieves do not keep written records. But whatever the total, the crown spent all its receipts from monastic treasure before war began in 1539, largely on patronage or conspicuous consumption.[12]

The crown realized only a fraction of the potential return from monastic lands and tithe rights. Frederick Dietz (1964) calculates that the crown received £789,400 from selling three-fourths of the properties seized in the Dissolution. Had they been sold at their full value of twenty years' rent they would have yielded between £2.0 million and £2.4 million, depending upon whether the sale price was based on net or gross annual income. Thus, the crown realized only 33 to 40 percent of the potential revenues it could have received from selling so much of the former monastic lands. Put another way, if the crown had been able to sell monastic lands at the going full-market rate, it could have financed its war deficit by selling only one quarter, rather than three-quarters, of those lands.

The crown received below market prices for the monastic lands it sold for two reasons. First, the crown wished to solidify lay elite support for the Reformation by giving monastic lands as gifts or selling such lands at cheap prices to reward its political allies. Second, the crown depended almost exclusively on lay assessors and administrators to evaluate and sell the monastic lands, thereby creating opportunities for self-dealing since the men who were prominent enough in each locality to administer great estates for the crown also were the most likely bidders on those properties. Then, once war came and the crown needed large amounts of cash quickly, Henry VIII was forced to put many manors on the market at the same time. Syndicates of London financiers were the only customers able to raise the capital to buy large blocks of manors as soon as the crown put them on the market. The absence of competitive bidding from multiple buyers allowed the syndicates to control the market and depress prices.

For similar reasons the crown also failed to realize its full potential annual income from the monastic estates it had seized and not yet sold. Dietz points out the difficulty in calculating that shortfall since Henry VIII "never had all the monastic lands in his hands at any one time, for much of the property and lands of the first monasteries to be suppressed had been alienated before the houses dissolved later came to the king's hands" (1964, p. 137). However, had Henry VIII been able to realize the full net income of seized monastic lands for himself, he would have been able to finance the entire cost of war without selling any monastic lands.[13]

Perry Anderson contends that Henry VIII's decision to attack France forced the sale of monastic lands; "the great bulk of this vast windfall was lost; and with it, the one great change of English absolutism to build up a firm economic base independent of parliamentary taxation. . . . One of the drabbest and most inconsequential foreign wars in English history thus had momentous, if still hidden consequences on the domestic balance of forces within English society" (1974, pp. 124–25).[14]

Anderson's view certainly is more accurate than the state-centered analysis. The growth in military expenditures has been interpreted as an indicator of state power by Michael Mann (1980, 1986) and Charles Tilly (1985). Mann believes that "the military aim of the state was truly functional, and so could be exploited for private state ends. The development of permanent fiscal machinery and mercenary armies provided opportunities for the enhancement of monarchical power" (1980, p. 198). Mann's view confuses England as an actor in interstate conflicts with the English monarch as an actor within the country. England did indeed become a European military "great power" by the end of the sixteenth century. However, that military strength did not aid English monarchs in their battles with domestic rivals.

Contrary to Mann, the mercenary armies, located on the Continent or on England's northern frontier, did not strengthen the crown against armed magnates within the country. England's armies were mercenary because the great lords, sitting in Parliament, would never have financed a native army located in England, which could be turned against them. The crown's armies were disbanded at war's end. Expensive fortifications were located abroad, or on the coast and border, not in places where they could be used to threaten magnate domination of the counties.

War not only failed to build the English crown's military strength against domestic elites; it also fatally weakened the crown in its effort to build political absolutism in England. War demands immediate resources to pay and supply armies and navies. Kings, because they must, make political agreements with those who can provide the cash, at the time when it is needed, to wage war. Henry VIII's schemes to preserve a permanent estate to finance political independence from Parliament and to build a royal bureaucracy that could have been the basis of an English absolutism were destroyed by his need to secure war finances. London merchants, the only source of ready capital, were able to refuse loans and demand the sale of clerical manors in return for financing his war making.

Henry's concessions to London merchants, in return for the capital to pay for war, were paradigmatic of the way in which the crown's positions in an international state structure weakened it in national-level elite conflict. Parliament was called into session time and again over the centuries covered in Mann's study (1980) because the crown needed quick access to the resources controlled by agrarian and urban elites. The crown's efforts to mobilize English resources for international war institutionalized Parliament as a forum for the organization of lay elite interests. War, and trade, indeed did foster the centralization of resources in a state organization that allowed England to compete with rival nations at the international level. However, that organization contained more than Theda Skocpol's state managers (1979) or Mann's "war party." Crown strategies for international competition with other monarchs created a state organization that mobilized magnates, and then broader elites, at the national level.

War, thus, was a regular event in the life of European monarchies and states.[15] Wars were initiated for a variety of reasons: hopes for territorial or financial gain abroad (initially within Europe but increasingly to control trade routes and command colonies), to protect a ruler's coreligionists or advance the cause of his religion, to force domestic rivals to suspend their opposition to the crown in order to face down a foreign danger. All the momentary calculations favoring a military campaign were undergirded by a culture of military prowess and valor. The social positions, privileges, and identities of kings and aristocrats were grounded in their self-proclaimed capacities to defend their subordinates, their territories, and Christendom from attack. Such a culture, and the resulting self-identifications, led European lay elites to discount the human costs of war and to see fortifications and military ventures as worthy investments of personal wealth and the social surplus.

European elites, then, had ample justification to initiate wars and they did so with great regularity. We can conclude that war making was "rational" or aided state formation only if we combine the particular and often opposed interests of distinct elites into a reified state. Elites made decisions to go to war that turned out to be catastrophic for themselves and that inadvertently aided their enemies. Our task as sociologists is not to override the complex effects of decisions taken within structures of multiple elites by subsuming all wars within master processes of state formation or master logics of rational choice. Instead, we must go forward with the difficult task of specifying the particular effects of each war upon the complex of elite and class relations.

Buying National Level Hegemony

We know that Henry VIII spent three-quarters of his Reformation windfall on war and patronage. His successors, Edward VI (1547–53), Mary I (1554–58), and Elizabeth I (1558–1603), spent the rest of the Tudor patrimony on political clients. By the start of Elizabeth I's reign, royal land holdings were back to their pre-Reformation levels of about one-tenth of the country's manors. By 1640, the crown held only 2 percent of English manors (Cooper 1967, pp. 420–21; Tawney 1954, pp. 91–97).

The Tudor monarchs bought an unprecedented degree of national-level hegemony with their patronage. Most peers and gentry, even those who were Catholic in their religion, became owners of lands or tithes that had once been church property and then had been seized in the Dissolution (Hill 1963; Bossy 1975). The king's courts and the county Commissions of the Peace gained authority over peasant land tenure and over the collection and allocation of tithes at the expense of clerical courts (Houlbrooke 1979, pp. 117–50 and passim; Sommerville 1992, pp. 111–28).[16]

The crown's sale of church lands and granting of clerical judicial powers to lay landlords gave lay landlords a material and political interest in supporting the Reformation. Any effort to revive the judicial authority of the Roman Church, or later of the Church of England, or to return an interest in tithes and former monastic lands to the clergy would have undermined a substantial portion of the lay elite's property holdings and income rights. Challenges by the pope and by English Catholics to royal supremacy of the church became challenges to lay elite wealth and lay control over the peasantry. As a result, English gentry of varying denominations opposed efforts by Mary I and later by popes to restore Catholicism and especially Roman authority over English religion. Even Catholic nobles and gentry "came to see how decisively their status was enhanced where plurality of religion became a condition of life. All in all, they were better off controlling the destinies of a minority sect in a country dominated by their Protestant counterparts, than playing second fiddle in a uniform society of the Catholic clergy's divising" (Bossy 1975, p. 32).

Henry VIII began, and Elizabeth I continued to ultimate success, the strategy of using the carrot of crown patronage and the stick of military attack to break the power of the magnates, who had been, along with the clergy, the other rival national elite of medieval England.[17] Elizabeth compelled magnates to disband their private armies and to knock down their fortified castles, replacing them with grander but indefensible palaces. She rarely had to use force; the generous use of royal patronage (made possible by the remaining stock of monastic properties) caused many magnates to orient their political activities toward the royal court and away from their home counties (Stone 1965, pp. 199–234, 398–424). The costs of patronage replaced military expenses as the chief drain upon royal finances.

Elizabeth initially made use of the remaining monastic lands to reward allies with gifts or sales at favorable prices. As the pool of crown lands dwindled, however, she turned to custom farms, trade privileges, monopolies in mining and manufacture, and revenue farms as further sources of subsidies for court favorites (Stone 1965, pp. 424–49). Each grant sacrificed the potential for royal revenues from customs, mining and manufacturing taxes, and land taxes in order to provide immediate patronage without spending current royal revenues. Grants were difficult to revoke, as James I and Charles I learned when they found many avenues for taxation blocked by the monopolies and privileges given away by Elizabeth I.

Elizabeth's success in directing the attention of great landlords away from provincial and military matters and toward the financial and political rewards of the royal court can be gauged from the relative immunity of the crown to armed challenge between 1558 and 1640. At the same time, court-oriented magnates expected lavish rewards for political loyalty to the crown. Patronage became the principal tool used by Elizabeth I and her successors to achieve national-level political consensus for their policies. The total value of crown patronage granted during the reigns of Elizabeth I, James I, and Charles I has been calculated by Lawrence Stone. His results are presented in Table 4.3.

The clamor for patronage, which continued and intensified under Elizabeth's successor, James I, was met by the granting or sale of offices that provided an income or opportunities for self-dealing to the occupants. Among the most valued offices were seats on the Subsidy Commission. The commissioners supervised the assessment and

TABLE 4.3. Crown Patronage, 1558–1641

Period[a]	No. of Years	Value of Patronage[b] (£)	Average per Annum (£)	No. receiving over £10,000[c]
1558–76	19½	268,000	13,800	11
1577–1603	25½	203,000	8,000	7
1603–1628	25½	2,174,000	107,500	45
1629–41	13	329,000	25,300	5

Source: Stone 1965, p. 775.

Notes
[a] The first two periods are the years of Elizabeth I's reign, the third period includes the reign of James I and the first two years of Charles I; the last period is during Charles I's reign.
[b] Values are expressed in pounds adjusted for inflation, with all amounts in 1603–1628 prices.
[c] Includes those receiving this amount as a total within one of the four periods. A single person, or family, could appear in the category for more than one period or could have received more than £10,000 over a period longer than that covered in a single period and so not be recorded in this column.

collection of the two principal parliamentary lay taxes, the subsidy and the fifteenth and tenth. Since the commissioners appointed the small landowners who did the actual assessment work and who determined what share of the total tax quota for the county was to be paid by each landholder, the commissioners were in a position to minimize the tax assessment on their own lands and on the holdings of their allies (Smith 1974, pp. 114–15).

The monetary value of an appointment as a subsidy commissioner is indicated by tax data from Sussex. Seventy families provided most of the commissioners in that county during the reigns of Elizabeth I, James I, and Charles I. The average subsidy assessment of those families fell from sixty-one pounds in the 1540s to fourteen pounds in the 1620s, a drop made even more dramatic by the fact that grain prices and land rents more than tripled in that period (Fletcher 1975, p. 203). Evidence from other counties indicates that commissioners paid the subsidy at a fraction of the rate of landholders not involved in the assessment process (Willcox 1946, pp. 112–13; Smith 1974, pp. 114–15).

One form of patronage, the granting of honors, did yield revenues for the crown. Once magnates' armies had been disbanded, knighthood became an honorific position. The crown rewarded loyal clients with 2,000 grants of arms between 1560 and 1589, and a further 1,760 grants between 1590 and 1639. James I named 1,161 new knights in the first year of his reign (Stone 1965, pp. 65–67). He also invented the new title of baronet, which out-ranked the degraded knighthood. The number of baronets was limited to 200, and an annual income of £1,000 was made a prerequisite for the office (pp. 67–97). English rulers received fees for granting titles, making such grants the only profitable form of patronage. Yet the profit was usually given to court favorites, who were given the right to name knights and baronets and receive the fee themselves (pp. 97–128).

The crown's distribution of patronage was governed by two imperatives. First, magnates were lavishly supported at court in order to draw them away from their provincial bases. Second, those who controlled votes in Parliament were rewarded for their ability to assist royal initiatives. As a result, the bulk of patronage was directed toward the few individuals who, at a given moment, were in a position to challenge the monarch's national-level domination. Nine men received 45 percent of the total value of patronage granted during the eighty-three years covered in table 4.3. Another twenty men took an additional 20 percent of the total (Stone 1965, p. 475).

Once the crown had exhausted the pool of monastic estates, profitable government offices were the principal reward available to royal clients. Yet the small size of the royal bureaucracy, the dearth of opportunities for new taxes, and the limited openings for trade and production monopolies—all due to the ability of landlords and merchants to prevent crown control of local governments and local economies—served to constrict the number of offices English monarchs were able to create for clients. Thus, Elizabeth I, James I, and Charles I were able to grant offices to only 117 of the 342 peers who held title between 1558 and 1641. For the 500 leading county landlords below the level of peer, there were only 100 available offices. Among the large number of "parochial gentry" only 1 in 30 secured a profitable royal office (Stone 1965, pp. 463–67). Among the 679 gentrymen of Yorkshire in 1642, only 22 held income-producing crown office (p. 467).

The narrow distribution of crown patronage reflected a preoccupation with preventing opposition on the national level. The value of royal favors, shown in table 4.3, was highest at the start of each monarch's reign, when the danger of armed challenge was the greatest. James I was the most lavish dispenser of patronage, since, as a Scotsman and a foreigner in the eyes of English magnates, he had the most difficult task of establishing legitimacy and finding allies.

Elizabeth I and her successors undermined magnates' political domination of county politics. When Elizabeth forced great nobles to disband their private armies, she eliminated magnates' capacity to intimidate lesser landlords. Peers who were at court for much of the year were unable to play an active role in county politics. While many still held county office, their membership on county commissions of the peace became largely honorary, rather than a basis for control over smaller landlords. The absence of the magnates and their armed men emboldened many lesser landlords to seek county office. The crown encouraged independence from magnates by granting local offices directly to county-based landlords. Peers lost the right to nominate candidates for all royal offices within their counties, undermining a key basis for their hegemony over county politics.

The crown prevented the reemergence of magnate domination by encouraging rival factions to compete for offices. A study of Somersetshire indicates a continuing royal effort to balance appointments of justices of the peace (JPs) between the two main factions, not only in the whole county, but also in each of the twelve sections into which the county was divided (Barnes 1961, pp. 40–97, 281–98). Detailed histories of Kent and Suffolk indicate a similar crown strategy (Everitt l966; Clark 1977, pp. 112–32, 341–47; MacCulloch 1977). The transition from magnate to crown appointment was followed by the growth in the size of commissions of the peace, as English monarchs sought to accommodate each faction and make it more difficult for one leader to control a whole commission. Thus, in 1561, Norfolk, Suffolk, Essex, and Kent all had roughly equal populations; yet Norfolk had twenty-four JPs, Suffolk had thirty-eight, Kent had fifty-six, and Essex had sixty-two. The first two counties were still dominated by magnates in 1561, while in the last two, several factions shared influence (Moir 1969, p. 29; Everitt 1966; Clark 1977, pp. 112–32, 341 -47).

Once the crown ended magnate hegemony within a county, it was forced to deal directly with numerous gentry, most of whom the crown could not afford to grant money-making offices or other significant patronage. As a result, the county commissions of the peace came to be dominated by men who were locally oriented, not because they wanted to be, but because they were locked out of opportunities at court.

While all JPs were oriented toward the national level in the sense that they were royal appointees, it is possible to classify JPs by the extent of their relative interests at the national and local levels. John Howes Gleason, in his study of JPs from 1558 to 1640, defines six categories of justices. First were the "dignitaries," men who were often magnates and held important royal offices. Even though almost all dignitaries were great landowners, they were oriented toward gaining and maintaining position at court and based their actions as JPs upon national-level political considerations. Such men were often absent from their home counties, living in London, and unable to influence the decisions of their fellow JPs (Gleason 1969, p. 49; Forster 1973, pp. 20–29). The second category, "courtiers," held second-level positions in the royal government. Like dignitaries, they were oriented toward the court, even though many dignitaries and courtiers used their court favor and wealth to build country estates for themselves.

The two intermediate groups of JPs consisted of lawyers and merchants. These men made their wealth in cities and often benefited from court favors. However, many merchants and lawyers had interests in and ties to towns and counties beyond London. Thus, JPs in those two categories must be classified as having a dual orientation, divided between the national court and local town and country networks. JPs in the gentry category, having inherited their landholdings, were not the beneficiaries of royal patronage (although some gentry had expanded their holdings by buying monastic estates from the crown). The final group of JPs was the clergy. Most clerics shared the gentry's local orientation, since they had been placed in office by gentry who held the advowsons for parish clerical offices (Gleason 1969, p. 49; Hill 1963, p. 58–59).

In the early years of Elizabeth I's reign, about half of the JPs were oriented toward the court (see table 4.4). By 1584, as a result of her efforts to expand membership and break magnate control of the county commissions, the portion of JPs oriented toward the court had fallen from a half to a third. That change was due to the addition of new JPs who were dually oriented professionals or locally based gentry. The total number of JPs in the counties of Kent, Norfolk, Northampton, Somerset, Worcester, and the North Riding of Yorkshire increased from 210 in 1562 to 330 in 1584. Of those totals, nationally oriented dignitaries and courtiers held 102 seats on the six county commissions of the peace in 1562, and 108 seats in 1584. In 1608, five years after Elizabeth's death, the predominance of gentry on county commissions is even stronger, up to 53 percent, or 205 out of 386 seats. The balance on county commissions in that year, 100 seats, reflects the success of her efforts to free county government from magnate policy in the early years of her reign. Locally oriented JPs made up 55 percent of the total number of JPs and constituted a majority on five of the six county commissions; only in the North Riding of Yorkshire did they remain in the minority (Gleason 1969, p. 49). The total number of locally oriented JPs doubled

TABLE 4.4. Composition of Commissions of the Peace in Six Counties, 1562–1636

Category and Orientation of JPs[a]	Year				
	1562	1584	1608	1626	1636
National orientation	49%	33%	26%	36%	29%
Dignitaries	32%	25%	19%	31%	25%
Courtiers	17%	8%	7%	5%	4%
Dual orientation	13%	19%	19%	13%	20%
Lawyers	9%	15%	14%	10%	16%
Merchants	4%	4%	5%	3%	4%
Local orientation	38%	48%	55%	51%	51%
Gentry	37%	47%	53%	45%	47%
Clergy	1%	1%	2%	6%	4%
Total number of JPs	210	330	386	389	356
Number of locally oriented JPs	80	158	212	198	181

Source: For the categorization of JPs, Gleason 1969, p. 49; the attribution of orientation is mine.

Note: The six counties are Kent, Norfolk, Northampton, Somerset, Worchester, and the North Riding of Yorkshire.
[a] Justices of the peace (JPs) who acquired their first lands during their lifetimes are listed under the category of their original source of income. Their heirs are listed under the same category if they continued their father's vocations; they are listed as gentry if they abandoned a profession for life in the country. Those who were born as gentry and entered the law or commerce are listed as gentry. Gentry who made careers in royal service are listed as dignitaries or courtiers.

in the six counties between 1562 and 1584, and increased another third by 1608. Elizabeth I's reign was the window during which control of the county commissions of the peace passed from magnates and other national-level actors to local gentry.

The Stuart monarchs proved unable to break the gentry's grip on JP offices. Gentry and their clerical allies retained a majority of seats on the six county commissions in 1626 and 1636. Despite the growth in the number of lay landowners in most counties in the sixteenth century, the concurrent expansion of the county commissions to prevent magnate dominance helped to maintain the existing ratio between the number of potential JPs and the number of seats open on each commission. The crown might remove a particularly obstreperous JP; however, few families of sufficient wealth were excluded permanently from service on their county commission (Gleason, pp. 65–67).

Norfolk provides an illustration of the limits upon the crown's ability to replace JPs. After the fall of the Howard family, the size of the Norfolk commission expanded from twenty-four members in 1562 to forty-seven in 1584, and sixty-five by 1626 (Gleason 1969, p. 49). Between 1558 and 1603, the Norfolk JPs were drawn from only 114 families, who were for the most part the largest landowners in the county. Sixteen families had members serve for three consecutive generations (Smith 1974, p. 58).

Whenever the crown sought to dismiss a JP, it was limited in its search for a replacement to the small group of gentry of significant wealth and local influence, the very families that provided the other members of the commission. If a substantial portion of a county commission adopted policies contrary to royal interests, the crown could not have replaced its members with new JPs of equal stature. The appointment of lesser landowners would have opened the way for a powerful JP to dominate his weaker colleagues and become a new magnate, thus posing a potential challenge to the crown on the national level. The hold that the gentry had upon county commissions was the price of the crown's national-level strategies.

The Limits of Horizontal Absolutism

Gentry filled the vacuums left by the crown's destruction of magnates' politico-military control within the counties and of the clergy's ability to regulate agrarian class relations. I address the fate of the peasantry and the development of agrarian capitalism in chapter 6. Here, I am concerned with the effects of gentry power upon national and local politics.

Gentry took advantage of magnates' removal from daily control of county politics to create new gentry-dominated networks. Peter Bearman (1993) has traced the evolution of political alliances and patronage networks in Norfolk from the Dissolution to the Reformation. The demise of the county magnates and the opening of patronage possibilities at court combined to sow confusion among gentry who previously had measured their political and social standing in terms of their kin and patronage ties to magnates.

The gentry's pursuit of status and patronage and the crown's efforts to undermine magnates combined to create a new political structure in Norfolk and most other English counties. The gentry sought royal favor both for financial advantage and to replace magnate-centered kin networks as an organizing basis of county politics. The crown's generous granting of favors shattered magnate authority but at the cost of surrendering control of future patronage decisions to factions organized within the county. Factional conflict paralyzed most decision-making in the Norfolk Commission of the Peace, the county's main governing body, by the start of the seventeenth century. That paralysis prevented the crown, a new county strongman, or a party from reestablishing political hegemony at the county level. At the same time, lay landlords were able to use petty sessions to enhance their authority over peasants at the local level.

Norfolk gentry overcame status and political confusion through the use of religious patronage. Spurred by Puritan zeal, a minority of late-sixteenth-century gentry started using the advowsons they had purchased to control the ideology of ministers rather than just to profit from parish revenues. Orthodox and Catholic patrons responded with ideological appointments of their own. Networks of gentry linked through the appointment of the same ministers (either simultaneously or in sequence) formed blocks defined increasingly by religious ideology in the decades leading up to the Civil War.

New religious identities allowed county gentry to give expression to their material interests as owners of former monastic lands and as inheritors of clerical powers to regulate land tenure. Those identities also allowed gentry to mobilize themselves in defense of their interests without having to subordinate themselves to crown, court sponsors, or magnates. Religious ideologies became the glue of gentry communities of self-interest as well as codes of moral behavior and expressions of faith in other-worldly salvation. The blocks of religious patronage identified by Bearman (1993) are the best predictors (better than an individual's own religious identity, his ties to the court, or his occupation) of affiliations and activism in the 1630s and during the Civil War.[18]

Factionalism undermined magnates' county bases, prevented the development of national or regional Catholic parties, and placed gentry in the position of petitioners and supplicants to the royal court. Thus, Henry VIII, Elizabeth I, and the Stuart kings achieved horizontal absolutism. The crown's position, however, was less absolute when it sought to collect taxes or to revive the fortunes of a national church.

County-based gentry came together to challenge each crown effort to aggrandize itself by appropriating gentry resources or by diminishing gentry authority. The gentry resisted repeated efforts by Charles I and Archbishop Laud to regain control over clerical appointments and to divert tithe revenues from lay holders of benefices to parish clergy and to the hierarchy of the Church of England. The royal and Laudian offensive took several forms. Laud won a ruling by the King's Bench in 1634 (in *Hitchcock v. Thornborough*) giving ecclesiastical courts the jurisdiction to order benefice holders to raise the portion of tithes going to the clerical incumbent. However, when Laud and other churchmen attempted to enforce that precedent in common law courts, they met with only limited success (Hill 1963, pp. 307–31). Charles also sought to retake former church properties in Scotland (with his 1625 Act of Revocation) and in Ireland through Strafford (pp. 332–36).

Laud's efforts in England provided little new revenue for the church; their main effect was to solidify Puritan opposition and to draw many less radical gentry (including some Catholic benefice holders) into opposition to Charles and Laud (Hill 1963, pp. 336–37 and passim; Bossy 1975, pp. 50–52 and passim).[19] Charles's attack on the Scottish Church served to unite the Scottish nobility with Presbyterians and against episcopacy. The events in Scotland also provided an object lesson for English gentry on the precariousness of their property rights if the crown should be able to reassert control of former clerical dominions. Strafford's campaign in Ireland reinforced the English gentry's fears along those lines.

English Absolutism and London Merchants

James's and Charles's efforts to extend the horizontal absolutism they inherited from Elizabeth were stymied first by the material interests of all gentry (regardless of their faith) in preserving lay and local control of clerical offices and tithes and second by the exhaustion of royal resources for patronage and the impossibility of paying off the vastly expanded number of influential men in county polities after the demise of magnate rule. A third handicap, which ironically was circumvented by the weaker French monarchy, was the crown's inability to create a rival elite to challenge gentry hegemony within the counties. The clergy of course had been fatally weakened in the Henrician Reformation. Magnate and then gentry hegemony in the counties prevented the creation of self-financing venal offices that could have funneled revenues to the crown and provided a counterweight to unpaid gentry JPs.

Merchants, who in England were concentrated in London, provided a potential source of money and allies for the crown. Marxist scholars traditionally believed such an alliance was impossible because capitalist merchants had intrinsic differences with absolutist monarchs.[20] Revisionist historians hold up those merchants who allied with Charles as Exhibit A for the inability of a Marxist class analysis, or indeed any broad structural theory, to explain the origins, loyalties, and consequences of the Revolution and the Civil War.[21]

In fact, "the merchants" were not a capitalist vanguard or royal lackeys or even (in another revisionist caricature) political bumblers, engaged in a Dutch auction of their support in return for favors from an increasingly hostile crown and Parliament. Robert Brenner, in his massive and magnificent study *Merchants and Revolution* (1993), finds that there were three largely distinct groups of merchants in seventeenth-century England: the merchant adventurers, the traders of the Levant, East India, Russia, and other chartered companies, and the interloper colonial-merchants. Brenner reexamines data on trade and finds that, overall, merchants prospered in the seventeenth century. The merchant adventurers lost ground relatively to the Levant–East India Company traders. The shift in economic and then in London political leadership was the result of declining continental European demand for the cloths that the merchant adventurers exported, while the rapidly growing home market for imported luxuries delivered great wealth to the investors in the geographically defined trading companies.

The merchant adventurers and Levant–East India traders both benefited from royal protections. The crown eliminated foreign cloth merchants from England, ensuring that the merchant adventurers would be able to monopolize a shrinking market; in that way foreigners, not English investors, bore the brunt of declining demand for cloth. The company traders benefited from royal monopolies that restricted entrants into their markets and, as Brenner emphasizes, from the even more important royal prohibition of artisans and retailers from foreign trade. This latter limit ensured that traders could demand a uniform and high markup on imported goods, preventing domestic merchants and retailers from undercutting their prices.

Brenner certainly demonstrates that the merchant adventurers and Levant–East India traders' profits were politically derived from royal concessions. While the crown repeatedly demanded increased customs duties in return for those concessions, and at times (especially in 1624–25) alienated the company merchants with unprecedented demands or outrageous antics, the two groups of chartered merchants remained dependent on the crown for their livelihoods.

The third group of merchants, the colonial-interlopers, were quite different. They were excluded from the great chartered companies because of the double handicap of limited capital and unimpressive social origins. Most were sons of lesser gentry or shopkeepers and manufacturers in London or involved as ship captains or traders with the American colonies. For a time in the early seventeenth century, the traders involved with the Americas were able to operate with little interference from the chartered merchants. Trade with the Americas depended upon the establishment and growth of permanent colonies, which, in turn, required the long-term investment of capital. The great merchants and landed elite had safer and quicker opportunities for profitable investment in eastern trade and by improving landed estates. American plantations were built by the lesser strata who became rich by selling provisions and slaves to American settlers and importing American tobacco and furs to Britain.

Only this third group of merchants were capitalists in Marxist terms or even in Weber's sense of economically oriented capitalism. Their prosperity depended upon the free import of American products to Britain outside the monopoly system of the chartered companies. (These colonial merchants also desired government help in excluding foreign traders, especially the Dutch, and in forcing the colonial settlers to buy only British provisions. Of course, slaves were vital to the "triangular trade" with the colonies and provided the labor for tobacco, and later sugar and cotton, plantations.)

The colonial merchants were unable to get Stuart monarchs to defend their interests against the established merchants, or even against foreign rivals. Later, when colonial shippers became interlopers in the East India trade, the crown attempted, albeit with little effect, to guard the East India Company's monopoly. The colonial-interloper merchants did receive a more sympathetic hearing from Parliament. A majority in Parliament represented interests opposed to the company merchants: The outports that had been decimated by the chartered merchants' centralization of trade in London, and manufacturers and growers, especially of wool, who sought wider markets for their products than were provided by the merchant adventurers and chartered companies. The colonial-interloper merchants also were linked by business and ideological ties to the great landlords who invested in and guided the Puritan colonies in the Americas.

The business and political links between colonial-interloper merchants and great Puritan landlords with American interests endured from the 1620s through all the conflicts of the 1640s. Indeed, they are central to Brenner's analysis of the Civil War. His study of merchants allows him to explain why the colonial-interlopers were stalwarts of the parliamentary cause (their economic interests depended upon defeat of the crown and a reversal of royal commercial and foreign policies), and why the company merchants generally were spurned by Parliament even though the crown's inconsistent and exploitative relations with its chartered merchants gave those merchants reasons to join the opposition. (Company merchants demanded policies that were costly to important parliamentary constituencies, leading Parliament to reject the basis upon which company merchants could have split from the crown and forcing those merchants back into the arms of a monarch who cared about them only as pliable sources of revenue.)

Brenner's book becomes more speculative when he turns to the motives of the great and lesser landlords who opposed the king. Brenner, like most Marxists and most revisionists, sees the Revolution of 1640–41 as the product of a virtual consensus among landowners who wanted political reforms to give Parliament the power to guard their (now capitalist) property interests against the crown. However, the crown and Parliament failed to reach an accommodation. The revisionists basically attribute the Civil War to Charles I's pigheadedness. Recently, John Morrill (1993) has made the important contribution of pointing out that Charles ruled a tripartite kingdom with distinct, English, Scottish, and Irish elites. The divergent religious and political-economic interests among the elites of the three nations and with the crown led to wars that extinguished any hope for a royal-parliamentary compromise and mobilized forces for a military challenge to the crown.

Brenner, following recent Marxist scholarship, presents the landed class as caught between a rock and a hard place. On one side was Charles I and his retainers who were unwilling to meet the revolutionary demands of 1640–41. On the other side were radical forces, first in London and then in the army, that had been unleashed by the ruling class split and who, in the eyes of some members of Parliament (MPs) and landlords, could be suppressed only if Parliament rallied around the king.

Brenner's study of the three merchant groups is useful for explaining why the Revolution sparked popular rebellion in London and why MPs and landlords divided as they did in facing the double threat of royal retaliation and the London mass movement. Historians commonly picture London as the site of radical politics in the 1640s, but as Brenner reminds us it also was the place where reactionary elite forces were concentrated. The city government was controlled by merchant adventurers and company merchants who were dependent upon crown patronage and who sided with the crown against a parliamentary opposition committed to eliminating the special privileges of the chartered companies. John Pym and his parliamentary allies therefore could not turn to the city government for aid when Charles I moved to arrest his leading opponents in December 1641.

Pym's landlord allies were dispersed throughout England and were themselves without arms, the end-product of Tudor monarchs' campaign to disarm magnates.[22] While the crown lacked a standing army of its own (as was demonstrated by the king's vulnerability to Irish and Scottish rebellions and his dependence upon Parliament or upon extra-parliamentary trade duties to finance military mobilizations), within the capital the king's minor advantage in arms seemed decisive. The crown was poised to arrest and prosecute the opposition before the landed elite beyond London could come to its rescue. Parliament's only potential saviors were to be found in London. The city government's reactionary, pro-crown cast gave popular forces within London further reason to come to the aid of Pym in hopes that Parliament might weaken the royalist oligarchy that maintained a lock on municipal power and resources.

Brenner's analysis leads me to a counterfactual speculation: Had the colonial-interloper merchants been in control of London government in 1641, or had the merchants who did hold power been allied with Parliament rather than the crown, then Charles I would have been left without allies in London and been forced to submit to Parliament's demands, thereby averting the Civil War. Alternately, if Pym and his allies had been defended by relatively conservative merchants rather than by radical popular forces, then landlords would not have been scared into the king's arms and the Civil War would have ended in Charles I's quick defeat. Nonetheless, the precapitalist, royal-dependent merchants who controlled London government in 1641 were necessary both for Charles's intransigence and for the popular countermobilization that together made the Civil War into a bloody and lengthy conflict with an otherwise unpredictably radical outcome.

Except for the London movement sparked by the reactionary city government, there was no base for a radical political movement in 1641. Nor did one develop in the course of the Civil War. Brenner concludes that "with the important exception of London (and of course the army), relatively few areas in the nation had experienced significant radicalization during the Civil War years. In fact, in view of the ideological hegemony exercised by local landlords over most of the countryside and the relative immunity of agricultural laborers to radical politics in this epoch, relatively little mass radicalization could have been expected at this time from rural England . . . under any conditions" (1993, p. 539).

Brenner's image of the Civil War is similar to that of the revisionists in that he sees alliances as opportunistic rather than principled. However, Brenner finds that they were enduring and strategic rather than shifting and tactical. The Civil War, for Brenner, was less a split within Parliament and more "the consolidation of critical alliances" (1993, p. 688). Brenner wants to argue that alliances were built upon both personalistic and class foundations. He makes much of the long-standing business, political, religious, and personal ties between Puritan colonizing landowners and the colonial-interloper merchants. Such links gave the landowner-parliamentarians confidence in 1641 and after that they could rely upon and control the London popular forces whom the colonial-interloper merchants mobilized against the crown. This alliance was further reinforced because the landowners and capitalist merchants (though often not the popular forces) had a common interest in an anti-Catholic militaristic foreign policy and a common desire for state stimulation of foreign trade and the domestic economy, and both groups demanded a Presbyterian or an independent religious settlement that would guard landowners' and merchants' control over former church properties and over the ministers in their congregations.

Brenner's critique of the revisionists could be deepened and strengthened by carrying his analysis of the merchants onto a renewed study of interests and networks among landlords. Much of that work already has been done. Christopher Hill's *Economic Problems of the Church* (1963) remains the definitive study of how the transfer of church lands, tithe rights, benefices, and advowsons gave the receivers and purchasers of such feudal holdings an interest in guarding their now "private" property against reassertion of income rights or judicial powers by the king and his Anglican hierarchy.[23] Thus, owners of former church properties came to assume similar political interests and a common range of religious identities and built ties through the hiring of congenial ministers for the benefices under their control.

Peter Bearman finds a similar reinforcing mix of class, patronage, and religious-ideological ties among proparliamentary gentry in Norfolk, superseding the old familial and patronage ties through which magnates controlled the county in the sixteenth century.[24] Hill's and Bearman's works point to a rural equivalent to Brenner's London-centered alliance of Puritan colonizing landowners and the colonial-interloper merchants.

Gentry may have made alliances based on localized and personalized networks; however, contrary to the antitheoretical assertions of the revisionists, the rural alliances were as enduring as the London coalitions and also had been formed decades before the Revolution. Social and political networks were not formed by chance or on whim. Decisions to extend political support, to appoint ministers, to invest money, to profess a faith, or to oppose a king or a county political machine were momentous. They were made to protect and hopefully to further one's life chances and those of one's family. Fateful decisions were made more confidently in concert with other like-situated and therefore like-minded individuals. As lines of tension deepened and conflicts sharpened, choices became more dangerous and less likely to satisfy. Royalists and revolutionaries were able to go forward, however, with the confidence that their immediate allies were partners of long-standing. When parliamentarians especially needed to broaden their alliance, they were faced with trusting allies of allies of allies. Brenner's book at least can explain why those far-reaching alliances were made. Further historical research, based on a willingness to treat even revolutionaries as rational and stable social beings, will identify the interests and networks that strung together the great antiroyalist alliance. Such research also will explain why that alliance splintered in the Commonwealth and Restoration, and why a much narrower agenda of reform endured through the Glorious Revolution.

Horizontal Absolutism and Elite Concentration

The strategy of horizontal absolutism launched with the Henrician Reformation proved a disaster for the cause of royal power. Every move by Henry VIII and his successors against potential challengers at the national level had the effect of ceding power over land, taxes, judicial authority, local government, and Parliament to a single gentry elite that proved too numerous for the crown to bribe with patronage. The crown's destruction of magnate political networks in the counties and of a Catholic hierarchy's control over a national organization with economic, judicial, and ideological powers led the gentry to seek new bases for determining their social standing and expressing their material and spiritual interests. The gentry did so through county political organizations centered on the Commissions of the Peace and through shared patronage over Protestant ministers. Together the new political and religious networks protected, as they gave ideological clarity to, the gentry's interests in preserving control over land against royal and revanchist clerical claims and in fortifying gentry primacy in county politics and, through ties to the colonial-interloper merchants, in the American colonies and eventually in London.

Horizontal absolutism, in the final analysis, consolidated all power in the counties in a single, gentry elite and provided the organizational and ideological means for that elite to define and defend its interests. We need to draw upon the subtle and complex analyses of Brenner, Hill, Bearman, and even Morrill to understand the outlines of the Civil War. A final understanding of loyalties and events in that conflict awaits further work along these several lines. The ultimate outcome of the Civil War, however, and the settlement that followed the Glorious Revolution (which, as the revisionists and Marxist all acknowledge, was similar to the proposed settlement between Charles and Parliament in 1641) was determined by the unfolding of English horizontal absolutism. That determination becomes even clearer in comparison with the different vertical development of absolutism in France. I now turn to France and return in this chapter's conclusion to a comparison of the English Revolution and Civil War with the French Frondes and 1789 Revolution.

France

From Crown Weakness and Failed Reformation to New Strategic Opportunities

At the outset of the sixteenth century great nobles were the key actors in French politics. Princes and dukes held the governorships of the major provinces (Harding 1978, pp. 127–34; Babeau 1894, 1:257–59). As governors, the great noble families exercised the crown's formal powers to appoint provincial and local officials. Governors built networks of clients by installing members of lesser noble families as judges of the provincial parlements, as tax collectors, as officers in the provincial military companies, and as holders of clerical offices and benefices (Major 1964; Harding 1978; Asher 1960; Peronnet 1977).

Great aristocrats and their networks of clients were the key obstacles to royal power in the *pays d'élection,* the provinces that formed the original domain of French kings. In the *pays d'état,* however, the peripheral provinces that had been incorporated into France only in the fifteenth century, nobles and clerics were organized collectively into provincial estates that enjoyed a high degree of autonomy from both the king and the great nobles who served as governors in those provinces. The different forms of aristocratic organization in the older and more recently independent provinces gave rise to two distinct fiscal structures in the *pays d'élection* and *pays d'état.* In the *pays d'élection,* the governor appointed assessors and collectors from among his clients. All aristocrats were formally exempt from the taille, the main tax on production and income. However, to the extent that peasants paid the taille, they were less able to pay rent to their landlord. As a result, aristocrats were eager to gain appointment for themselves or their allies to tax offices so that they could use those powers to place the tax burden on other landlords' tenants (Marion 1974; Buisseret 1968, pp. 57–60). In all provinces, seigneurs sought to extend their formal exemption from the taille to cover lands that they had leased to tenants as well as lands they farmed directly with tenant or hired labor. When landlords gained such exemptions, they were able to charge their exempt tenants higher rents than those who leased taxable lands (Saint-Jacob 1960, pp. 126–30; Varine 1979).

Nobles, clerics, and bourgeois in the *pays d'état* were organized into estates. Artifacts of their independent history, the provincial estates retained the right to vote as corporate bodies on the rate and total amount of the taille in their provinces. The estates' collective organization and their equitable allocation of the tax burden among all localities prevented governors in the *pays d'état* from following the strategy of their counterparts in the *pays d'élection* and playing off lesser aristocrats against one another in competition for the offices that would allow them to saddle one another's peasants with the provincial tax obligation. The provincial estates' superior capacities for organizing resistance to royal revenue demands was reflected in the amount of the taille collected in the various provinces. The *pays d'élection* and *pays d'état* had roughly equivalent populations and levels of agrarian production, yet the taille from the former group of provinces was ten times that from the areas where estates remained intact throughout the sixteenth century (Buisseret 1968).

Whereas governors were better able to organize client networks and collect taxes in provinces without estates, their capacities did not automatically translate into higher revenues for the crown. Much of the income collected by governors in the *pays d'élection* was spent within the provinces on armies commanded by and loyal to the leading aristocratic families, and for patronage for the governors' clients (Parker 1983, pp. 1–45; Kettering 1986).

The crown was unable to penetrate elite structures in most provinces in the centuries before the Reformation. Many of the *pays d'état* were border provinces, in which crown interference could have precipitated an alliance between disgruntled aristocrats and expansionist foreign powers. The other *pays d'état* were dominated by powerful magnates, with the exception of Provence. The especially powerful Provencal clergy was the main fiscal beneficiary of noble divisions. More of the *pays d'élection* were marked by factional conflicts, and in those provinces the crown was able to establish relatively powerful intendants and to collect the most taxes.[25]

The French crown's failure to achieve a Reformation or to consolidate control of the Catholic Church under royal administration deprived the monarch of a financial windfall with which to purchase the loyalties of lesser elites and thereby disrupt the hegemony of magnates or of corporate bodies within the provinces. French kings did realize two strategic opportunities, however, from their failure to master the religious conflicts engendered by the Reformation. First, the crown could put a pious face on its political weakness and present itself to the pope as protector of the Catholic Church against Protestant heretics and noble appropriators. The papacy responded to those overtures by granting French kings measures of fiscal and political control over the French Church that, while less than what Henry VIII was able to seize for himself, proved more durable because they did not have to be shared with lay allies of a Reformation. Second, the French monarch widened the fissures that religious differences had opened in formerly stable magnate blocs and in urban oligarchies by inserting new bodies of venal officials into provincial, urban, and ultimately national polities.

French kings combined the two strategies of heightening religious conflict and developing venality to produce a vertical absolutism in France. For a time, the synergy of those two strategies propelled the crown toward greater power at the expense of the aristocracy. The ultimate indication of noble weakness came in the Frondes. From the second half of the seventeenth century on, however, the crown's strategic opportunities narrowed. This analysis of French elite conflict proceeds in stages, beginning with an examination of the achievement of French vertical absolutism through the Wars of Religion and the extension of venality in the first half of the seventeenth century. I then explain the failure of the noble Frondes of 1648–53 in terms of the structure of elite and class relations created by vertical absolutism. The crown's victory in the Frondes was followed by a century of stalemate and a deepening fiscal crisis for the crown and for much of the aristocracy. I am concerned with explaining the reasons for that stalemate and why it endured as long as it did. That analysis of stability in crisis allows for a dissection of the causes and course of the revolutionary destruction of the ancien régime that began in 1789.

Venality and the Wars of Religion

During the sixteenth century French kings moved to enhance their income and weaken the power of the great aristocratic families and provincial estates by enlisting as allies the individuals and corporate bodies who were excluded from the dominant political networks of each province. The institution of the venal office provided a basis for the crown to establish direct fiscal and political links with local elites and to fortify its new allies against entrenched aristocrats and officials within the provinces.

Venality was a royal grant of an office for a fixed term or for the life of the incumbent in return for an initial, and often an annual, payment by the officeholder. The crown realized an increasing stream of revenues from the sale of venal offices. During the sixteenth century, sales of offices surpassed loans as the major source of extraordinary royal revenues (Parker 1983, pp. 13–39). By 1633, half of all crown revenues (both ordinary and extraordinary) were derived from the sale of venal offices, and from the *paulette,* an annual fee paid by incumbent officeholders beginning in 1604 in return for royal recognition of their right to resell or bequeath their venal posts (Treasure 1967, p. 54).

The crown profited politically, as well as financially, from the growing corps of venal officers. A growing majority of men who bought seats in parlements and in the lesser provincial courts during the sixteenth century were landed aristocrats from the province in which they held office (Dewald 1980, pp. 69–112; Parker 1980, pp. 56–95; Tait 1977, pp. 1–20; Kettering 1978, pp. 13–50). With the security of permanent tenure in office, judges asserted their independence from the magnates who formerly had passed upon their appointment to office. The parlements became an alternative locus of aristocratic organization on the provincial level that the crown could employ to ratify and enforce royal decrees, thereby circumventing governors and their cliques.

The crown's venal strategy was less successful in the *pays d'état* where provincial nobles were broadly represented in the estates (Freville 1953, pp. 22–25). As a result, the crown was unable to identify an excluded group of nobles to favor with venal offices. In those provinces, estates remained the locus of aristocrat politics, while the parlements were confined to a subsidiary role and excluded from the most lucrative political activities. The political weakness of parlement judges in the *pays d'état* was reflected in the stagnant and falling prices of their seats, in contrast to those in the *pays d'élection* whose offices rose in value with their growing capacity to challenge the governors (Hurt 1976).

Sixteenth-century French kings also sought to build venal clienteles in urban areas as a way of undermining the autonomy of the independent or magnate-controlled oligarchies that dominated French towns. Kings gained revenues by revoking and then selling back town monopolies and privileges. That strategy was not successful, however, in areas where towns had the independent military power or the magnate support to defy royal edicts. In those municipalities the crown established new bodies of judicial and fiscal officers in competition with the old oligarchies. The new venal offices were purchased mostly by merchants and manufacturers excluded from the old elite. The crown gained revenues from the office sales and transformed the urban purchasers into a political bloc whose capacity to protect their venal investment depended on a continuing alliance with the crown against the oligarchs. By undermining the old oligarchy's political hegemony, the crown made itself the arbiter between two parties, each dependent on the monarchy to recognize the powers and income rights attached to their offices (Parker 1980; Westrich 1972).

The crown pursued a similar strategy with respect to the Catholic Church. At the outset of the sixteenth century most clerical offices and benefices were under the de facto control of provincial aristocrats who named family members and other allies to church posts, often in return for a share of the appointee's official income. Magnates negotiated directly with Rome to gain papal approval of their candidates for archbishop and bishop, who in turn appointed lesser church officials. The crown's lack of authority over the church, and over magnates, was also reflected in the tactics of nobles who had converted to Protestantism. Those Huguenots also sought allies from abroad in their efforts to wrest control of clerical revenues and offices from Catholics and apply those resources to their own and their coreligionists' needs.

The French monarch exploited the religious schism among the aristocracy to gain greater control of clerical offices and revenues. King François I outflanked the divided provincial aristocrats by presenting himself to the pope as the protector of French Catholicism. In the 1516 Concordat with the pope the crown conceded to the papacy annates (an annual share) on benefices in return for royal control over the appointment of bishops (Shennan 1969, pp. 16–19; Blet 1959, 1:88–99). The crown used this vast new source of patronage to draw aristocrats away from their magnate patrons with appointments to bishoprics. Crown favorites were able to build their own patronage networks by installing supporters in the clerical offices under their control (Bergin 1982). The number of bishops from magnate families declined during the reign of Louis XIII (1610–43) and were replaced by candidates from the *noblesse de robe*. Richelieu and Mazarin, the king's chief ministers, appointed many of their own clients to high church offices (Bergin 1992). At times the crown supported Protestants' claims upon benefices as a way of stripping hostile provincial Catholics of clerical revenues (Salmon 1975; Guery 1981).

French kings used their alliance with the pope and their growing control over the clerical hierarchy to compel the bishops at their annual assembly to vote increasing "gifts" to the crown. The crown's revenue from the church rose from 379,651 livres in 1516 to 3,792,704 livres in 1557 (Carrière 1936, pp. 250–57). The crown and papacy increased their share of church revenues at the expense of the clerics themselves and their aristocratic patrons. However, when the crown sought to appropriate clerical properties for royal use or sale, it was opposed by all bishops—crown appointees who filled church offices with their own allies, as well as those still under magnate domination (Cloulas 1958).

While French monarchs gained increasing revenues from the sale of venal offices during the sixteenth and early seventeenth centuries, the crown received a decreasing portion of the taxes and duties that venal officials collected. In order to make venal offices financially attractive to potential buyers, and to retain the loyalty of the original and subsequent holders of those offices, the crown was forced to allow venal tax collectors and judicial officers to collect "commissions" on the revenues destined for the crown. Those commissions ranged from 17 percent to 25 percent in the early seventeenth century and rose to over 40 percent by the eve of the Frondes in the 1640s (Dessert 1984, pp. 46–63).

The crown's restricted political control over the aristocrats who were the main purchasers of venal offices resulted in contradictory results for the monarch: increasing income from the sale of offices at the cost of limiting returns from the taxes that venal officials had been appointed to collect.[26] The crown's massive sale of venal offices created the financial and social bases for local nobles to distance themselves from the great nobles who had dominated their provinces. Where seigneurs previously had turned to the princes and *ducs et pairs* for patronage and social prestige (Major 1964; Lefebvre 1973), they now became able to expand their family fortunes by investing in venal offices. Membership on a provincial court provided office-holding nobles with status and political power independent of their ties to great aristocratic families.

French kings, by creating corps of venal officials in the provinces, succeeded both in subverting the capacities of great nobles to mobilize lesser elites to challenge the crown on a national level and also in undermining the crown's ability to expand its ordinary revenues from taxes and duties. Once seigneurs were installed in venal offices, they had an interest in opposing the creation of new positions that would compete for the revenues and powers previously reserved to them. Thus, while the crown forged ties of obligation and dependency with venal officeholders, it also created a constituency with an interest in preventing it from further expanding its venal administration.

While venality freed provincial nobles from dependence upon the great nobles, it did not make them automatic allies of the French crown. Unlike English monarchs who spent their windfall from the sale of monastic properties to entice the great magnates to depend on the crown, sixteenth-century French kings did not have the wealth to support notables at court. Instead, the crown used its political power to create nonseigneunal sources of income, but then it appropriated much of that income for the royal account. French kings, in their fiscal duress, made themselves both the patrons of and competitors with venal officials.

Wars of religion were the archetypal conflicts of sixteenth-century France. French kings profited from the struggle between Protestant and Catholic nobles to control provincial institutions, clerical tithes, and urban governments by alternately supporting one or another faction in return for the lion's share of the resources seized by the crown's allies from the losing side. In towns, factions often shared the same religious orientation and merely competed for political power and control over urban revenues (Parker 1980, pp. 46–94). Provincial and urban conflicts, while usually couched in religious terms or justified as the defense of ancient rights by provincial and corporate bodies, were precipitated when the crown attempted to expand its revenues by empowering one faction to collect taxes or control resources previously under the authority of a rival.

Provincial and urban factions that were on the losing side of the monarch's venal establishments sought allies within and outside the French nation. In contrast to sixteenth-century English monarchs, who succeeded in preventing foreign interventions in domestic politics, French kings were often confronted by political enemies who enlisted foreign armies in their cause (Parker 1983, pp. 27–45). The weakness of the French "state" is demonstrated by the frequency with which monarchs had to make concessions to domestic opponents to avoid creating an opening for foreign intervention (Major 1964). By threatening to ally with Protestant foreign powers, an array of mostly Catholic nobles and parlementaires forced the crown to call a national Estates General in 1614 which, at least temporarily, restricted royal authority to create new venal offices (Hayden 1974).

Most sixteenth-century struggles were confined within the French nation. Factions raised their own armies to protect privileges against encroachments by the crown and its new venal allies. Although French monarchs succeeded in weakening the capacities of great nobles to mount armed challenges, venality created new opportunities for armed resistance to coalesce (Beik 1985; Harding 1978). Many of the "antistate" rebellions catalogued by Charles Tilly often were instigated and fought by nobles and officeholders who sought to protect their venal privileges from the next generation of royal concessionaires.

French kings were limited further, as were their English and other European counterparts, by the fiscal pressures created by the dramatic escalation in the costs of war in the seventeenth century. Military expenses rose from 5 million livres a year in the first decade of the 1600s to 16 million in the 1620s, 33 million in 1635, and 38 million in 1640 (Parker 1983, p. 64).

French kings sought to pay war expenses by selling new posts to aristocrats and urban merchants eager to buy into the political power and growing market value of venal offices. In 1602 the crown legalized venal officeholders' already de facto rights to sell or will their offices in return for payment of the *paulette*.[27] However, incumbent officials had an interest in preventing the creation of new positions that would compete with their authority and access to resources. Parlement judges renewed the demand, which the crown had agreed to at the 1614 Estates General and later abrogated, that the crown not create any new judicial bodies and refrain from selling additional seats in the existing judicial chambers (Kettering 1982). Urban and provincial officials used tax strikes to force the crown to rescind sales of new venal posts. As a result, crown revenues from the sale of offices, which had peaked at 30 million livres in 1639, collapsed in the following two decades, bottoming out at an insignificant 800,000 livres in 1661 (Dent 1967, pp. 247–50).

The limits of venality, and of the vertical absolutism French kings created with that strategy, are reflected in the origins and outcomes of the Wars of Religion and the 1614 Estates General as well as the Frondes. The elections to the Estates General of 1614 provide a measure of royal authority over nobles, clerics, and urban elites in the various French provinces. Royal control was weaker over delegations from the *pays d'état* than over estates from the *pays d'élection*. That contrast confirms my earlier observation that provincial estates that retained control over the allocation of the taille within the province were better able to prevent the crown from co-opting aristocratic and urban factions. For those provinces the crown was forced to buy each estate's votes by promising to reduce provincial and urban taxes and demands on clerical tithe revenues (Hayden 1974).

The monarchy also was limited in the demands it could make on the delegations from the *pays d'élection* that were dominated by venal officials and clerics it had appointed. When the crown sought to compel those estates to agree to higher taxes in return for the renewal of the *paulette* that guaranteed their rights to sell or will their offices, venal officials united with the magnates to preserve their particular interests against crown appropriation (Hayden 1974). The 1614 Estates General demonstrated the partial achievements of the crown's venal strategy. Venality divided provincial aristocrats, weakening the magnates' regional bases and thereby limiting their capacities to challenge the crown at the national level. However, after the initial windfall from the sale of offices, venality was a fiscal failure. Each royal effort to tax the fruits of venal privileges or to sell the same privileges to new purchasers drew aristocrats and venal officials together in a common defense against the interlopers who would weaken both their positions.

The crown faced comparable difficulties in exploiting financially the religious differences between Catholics and Protestants. Protestants were concentrated in a few provinces and several towns (Parker 1978). The crown allowed Protestant domination in those areas in return for fiscal concessions. Protestants took advantage of royal support to subordinate or expel Catholic officials in the provincial estates and parlements and urban governments. Catholics organized into the Ligue to prevent the further expansion of Protestant power and to retake areas under Protestant control, sparking the Wars of Religion in the latter part of the sixteenth century.

The Ligue undercut the degree of control over the Catholic Church that the crown had obtained with the 1516 Concordat. Bishops fearful of losing properties to Protestants in concert with the crown turned to the Ligue nobles for protection (Hoffman 1984, pp. 7–44; Tait 1977). Thus, in the majority of France that remained Catholic the crown lost authority within the church.

The Wars of Religion also affected urban politics Municipal bodies were split along religious lines. Once the Ligue or Huguenots gained hegemony within a municipality and expelled their opponents, the crown was no longer able to play off opposing factions and governing bodies against one another. Instead the crown was forced to negotiate with militarily powerful parties, gaining limited cash payments in return for grants of near-total municipal autonomy (Parker 1980; 1983; Gascon 1971; Westrich 1972).

Religious conflict, and the crown's attempts to extract revenues from venal officials, led to a common political outcome. In both instances provincial and municipal factions found that they could better protect their interests by amalgamating into parties, often in alliance with magnates, than by seeking to compete with rivals for crown protection. The only way the crown could unpack those reconstituted provincial cliques was by increasing patronage to lure critical actors away from their allies. Thus, King Henri IV paid 24 million livres to Ligue leaders to induce them to disarm and guaranteed Protestant towns immunity from taxes in return for their toleration of Catholic landlords and clerics in their regions. Those concessions prevented the further combination of provincial parties into national blocs that could have challenged Henri IV's throne. However, the king was unable to pay for both domestic concessions and foreign war. He was forced to end his war against Spain, permanently dashing hopes of expanding the boundaries of France (Parker 1983, pp. 46–94).

The French kings of the early seventeenth century "neither taxed nor spent at will and local elites retained a great deal of control over the practical workings of the [fiscal] system" (Collins 1988, p. 2). However, unlike the English monarchs who had lost their hold over the gentry-JPs with the elimination of magnate power, the French kings had been unable to dislodge the great nobles' provincial power. French monarchs found that they needed to ally with the most powerful provincial nobles if they hoped to extract further resources from the lesser aristocrats within each province. Provincial governors appointed from among the great aristocratic families became the main instrument of royal policy at that time.

The most successful governors, in terms of preventing fiscal or military rebellion within their provinces, were those men with independent networks of clients made up of lesser landlords and provincial officials to whom they afforded political and military protection (Harding 1978; Bonney 1978). By siding with their clients to prevent the creation of new competitive venal offices, governors ensured that the incomes and market values of existing offices escalated dramatically, A seat in the Parlement of Provence at Aix worth between three thousand and six thousand livres in 1510 rose in value to between forty thousand and fifty thousand livres in 1633, an increase of

400 percent after accounting for inflation (Kettering 1978, pp. 221–25). Similar increases occurred in other provinces and for other offices (Dewald 1980, pp. 131–161; Collins 1988, pp. 80–87). Governors used their influence over appointments to the shrinking supply of new or vacant offices to reward their clients. Additionally, governors maneuvered to ensure that their allies among venal officials controlled the parlements, lesser courts, and urban councils.

Governors found that they could best advance their political and financial fortunes by acting as mediators between crown and provincial interests. When governors were able to head off sales of crown offices and tax increases, they won the loyalty of urban and provincial officials who had been threatened by the crown's fiscal demands (Harding 1978). Governors were able to compound their political control by supporting the crown's demands for tax increases and then rebating most of the increases to favored allies in the form of commissions for collecting the taxes. This allowed governors to punish obstreperous officials by excluding them from the largesse made possible by the new taxes. As long as governors were able to buy the loyalty of a majority of their parlements, lesser courts, estates, and urban councils, they could prevent a unified opposition by those provincial bodies.

During the first half of the seventeenth century the crown sought to regularize its grants of patronage, and use that largesse to build parties of royal supporters in the provinces independent of the armed magnates. Beginning in 1634, the crown appointed permanent intendants in each province to organize the collection of revenues and the distribution of patronage. Intendants focused their efforts on circumventing the trésoriers who were charged with collecting the taille. The trésoriers had been allied with the provincial magnates and later were often sponsored by the Ligue or Huguenot factions that dominated a province. Intendants tracked the crown's earlier venal strategy by appointing to serve as tax-collecting *élus* those nobles and urban financiers who were at the margins of provincial and municipal factions.[28]

The *élus* organized teams of tithe assessors and collectors in each of the elections, the subdivisions of the provinces of the *pays d'élection*. *Élus* realized lucrative incomes from their offices by collecting fees and by acting as tax farmers, advancing the crown a fraction of the tax levy in return for the right to collect the tithe or other tax within a province. Intendants used the lure of appointment as an *élu,* or of being allowed to join a tax farm syndicate, to build networks of supporters.

Intendants were less able to manipulate and divide the more cohesive nobles of the *pays d'état.* The estates and parlements in those provinces often refused to register the contracts intendants made with tax farmers. Resistance by the estates made it difficult for the tax farmers to collect the taxes within the *pays d'état.* As a result, aspiring tax farmers entered bids on tax farms that were often less than the amount the estates previously had agreed to pay the crown (Buisseret 1968).

The intendants were most successful at weakening the powers of autonomous towns. Provincial estates and parlements resented the challenge posed by municipal governments' claims to authority over their towns' hinterlands, whereas the intendants sought to limit municipal fiscal autonomy as a way of tapping the towns' income and assets for the royal treasury. The intendants used the threat of being subordinated to provincial government to extract ever greater forced loans from towns (Bordes 1960; Parker 1983).

Royal revenues increased in the decades after the establishment of provincial intendants. Direct taxes, primarily the taille, *taillon,* subsistence, and *étape,* rose from 36 million livres in 1635 to 72.6 million in 1643, whereas arrears fell (Parker 1983, p. 64). A majority of the tax collections, however, were used within the provinces by the intenants to pay *élus* and to maintain the loyalty of aristocrats, venal judges, and other former allies of the magnates.

The royal intendants constantly needed to bribe their own appointees because crown officials in the provinces were overwhelmingly drawn from the ranks of the aristocracy.[29] Few Frenchmen who were not aristocrats could afford to purchase venal offices or tax farms, and only if an intendant recruited a substantial portion of the provincial aristocracy to royal office could he splinter a province's opposition to tax demands. The crown was caught between two opposing imperatives: the need to raise money to support the royal court and foreign military ventures, and the need to prevent a unified opposition from coalescing in the provinces or towns. The former objective required reducing the profits from offices and forcing provincial nobles to accede to the appointment of new corps of tax collectors. The latter goal could be met only by granting offices and other concessions to enough nobles and venal officials to counterbalance those still outside the intendants' political networks.

Crown success in fulfilling its two contradictory needs varied with the demands of war. When France was at peace and military expenses were low, as in the years following the Wars of Religion, the king could afford to divert a greater part of royal revenues to buying aristocrats' loyalty and consolidating royal parties under provincial intendants. But, as war expenses rose and the secular depression deepened in the mid-seventeenth century, the crown was forced to abandon clients and impose new demands on venal bodies and provincial estates. The fiscal squeeze became acute in the 1640s: War with Spain escalated while direct tax revenues that had peaked at 72.6 million livres in 1643 fell to 56 million in 1648 (Parker 1983, p. 64). The shortfall was made up through the sales of offices and other fiscal expedients. Such techniques could not be sustained. Total government revenues fell by 28 percent from the 1650s to the 1660s and did not recover until the end the end of the 1720s (see chapter 5, esp. table 5.4). Thus, while "the intendants served to accelerate the flow of resources to the central government" (Tilly 1981, p. 205) in the decades before the Fronde, the increase in state income and capacities provoked political reactions that led to the unraveling of the intendants' politico-fiscal networks. The rise and fall in pre-Fronde crown revenues were artifacts of a venal strategy that affected the structure of elite relations in civil society in ways that in turn limited the efficacy of the crown's administrative organs.[30]

The Frondes

The Frondes, the series of revolts against crown authority in the years 1648–53, must be seen as a consequence of the crown's fiscal crisis. The Frondes were aimed at limiting the crown's ability to establish new offices or to issue decrees that would undermine the existing powers of venal bodies. Frondeurs were virtually unanimous in demanding the abolishment of the office of intendants. The Parlement of Paris articulated the Frondeurs' sentiments by demanding that judges retain their power to decide whether to register, amend, or reject royal decrees. Provincial parlements echoed that position within their provinces. The parlements were supported by a variety of provincial and urban groups. Venal officials threatened by governors and intendants' efforts to augment crown revenues were the principal supporters of the Frondes. Some of the most powerful governors stood with their clients and against crown policies that would have interjected intendants into provincial politics, undermining the governors' bases of authority (Harding 1978, pp. 199–212; Moote 1971; Bonney 1978).

The uprisings were led by parlementaire judges in three provinces and joined there and in other provinces by a changing array of magnates and their clients, provincial estates, urban merchants and officials, Protestant and Catholic clergy, and peasants. The rebellions threatened the monarch's powers and reign. Sharon Kettering (1982), in a comparison of the provincial parlements that joined the Frondes with those that remained loyal to the crown, finds that venal judges revolted when they had both the motive and allies. Motive was available to parlement judges in most of France as their incomes and perquisites were squeezed by intendants who championed rival courts under their control. However, judges acted on their grievances only when they were able to exploit political schisms opened by provincial intendants. In the three provincial cities where judges revolted—Aix, Rouen, and Bordeaux—intendants had antagonized large sectors of the urban administrations. Urban officials often were linked to the judges by family and patronage ties, creating a cohesive oppositional bloc.

Provincial governors proved unable to counter the Frondeurs' insurrections. The crown's venal strategy had weakened the governors' hold on provincial officials. Such officials no longer needed the governors to maintain tenure in their personal offices. Instead, venal corps looked to governors to prevent the establishment of rival corps that would erode the income and value of their offices. As previous discussed, governors were able to fulfill that political role in the first third of the seventeenth century, when low military expenses allowed the monarch to spend its income on building political blocs around loyal governors. Once the crown limited patronage and multiplied offices in response to the fiscal pressures of the late 1630s and 1640s, governors had little to offer the old venal corps. The governors seated in Aix, Rouen, and Bordeaux reacted to their inability to protect provincial clients by currying favor at the royal court, allying with the intendants to squeeze the provincial and urban venal corps (Kettering 1986, pp. 99–140; Bonney 1978). However, the governors and intendants were unable to build new clientage networks that could challenge the alliance of parlement judges and nobles at the local level. The governors were forced to call on royal armies to battle the judicial Frondeurs.

Other governors, led by the Condé prince, sought to reconstitute their provincial clienteles by opposing the crown. Condé calculated that, with royal troops tied down in the war with Spain, he and his fellow magnates could meld their armies into a military force capable of overwhelming the crown's scattered troops still in France (Westrich 1972). Condé and his fellow magnates rallied provincial nobles, urban merchants, and officials excluded from crown patronage, creating a revolutionary coalition far stronger than the isolated parlementaire parties of the initial urban Frondes.

The Frondeurs were unable to unite and sustain a rebellion despite venal officeholders' shared interest in limiting crown power. Although the Frondeurs began the rebellion with superior military forces and strategic advantages, they were defeated because the crown reached accords with particular opponents and thereby isolated and then defeated the remaining rebels (Moote 1971, pp. 316 54; Kettering 1978, pp. 277–97).

Michael Mann errs in accounting for the divergent outcomes of the Civil War and the Frondes by emphasizing the preexisting military capacities of the monarchs. He contends that the French kings commanded armies that could be turned against domestic as well as foreign enemies, while English monarchs concentrated their military investments in a navy more appropriate for an island kingdom (1986, p. 478). In fact, both sides in the civil wars in both countries were able to raise armies large enough to challenge their opponents. The French Frondeurs lost for the same reason the English royalists lost: Crucial allies deserted them, neutrals rallied to their enemies, and they lost the capacity to raise taxes or loans to sustain their cause. Thus, to understand the Frondeurs' defeat, we must explain why some provincial elites broke with their fellow aristocrats and submitted to crown rule, thereby providing the crown with the necessary armies and fiscal resources to outman and outlast the Frondeurs' forces.

The Frondeurs' ultimate defeat demonstrated that whereas the crown had failed to organize venal officials into a reliable and continuing revenue source, venality did undermine national oppositional coalitions. As I show in chapter 6, a century of venal administration weakened the direct seigneurial relation between landlords and peasants. Even those nobles who derived most of their income from peasant rents found that their land and income rights were upheld and mediated by venal officials. French lay seigneurs, as a result, never were able to establish direct domination over peasants ummediated by rival feudal elites.[31]

French agrarian class relations retained the characteristic feudal form of multiple elites regulating and profiting from agrarian production. French monarchs' absolutist strategies weakened clerical and magnate control over land tenure, while empowering new, venal elites, above all the parlement and lesser judges, to intervene in landlord-tenant relations. Rather than a single class of landowners as in England, several French elites jostled for the rights to collect taxes and rents from the peasantry. After a century and a half of crown manipulation of provincial elites, and after the reorganization of aristocratic power within venal offices, each elite's authority came to rest upon royal grants of "privileges which were subject to differing interpretations and which were defined in reference to the king" (Beik 1985, p. 219).

Once the Frondeurs had rejected crown regulation of crown-granted privileges, provincial factions were left to sort out their overlapping jurisdictions. As a result, the weaker elements within the Frondeur coalitions fared less well in competition with provincial rivals than they had when subordinated to the crown and intendants. Officials and nobles whose positions the crown had most recently established and who were not clients or allies of the leading Frondeurs were the least likely to have joined the Fronde, or most likely to abandon quickly the rebels' common front (Kettering 1978; 1982, pp. 294–304; Moote 1971; Bonney 1978, 1981).

Frondeurs had reasons to fight each other as well as the crown. While the crown's venal strategy had failed to pacify provincial elites, it had precluded the formation of a common front of similarly situated nobles in opposition to the royal court. The inability of French provincial elites to act as a class, demonstrated by their conflicts with one another over privileges, was confirmed by their failure to suppress the massive peasant resistance during the Frondes. The crown's venal strategy had diminished the seigneurs' capacities to collect rents and to exercise military domination over peasants and substituted instead state-mediated taxation collected by venal offices. As a result, when peasants went on tax strikes against the crown under the cover of the elite Frondes, Frondeurs' venal incomes from tax collection were lost. Frondeurs had few cash reserves and were unable to support the private armies needed to defeat both the crown and peasant rebellions. In the end Condé was forced to sue for peace because his party was bankrupt (Parker 1983, pp. 95–117). The monarch, by contrast, could raise funds from great financiers whose investments in royal debt required the crown to dominate the provinces to insure repayment. Financiers provided the crown sufficient resources to outlast and defeat the Frondeurs (Bonney 1981, pp. 213–14, 228–41; Parker 1983, pp. 95–117).

The Frondeurs' inability to sustain armed resistance against the crown or to defeat peasant rebellions resulted from the crown's establishment and manipulation of venal offices that had fused the powers of the various elites into a single state structure. "The rulers could not subtract their sphere from the larger polity because their authority was based on a system of shared power and graduated privilege which was presided over by the monarch. Without the king there could be no hierarchy of authorities and no 'division of labor' among them. Yet there was no possibility of a royal 'takeover' either because the king relied on his social allies within the province and had no alternative to their rule" (Beik 1985, p. 219). The fiscal crisis of the early seventeenth century demonstrated the limits of crown control over provincial nobles, just as the Frondes proved that aristocrats and venal officials could not form a class outside the absolutist state. The political settlement achieved after the Frondes was not the monarch's victory over the aristocracy, or of state bureaucrats over civil society, but the accommodation of formerly autonomous feudal elites within a single state structure.

The contrast in the outcome of the French Frondes in comparison with the English Revolution and Civil War exposes the predictive and explanatory limits of the three theoretical perspectives presented earlier in this chapter. The English Revolution was indeed a conflict between a state elite and a gentry class whose interest was defined by its new monopoly of control over agrarian production. In that confrontation, the military and administrative capacities emphasized by state-centered theorists proved less powerful than the gentry's ability to pursue its interests with respect to the peasantry without reference to the royal state's grants of authority. Even when Parliament and the gentry split into opposed factions in the Civil War, Charles I was unable to recruit enough allies from among the gentry, London merchants, or county yeomen to win. The king was such an uninviting ally because he was not vital to the maintenance or expansion of any elite's economic power. The king lacked the resources to sustain a patronage network sufficient to dominate national politics, and therefore a crown victory would have harmed more gentry, yeomen, and merchants than it could have aided.

The Frondes, in contrast, fit less well into the archetypal struggle between tax-collecting state officials and tax-paying state subjects. The French crown's inability to achieve horizontal dominance over national rivals forced it to cede areas of sovereignty to the institutions now controlled by other elites. The French crown could weaken rival elites only by creating more sovereign institutions, and thereby new venal elites. The Frondeurs' defeat was less a consequence of the crown's independent capacity to deploy force and more a consequence of the embedding, over two centuries, of each elite's interests within a vertically organized state. Antistate rebellion failed because most elites were sited within that state and could express their interests only through it.

Perry Anderson (1974) is correct in describing the absolutist state as a redeployment of the feudal ruling class. However, in looking to the struggles between peasants and landlords for the dynamic of state formation, he is unable to explain the differences in the rise of English and French absolutism, or the early demise of the former. Both Anderson's class analysis and Marx and Engels's relative autonomy model lead us astray in depicting the bourgeoisie as external to, if for a time dependent upon, the absolutist state. The bourgeoisie emerges differently in my analysis. The varying sites at which it organized and defended its interests in the two countries appear less the product of an autonomous process of capitalist development and more the result of openings created by the particular paths of elite conflict and absolutism in England and France. In England, elite conflict created a structure of gentry class rule outside of, and hence capable of destroying, absolutism, and it set up an opportunity for London merchants to oppose the king. In France, vertical absolutism created narrow opportunities for holders of capital to buy offices and to invest in state debts and precluded a broad alliance of officeholders and landlords against the crown. The nature of the seventeenth-century French bourgeoisie forced it to define its interests with the state in the Frondes, while the locally based English gentry was divorced from the state. Bourgeois strategies in the two countries were determined by that class's structural location, not by an absolute measure of strength or maturity. Possibilities for bourgeois political agency developed as artifacts of conflict among elites.

The state was not an actor or an interest in early modern England and France. Instead, the differing horizontal and vertical forms of absolutism were outcomes of the long chains of conflicts among complexes of actors analyzed in this chapter. Horizontal absolutism compressed the transformation of elite relations in the English polity and, as I show in chapter 6, produced capitalist class relations in the economy in the same short period.

Vertical absolutism and political stalemate were the results of a different train of elite conflict in France. The following sections of this chapter trace elite conflict in France after the Frondes to explain why stalemate lasted as long as it did, and why the Revolution of 1789 occurred when it did and with particular consequences for subsequent elite and class relations in France.

Elite Stalemate: The Limits of Conflict and Class
Formation in the Ancien Régime

The Frondes were a decisive political, as well as military, defeat for provincial magnates. Their outcome revealed that no one save the monarch was able to guarantee seigneurial land rights and official privileges against the claims of rival elites or of rebellious peasants. The peasant rebellions that accompanied the elite Frondes demonstrated the further inability of provincial and urban elites to defend their class interests without crown aid.

The crown had become ever more implicated in seigneurs' surplus extraction in the century leading up to the Frondes. First, a growing portion of aristocratic income came from state offices rather than from manorial dues. Second, in the century leading up to the Frondes, seigneurs had made increasing use of royal edicts and parlement decisions in their efforts to raise peasant rents and expand the portion of the estate under direct aristocratic control (Dewald 1980, pp. 162–201; Mousnier 1970, pp. 215–30). Frondeur nobles threatened both those props when they rebelled against the crown. Intraclass disputes, therefore, disrupted aristocrats' seigneurial as well as their official income sources. Peasants took advantage of elites' challenges to one another's income and judicial rights during the Frondes by engaging in rent strikes or reasserting ancient rights. Seigneurs lacked the independent military or judicial apparatuses to put down the rebellions and reassert their seigneurial claims. Aristocrats could restore their income bases only by becoming clients of a magnate or monarch with the military power to enforce extraction against peasants.[32]

After the Frondes, rebellious nobles hastened to demonstrate their loyalty to the crown and sought to attach themselves to the royal offices that could guarantee their income and political standing. The crown expanded the number of sinecures available to provincial aristocrats while seeking to prevent magnates from appropriating those offices and thereby reconstituting autonomous clientages (Kettering 1986). The crown reintroduced intendants, crown appointees who rivaled the governors in their control over provincial institutions. Unlike the governors, intendants were not natives of the province in which they served. Crown favorites often held several intendancies before ascending to higher positions at the court (Emmanuelli 1981; Gruder 1968; Babeau 1894, 2:14–24). Intendants were creatures of the court who furthered their careers by being loyal servants of their monarch's interests, unlike the governors who had property and political interests to preserve in their home provinces.

Intendants did not need to risk new Frondes by attacking the existing privileges of governors, aristocrats, and officials. Rural and urban elites depended upon military aid from armed companies under the intendants' control if they were to reestablish their authority over the peasant and urban rebels who had threatened their privileges during the Frondes. Intendants made loyalty to the crown, and the collection of the taille and other direct taxes, preconditions for aid to seigneurs in their battles with peasants.

An analysis of the responses the crown made, through its provincial intendants, to peasant rebellions in the half century after the Frondes, reveals that the monarch differentiated between loyal officials and autonomous seigneurs. After royal troops suppressed uprisings, fiscal officers loyal to the intendant were aided in extracting both taxes in their localities and rents on their own estates, whereas autonomous seigneurs and corporate bodies were held responsible for overdue taxes and left to fend for themselves in recovering lost rents (Bernard 1964). Thus, provincial elites found fiscal office to be both a lucrative investment and the way to prove and benefit from loyalty to the crown.

Under the threat of military terror, peasants were induced to pay taxes that increased absolutely and as a portion of agrarian production, doubling official income and raising rents on many estates as well in much of France in the decades after the Frondes (Dontenwill 1973; Jacquart 1974; Mireaux 1958; Venard 1957; Wood 1980). As Perry Anderson (1974) argues, the upward displacement of feudal military power into a complex of provincial forces commanded by envoys from the royal court did increase the absolute and relative surplus taken from the peasantry. However, that shift in the organization of military forces was caused most directly by a venal strategy directed by some fractions of the aristocracy toward gaining power and income at the expense of other elites. Seigneurs' decreasing ability to extract rent directly from their tenants, and their transformation into venal officials and financiers, were consequences of those earlier elite conflicts rather than of any increase in peasants' capacity for class struggle. The peasant rebellions of 1650–53 were precipitated by the breakdown of ruling class organization in the Frondes and exposed the untenable position of those aristocrats least tied to the central fiscal apparatus.

The increasing flow of revenues through the fiscal apparatuses directed by the intendants created new opportunities for aristocrats to find a source of income beyond the seigneural dues from their estates. Within the *pays d'élection,* the most lucrative posts were those of the receivers, who collected the direct taxes in each diocese. Receivers profited from their offices in two ways: first, by collecting a commission that ranged from 16.6 percent to 24.5 percent of the amounts collected and, second, by being allowed to hold the tax receipts until they were needed by the crown. Generally, half of the monies were sent to the king, whereas the other half was spent within the province. That second half remained in the receivers' hands for months or years, creating an interest-free "float" that receivers invested in their own businesses or loaned out for profit (Beik 1985, pp. 245–78; Chaussinand-Nogaret 1970; Dessert 1984).

The political dynamic set in motion by the expansion of the tax collection apparatus after the Frondes was quite different from that spawned by the creation of venal offices in the previous century. Venal offices were about authority; each new office encroached on the prerogatives of already entrenched seigneurs, officials, and corporate bodies. Although the first venal officials perceived the crown as their ally in struggles against the provincial blocs headed by magnates or against the urban oligarchies, venal officials quickly came to understand that the fiscal return to the crown from new offices was bought by undermining the political and financial value of their offices. Venality was about the division among members of the ruling class of political authority and the income rights tied to those feudal claims.

Venal officials sought to magnify the power and resources of their offices, and of the institutions within which their offices were embedded, by allying with more powerful patrons from above and by recruiting clients from below. Such patronage-clientage alliances acknowledged rather than challenged the central power of the king. The paucity of strategies open to aspiring politicians, and the zero-sum nature of conflicts among patrons and their clienteles, are indications of the long-term stalemate in elite relations in the century after the defeat of the Frondes.

Patrons needed to buy the support of clients since the lack of new offices and the inability to dislodge existing elites from their sinecures limited the rewards that kings, ministers, governors, or intendants could offer to lesser elites. When a patron failed to meet clients' expectations for offices or largess, then clients went shopping for new patrons.[33]

The post-Fronde political settlement overcame for a time the contradictions of venality. Existing offices were preserved, even as their capacity to defy royal decrees was lost when provincial elites lost their ability to coalesce into oppositional parties. The new competition for jobs as tax collectors had little to do with authority and privilege. All aristocrats were formally exempt from direct taxes, regardless of their official positions, and tax collection was carried out within parameters set down by the intendants after negotiation with, and intimidation of, provincial parlements and estates.

The crown had given vast patronage to great nobles in the sixteenth century in order to bind the provinces dominated by those nobles into the developing royal state. The factionalism of the Wars of Religion, which the crown had played to its benefit, escalated out of crown control in subsequent decades. "Great nobles of the sixteenth century were able to turn royal government into a hotbed of rival influences, creating political conflict and even civil war" (Kettering 1986, pp. 141–42).

The crown under Richelieu, and then Mazarin and Colbert, sought to undermine magnate power with two parallel strategies. One (discussed above) was the creation of intendants and new corps of venal officeholders to rival the old provincial institutions and blocs headed by magnates. The second strategy was to weaken the capacity of all political patrons to assemble vast clienteles. The institution of the permanent *paulette* in 1604 (the right to bequeath or sell venal offices in return for an annual tax payment to the crown on the value of the offices) sharply reduced the number of offices available to the crown and to magnates for patronage. Magnates never were able to create new avenues for patronage and were weakened permanently. The crown developed a new, fiscally based system of patronage through tax farms and loan syndicates. Fiscal maneuvers became central to the politics of the final century of the ancien régime.

Aristocrats no longer vied for fiscal authority after the Frondes. Instead, they bid for tax farms, the right to collect set taxes within a jurisdiction in return for advancing the crown the amount due to be collected from the taxes. Thus, the receivers' commissions, and their ability to float tax receipts, were actually interest on loans. In contradistinction to the pre-Fronde *élus,* who were given venal offices with the same authority as the older venal *trésoriers* in return for a one-time loan to the crown (Mousnier 1959), almost all tax farms after 1653 were granted for only one or two years at a time. Upon the expiration of the loan and the farm, the crown took new bids from incumbent or rival financiers for loans against the farm of the particular direct taxes of a diocese, election, or province.

Ironically, the crown's inability to liquidate its debts and pay back the tax farmers insured the stability of Louis XIV's fiscal system. Tax farms were, in their operation, pyramid schemes. The paper value of farmers' investments increased exponentially. However, the scheme participants, the tax farmers, could liquidate their positions only by selling their shares of a local, provincial, or national tax farm to another farmer eager to expand his investment or to a newcomer. The rising nominal value of the tax farms would crash if the demand by farmers seeking to cash in their investments exceeded the supply of new capital entering the system. Tax farmers as a whole had limited leverage because a refusal to reinvest their profits would cause state bankruptcy. At the same time, the crown could never find an alternative source of funds that would allow it to buy out the existing corps of tax farmers.

The crown was able to afford to pay tax farmers commissions ranging up to 25 percent because little of that amount was ever paid out. Instead, it was added to the crown's paper debt, and to tax farmers' paper assets (Harsin 1970). From another perspective, the crown could not afford to offer smaller commissions. During wartime, when the crown incurred an operating deficit, it needed to induce aristocrats and domestic and foreign merchants to invest their seigneurial income and profits from manufacture and trade in the state, as well as to retain the previous investments of tax farmers. Thus, tax commissions had to exceed the return on other investments, not only in France, but also abroad. Much of Louis XIV's debt was financed abroad, with French tax farmers serving as conduits for foreign investors in state debts. Indeed, the principal reason why France was able to fend off the combined forces of its English and continental enemies in the "Second Hundred Years Wars," the series of conflicts that continued almost unabated from 1672 to 1783, was the superior fundraising capacity of the tax-farm system (Chaussinand-Nogaret 1970; Mousnier 1984; Parker 1983). Indeed, during the last decades of the seventeenth century, total French royal revenues exceed that of all its enemies combined. Only in the 1780s did British state revenues approach those of France.[34]

A pyramid scheme cannot be sustained over the long term if investors seek to withdraw even a part of their money. Almost no individual farmers or foreign investors liquidated their shares in the financial syndicates. But, not all the profits from tax farms were reinvested. Tax farmers did spend part of the annual commissions they received on their tax-farm investments, to support their familial consumption. The French crown was able to avoid bankruptcy from 1653 to 1709 because it found new sources of real income large enough to hold tax farmers' capital and to support the rich lifestyles of the tax farm investors (Dessert 1984, pp. 160–61).

At first the crown realized an increase in direct taxes in the *pays d'élection;* however, the return from the taille stagnated after 1676. Further royal revenues came from two sources: first, from the *pays d'état* and towns that were no longer able to guard their autonomy and, second, from indirect taxes. The new forms and sources of revenue illuminate the changing structure of relations within the ruling class in the late seventeenth century.

The only corporate bodies that emerged from the Frondes without a significant loss of power were the estates in the *pays d'état.* They had not challenged crown authority, and, therefore, they retained their ancient rights. Further, their capacities to mobilize independent armed forces had not been bound up in the magnate clientage networks that had been broken apart in the Frondes. A number of autonomous towns also had stood apart from magnate parties and supported the crown, thereby escaping the political disorganization and royal retribution that followed the Frondes (Asher 1960; Beik 1985; Bordes 1972; Mousnier 1979).

Despite their success in maneuvering through the Frondes, the estates and urban governments lost many of their autonomous rights in the decades after the return of domestic peace in 1653. Those bodies lost out, not because they became weaker, but because the crown became stronger. Once the aristocrats and officials of the *pays d'élection* had been accommodated within the new fiscal and political structures headed by allied governors and intendants, the crown could challenge local and provincial privileges without sparking resistance from beyond that territory. As a result, intendants could increase fiscal demands on the estates of the *pays d'état* in the knowledge that resistance would remain localized and thus easily overcome by royal troops. Isolated provincial aristocrats shied away from challenging the crown under such conditions, and armed rebellion fe1 1 off drastically in the decades following the Frondes (Baxter 1976; Beik 1985; Bernard 1964).

A similar dynamic weakened urban autonomy, especially in those towns dominated by Protestants. The king and magnates had championed urban and Huguenot privileges as a way of denying one another military and fiscal control over particular regions. With the demise of provincial blocs, urban autonomy no longer served the interests of either the crown or aristocrats. Both sought to extend taxes in those areas to provide the fiscal base for new loans, new tax farms, and new commissions (Bonney 1978; Bordes 1972). The demise of religious competition also weakened the structural basis for clerical autonomy. Seigneurial control over benefices was regularized, allowing the crown to claim an enlarged share of clerical revenues (Blet 1972; Dent 1975).

Provincial estates and urban governments were transformed into tax farmers. The crown used its military power to compel those corporate bodies to advance loans. In return, the crown provided the military support for the estates and town governments to collect the higher taxes that would allow the new tax farmers to realize a return on their loans (Bordes 1972; Temple 1966). As in the *pays d'élection,* much of the tax farmers' profits from higher taxes in the *pays d'état* was reinvested in larger loans, allowing further taxes and compounding the farmers' commissions.

Indirect taxes provided the greatest source of new revenues for the crown in the century after the Frondes (Dessert 1984, pp. 161–66). Until the Frondes they had been a minor part of the royal budget. However, by 1725 they contributed a plurality of the crown's 204 million livres of revenues. In that year, the crown realized 99 million livres from indirect taxes on salt and tobacco and from customs duties and tolls, compared with 87.5 million livres from all the direct taxes. The crown's post-Fronde military hegemony had allowed it to extend indirect taxes to previously exempt regions. The lucrative commissions and high interest rates available to farmers of the indirect taxes created constituencies throughout France that gained from, and therefore supported, increased taxes (Matthews 1958, p. 81; Beaulieu 1903).

Reorganizing the Opposition

Tax farming joined the crown and the aristocrats who invested in and operated the farms in a common project of extracting a surplus through taxes. The stagnation of seigneurial revenues and dramatic rise of tax receipts in the century after the Frondes provides a material demonstration of Anderson's (1974, pp. 18–19) hypothesized "displacement of politico-legal coercion upwards. . . . Diluted at the village level, it became concentrated at the 'national' level."

If tax farming changed the nature of surplus extraction in seventeenth-century France, it did not do so, as Tilly (1981) claims, by creating a new corps of extractors. Instead, the existing aristocracy was reorganized on a national basis. Access to the surplus came to depend less on the familial inheritance of a fief, and more on membership in a financial syndicate. Yet it would be a mistake to view tax farmers as aristocrats in the process of becoming capitalists, as Wallerstein and at times Anderson claim. Financiers, by their investments in tax farms, merely purchased the right to a portion of a surplus extracted from the peasantry by force. The funds that financiers accumulated through their participation in tax farms were not transferable to other enterprises, because those funds existed neither as liquid capital nor as productive investments in surplus-producing enterprises. All the monies loaned to the crown and the profits from the farms were spent on military ventures at home or abroad or on consumption by the crown and its officeholders.

Individual financiers could quit a tax farm, provided their stake was small enough to be purchased by an outsider. However, almost all investment alternatives, in the embryonic capitalist sector or in loans to countries other than France, were less lucrative than the commissions earned by tax farming. There is no evidence of any financier ever voluntarily reducing or liquidating his position in a farm, and records testify to an unending stream of petitioners hoping to join the existing corps of tax farmers (Dessert 1984).

New investments in state loans were limited only by the political power of existing farmers, who shared an interest in preserving their control over the forms of feudal surplus extraction embodied in direct and indirect taxes. Although the crown and tax farmers shared a class interest in extracting as great a surplus as possible from peasants and from trade and manufacture, they were in competition with one another over the assignment of that surplus in the form of commissions and interest to the farmer-financiers and as loans and tax receipts for the crown and those officials authorized to spend revenues on the monarch's behalf.

With all the different factions and corporate bodies of feudal France incorporated within one or another tax farm, the crown was dependent on that class to extract the surplus. There was no other class with which the crown could ally. At the same time, the crown was concerned with preventing the reemergence of provincial blocs that could have demanded a higher return on, or greater control over, the local resources they extracted. The crown prevented intendants or governors from organizing such blocs by periodically reorganizing tax farms and transferring the intendants and financiers who organized those bodies to prevent them from joining with the local tax collectors into a party able to act on the national level.

The changing career paths of intendants illustrate the development of the crown's reorganizing strategy. In the first decades after the Fronde, most intendants spent the first decades of their careers in a single province before moving to the royal court and appointment to the Council of State. After Louis XIV's death in 1715, the majority of intendants served in several provinces, often for under a decade in each post, before achieving higher office in the royal councils. The promise of a final appointment to high court office ensured that intendants retained loyalty to the crown and did not seek to build personal bases in a province. That purpose was also furthered by choosing intendants from among the children of court officials who lacked ties to provincial families (Emmanuelli 1981, pp. 60–61 and passim.).

The differing tenures of intendants reflected their different political tasks in the seventeenth and eighteenth centuries. In the seventeenth century, the crown was concerned with undermining the privileges claimed by the estates, towns, and venal bodies of each province. Those claims could be countered only by building an alternative structure of interest in the tax farms. Seventeenth-century intendants often invited opponents of crown policy to buy into the tax farms. In the later period, however, once bodies of tax farmers were created within each province, the crown was concerned with preventing syndicate heads from becoming the loci of new provincial interests and opposition. Intendants were saved from the temptation of joining such a bloc by frequent transfers.

Intendants who served in several provinces were also able to aid the crown by integrating aristocrats into tax farms that spanned provincial lines. The crown used intendants to encourage the great financiers to bid on farms in other provinces. The great expansion of indirect taxes at the end of Louis XIV's reign and afterward provided new opportunities for financial alliances across provincial lines. The crown periodically reorganized the bundles of local units included within the farms of each direct and indirect tax. As a result, links between the national heads of syndicates located at the court and the aristocrats who manned the tax collection machinery in the localities were constantly disrupted (Dessert 1984; Matthews 1958).

The crown's reorganizing strategy, like its earlier venal strategy, was successful at disrupting provincial oppositional blocs. Yet, while the crown was able to outmaneuver its actual national political rivals in the pre-Fronde era and prevent the emergence of new opponents after the Frondes, it was unable to substantially reduce the major share of the surplus that remained in the hands of locally based venal officials and tax farmers. Just as the Frondes demonstrated the limits of crown control over local officials (at the same time revealing the impossibility of challenging the crown's national-level hegemony from a provincial base), the crown's inability to resolve the fiscal crises of the eighteenth century demonstrated that national officials and financiers were still a part of, and therefore dependent on, the locally based aristocrats engaged in direct surplus extraction.

The Limits of Eighteenth-Century Capital

The Wars of the League of Augsburg (1689–97) and of the Spanish Succession (1701–14) brought the French crown to the point of bankruptcy. Each year's deficit, induced by military expenses, was met with new loans from the tax farmer-financiers, thereby increasing the portion of tax receipts needed to meet the interest on loans. The crown's efforts to raise new revenues, both to meet annual expenses and to raise credit through new tax farms, were failures. Neither a capitation imposed in 1695, nor the *dixième,* established in 1710, raised significant revenues. The inability to raise taxes was due to a long-running agrarian depression that made it impossible for peasants to pay higher taxes without defaulting on their seigneurial rents.[35] Aristocrats had the power to ensure that they would not have to cover the crown's deficit, either by extending direct taxes to previously exempt noble income, or by giving priority to the collection of land taxes over seigneural rents (Dessert 1984, pp. 160–66; Bastier 1975; Jacquart 1974).

The crown's debt, which had stood at 170 million livres in 1648, rose to 413 million in 1707 and 600 million after Louis XIV's death in 1715 (Bosher 1970, pp. 13–15).

By 1709, the crown's obligations to pay venal salaries, tax farmers' commissions, and interest to the financiers so exceeded annual revenues that even taking into account the fact that most of those payments were reinvested in state debt, financiers were unable to see how they could realize a return on new loans and refused to finance the crown's debt in that year. The crown was forced into de facto bankruptcy (Dessert 1984, pp. 210–36).

The crown found short-term relief by attacking its politically weakest creditors. Three-quarters of the financiers were tried for fiscal irregularities and forced to pay fines and surrender much of their investments in state debt. The crown's previous annealing strategy had ensured that financiers were isolated from regional political networks and so could be eliminated without arousing provincial oppositions. The creditors slated for prosecution were those who lacked access to new sources of credit and, therefore, were only a sump for crown revenues. The sixty-one financiers who survived the purge of 1709–16 were spared, not because they enjoyed provincial political backing but because they were indispensable. That elite fourth of the financiers held 85.3 percent of the total value of tax farms by 1709 (Dessert 1984, pp. 210–36). Those financiers' share of the tax farms had increased in previous decades because they dominated access to French and European credit.

The liquidation of all but the greatest financiers narrowed the crown's subsequent room for maneuver. Unable to raise taxes, and with all current revenues claimed by venal officials and tax farmers, the crown was dependent on the sixty-one financiers' willingness to inject new capital into the system. However, those financiers had no reason to loan the crown more money unless they could increase their share of the annual revenues at the expense of entrenched provincial officials. In the face of that impasse, the regent who ruled during Louis XV's minority was attracted to an ingenious scheme devised by a Scottish financier, John Law. Law suggested that if venal officials' and tax collectors' investments in their offices could be severed from their control over revenue sources and converted into publicly traded debt, the crown could overcome the capital shortage.

The regent chartered Law's private bank in 1716 and converted it into the royal bank by buying all its shares in 1718 (Hamilton 1969, p. 145; Harsin 1970, pp. 277–78). The bank was granted the right to issue notes, which were given value by the regent's declaration that tax farmers were required to accept them as payment for taxes without discount. The regent granted Law a monopoly on all trade in Louisiana and Canada, as well as Paris rentes, to provide backing for the notes that Law had issued. The established financiers, who had opposed the establishment of Law's bank, sought to bankrupt it by presenting the notes they had collected through their tax farms to Law for conversion into gold. Law and the regent finessed that demand by debasing the gold content of the Louis d'or while maintaining the value of the notes by decree (Matthews 1958, pp. 62–65; Luthy 1959, 1:298–303).

Between 1718 and 1720, the crown transferred all tax farms, control over the remaining colonial monopolies, and the power to mint coins to Law's bank. Those income sources provided the backing for Law to convert all the notes already issued by his bank, as well as the face value of all French officials' investments in their offices, into shares in his bank. Venal officials and tax collectors initially acquiesced in Law's System because they retained their powers and continued to receive commissions on the revenues they collected for the crown. At first they profited because their investments in offices and their commissions on tax receipts were now denominated in shares from Law's bank that rose in value through February 1720 (Matthews 1958, pp. 65–69; Luthy 1959, 1:300–315).

Law's reforms benefited the crown and the small number of capitalists in France. The crown gained because Law devised a way to inflate the money supply, allowing the crown to generate its own credit, without having to depend on specie held or imported by the great financiers. Inflation, and the market in credit created by Law's public bank, caused a decline in real interest rates and made capital available to merchants and manufacturers. Law began to aid the free flow of goods within France and to eliminate some tax officials by consolidating and reducing internal tariffs and abolishing some minor taxes (Matthews 1958, pp. 68–69; Luthy 1959, 1:295–315).

The need to accommodate provincial officials, rather than the ineffectual opposition of politically isolated financiers, caused the collapse of Law's System in 1720. Law, like his predecessors the financiers, needed to maintain local officials' profits. However, once those officials' escalating profits and investments were converted into marketable securities in 1718, the inadequacy of the totality of state revenues, now funneled through Law's bank, to support all the local officials became apparent. The value of bank shares crashed in spring and summer 1720 (Matthews 1958, p. 69).

The collapse of Law's System illuminated the true balance of power in the last century of the ancien régime. Neither financiers, nor Law and the regent, were able to revoke provincial aristocrats' feudal claims, derived from offices and seigneuries, on state revenues. Even though bourgeois manufactures and merchants benefited from inflation, that inflation could not be sustained once provincial officials realized that the value of their offices and concessions was being undermined.

The Limits of State Extraction

Ironically, the crash of Law's bank was a financial boon to the crown. Because debt was denominated in bank shares, most state debt was wiped out in the crash, eliminating financiers' existing claims on state revenues. The continuing corps of provincial officials, however, retained their capacities to appropriate tax revenues through the Law years and after. The diminution of state obligations, combined with a long period of relative peace and low military expenses from 1714 until 1740, allowed the crown to establish a more secure fiscal foundation.

With the fall of Law's bank, taxes were once again paid in specie. Deflation created a new shortage of revenues and made the crown once again dependent on those financiers with access to large amounts of capital. In 1726, sixty tax farmers were institutionalized as one monolithic syndicate (Matthews 1958, pp. 70–76). The Company of General Farmers (CGF) assumed the same role as the corps of financiers in the pre-Law era. The one great advance in tax farmers' internal organization was the elimination of venality from their own ranks. No single farmer enjoyed rights to a particular portion of the tax farm. Instead their investment in the corporation gave them a proportional right to the returns generated by a bureaucratic staff hired to manage the farm. The actual tax collectors in each locality remained venal, and neither crown nor tax farmers gained any new control over those officials after 1726. Bureaucratic control was exerted only after the revenues, minus deducted commissions, had been collected in the central office of the tax farmers.

The CGF's bureaucratic internal organization frustrated crown attempts to gain leverage by annealing relations between local tax collectors and the tax farmers. The CGF faced the crown as a single unit, bargaining only over the interest rate and amount of the loan. The crown's leverage decreased further when it fought the Seven Years' War (1756–63). The crown's annual deficit mounted from 67 million livres in April 1756 to 118 million in 1759. Although the state declared partial bankruptcy in 1759, deficits continued to accumulate at 200 million livres a year for the remainder of the war. Simultaneously, France lost its colonies in India, Canada, West Africa, and the West Indies to England. French intervention in the American War of Independence compounded the deficit; by 1788 debt service to the CGF was absorbing half the state's annual revenues (Matthews 1958, pp. 222–27; Anderson 1974; Bosher 1970, pp. 23–24).

The CGF, like the financiers under Louis XIV, used the crown's periodic fiscal distress to demand high interest rates and to fend off efforts by the king's controller general to regulate its activities. All controllers general until Turgot in 1774–76 were given an interest in the CGF from which they received at least 50,000 livres annually. As a result, no controller general until Turgot used his power of countersignature to supervise the CGF.

As the overall profits of the CGF mounted, syndicate shares escalated beyond the resources of most bourgeois. The mere 223 general farmers who monopolized the CGF from 1726 to its end in 1791 were drawn from only 156 families, and the few bourgeois among the farmers increasingly intermarried with old nobility.[36] The CGF became "a peculiar class of rentiers which, in return for a guaranteed annual income, invested its entire wealth in the permanent government debt" (Matthews 1958, p. 249).

The tight organization of the CGF prevented the crown from taking advantage of the surge in tax revenues that accompanied the post-1750 expansion of French agriculture, commerce, and industry. From 1725 to 1788, indirect taxes rose from 99 million livres to 243.5 million; direct taxes from 87.5 million to 179.4 livres, and total royal revenues from 204 million to 460 million (Matthews 1958, p. 81). The rise in tax revenues benefited the aristocrats who held local offices as well as the CGF investors.

The additional revenues were raised by imposing new taxes on urban residents who had lost their autonomous rights and tax exemptions by the eighteenth century (Temple 1966; Bordes 1972), and by increasing the burden on the lands and incomes of peasants and investors in agriculture. The aristocracy's long-term transformation from seigneurs into state officials was reflected in the shrinking portion of agricultural land held as seigneurial domaines, and hence exempt from taxes. Thus, most of the lands bought by commercial investors were subject to taxes, even when those bourgeois gained noble status for themselves (Bastier 1975; Dontenwill 1973; Leon 1966; Le Roy Ladurie 1975; Saint-Jacob 1960).

Tax farmers and venal officials were the primary beneficiaries of rising tax revenues. From 1776 to 1787, direct and indirect taxes increased by 96 million livres, of which only 23 million were received by the treasury (Bosher 1970, p. 90). The remaining 73 million were retained by tax collectors as commissions. Office, rather than noble status or estate, had become virtually the only avenue to greater incomes in the late eighteenth century, as venal offices and especially tax farms became increasingly closed to new, bourgeois aspirants.

Tax collectors became so adept at identifying and making claim to increased peasant production that landlords' parallel efforts to reassert ancient rights to tenant dues faltered because tax agents had made prior claim to those revenues. Studies of the eighteenth-century "seigneurial reaction" demonstrate that landlords' grandiose claims yielded relatively minor revenues, and that the rising peasants' tax burden was the chief reason.[37] Similarly, the increase in tax revenues was barely slowed in regions with the strongest seigneurial reaction (Behrens 1963; Villain 1952).

Crown officials made various attempts to weaken the hold of venal officials and the CGF upon state revenues in the last decades of the ancien régime. The crown also sought without success to tap the income of clerics and their aristocratic sponsors (Tackett 1977; 1979). Such reforms would have benefited the bourgeoisie by allowing them to invest their assets in the state, or to engage in enterprises free from feudal extractions. Historians disagree over the role of bourgeois pressures in engendering those reforms.[38] What is beyond dispute is that until 1789 neither the bourgeoisie nor the crown had the power to institutionalize any reforms that threatened any but the most marginal powers of officials and tax farmers.

Turgot (1774–76) was the first controller general to use his power of countersignature to limit the autonomy of the CGF, and to refuse personal enrichment from company funds. He embarked on a variety of reforms designed to enlarge the crown's share of tax revenues by suppressing some venal and commissioned tax-collector offices, and to free some forms of trade and manufacture from venal pillaging—most notably by removing commercial transport from tax-farmer control and by deregulating the grain trade (Phytillis 1965, p. 12; Luthy 1959, 2:411). Turgot was dismissed before those plans could come to fruition. Controller General Necker (1777–81) revived Turgot's plan to place his own supervisory agents in the CGF, and then to extend their powers of audit and inspection to cover venal tax collectors. Both controllers general sought to suppress venal offices and force tax farmers into bureaucratic positions from which they could be controlled or dismissed by the crown (Bosher 1970, pp. 145–62).

Turgot's and Necker's reforms aroused massive opposition from the aristocracy. The Parisian and provincial parlements refused to register their edicts. Holders of sinecures at court and in the provinces united to force Necker's three successors to reverse all of the reforms and guarantee their privileges (Bosher 1970, pp. 180–81). A wave of officials who had "borrowed" royal funds were forced into bankruptcy when the crown demanded repayment during a cash crisis of 1787. Few venal offices were suppressed, even under the dire fiscal conditions in the two years before the Revolution. Turgot and Necker's inability to institute more than minor reforms exposed the sharp limits upon the crown and upon new elites in challenging the control of venal officials and tax collectors over state revenues. Elite conflict had little effect upon French social structure until it sparked and interacted with class struggles in the Revolution.

The Making of the French Revolution

The configuration of elite and class relations, and hence the consequences of urban and peasant rebellions, were quite different in 1789 than they had been at the time of the Frondes.[39] The "revolt of the aristocracy" of 1787–89 was like the Frondes in that it was a response to crown challenges of aristocratic privileges. The causes of aristocratic grievance, however, were different in the 1780s from what they had been in the seventeenth century. They concerned taxation and fiscal reform more than challenges to the authority of long-established venal offices. The drastic increase in royal debt, caused by France's intervention against Britain in the American Revolutionary War, created an insoluble state fiscal crisis. Efforts by Controller Generals Turgot and Necker to finance state debts by taxing the aristocracy and clergy caused implacable opposition by provincial elites.[40]

Provincial nobles incited popular riots against royal officials in 1788, forcing the crown to agree to call an Estates General in 1789 for the first time in more than a century (Soboul 1974, pp. 105–6). However, the popular forces unleashed by the aristocracy proved to be its undoing. When the Estates General were chosen, the largely conservative representatives of the clergy and aristocracy were foiled in their efforts to use the convention to regain power at the expense of the crown and great financiers. The Third Estate seized the initiative, meeting as a National Assembly and passing legislation guaranteeing state debt, and abolishing aristocratic and corporate privileges and most feudal obligations, while preserving private ownership of estates and tenancies. Those measures reflected the interests of the big financial capitalists and lawyers who held most of the state debts and of provincial bourgeois who were excluded from the most lucrative offices of the ancien régime and who profited from land holdings but not from the old aristocrats' feudal privileges.[41]

Most leading aristocrats and clerics rejected the new legislation and supported royal efforts to call troops to Paris to dismiss the National Assembly. Those royal efforts were blocked by the popular forces that had first mobilized to block real and imagined stratagems on the part of provincial aristocrats. The Great Fear of summer 1789 fatally undermined aristocratic control of the countryside, while revolts in provincial towns ended both aristocratic and royal authority in the provinces. Most critically, the Paris bourgeoisie mobilized "sansculottes" who took to the streets at key moments to counter the troops under royal control, forcing the crown to allow the National Assembly to remain in session (Lefebvre [1932] 1973; Soboul 1974, pp. 119–58).

The strategic unfoldings, though not the structural consequences, of the French Revolution were similar to those of the English Civil War. In both instances, the presence of mass forces in the capital, mobilized by a particular elite, led "rump" national legislatures to enact and implement legislation more radical than would have passed in the absence of mass action (Traugolt 1995; Brenner 1993, pp. 393–459 and passim; Soboul 1974). Popular forces both in France during the 1790s and in England in the 1640s were more effective at disabling the monarchs and their elite allies than at advancing their own interests. By contrast, the popular Frondes harmed the elite Frondeurs more than the crown, while also accomplishing little for the nonelite rebels.

Elites during both revolutions made momentary concessions to win popular support: In England, Parliamentarians gave commercial concessions and control over London city government to interloper merchants and their less wealthy shopkeeper and commercial allies. In France, the National Assembly ratified popular control over the Parisian government, supported popular coalitions in provincial cities, imposed price controls on food for the masses, and abolished agrarian feudalism even though peasants remained obligated to pay most land rents.

The ultimate elite victors of the revolutions in both countries moved to demobilize their nonelite allies once they were confident they had defeated the royalist forces. In France, the National Guard and army were firmly under elite control and so were easily used to suppress mass risings in 1794–95 and to implement the White Terror of 1795. In England, the independent New Model Army continued to set state policy on its own even after the execution of Charles I, being demobilized only with difficulty and at great expense in 1648. Again, the Frondes stand in strategic contrast to the two revolutions. Because elite Frondeurs were endangered more than the crown by the popular Frondes, aristocrats' armed forces joined the royal army in suppressing the popular Frondes.

The structural consequences of the French Revolution were dramatically different from the consequences of both the Frondes and the English Revolution. As discussed above, the English gentry's ownership of private property in land, and its control over county government to protect those property rights, was absolute and settled before 1640. The English Revolution was a successful gentry response to the crown and allied clergy's efforts to construct rival mechanisms of political domination and economic extraction in the provinces. While the gentry divided during the Civil War over an array of issues and in pursuit of personal advantages, at no point did either side in the Civil War threaten the organizational bases for economic exploitation and political domination by the landed elite. Parliamentarians, royalists, and neutrals retained their common organizational capacities and therefore, once Charles I was executed, regained a common interest in demobilizing and subordinating popular forces.

No single French elite of the seventeenth and eighteenth centuries matched the English gentry in its control over a distinct organization of political domination and economic extraction. However, by 1789 several small elites were able to achieve organizational capacities that were more threatened by the king and his noble and clerical allies than were aided by continuing subordination to the crown. Financiers, manufacturers, and some landowners came to share an interest in the defeat of the first two estates and the capacity to preserve their organizational integrity without royal support. The royalist elites in France, unlike Charles I's allies during the English Civil War, were so dependent upon the crown for recognition of their official bases of power and income that they could not survive the temporary victory of the popular revolution in any form. The "bourgeois" victors of the French Revolution created new state-based mechanisms of patronage and extraction for themselves.[42]

The new elites concretized their own organizational capacities through the revolutionary state in the early 1790s. The possibilities of a counterrevolution by the old elites of the ancien régime ended with the Republic's war victories in late 1793. The new elites then moved to demobilize popular forces in Paris and the provinces with the executions of Danton and the Indulgents, the drafting of sansculottes to the war front (removing them from Parisian politics), the subordination of popular organizations within the Jacobin Club, and the Terror in 1793–94. Those actions against popular forces proved fatal for the Jacobins of the National Assembly and of the Committee on Public Safety (personified by Robespierre) who could not call upon street forces to save them when they were marked for execution in the Thermidorian reaction of July 1794 and in the subsequent White Terror.[43]

The 1794 reaction, like the 1648 denouement of the English Civil War, killed *individual members of elites* who belonged to losing factions without disrupting the political and economic hegemony of *whole elites:* Hegemonies determined in England by elite conflict before the Revolution, in France by elite conflict during the Revolution. The consolidation of a new elite and class structure in England before the Revolution minimized the long-term effects of popular participation in that revolution and the Civil War. The heightened and unresolved elite conflict in France from 1787 to 1793 made mass revolutionary action critical to the outcome of elite and class conflict and thereby made the long-term consequences of the French Revolution far more significant than were those of the English Revolution and Civil War (not to mention the insignificant structural effects of the failed Frondes).

Internal Conflicts and Foreign Wars in State Formation

Elite conflict precipitated each of the mass mobilizations in early modern England and France. Nonelites mobilized in England and France only when and to the extent to which they were encouraged by elites who allied with them to advance their positions in elite conflicts. Elites were effective allies and helped to sustain mass action as long as the elite allied with popular forces remained unified and was able to command resources for an extended time.

The English and French Revolutions were instances when an elite both was threatened with extinction and had the resources to mobilize nonelite forces and so sustain revolutionary conflict over years. The French bourgeoisie used its alliance with peasants and sansculottes to realize a dominant position in the polity, subordinating their remaining rival elites and then, in the counterrevolution, their nonelite allies. The English gentry and allied London merchants constructed their revolutionary alliance to protect positions of dominance won in a century of elite conflicts beginning with the Henrician Reformation.

The states that emerged from the English and French Revolutions reconfirmed and enthroned, respectively, new structures of elite and class relations created by the long sequences of elite and class conflicts initiated by the Reformation. These conflicts were fought among elites and classes within each nation-in-formation. In other words, the processes of state formation in early modern England and France were determined primarily by internal factors. Domestic elite and class conflicts, not foreign wars or international economic opportunities, molded the two states' capacities and relations with civil society.

English and French elites disagreed over whether their nations should fight a war because elites differed in the benefits they derived from war and in the share of military costs they had to shoulder. The monarch or "state elite" was not always the militarist. Kings Charles I and Louis XIV were less eager to mount wars against their foreign enemies than were the majorities of the Parliament and National Assembly.

War making, as Charles Tilly teaches us, made increasing claims upon societal resources throughout early modern Europe. Resources were mobilized within city-states and nations-in-formation through mechanisms already determined by previous elite conflict. Those mechanisms changed only in response to further elite and class conflicts, not merely because of the inflation of military costs. Political entities whose internal relations created less capable institutions for mobilizing men and money for war were subject to conquest by stronger powers. In those cases, military defeat could propel a territory in a new direction of political development as a subunit of a state or empire. (Although, as revealed in the discussions of Florence in chapter 3 and the Netherlands in chapter 5, once elites became consolidated and conflict became subdued, structures of social relations were little changed as Florence and the Netherlands passed in and out of foreign control.) For the "winners" and survivors of European military contests, war had a highly limited effect upon elite and class relations, effects that were specific to and predictable from each country's social structure.

Similarly, opportunities for trade and colonial plunder were taken by already existing elites limited in their strategic opportunities abroad as at home by their positions within domestic social relations. In neither England nor France were merchants or colonists decisive actors in elite or class conflicts. Indeed, as we will see in the next chapter, the development of foreign trade and conquest in early modern Europe were determined by the preexisting, and still primarily agrarian, structure of elite relations in each country. Only in the nineteenth and twentieth centuries did transnational markets come to have an independent effect upon social relations in the leading capitalist nations.

5

A Dead End and a Detour

Spain and the Netherlands

S PAIN AND THE NETHERLANDS CHARTED paths of political and economic development different from those of England and France. Britain and France, even while they became the most powerful nations of Europe economically and militarily in the seventeenth century, were latecomers to imperialism. Britain and France benefited from and were affected by their colonies only marginally before the late seventeenth century, while Spain in the sixteenth century and then the Netherlands in the seventeenth century sustained great power status within Europe and were enriched by their non-European holdings.[1]

This chapter begins by asking why empires in general, and the Spanish Habsburg empire in particular, did not become the locus of capitalist development in early modern Europe. Why was the Habsburg imperial elite unable to sustain control over the subordinate elites of non-Castilian Iberia, Italy, the Low Countries, and the Americas?[2] As I answer those questions, I hope to explain why empires were weaker, politically and militarily, as well as economically, than the emerging states of Britain, France, and the Netherlands.

Spain in the sixteenth and seventeenth centuries was not a nation-state; instead, it was a collection of monarchies encompassing present-day Spain, other European territories, and American colonies. Elite relations in such an empire were transnational.[3] War sometimes incorporated regional and foreign elites within a Spanish polity and at other times allowed certain elites to gain autonomy or independence from a social system centered on Madrid.

The Spanish economy benefited from colonial plunder to an extent unmatched by any other European entity in the sixteenth or seventeenth century. Yet, by 1557 the Spanish state was bankrupt. Although Spain and its Habsburg rulers remained a leading European power for another century, and Spain the dominant power in the Americas well into the eighteenth century, this greatest European empire since Rome was outmaneuvered militarily and bled economically by smaller polities.

The first beneficiary of Spain's weakness was the Netherlands. We must ask: How did the dynamics of elite conflict differ within empires such as Spain's from the

English and French trajectories of elite consolidation? Did war and American treasure open possibilities for elite conflict and paths of state formation unavailable within the more isolated English or French social systems?

The Netherlands escaped in stages from the Spanish polity to become the leading trade entrepôt and Asian colonial power of the seventeenth century. The Netherlands' peculiar position within a decaying empire created a unique nonfeudal social structure. Each Dutch elite constructed its own statelike institutions that were only partially restrained by their nominal positions within the Dutch Republic. Various Dutch elites enjoyed the institutional bases to pursue their own foreign military and mercantile policies. One elite, the Amsterdam merchants, did so with great success in the seventeenth century, using profits from European trade, manufacture, and an Asian empire to deploy a military force capable of defending its interests in Europe and beyond. We must ask: Was the fate of Holland as a great power, and of its ruling elite's political and economic position, determined more by international trade and armed warfare than by domestic elite and class conflicts? Was the rigidity of elite relations in the Netherlands responsible for the Dutch Republic's inability to counter Britain's commercial and military challenges in Europe and Asia in the late seventeenth and eighteenth centuries?

This chapter presents the outlines of answers to these questions about Spain and the Netherlands.[4] In so doing I can address the saliency of elite conflict as a determining force in two polities far different from the central comparison of English and French state formation in chapter 3. We will then be able to address the continuing debate over the relative causal roles of domestic social relations as opposed to international geopolitics and the movements of the capitalist world system in the formation of the British, French, Spanish, and Dutch polities.

Spain

Spain could be described as rich in both coercion and capital. Its rulers controlled the largest expanse of territories in Europe, save for Russia. Once it conquered colonies in the Americas, the Spanish crown realized more revenues than any other institution in Europe. Spanish revenues increased 500 percent from 1504 to 1577. By the 1560s Castile had surpassed France to become the richest crown in Europe, a position it held until 1620 when France regained first place.[5] Despite its geopolitical and financial resources, Spain was overwhelmed militarily by rivals with fewer armed forces. Its wealth did not spur capitalist or any other sort of economic development. Why?

Imperial Formation and Spanish Elite Conflict

The Reformation, or more accurately the almost total lack thereof, provides a starting point for understanding Spain. The stasis of Spanish elite relations never was disrupted by Reformation. The opportunities created by American conquests and by the influx of gold and silver combined to preserve rather than transform the structure of elite and class relations forged in the Christian "reconquest" of Spain from Muslims.

"Spain" was a conglomeration of several kingdoms, which in turn were built up over centuries through the reconquest of lands held by Muslims. Immanuel Wallerstein, quoting Jose Maravell, observes that "because Spain was built on a reconquest, feudalism as a political form was weak.' [This weakness] provided favorable terrain for the development of 'state' forms'" (1974, pp. 166–67). Wallerstein and Maravell are correct that the Castilian aristocracy, unlike the aristocracies of the other kingdoms incorporated within the Spanish empire, had at best weak representative bodies to voice their interests before the crown. Feudalism, however, assumed a variety of forms across Europe.

The Castilian aristocracy was led by the relatively few great families of grandees (*caballeros* and *titulos*) who were linked to one another by marriage, business, and patronage ties.[6] Castilian aristocrats had common interests in preserving their judicial powers over peasants and lands, their exemptions from royal taxes, and their control over military and civil offices and the revenues and opportunities for graft that accompanied those positions.[7]

Castilian aristocrats provided the armed forces needed to reconquor Muslim Spain and were rewarded with the lion's share of the lands seized in the centuries-long struggle (Lynch 1991, pp 1–26). "Since the late Middle Ages, successive Castilian kings and queens had coaxed the nobility away from rebellion by giving it effective control over the internal economy and local politics of Castile" (Phillips 1979, p. 77). Crown efforts to limit aristocratic authority with corps of bourgeois officials sparked the fourteenth-century Castilian Civil War. The king was killed and replaced by his half brother, who returned high state and clerical offices to the aristocratic families that claimed those posts. The new king also revoked towns' autonomous rights in the aftermath of the Civil War. Aristocrats thus regained control over those towns that had sided with the monarchy in the Civil War.

The Castilian crown next attempted to check aristocrats' power by supporting peasant demands during the spate of uprisings from 1460 to 1472. Aristocrats crushed all the uprisings. While peasants won minimal concessions, the crown made no advances in limiting aristocratic privileges in the course of the uprisings (Payne 1973, pp. 141–69).

King Ferdinand and Queen Isabella and their Habsburg successors were highly realistic in their appraisals of aristocratic power. They did not provoke further uprisings in Castile. As they moved to incorporate other kingdoms within an imperial monarchy, these monarchs did so by preserving all the privileges of the incumbent nobilities. The kingdom of Aragon, which itself was a combination of Aragon, Catalonia, and Valencia, and later Portugal were brought into the Iberian empire not by conquest but instead through accords between the Castilian monarch and the aristocracies of each of those kingdoms. Aragonese and Portuguese nobles recognized the Castilian monarch's right to wear plural crowns in return for royal recognition of the aristocracies' broadest claims of ancient rights to tax exemptions, local judicial authority, and power for their representative bodies to veto royal initiatives (Bush 1967, pp. 48–58; Kamen 1991, pp. 17–32; Lynch 1991, pp. 67–68 and passim; 1992, pp. 17–52; Payne 1973, vol. 1; Vilar 1962, vol. 1).[8]

The Spanish crown challenged the power of the clergy and succeeded in claiming a growing share of clerical tithes and in appropriating much of the church's property.

Crown appropriations of clerical powers and properties began during the Castilian Civil War and continued in the following centuries. The crown was able to weaken the church for two reasons. First, clerics lost land and tithe rights when they backed losing parties in the fourteenth-century civil war. Second, the pope granted the crown the power to appoint all Spanish bishops and the right to receive a growing share of clerical revenues in recognition first of Ferdinand and Isabella's reconquest of Spain, then of their successors' vigor in combating Protestants, Jews, and Muslims through warfare and through the Inquisition, and finally of the crown's efforts to convert heathens in the Americas (Bush 1967, pp. 44–48, 58–61; Lynch 1991, pp 1–26, 342–85; Payne 1973, pp. 205–6).[9]

The Spanish Church became, after the Castilian peasantry, the largest source of crown revenues in the seventeenth century. Averaging revenues from 1621 through 1640, Castilian taxes (which fell almost exclusively on peasants and laborers) yielded 38% of crown revenues, followed by 15.6% from the Spanish Church, and only 10.7% from American bullion (Kamen 1991, p. 218).[10] The crown's clerical revenues came, however, at a political cost. As the crown weakened, the clerical elite it lost a potential counterweight to the great nobles. Much like the English crown following the Henrician Reformation, Spanish monarchs found they lacked non-noble allies with either the administrative capacity or the local political authority to reap the full benefits of clerical lands and tithes for the crown. Much clerical land was leased to nobles on favorable terms, with corrupt payments passing between nobles and clerics who often were related to one another (Lynch 1992, pp. 348–82; Phillips 1979, p. 110).

The Castilian Cortes is a clear barometer of elite relations and of the crown's perpetual inability to gain leverage over the great aristocrats in the core territory of the Habsburg empire. The aristocracy and clergy defected from the Cortes in 1538 because those two elites were so secure in their privileges that they had no need of a representative institution to protect their tax exemptions and declined to gather as a body that would give the crown a target to ask for fiscal grants.[11]

The Cortes remained the forum at which the crown received tax revenues and loans from towns in return for continued liberties.[12] The crown was so weak, even within Castile, that it found it increasingly difficult to impose taxes on towns through the Cortes from the late sixteenth century until its abolition by the crown in 1665. The crown therefore allowed the aristocracy, the only elite capable of breaking the urban bourgeois, to gain majorities, and in some towns monopolies, of municipal offices during the sixteenth and early seventeenth centuries (Bush 1983, p. 87). At the end of that process, most Castilian towns were ruled by coalitions of nobles and rich commoners formalized under systems of *mitad de oficios,* which divided the spoils of office and ensured unity between the two elites against revenue demands from the crown and ensured the subjugation of nonelites within the towns (Lynch 1992, pp. 348–82).

Charles V and his successors extended to their dominions in Italy and then throughout the Holy Roman Empire the Iberian strategy of guaranteeing local privileges and offering fiscal concessions and patronage in return for aristocratic recognition of the Habsburgs' multiple crowns. The Habsburgs made so many concessions to the princes, aristocracies, and autonomous towns that they "ruled" as Holy Roman emperors (Bush 1967, pp. 345–49) that those territories yielded virtually no revenue to their nominal imperial ruler (Kamen 1969; 1991, p. 218).

The Ends of Empire: The Americas

A few decades after they "discovered" and looted the Caribbean, the Spanish colonialists organized themselves into colonial oligarchies capable of financing and mounting the conquest of Mexico and later of Peru. The conquistadors depended on the Spanish crown mainly to adjudicate among their competing claims to American lands, natives, and offices. The conquistadors and their patrimonial heirs shared the treasure they extracted from American mines with their sovereign in Madrid in return for royal recognition of their titles over vast tracts of land and their dominion over multitudes of Indians. Spanish-American elites became less dependent upon their sovereign's imprimatur once they resolved their conflicts and congealed into stable oligarchies over the course of the sixteenth and seventeenth centuries. At the same time, Spain became increasingly unable to secure American coastlines and Atlantic shipping routes against pirates or rival European powers (Lynch 1991, pp. 386–428), and as a result the metropole's commercial hold over their American settlers diminished. With the loss of both political and economic control came a decline in the crown's share of American treasure.

Schoolbook stories about Queen Isabella pawning her jewels to pay for Columbus's journey in 1492 mask the true source of funds for American exploration and conquest.

> Resources for conquest and settlement came, for the most part, from private individuals. . . . The crown and its officials had met some of the small cost of Columbus's first voyage, but merchants and nobles flocked to lend support to his much larger second expedition of 1493, and they provided the funds for all later ventures. Partnerships of merchants, nobles and soldiers competed for royal licenses to explore and to organize new settlements, guaranteeing shares of their gains to the crown. Capital to provide the ships and their stores, and the colonists' armament, was raised in Spain itself for the early expeditions, but by 1506 a few of the colonists had accumulated sufficient fortunes from the gold of Espanola to mount the conquests of Cuba, Jamaica and Puerto Rico. . . . The series of expeditions after 1516 which culminated in Cortes's conquest of Mexico were backed by Cuban resources; and the wealth of Mexico paid for the northward and southward extension of exploration and gave some backing to the conquest of Peru. The net investment of Spanish resources in the New World itself, therefore, was significant only in the first fifteen years after Columbus's arrival (Davis 1973, pp. 39–40).

The crown rewarded New World explorers and conquerors, and adjudicated among their competing claims, by awarding *encomiendas*. An *encomienda* was a grant over the Indians in a territory. The holder of the *encomienda* got the right to the forced labor of the Indians within the territory of the grant as well as to any gold and silver already held by the natives or which the natives could be compelled to mine for their overlord. (The *encomienda* holder also was supposed to see to the Indians' conversion to Christianity.)[13]

Charles V and his ministers realized within two decades of the conquests of Mexico and Peru that Ferdinand and Isabella, and then Charles himself, had given away the store in granting *encomiendas* to the colonists. Holders of the grants quickly drafted the natives under their control to find treasure. The rigors of mining combined with the introduction of European diseases to wipe out the Indian populations on the Caribbean islands conquered by the Spanish and then to kill off over 80 percent of the Indian population of Mexico (Davis 1973, p. 54). Charles V, perhaps prodded by his clerical retainers, seems to have became disturbed at the deaths of so many heathens before they could be converted to Christianity. But he exhibited far more distress over his meager 26 percent share of American treasure shipped back to Spain.

Charles V sought to solve both problems in the 1540s by narrowing the privileges granted to colonists. *Encomiendas* were made to expire upon their holder's death. Charles V transferred control over Indian labor from the holders of *encomiendas* to state officials.

The crown should have been the main beneficiary of treasure mined from the vast new deposits discovered at Potosi, Peru, in 1545 and at Zacatecas, northern Mexico, in 1546. While the crown now had formal control over Indian labor, Charles V's representatives in Mexico and Peru remained totally dependent upon the settler oligarchy for the resources necessary to work the new mines because the Spanish crown remained mired in a permanent fiscal crisis. Just as Ferdinand and Isabella had to rely upon private capital to explore and conquer America (and then reward the financiers and conquistadors with *encomiendas*), so too bankrupt Charles V had to call upon American capital to open and operate the new Mexican and Peruvian mines. Charles V's successors also were dependent upon capital from the colonial oligarchy to mine the deposits discovered in Mexico in the 1670s.

Capital trumped control over corvée labor in the mines of Mexico and Peru. The great mines of the 1540s and 1670s, as well as the lesser mines discovered in between, all were controlled by the American financiers who paid for the mining equipment (and for the German technicians who immigrated to Mexico and Peru to set up and operated the pumping and crushing machines). Silver was extracted from low-grade ores using the mercury amalgamation process. The two largest known deposits of mercury were in Spain; American mine owners quickly gained control over Spanish mercury production. State officials became glorified press gangs and crew bosses for the mine owners, supplying masses of Indian laborers who were trained and provisioned at the mines (Davis 1973, pp. 50–53).

Ferdinand and Isabella's decisions to grant *encomiendas* and thereby create an American oligarchy would not have been irredeemable if their royal successors had had the resources to finance new mines on their own, or even to create and reward an independent corps of officials in America. The crown never was able to generate a surplus large enough to pay the huge start-up costs of new mines and certainly could not weather the frequent losses that mine owners incurred when the amount of silver or gold that could be extracted with existing technology fell off. Thus, the bankrupt Spanish crown had to surrender the lion's share of American treasure to the only elite willing and able to finance the great mining enterprises in Mexico and Peru.

The crown received between 25 percent and 30 percent of the gold and silver mined and stolen in America from the start of significant treasure imports in 1503 until 1580. The crown's share fell with the vast increase in mining output after 1580, dropping to the 15% range, and then catastrophically (for the crown) to 10% or less after 1615. For the five years from 1656 to 1660, the crown received 600,000 pesos of treasure out of 5.216 billion produced. The crown's share of American gold and silver amounted to 4% of royal income in 1510, rose to 7.5% in 1577, and then to a peak of 16% of receipts in 1591. The crown's take then declined to an average of 6% of income for 1621–40 and fell to an insignificant 1% for 1656–60.[14] American elites took advantage of the Habsburgs' weakness and preoccupation during the Thirty Years' War against the Netherlands, France, and Britain (and at the end of the war with the revolt of Portugal) to withhold an ever greater share of declining bullion production, sealing Spain's doom in its fight to retain its European empire.

Would it have been possible for Spanish monarchs to have undermined the American oligarchs by offering competing mining concessions or land grants to rival elites in Europe? Charles V and his successors laid the basis for such a strategy by granting the merchants of Seville a monopoly on trade with the Americas (Davis 1973, pp. 62–63). As long as the crown maintained control over the military and merchant fleets sailing to America, it could have used its naval hegemony to concentrate all the advantages of transatlantic trade on a merchant elite in Seville. Then most of the profits from American mines and plantations would have accrued to Seville, leaving the American oligarchs in a perpetual state of underdevelopment and dependence on Spain for finished goods and mining and farming equipment. American oligarchs never would have generated the surplus to develop and operate the new mines. Instead, the Seville merchants would have been the nexus of Spanish-American wealth much as London merchants were the primary beneficiaries of British-American colonial settlements. A powerful commercial elite in Seville could have been a counterweight to the entrenched rural nobility of Spain, allowing the crown to play off competing elites against one another as French kings were able to do so ably.

The Seville merchant elite never became a major political or economic force within Spain. The crown lost the dual opportunities to subordinate American settlers to a metropolitan commercial elite and to create a counterweight to the rural aristocracy. Seville's trade monopoly did not foster much industry within Spain because land and labor remained locked in feudal relations of production under aristocratic control.[15] Seville became nothing more than an entrepôt, sending American gold and silver onto the real centers of European production (mainly to France and the Netherlands and later to England) and receiving manufactured goods (and even French agricultural products) for shipment onto Spanish America (Davis 1973, pp. 143–56; Kamen 1978; Wallerstein 1974, pp. 187–99).

American treasure, in the absence of opportunities for productive investment, stimulated inflation within Spain that further reduced the possibilities for constructing domestic manufactures that could compete with the cheaper products of established industries in the relatively low-inflation economies of France, the Low Countries, or Britain. The Spanish crown, under constant fiscal duress and without the immediate possibility of profiting from new domestic industries, milked transatlantic trade as a cash cow.[16]

American settlers responded to high taxes and the dearth of Spanish manufactured goods and the dearth of Spanish entrepreneurs with either the capital or the know-how to become partners in American ventures by fostering direct commercial relations with their real trading partners in Europe and by building domestic industries to meet the settlers' needs for agricultural and manufactured goods. The 1630s were the turning point. Silver shipments to Spain through official channels dropped off abruptly along with trade. Dutch and British piracy disrupted official convoys, while merchants from those nations became ever more aggressive at undercutting the official markets of Seville. By 1686, only 5.5% of Spanish American trade was with Spain (and an additional 17% with Genoa, compared to 39% with France, and the remaining 37.5% with Britain, the Low Countries, and Hamburg (Lynch 1989, p. 20).

Spanish-American commercial separation from the mother country was matched by Mexican and Peruvian political autonomy from Madrid. The share of Mexican state revenue shipped to Madrid or to the new colony in the Philippines fell from 55% in 1611–20 to 21% by 1691–1700 (TePaske and Klein 1981, p. 133). In Peru, state revenues declined 47% from 1650 to 1700, and remittances to Spain fell 79% (Lynch 1989, p. 13). Spanish colonialism became a significantly lighter burden on Mexico and Peru in the course of the seventeenth century.

Seville's own merchants were rapidly displaced as managers and beneficiaries of the entrepôt's American trade by Genoese who outclassed their Spanish competitors in their access to capital and their commercial connections to markets throughout Europe. The Habsburgs welcomed the Genoese since they had a far greater capacity to buy state debt than did the hapless Spanish merchants of Seville (Muto 1995). The political and financial benefits of servicing crown debts then accrued to the Genoese, further retarding the Seville merchant's development as a national elite.

Seville merchants were blocked at every turn by the rigidity of Spanish elite and class relations. They were unable to mobilize the factors of production and the political power necessary to take advantage of the opportunities to spur manufacture opened by American treasure and American markets. The Seville merchants gained neither financial nor political leverage over the imperial government or any measure of control over American oligarchs and the colonial governments, The weakness of the Seville merchant elite, which could have acquired the wealth and power of the aristocracy and clergy through real hegemony over Spanish-American markets, extinguished the Habsburgs' last opportunity to foster political realignment within Spain.

Fiscal Limits and Imperial Decline

The Netherlands were the only exception to the Habsburg policy of accommodation. The particular pattern of elite relations across the Netherlands, combined with Spanish fanaticism in challenging Dutch Protestantism, made the Low Countries an unusually inviting target for Habsburg efforts to impose imperial rule and extract resources. The Spanish were fought to a stalemate and eventually forced to recognize Dutch independence, despite the Habsburgs' willingness to apply tactics of mass terror against the civilian population of the Netherlands.

The Spanish were defeated primarily by fiscal rather than by military factors. The trade-offs made by Castilian monarchs, and later by the Habsburg emperors, to win aristocratic and clerical support for their regimes restricted their governments' abilities to raise revenues as severely as if full-blown political feudalism had survived in Spain.

The total revenues received by the Spanish crown between 1504 and 1718 rose 843 percent from 1504 to their peak in the period 1641–60.[17] They then declined rapidly in the subsequent two decades, falling by a third from the peak in the 1650s

TABLE 5.1. Spanish Crown Revenues, 1504–1718

Years	Revenue in British Pounds (×1,000)
1504	558
1565	2,154
1577	3,346
1588	3,654
1607	4,808
1621–40 average	4,500
1641–60 average	5,263
1674	3,485
1703–1704 average	1,076
1705–1707 average	1,879
1707–1709 average	2,106
1709–1711 average	2,364
1711–13 average	1,560
1713–16 average	3,152
1717–18 average	3,273

Sources: Data sources for the sixteenth and seventeenth centuries and bases for the conversion of ducats into British pounds are given in table 5.4. Data for the eighteenth century are from Kamen 1969, p. 228.

TABLE 5.2. Changes in State Revenues for Britain, France, Spain, the Netherlands and Spain, 1515–1790s

	% Change in Revenue			
Years	Britain	France	Netherlands	Spain
1515 to 1600s	+371	+35		+762
1600s to 1670s	+175	+274	+476	−28
1670s to 1790s	+2287	+111	−38	−6

Sources: Data sources are given in table 5.4. The dates of comparison for Britain are 1502–1505 to 1604–1613; 1604–1613 to 1672–85; and 1672–85 to 1795. For France the dates of comparison are 1515–47 to 1600–1609; 1600–1609 to 1670–79, and 1670–79 to 1780–19. The Netherlands did not exist in 1515, so there is no basis for the first comparison. The other comparisons are of 1600–1609 to 1675, and 1675 to 1794. For Spain the dates of comparison are 1504 to 1607, 1607 to 1674, and 1674 to 1718.

to 1674. The crown's fiscal position never recovered. Revenues declined further. Revenues in 1718 still were 6 percent below the level of 1674 (see table 5.1).

The Habsburg empire was unique in early modern Europe in that it experienced an absolute as well as a relative decline in fiscal strength.[18] Spain's decline was compounded by the fact that the centuries of its decline coincided with dramatic absolute increases in French state resources, and especially in Dutch and British governmental revenues (see table 5.2).

The Netherlands' exponential rise in revenues combined with Spain's absolute decline in income to allow the Dutch to close most of the gap in revenues with their former ruler. The Dutch Republic's revenues rose from 8 percent of Spain's in the

1580s to 18 percent in the 1600s and to 44 percent in the 1630s and 143 percent in the 1670s.[19] Spain's shrinking revenues had to be spread thinner than the Netherlands's growing resources. The Habsburgs needed to pay for armies and navies to guard possessions in Iberia, the Mediterranean, Italy, Germany, the Low Countries, the Atlantic, and the Americas, while the Netherlands needed to field armed forces only at home, in the Atlantic, Brazil, and Asia.[20] Although the Netherlands was involved in repeated wars from 1567 until 1748, it fought only one war at a time. (The single exception to that was 1645–47, when the Dutch fought both the Spanish in Europe and the Portuguese in Brazil. The Dutch quickly lost Brazil to its lesser rival and could not mount an expedition to reclaim the colony at the same time that it was at war with Spain. By the time peace came in Europe, Brazil was irretrievably lost.)

Spain, by contrast, was often involved in multiple wars against its French, British, German, and Ottoman rivals at the same time that it sought to subdue the rebellious Dutch. Thus, it becomes easy to explain the outcomes of the Spanish-Dutch wars. Spain quickly defeated the Dutch resistance when it sent a large army in 1567. The Dutch were able to mount only raids and piratical naval attacks against the Spanish in the following years. However, countering even such a low-intensity war, when added to the other costs of empire, pushed Spain to the fiscal brink. Spain became increasingly unable to pay or provision its troops in the Netherlands. The Spanish crown was forced into de facto bankruptcy, and its army in the Netherlands disintegrated, after a single Dutch victory in full-scale warfare: the breaking of the Spanish siege of Leiden in 1574. A combatant with greater resources would have been able to reprovision and reinforce its army and thus fight on. Bankrupt Spain could not do so after 1574.

The Dutch gained ultimate security over their territories in the 1590s because Spain decided to shift troops from the Netherlands to intervene in France in a futile effort to keep Protestant Henry IV off the French throne. The Dutch won security from Spanish attack because the declining Habsburg empire could not fight both wars at once. Spain finally recognized Dutch independence when the Habsburgs were forced by financial bankruptcy and the overwhelming fiscal and demographic advantages of Britain and France to conclude the treaties ending the Thirty and Eighty Years' Wars. Those 1648 treaties also marked the end of Habsburg pretensions to empire within Europe. One branch of the family was confined to the ever more meaningless crown of Holy Roman emperor and to rule of an Austrian Empire that was becoming as peripheral militarily as it had always been economically. The Spanish Habsburgs were confined to Spain and its American colonies.

Class Relations and Economic Stagnation in the Spanish Empire

Spain's process of imperial formation molded the structure of elite and class relations within each imperial unit as well as in the empire as a whole and determined Spain's economic peripheralization, fiscal stagnation, and geopolitical decline. We have seen that in each Spanish province, and in both the European and American components of empire, the Habsburgs gained acquiescence for their claims by favoring a single elite. That elite, in most parts of the empire, was an aristocracy that used its royal

backing to sustain or intensify feudal exploitation of peasants and to sap urban bour-
geoisies of their political autonomy and block opportunities for productive capital investment. Throughout Spain the favored elite collaborated with the crown to loot the
church financially, even while indulging the papacy and the most reactionary elements
of Catholicism in their desires to enforce religious orthodoxy on Protestants and non-
Christians.

Spain's imperial ambitions retarded agrarian economic development as much as
it stymied industrial and commercial expansion. The aristocracies of Castile and of
most other Spanish provinces enjoyed even greater control over land and over peasant labor than did the British gentry. Yet, Spanish landlords did not use their local political hegemony to transform agrarian relations of production in the same way as the
English gentry. Spanish grandees were able to sustain feudal modes of exploitation
because their control over land and rights to collect rents from peasant farmers never
were challenged by rival elites. Capitalist agriculture, the foundation of economic development in Britain, did not come to Spain because Spanish landlords never had to
revise their land tenure arrangements to fend off challenges from peasants or from
rival elites.

The Habsburgs were thrown into perpetual fiscal crisis by their multinational
crowns and the several armies and navies needed to defend their various sovereign
claims from revolt and from Great Power attack across Europe and in the Americas.
As a result, the Habsburgs were continually constructing ad hoc deals for cash infusions with financiers across Europe and therefore never were able to privilege a single
merchant elite and thereby reap the fiscal benefits of a rapidly developing commercial or industrial center. Thus, even in northern Italy, where they were allied with urban
oligarchies rather than rural aristocracies, the Habsburgs were limited in the markets
and territories they could bestow on the Italian bourgeoisie. Much of Habsburg territory became economic hinterlands for the French, Dutch, or British who could undercut the Italians, ensuring that the Genoese would become a sink rather than a
source of Spanish wealth.

The lack of a privileged and therefore loyal nonaristocratic elite left the Habsburgs with no room for maneuver against any aristocratic oligarchy within Spain or
in the Americas. The Dutch perhaps could have become such an elite for the Habsburg empire. However, the Habsburgs' heavy dependence upon papal support, and upon
the Spanish clerical resources freed for the crown by that support, made it impossible for the Spanish to make even the minimal concessions necessary to fend off
Dutch revolt.

The structural bases of the Habsburg empire left no room for any imperial initiatives but enormous grants of local autonomy to unified provincial aristocracies in
return for the mere recognition of Habsburg sovereignty. Each attempt at constructing a different, more financially lucrative or more politically malleable arrangement
was blocked by the complex of existing relations among crown, local aristocracy, and
transnational Roman Catholic Church. Spain never could concentrate power over its
empire in a single elite, and therefore the wealth of empire never flowed to a single
site. Thus, the Habsburgs had no mechanism to tap the riches of their dominions to
meet the costs of empire or to encourage capitalist accumulation and development.

The Netherlands

The Netherlands of the seventeenth century, like the Italian city-states in the centuries of the Renaissance before that, became the dominant commercial center of Europe. In addition, the Dutch Republic was a major military force in continental Europe and through its chartered United East Indies Company (*Vereenigde Ooost-Indische Compagnie;* hereafter VOC) was the hegemonic colonial power in Asia.

Giovanni Arrighi (1994) aptly summarizes the bases of Dutch commercial hegemony in seventeenth-century Europe.[21] Taking advantage of an opening in the world system left by the decline of the Spanish empire and with it of Genoese financial hegemony, the Dutch developed a strategy and built the organizations that were suited to their location "in the place and at the time that were both just right in catch 'the wind actually blowing'" (p. 133). First, the Dutch centralized in Amsterdam warehouses the major supplies of key commodities, allowing merchants to release limited amounts of each commodity upon markets in ways controlled to maximize profits. Second, Dutch businessmen made Amsterdam the financial as well as commercial center of the European world system when they developed the Amsterdam Bourse, the first and for several key decades the only permanent stock exchange. Third, and most crucially to sustain the first two initiatives, the Dutch created joint-stock companies "with exclusive trading and sovereignty rights over huge overseas commercial spaces" (p. 139).

Arrighi (1994, p. 140 and passim), following Braudel (1977, pp. 85–86), gives the 1610s to the 1730s as the era of Dutch economic hegemony. Jonathan Israel (1989; 1995) places the period of Dutch primacy in world trade a few decades earlier. Israel with great historical specificity ties Dutch trade success to the political fortunes of the Republic. Spain's virtual abandonment of the reconquest of the northern (Dutch) Netherlands in favor of war with France in 1590 allowed the Dutch to decisively capture the Baltic trade from the English and the Hanse and to blockade the southern ports of the Netherlands, thereby ending Antwerp's role as a major port and center of manufacture to Amsterdam's benefit. The Dutch decline began with the end of the War of Spanish Succession in 1713. The British gained all the advantages of peace, winning trade concessions in Spain at the Netherlands' expense as well as commercial control over Spanish colonies in the West and East Indies, which became the basis for an expanded British empire and for British trade hegemony.

Descriptions of Dutch trade hegemony, or of what Arrighi calls the "Second (Dutch) Cycle of Accumulation," beg the question of why the Netherlands rather than any of its rivals was the nation able to take advantage of openings in the European economy at the end of the sixteenth century. Also unanswered is why the Dutch could not adapt to geopolitical changes at the end of the seventeenth century and so lost commrcial primacy to the British. It is not enough to argue that "there was nothing the Dutch merchants could do to contain, let alone reverse, this tidal wave of mercantilism. Such a containment was well beyond their organizational capacities" (Arrighi 1994, p. 142). The Dutch had been able to foreclose such mercantilist strategies by their rivals in the first part of the seventeenth century. Indeed, the Dutch themselves facilitated mercantilism in the late seventeenth and the eighteenth centuries by exporting capital and technical know-how to rivals.

The Russian shipbuilding, sailcloth, and rope-making industries, established by Peter the Great, were all based on the Dutch model. The adoption of Dutch multiple-blade saws in Russia and Scandinavia broke the hegemony of the Zaan timber and accelerated the decline of Dutch shipbuilding. Sweden acquired not just Dutch tobacco-processing techniques but whole workshops, transferred lock, stock and barrel, complete with workers, from Amsterdam. Durch fine-cloth weaving techniques were adopted in Prussia, Savoy, and Spain. By 1719 a colony of three hundred Dutch *laken* workers was resident in Guadalajara, invited by Philip V on favorable terms. Down to 1740 it was generally the declining United Provinces, rather than the rising industrial power of Britain, which set the trends in European industrial and technological innovation. (Israel 1989, pp. 384–85)

Why did the Dutch lose control over their own as well as the Spanish colonial empire? Why did the Dutch export industry and capital rather than maintain them in mercantilist fashion at home?[22] Why were the Dutch no longer able to buy a first-rank army and navy capable of rivaling those of the other European powers? To answer these questions and explain the decline of Dutch power in the eighteenth century we must look first, as for the Florentines in chapter 3, at the internal dynamics of elite conflicts.

Elite, Class, and State Formation in the Netherlands

The northern Netherlands came under the sovereignty of an independent count after the collapse of the Carolingian empire.[23] The count and lesser aristocrats exercised only weak control over the peasants who tilled their lands. Peasant freedom was the result of the ways in which the northern Netherlands were settled and ruled. Dutch farmland in large part was reclaimed from the sea. Reclamation work was initiated and financed almost exclusively by peasants, who elected their peers to drainage boards (*waterschappen*) to plan the dikes and canals needed to reclaim lands and control flooding. To raise revenues, the counts of Holland sold land to intermediaries,who often resold it to peasants, keeping only tithe rights. Thus, in most of the northern Netherlands, nobles and other landlords exercised no juridical control over peasants or land, receiving only rents and tithes.

The absence of feudalism in the northern Netherlands shaped elite as well as class relations. Elites lacking juridical or financial controls over land and peasants withered in political and economic importance. The clergy was an unusually weak elite in all Dutch provinces. Clerics exercised little juridical authority. The church collected few tithes. Most parish priests did not enjoy benefices and had to depend upon fees from religious services for their livings (De Vries 1974, pp. 41–43). Both contributing to and as a consequence of those weaknesses, there were relatively few clerics in residence in the northern Netherlands.

As the Dutch became increasingly attracted to humanism and then to Protestantism, their estrangement from the Catholic Church led them to reduce payments to priests for religious services. Catholic priests responded to declining incomes by assuming multiple livings, which meant that parish priests (and Catholic influence) became increasingly absent in the north (Israel 1995, pp. 74–105). Each province of the Dutch Republic sold lands once owned by the Catholic Church and by exiled Catholic nobles in the decades following the Spanish withdrawal from the northern Netherlands after 1590 (pp. 337–41). Those property transfers further consolidated agricultural lands in the hands of urban merchants and rich peasants in Holland and Zeeland, the two wealthiest Dutch provinces.[24]

The nobility was the dominant elite in the less populous and poorer Dutch provinces. "In Friesland and Groningen, the rulers were gentleman farmers.[25] Gelderland was dominated by rural nobles, whereas hedge squires governed in Overijssel and neighboring Drenthe" (T'Hart 1993, p. 25). Those noble elites were the main beneficiaries of the sale of Catholic lands after 1590 in their provinces. The unitary elites of those provinces exercised only limited, nonfeudal control over peasants, deriving income from renting the land they owned and from political offices.

In Holland, by far the richest province of the northern Netherlands, the nobility was a weak elite. Noble families were easily bankrupted by war or other extraordinary expenses since they received relatively little income from their lands. "In Holland, around 200 families comprising the province's nobility, in 1500, possessed approximately 5 per cent of the total cultivable land. . . . The church too lagged behind, owning under 10 per cent" (Israel 1995, p. 108).

Weak nobilities and clergies proved uninviting allies for the parade of rulers who claimed sovereignty over the northern Netherlands. Independent counts in the eleventh through fourteenth centuries, the counts of Burgundy beginning in 1425, and then the Habsburgs who ruled after 1482 were mainly concerned with extracting revenues from the Dutch provinces. The provinces in which nobles were strong made only minor contributions to state revenues. Under the counts and the Habsburgs the noble-dominated provinces (all the provinces except Holland and Zeeland) contributed 20 per cent of the tax quota (Israel 1995, p. 286). The real money, and therefore the political interest of the counts and the Habsburgs, was focused on cities, especially those of Holland. The counts and the Habsburgs generally spurned the weak nobles of Holland and Zeeland and the poor nobles of the other provinces in favor of cities with the money to buy autonomy and privileges in return for steady payments to their sovereign.

Autonomous cities were the great beneficiaries of royal, noble, and clerical weakness in the northern Netherlands, just as cities had benefited from stalemates among great powers and between aristocratic factions in northern Italy. The political stalemates of northern Italy led factions to "reach down" to recruit allies from below, building new elites first from lower strata of nobles and then from among wealthy commoners in the process. The polities of northern Italian city-states became multitiered and marked by shifting factions. It took centuries for political structures and elite and class relations to become rigid in Florence and the other city-states.

The absence of feudal agrarian relations in Holland and the other northern Netherlands provinces, and the resulting paucity of elites (few nobles, a weak clergy, hardly any "state" officials in Holland and Zeeland, and almost nothing but nobles in the other provinces), short-circuited the opportunities for factional conflict. As a result, Dutch urban merchants were able to achieve hegemony within their towns without having to reach down for allies. Towns gained charters of autonomy, and urban elites institutionalized their power, in return for paying set quotas of taxes to the ruling counts and later to the Habsburgs.

Alliances among towns in Holland were cemented by shared opposition to three enemies: the sea, the Hanse, and retrograde nobles increasingly based in the south. Towns (and villages as well) needed to cooperate if they were to complete the massive dike and canal projects that were needed as much to preserve existing towns, farmlands, and their water supplies from flooding or salinization as they were to open new lands and waterways for settlement and transport.

Merchants from the coastal and inland towns of Holland needed to overpower the Hanse if they wished to expand their share of the "bulk" Baltic trade in grain, timber, salt, and herring, and to gain access to the "rich" trade in bringing "spices, sugar, dyestuffs, Mediterranean fruit and wine, and Spanish American silver . . . to the North" (Israel 1995, p. 312). The Hanse, in alliance with German princes and the Holy Roman emperor, also was a rival with Holland for control of what eventually became the Dutch provinces of Gelderland, Overijssel, Drenthe, Friesland, Groningen, and East Friesland (pp. 18–35).

Success in overpowering the sea and the Hanse gave Amsterdam and the other major cities of Holland control over the countryside and of the emerging States General of Holland, the collective directorate and developing administrative arm of Holland's merchant-ruled polity. The declining aristocracy made several attempts to regain power at the expense of Holland's towns. The 1350 Civil War resulted in a decisive victory by the Cabeljauwen (codfish), an alliance of urban merchants with the count and his noble retainers, over the Hoeks (hooks), a rival coalition of declining aristocrats and urban guildsmen who were becoming economically and politically subordinated to the urban merchants.

The Hoeks and the social groups they represented mounted periodic uprisings, often in alliance with outside forces such as the Hanse. However, they never had a realistic chance of overturning the merchant-dominated ruling oligarchy of Holland. Guilds in Holland were as strong as those of Florence and received similarly strong charters and monopolistic privileges from urban oligarchies eager to quiet popular dissent and uprisings during times of civil and foreign war (Israel 1995, pp. 119–21 and passim.). Despite their internal cohesion, Dutch guilds lacked the elite allies necessary to leverage their disruptive street potential beyond economic concessions into a political role in urban or state organs. Peasants had no reason to join the Hoek forces since the nobles at the head of the Hoeks would have been more demanding overlords than the tax collectors, merchants, and rentiers of the Cabeljauwen.

The merchant-regent elite of Holland and the elites of other Dutch provinces faced their ultimate threat from Spain. Spain made increasing fiscal demands on Holland to support the costs of defending the entire Netherlands and for war against France. Beginning in the 1550s, and continuing until 1648 when the United Provinces won Spanish recognition of their independence in a formal peace treaty, Holland with greater or lesser support from the other provinces resisted those demands. The struggle against Spain drew popular as well as elite support because it also was about the desire of Dutch Protestants for religious freedom against the fanatical efforts of Spain to impose Catholic conformity upon all Habsburg subjects. The "Eighty Years' War" between Spain and the Dutch was marked by periods of intense and brutal conflict, years of less violent resistance, and times when Spain offered truces in hopes of regaining the financial and military means to recapture the northern Netherlands.

The Dutch won their war for independence in part because Spain became progressively weaker in the sixteenth and seventeenth centuries. The Dutch also were aided by Spain's enemies, France and Britain. Yet, the Dutch did not merely outlast an exhausted Spain to become an independent backwater as did Portugal. The Dutch emerged from their war as a major military and colonial power and with Amsterdam as the financial and industrial capital of Europe.

Capital into Coercion in the Dutch Polity

War furthered the interests of the Amsterdam-Holland merchant oligarchy[26] in three ways. First, the war undermined Amsterdam's main commercial rival Antwerp. War gave the Dutch an excuse to blockade Antwerp, cutting it off from trade and shifting commerce to Amsterdam. Second, Spain's embargo against the Dutch led them to create their own colonial system and to develop a trading system for luxury goods from the Indies centered on Amsterdam (Adams 1994b, pp. 327–32).

Third, war facilitated merchant hegemony within Holland. The revolt against Spain in 1572 was accompanied by a purge of pro-Habsburg Catholic and noble officeholders from town and provincial governing bodies, most drastically in Amsterdam (Israel 1995, pp. 337–41). Popular and elite reaction against Catholic allies of the Habsburgs eliminated Catholics from the polity of the United Provinces by the 1580s. The ferocity of the Spanish terror against Protestants in the south led to a flight of Protestants and of Protestant capital to the north in the same decades. The post-1572 ruling elite was almost uniformly Protestant, removing religion as a basis for division within the governing bodies of the Republic and its provinces.[27]

The cohesion of Amsterdam's ruling elite gave it the capacity to raise large sums of revenue quickly and consistently and to apply those revenues to pursue its geopolitical and economic interests. Dutch provinces and cities preserved their own independent armed forces throughout the centuries of the Republic. There were five separate Dutch navies, each financed by customs duties and excise taxes raised from within the territory controlled by the town or province to which the navy belonged.[28] In addition the West Indies Company (hereafter WIC) and the VOC had their own fleets and armed forces as well. All efforts to consolidate the five admiralties, or even to place them under a genuine central command, foundered. Similar attempts to control WIC and VOC forces through the stadtholder or any other appointee of the States General repeatedly failed as well. The stadtholder's nominal control over all land armies was undermined by the fact that each company was financed by a specific province and by the willingness of Holland especially to disband its troops when the stadtholder's foreign policy became too aggressive or otherwise did not conform to the desires and interests of the Amsterdam regents.[29]

The stadtholder and the States General were stymied in their efforts to centralize control over the military by their inability to create a national fiscal system. Towns had their own mints; merchants prevented devaluation because they relied upon strong coinages for international trade. Thus, devaluation, an effective short-term (if ultimately counterproductive) method for sovereigns to raise funds, was not available to the Dutch Republic. Most customs were controlled by provinces and towns; Holland regents, especially those with heavy investments in the VOC, undermined the States

General's 1625 scheme to consolidate customs into a Republic-wide tax farm. The national government raised only 20 percent of its own revenues from lands and taxes under its direct control. The other 80 percent of national taxes were paid by the provinces according to a quota system (Israel 1995, pp. 285–91). If any province refused to pay or reduced payment, all the other provinces were allowed to reduce their receipts in proportion to the recalcitrant province's payment.[30]

Holland, because of its relative wealth and because its economy was concentrated in trade and urban production, which were easier to trace and therefore to tax, provided the majority of Dutch revenues. From 55 to 65 percent of the Republic's revenues came from Holland in the period 1586–1792, and even so its wealth was underassessed relative to the other provinces (Israel 1995, pp. 286–87). If we add each province's and admiralty's spending on its own behalf, as well as the military expenditures of the WIC and VOC, which were largely owned and controlled by Hollanders, then it becomes clear that the Dutch "state" was financed in large part by Holland.

When the several city elites of Holland agreed on foreign military and trade policy, they had the means to finance the armed forces necessary to pursue their interests. Often the other provinces through the stadtholder or the States General went along with Holland's desires, either because there was a genuine unity of interest (most notably in the war for independence against Spain and in the efforts to counter Holy Roman or Hanse influence) or because Holland had the means to bully the others to follow their lead. When Holland's elites were divided, national policy was paralyzed. Under those conditions Amsterdam (often in concert with Rotterdam and other Holland "peace" cities) used its fiscal power of refusal to force the Dutch Republic to make peace (or Amsterdam sent its own diplomats to negotiate a peace, which it imposed upon the Republic). Conversely, Amsterdam and allied towns or the WIC and VOC could finance their own armies and navies to pursue their own foreign interests (again often accompanied by diplomacy mounted by Amsterdam diplomats who did not consult with the Republic's executive or legislative organs).[31]

The Holland elites got the foreign policy they desired, and they were able, as well, to finance the wars fought in their interests to enrich themselves. Within Holland, taxes and duties fell upon urban workers. Urban merchants' growing investment in farmland reinforced their preference for taxes and duties on consumers over taxes on land or urban property. "High taxes persisted in Holland because local elites never supported such lower-class revolts as occurred" elsewhere in the Netherlands or Europe (T'Hart 1993, p. 150). The early unity of Holland elites and the resulting absence of reaching down for support in factional conflict allowed those elites to use the fiscal system to enrich themselves without fearing popular opposition.

Holland, like Florence, financed extraordinary war costs with bonds backed by taxes. War led to a massive increase in governmental debt in the first half of the seventeenth century. The indebtedness of the Dutch Republic itself rose from 4.9 million guilders in 1617 to 13.2 million in 1648. More significant was provincial debt (mainly from Holland and its cities), which rose from 1.5 million guilders in 1621 to between 130 million and 140 million guilders in 1650 (Adams 1994b, p. 340). Holland's wealth (and elite unity and lack of popular revolt) insured fiscal stability and allowed the province and its cities to reduce the interest rates it paid on bonds from 8 percent in

1606 to 4 percent by 1655 even in the face of the huge and rapid rise in debt (T'Hart 1993, p. 163).[32]

Holland's debt, like the debt of all nations with stable currencies, transfered wealth from taxpayers (who were, in the main, urban consumers) to bondholders. The ruling elite were the greatest investors in provincial and urban bonds; however, Holland's growing middle class came to have an increasing proportion of its wealth in bonds, especially as the elite came to monopolize opportunities for investment in land and manufacture as it always had in foreign ventures. There were 65,000 investors in Dutch debt by the 1660s (T'Hart 1993 pp. 173–74). Middle-class investors supported the Holland elites' rule since they shared an interest in the stability of the provincial and town governments that paid them interest.

Elite Rigidity and Geopolitical Decline

The Dutch elites derived a growing share of their income in the eighteenth century from their control over offices (Israel 1995, pp. 1006–1012; Adams 1994a) Offices came under the permanent control of families whose patriarchs were able to name their heirs as successors. Major offices also carried with them the right to name lesser family members or clients to lower offices or to positions in the WIC and VOC. Dutch offices were not formally venal as in France. Instead, the ruling families of each city formulated "contracts of correspondence," dividing city offices among families with "written succession rules, which laid out systems by which all eligible elite families would take turns at getting mayoralties, East Indies Company directorships, and other corporate privileges" (Adams 1994a, p. 516).

Holland's polity in the eighteenth century was even more rigid (though differently structured) than that of the Spanish empire, and far less open to conflict and change than those of England and France. As in the Italian city-states once the era of reaching down ended, all governmental and state-chartered corporate spoils in Holland were divided among families through a system of rotating offices that generally excluded families outside the oligarchy. The Dutch system lacked any of the features that in other countries fostered the "circulation of elites." The contracts of correspondence prevented factionalism (Adams 1994a, pp. 516–17) of the sort that pushed weak elites out of power in Italian city-states and in England at the levels of hundreds, counties, and Parliament or that degraded the power and value of some corps of venal officials in France and Spain. The contracts of correspondence blocked the creation of new offices that might have provided access to power for rising bourgeois, while the absence of venality prevented regent families that had done badly in business from selling their offices to rising families, as happened in France, Spain, and Medician Florence. The unity and power of each city's elite also prevented a national sovereign from cashiering some elite families and elevating allies, as happened in monarchical Spain, France, and England, and in Medician Florence.[33]

The rigidity and isolation of Holland's oligarchs was highlighted when "the falling birthrate of the regency in the eighteenth century . . . produced demographic shortfalls of men from regent families deemed suitable for high offices, and dramatic and persistent vacancies in town councils. . . . [In response] the regents simply recognized and accepted the shrinkage of the [number of offices in] the state body" (Adams 1994a,

p. 517). The oligarchs did not add new rich families to their contracts of correspondence. The oligarchs' rigidity reflected not only greed but also fear of starting a process of political devolution that could undermine their hold on state offices and powers.

The Dutch national state was weak when measured against the Weberian ideal of a rational bureaucratic state. Yet, the weakness of the Dutch state was the basis for the Amsterdam elite's international commercial success in the sixteenth- and seventeenth-centuries. Thus, to answer the questions posed at the outset of this section: The regent elite of Amsterdam was unique in later sixteenth- and seventeenth-century Europe in the extent to which it controlled a statelike apparatus without having to compromise with the interests of rival elites or make concessions to reach down to social groups below. As a result, the Amsterdam elite was able to concentrate the resources of its city and hinterland upon military and colonial projects of specific interest to themselves. The regent elite thus was able to take advantage of the northern Netherlands' geopolitical position in Europe, and of the wars engendered by that position, to preserve and to make ever more lucrative their local authority as well as their position at the apex of the seventeenth-century European world system.

The "weakness" of the Dutch state was the basis of the Amsterdam elite's strength. T'Hart concludes her study of the Dutch state by noting that "as control over revenues was diffuse, monopolization of taxation did not occur. . . . Holland frequently failed to act as a centralizing power as it was divided by inter-city rivalries itself. . . . A further reason for the weakness of the bureaucratization process was the absence of a powerful nobility. Nobles did not dominate military institutions, or the civil service" (1993, p. 221). Because the Dutch state was weak in formal bureaucratic terms, the Amsterdam elite was easily able to direct governmental resources and powers in the era of its Golden Age.

The Amsterdam elite's ability to engage in unrestricted self-dealing at both the local and the international level created rigidities that eventually disadvantaged the Dutch in their competition with rivals, most notably the British, in the eighteenth century. Like the Italians, the Dutch oligarchs created business forms designed as much to preserve their local power as to take advantage of foreign openings. It was these structures, created through local politics, that explain the rise and then rigidity and decline of the Dutch as mercantile, military and colonial powers.

Julia Adams (1994a, 1994b, 1996) offers the best explanation for the ways in which organizational rigidities undermined the Dutch in commercial and military competition with the British. She shows how the organizations of the WIC and VOC paralleled those of Holland municipal governments, with specific families given permanent control over particular chambers, offices, and trade concessions in the two companies. Each trading company had a monopoly on trade in its hemisphere and did not have to worry about Dutch competitors, unlike the British East India Company, which contended with various British rivals that were granted royal charters. WIC and VOC became the sole repositories of Dutch investment in colonial trade ventures and thus were able to outgun and outbid British and other European competitors for trading rights and colonies.

The insulation of VOC and WIC from local competition and from revenue or political demands on the part of the Republic or provincial governments became a liability when each company needed temporary infusions of naval and armed forces to defeat colonial rebellions or to fend off the British. WIC was fatally undermined by a successful uprising of the predominately Portuguese settlers in Brazil in 1645. The WIC directors' isolation from the Republic's government and from the elite blocs that controlled VOC and the Amsterdam government meant that WIC was unable to call upon Dutch forces to retake Brazil in 1649 (Adams 1994b, pp. 337–42; van Hoboken 1960). WIC never recovered after losing its largest and richest colony; the British became the dominant commercial and military power in Latin America thereafter.

The political and economic isolation of VOC from the Dutch state and from other elites prevented the company from claiming the fiscal and military resources necessary to defend its trade routes and colonies. VOC was unable to prevent a competition between itself and the five Dutch admiralties to cut customs rates to lure commerce to its own ports. As customs rates fell in the eighteenth century, VOC and the admiralties lost the revenues needed to compete against the growing British navy.

Holland's ability to aid VOC against the British was further undermined by a long-running dispute between Amsterdam and other Holland towns over the assessment of property taxes. Such taxes were based on a 1632 assessment that had the effect of reducing the burden on Amsterdam as real estate values in that city rose in the century after 1632, while increasing the burden on the other parts of Holland as their real property values declined after 1650. Amsterdam regents refused to consider a new assessment that would have increased their tax burden (Aalbers 1977), even though their refusal left Holland unable to tax the new stores of wealth that could have financed an effective military counterforce against Britain and perhaps preserved the VOC's commercial advantage.

A governmental system designed to block challenges to any elite interest had the effect of undermining the greatest elite interest of all—VOC's commercial position. As a result, VOC was unable to finance itself or call upon the Republic for the resources needed to fight the British takeover of Bengal in 1759. Britain easily defeated the Dutch and seized many VOC and WIC ships and colonial bases in the Fourth Anglo-Dutch War of 1780–84. WIC was bankrupt by the end of the war and liquidated in 1791, while VOC lost hegemony over intra-Asian trade and the spice markets to the British (Adams 1994b, pp. 342–47; Israel 1995, pp. 1096–1115).

Because VOC possessed the legal and politico-military power to prevent Dutch interlopers from participating in either intra-Asian or long-distance spice trades, it was able to reap superprofits from its ability to set the terms of trade within Asia and to manipulate the European spice market in the late sixteenth and the seventeenth centuries. VOC directors in Amsterdam also used their uncontested monopoly on Dutch shipments from Asia to Europe "to enforce conventional limits to profiteering" (Adams 1996, p. 22). Since all goods and monies made in the Dutch East Indies were shipped through Batavia and on to Amsterdam in the sixteenth and seventeenth centuries, Batavian officials could keep track of the illicit profits their agents in satellite colonies sought to repatriate, as could company officials do for all their agents in Asia by watching what personal goods and remittances came back to Amsterdam in the fleets from Batavia (Adams 1996).

Once rising British and declining Dutch and VOC military power made the British East India Company a competitor in Asia, VOC lost control over its agents in the East Indies. Underlings, however, could engage in self-dealing with the British, repatriating their profits on British as well as Dutch ships. Thus, VOC's directors lost much

TABLE 5.3. Total and Urban Populations of the Netherlands and Its Rivals

Country	1500	1600	1700	1800
Total Population (×1,000)				
Netherlands	950	1,500	1,900	2,100
England and Wales	2,600	4,400	5,400	9,200
Spain	6,800	8,100	7,500	10,500
France	16,400	19,000	19,000	27,000
Urban Population (×1,000)				
Netherlands	150	364	639	604
Belgium	295	301	486	548
England and Wales	80	255	718	1870
Spain	414	923	673	1165
France	688	1114	1747	2382

Source: Data from De Vries 1984, pp. 30, 36.

Note: Urban population is the total of all cities with at least 10,000 inhabitants. DeVries uses "Netherlands" to refer to the territory of the Dutch Republic and "Belgium" to refer to the southern Netherlands.

of their control over agents in Asia, and VOC officers in Batavia lost leverage over agents in the lesser colonies (Adams 1996).

The Spanish and Dutch Polities in Comparative Perspective

The decline of Amsterdam as the commercial center of Europe, and of WIC and VOC as colonial powers, were not due to the Dutch Republic's small size relative to Britain, France, or Spain. Only Britain was able to benefit significantly from the Dutch decline in the eighteenth century. While the Netherlands had by far the smallest population of the four countries, its main commercial and colonial competitor was the next smallest, Britain, rather than the two giants of Europe, France and Spain (see table 5.3). Furthermore, the Netherlands retained its commercial superiority through the sixteenth and seventeenth centuries even while England's urban population rose to equal and then surpass that of the Netherlands. The stagnation and decline of the Netherlands' urban population in the eighteenth century was a symptom not a cause of Dutch decline, just as the stagnation of Belgium's urban population in the sixteenth century had been a symptom rather than a cause of the southern Netherlands relative and then absolute decline relative to the northern Netherlands.

The Dutch Republic had the fiscal capacity to equal if not to exceed British military expenditures throughout the seventeenth century. Dutch commercial hegemony and the military power to back it up was maintained even in the face of the vastly greater revenues taken in by the French state. The Dutch fell behind the British in governmental revenues only after 1700. That Dutch fiscal decline, like Dutch demographic stagnation, was an effect not a cause of the loss of commercial hegemony (see table 5.4).[34]

In keeping with these data on state revenues, the history of each polity presented in this and the previous chapters demonstrates again and again the difficulties of using tax revenues or the number and powers of officials as measures of state capacities.

TABLE 5.4. Governmental Revenues of Britain, France, the Netherlands, and Spain, 1515–1790s

Years	Revenue in British Pounds (×1,000)			
	Britain	France	Netherlands	Spain
1515	126	1,800		558
1560s	251	1,280		2,154
1570s	224	2,620		3,346
1580s	293	3,040	302	3,654
1590s	494	2,130	473	
1600s	594	2,430	867	4,808
1610s		3,070	788	
1620s		4,310	1,516	4,500
1630s	605	8,400	1,958	4,500
1640s		9,580	1,799	5,263
1650s		10,570		5,263
1660s	1,582	7,640		
1670s	1,634	9,080	5,000	3,485
1680s	2,067	9,940		
1700s	5,900	7,870		
1720s	5,500	10,380	3,600	3,273
1740s	8,900	13,150		
1750s	7,100	12,430	4,860	
1770s	10,400	16,450		
1780s	17,000	19,160		
1790s	39,000		3,690	

Sources: Data for England are from Mann (1980, pp. 174, 193) from his columns in current prices. The amount for 1515 is Mann's average annual revenue of 1502–1505. The 1560s total is the average annual revenue of 1559–70, that of the 1570s is the average annual revenue of 1571–82, that of the 1580s is the average annual revenue of 1583–92, that of the 1590s is the average annual revenue of 1593–1602, that of the 1600s is the average annual revenue of 1604–1612, that of the 1630s is the average annual revenue of 1630–40, that of the 1660s is the average annual revenue of 1660–72, that of the 1670s is the average annual revenue of 1672–85 and that of the 1680s is the average annual revenue of 1685–88. The amount given for each decade from the 1700s to the 1790s is Mann's total for the mid-year of that decade.

Data for France are from Hoffman (1994, pp. 238–39). The 1515 amount is the average annual gross regular tax revenue during the reign of Francois I (1515–47). The other amounts are the average annual central treasury receipts of that decade.

Data for the Netherlands for 1585–1647 are derived by adding together T'Hart's data (1993, pp. 60–61) data for ordinary costs, standing war establishment (excluding navy) and extraordinary war expenses (including navy). Data are the average for each full decade except the 1580s, which are the average of 1585–90 and the 1640s, which are the average of 1640–47. The figure for the 1670s is the Generality's war expenditures for 1675 from Israel 1995, p. 818. Dutch totals for the sixteenth and seventeenth centuries are not exactly comparable to the other countries since nonmilitary expenditures are excluded, while military costs paid for with loans rather than tax revenues are included. Thus, Dutch totals probably are somewhat higher during wartime and somewhat lower during peacetime than if strictly comparable data were available. Dutch data for the eighteenth century are from Veenendaal 1994, p. 137, and are for total revenues, offering a strict comparison to the other countries. The 1720s figure is the total for 1720, the 1750s figure is the total for 1758, and the 1790s figure is for 1794.

Data for Spain up through the 1670s are from Thompson (1994, p. 157). He gives income as revenues actually received by the crown from its dominions in Europe and the Americas. Amounts spent on behalf of the crown and accounted for are included, but not revenues collected and spent by local officials and not accounted for to the crown. The amount for 1515 is crown income for 1504. The figures for the 1560s, 1570s, 1580s, and 1600s are the annual amounts for 1565, 1577, 1588, and 1607, respectively. The 1620s and 1630s figure is the annual average for 1621–40, the amounts for the 1640s and 1650s is the annual average for 1641–60, and the 1670s figure is that of 1674. The amount for the 1720s is the annual income for 1718 from Kamen 1969, p. 228.

Notes: All figures in this table are in British pounds at current prices, not adjusted for inflation. The French totals in livre tournois, the Dutch totals in guilders, and the Spanish revenues in ducats were converted into pounds, following Braudel and Spooner 1967, p. 458, by comparing the silver content of each currency. Thus, the French totals were divided by 5 for the period before 1560, by 8 for the 1560s and 1570s, by 10 for 1580–1629, by 11 for the 1630s, by 12 for 1640–19, by 15

France is the prime illustration. French state revenues were far greater than those of England or the Netherlands throughout the seventeenth century. Yet a French fiscal advantage of more than 4:1 over the Netherlands and 13:1 over England in the 1630s yielded at best military parity. France's advantages in gross population and revenues were dissipated by the myriad ways in which "state" military powers and resources were appropriated by a variety of officeholders and financiers at the local, provincial, and national levels. Collins (1988, pp. 114–35) found that only 20 percent of state revenues in the first half of the seventeenth century made it to the central treasury in Paris. The rest was supposedly spent on behalf of the crown; some no doubt was for military expenditures, but most was taken by provincial officials for their own purposes.

Each institution of the Dutch polity and economy, and therefore every Dutch commercial and military enterprise, was organized in such a way as to preserve the particular interests of the unchanging set of elite families with permanent control over those institutions.[35] While the Dutch were conquering trade routes, markets, and American and Asian colonies that were relatively "empty" of European competitors in the sixteen and early seventeenth centuries, the self-serving autonomy of each family did not impede Dutch commercial hegemony. Instead, the same locally based alliances and privileges that protected each family's interests also allowed elites to mobilize resources to realize their common goals. Once the Dutch had filled all the open spaces for profit in the seventeenth-century world economy, and as the British especially sought to vie for opportunities the Dutch had monopolized, Dutch elites undermined their collective ability to mobilize resources for trade and military wars as each regent elite family moved to guard its own interests. "State" officials were able to use the revenues collected by their offices for their own purposes even as their self-dealing sapped the Republic and the WIC and VOC of the ability to maintain commercial and military advantages abroad.

Braudel, Arrighi, and Wallerstein then are half-right as each in his own way explains the rise and decline of Dutch commercial hegemony in terms of shifts in the nature of the European or world system. As I noted before, however, they are unable to explain why it was the Dutch rather than the previously dominant Genoese who waxed in the sixteenth century. Nor can they explain why it was the British rather than the richer and already established Dutch who led the world economy in its eighteenth-century phase. Both shifts in international commercial leadership are explained by the particular capacities that the elites of each nation brought to the struggles for commercial and military hegemony in each era.

The rigid and compartmentalized Dutch elites brought the same qualities to war and commerce in both periods. The Amsterdam elite's autonomy from other elites and

NOTES TO TABLE 5.4. (*cont.*)

for 1690–1719, by 19 for the 1720s, and by 22 for 1730–19 to convert livre tournois into pounds. Dutch totals in guilders were divided by 10 for the entire period to yield British pounds. Castilian ducats were divided by 2.66 up to 1620, by 3.8 for 1620–50, and by 6.6 in the eighteenth century to yield an equivalent in British pounds.

Any system for currency conversion is problematic. I have used the Braudel-Spooner method because it reflects accurately the fiscal resources and military buying power of each state, since many troops were mercenaries and were bought on a transnational market as were some munitions. Similarly, tax revenues and currencies were augmented by international loans denominated in gold or silver. The Braudel-Spooner tables have the additional virtue of being complete and consistent for the entire period under study.

classes and from an overarching state was a decisive advantage in the initial scramble for trade routes and colonies. The same elite structure reduced the resources the Dutch could mobilize for the more intense and crowded geopolitical and trade battles of the eighteenth and nineteenth centuries.

Elite conflicts were rapidly resolved in the Netherlands and yielded a structure of social relations that was rigid and produced a certain form of resources mobilization that was advantageous for Dutch power in one era and subversive of Dutch hegemony in the next. Florentine elite conflicts, which took centuries longer to produce a single hegemonic elite, also produced a social structure that aided Florentine commercial and geopolitical interests at one time while making it impossible to adapt to new challenges later. Spain's imperial successes made that nation's elite and class structure more rigid, which in turn undermined Spain's capacity to use its domestic resources or its windfall of American treasure to expand or even to preserve its empire.

England and France had multiple elites, engaged in conflicts with dynamic effects on their polities. Chapter 6 turns to the as yet unanswered questions: How did the new structures of elite relations, which were crystallized in the aftermaths of the English Civil War and the 1789 French Revolution, affect class relations and therefore the economies of England and France? In other words, what effect did the elite conflicts analyzed in chapter 4 have upon the development of capitalism in England and France and upon their commercial and military rivalries?

6

Elite Defensiveness and the Transformation of Class Relations

England and France

THE CONFLICTS ENGENDERED BY THE Reformation and the subsequent concentration of certain elite powers within statelike structures posed mortal dangers to the privileges of the rural aristocracies of England and France. Chapter 4 traces the differing institutional Reformations in Britain and France and the varying absolutisms created in each nation. The task of this chapter is to explain how landlords responded to the new dangers and how those responses transformed agrarian class relations in the two countries.

Many landlords were unable to meet the challenges posed to their manorial positions by elite conflicts. Those nobles lacked the strategic openings or the capacities to initiate actions that could alter class relations on their manors in ways that would fend off threats from rival elites. Such landlords lost their elite positions. Other landlords sustained their positions but lost portions of their incomes to rival elites or to their tenants. Most French aristocrats, and a minority of British landlords, fall into these two categories.

A majority of British landlords, and a minority of their French counterparts, were able to devise and implement new strategies to fend off challenges from rival elites and at the same time gain control over land and labor in ways that allowed those landlords to realize unprecedented incomes from their estates. The new modes and relations of production were capitalist in the fullest sense of every definition of that term. Capitalist agriculture provided the basis for sustained economic development in ways that the forms of urban, corporate, and transnational enterprise examined in previous chapters did not.

This chapter explains the interrelated developments that resulted in the creation of capitalist class relations, capitalist modes of production, and capitalist economic development in England and France. I begin by comparing the ways in which English and French landlords responded to the threats that the elite conflicts analyzed in chapter 4 posed to their seigneurial incomes and powers. My goal is to identify the factors that can account for the differences in landlord strategies within and between England and France. I then turn from elite to class conflicts. I inventory the range of peasants' responses to the challenges posed to their long-standing rights by landlords and other elites. I explain how previous elite and class conflicts affected the strength of peasant communities and how the total structure of elite and class relations determined the efficacy of each form of peasant action.

Class and elite conflicts interacted to create new structures of land use, labor control, and income distribution. The third section of this chapter describes the agrarian relations of production that emerged in the seventeenth century. I also compare the distribution of agrarian income in the two countries. I conclude by explaining how the different English and French agrarian regimes affected economic development in the seventeenth and subsequent centuries. I highlight, at appropriate points in the chapter, the most significant ways in which my explanation of agrarian change and capitalist development differs from previous class analyses and demographic, regional ecology, rational choice, and developmental models of the transformations in England and France. Readers who want more extended critiques of those earlier works will find them in the endnotes, where they do not disrupt the thread of my argument.

Landlords Respond to Elite Conflict: Strategies for Control of Land in England and France from the Reformation to the 1640s

Medieval landlords were protected because they were limited by the authority that rival elites exercised over the tenants on the lords' manors. Recall that kings, clerics, and overlords sustained separate legal systems to guard their own claims to shares of peasant production. The commanders and beneficiaries of royal, clerical, ducal, and baronial courts sought to enlarge their incomes and authority at the expense of manor lords even as the intellectual architecture of their legal and fiscal claims assumed the continued existence of manors and landlords. Feudal elite conflicts were about the relative authority and income shares of existing elites. While royal dynasties were overthrown by rivals and some families lost noble titles or control over ecclesiastical offices, elite combatants never could challenge the permanence of the titles and positions that defined the contestants in medieval elite conflicts.

The elite conflicts that followed the Reformation differed fundamentally from those that came before in that they overturned the judicial and fiscal rights of clerics and manor lords and challenged peasants' tenure rights. The English clergy's very right to regulate and appropriate agrarian production was seized by the crown and then largely sold or ceded to lay landlords in the aftermath of the Henrician Reformation. Royal judges in both England and France overruled manor courts in the sixteenth and seventeenth centuries. Such challenges threatened the legitimacy of seigneurial justice and therefore of landlords' abilities to preserve their incomes and statuses. In so doing, kings and their retainers went beyond the pre-Reformation jurisprudence that guarded royal and clerical claims to peasant incomes (and ensured that peasants had the security to meet those claims). Elite conflicts left English and French landlords with varying capacities to respond to royal challenges and to peasant resistance. The remainder of this section identifies the differences in seigneur's capacities with respect to rival elites; the next section addresses peasants' efficacy, in England and France.

England

The English crown's success at building horizontal absolutism by subordinating the clergy and subduing the great magnates turned the elite, locally based lay landlords, into a new class, the gentry, with unmediated access to peasant labor and to agrarian production. The gentry's hegemony within the counties was challenged by the crown, by the Church of England, and by resurgent and aspiring magnates time and again from the Reformation through the Civil War. Many of those challenges were over the control of parliamentary and local offices, and over the allocation of status and the alignment of political factions. Each elite's survival and attainments were grounded ultimately in its control of resources, with land and agrarian labor being the preeminent sources of wealth in early modern England.

The gentry's paramount interest was in fending off claims to the income from their estates by the crown and the clergy. The main challenges came from the crown in efforts to guard peasant incomes and land tenures so as to better tax that majority of subjects, and from the clergy in an attempt, aided by the Stuart kings, to reassert rights to the lands, tithes, benefices, and advowsons that once belonged to monasteries and had been sold to laymen in the aftermath of the Henrician Reformation.

The gentry responded to royal and clerical assertions by obliterating the manorial institutions that provided the juridical bases for the claims of those elites to agrarian resources. The gentry used five strategies to extinguish peasant land rights and to convert their income and use rights on manors into private property: They denied clerical courts jurisdiction on manors where laymen held benefices (tithe rights), they limited royal judges' interventions into landlord-tenant disputes, they allied with freeholders to boycott manor courts, they used the process of ascertainment to extinguish copyholders' land rights, and they used enclosure to convert common lands into private property.

Landlords needed private bills from Parliament or support from the Chancery and the constant assistance of their county justices of the peace to implement those five strategies. Gentry success in guarding their incomes and rights from the predations of rival elites thus depended upon their collective power in Parliament and their control of each county commission of the peace. The crown's strategy of horizontal absolutism had the unintended effects of ceding to the gentry enough power in Parliament to win the legislation they wanted and of cementing gentry control over most county commissions of the peace.

Recall how the removal of most clerical lords from Parliament after the Henrician Reformation weakened crown control over that body. As Henry VIII and especially Elizabeth I undermined magnate power in the counties, the great lay lords became less able to control lesser lords and to mobilize them to support magnate bids for power in Parliament or on the battlefield. Members of Parliament became more independent of national factions and more focused on the local interests of the gentry, who came to control elections in most counties.

The Parliaments of the Tudor and Stuart eras functioned as conduits between the crown and influential constituents. Constituents demanded that their members of Parliament (MPs) fulfill local needs by winning royal favors, passing particular local and private bills, and winning appointments to offices for local men. The crown fulfilled

MPs' local political needs and thereby often won votes for taxes and other national items, by granting the patronage and approving the bills MPs requested.[1] One form of patronage was crown approval of private bills or Chancery decrees for enclosure and ascertainment.

The crown sacrificed its ability to regulate peasant land tenure at the local level to win the parliamentary support needed to fend off challenges at the national level and to gain tax revenues to fight foreign wars. Similarly, the crown used circuit and county judicial appointments as patronage. Further, the crown expanded the membership of county commissions of the peace and gave an increasing share of those offices to locally oriented appointees both to undermine magnate hegemony over the commissions and to win local acquiescence of the crown's national-level and foreign policies (see table 4.4).

The gentry took advantage of the decline of magnate power (which increased gentry leverage over MPs, who then were freed from magnate protection and domination), and of the crown's need to trade local favors and offices for parliamentary and more general national-level political support, by demanding and receiving legislative and judicial support for assaults on tenant rights. Enclosure is the best known and was the most dramatic method for extinguishing manorial and common rights and creating private property. Enclosure, however, often was the culmination of a long process of challenging and reducing peasant tenures. The timing of enclosure indicates the end of agrarian class struggle on a manor and the final creation of private property.

Almost half (47.6%) of all land enclosed in England from the Reformation to 1914 was enclosed in the seventeenth century. "There was almost twice as much enclosure in seventeenth-century England as in any other century, including the eighteenth" (Wordie 1983, p. 502). Relatively little of that enclosure was by parliamentary acts. Most sixteenth- and seventeenth-century enclosures gained the needed legal recognition from Chancery decrees. Acts and decrees both often confirmed previous enclosures that were accomplished by limited agreements among some landholders on a manor or by "unity of control" in which a single landowner bought up or otherwise gained control of all the tenant holdings and other rights on a manor.[2]

Landlords became able to enclose so much land in the seventeenth century because they had removed many impediments to enclosure in the first century after the Reformation. The Reformation did not abolish clerical courts, but the authority of those courts was weakened. As monastic assets were sold, laymen came to hold a majority of benefices and advowsons in England (Hill 1963, pp. 144–46). Lay owners of benefices could turn to lay, rather than clerical, judges for interpretations of their rights. A lay owner of a manor and benefice would see the profit from a degradation of peasant tenures outweigh the income loss from a reduction in the value of a benefice. The arguments of such benefice owners in lay courts, or more often the absence of such owners from court since their "unity of control" of manor and benefice removed any legal dispute, differed from the position clerics took in church courts. Thus, most peasants lost a clerical advocate of their land rights when benefices passed to laymen. After 1549 Parliament passed laws limiting the authority of clerical courts to rule on questions of tithes and manorial tenure, regardless of the circumstances (Hill 1963, pp. 84–92; Houlbrooke 1979, pp. 121–22).[3] Peasants who leased lands for fixed terms or at the will of the lord were the principal victims of the withdrawal of clerical court jurisdiction over tenant rights. Without the intervention of church courts, landlords could increase rents or evict tenants at the expiration of a lease (Kerridge 1969, pp. 38–40).[4]

Copyholders were in a stronger position than mere leaseholders since their rights were guarded by each manor's court, which determined that manor's customary level of rent, length of lease, and rights to renew a lease and pass a copyhold to an heir. Copyhold leases, before the Reformation, typically were for terms of years (most commonly forty, sixty, or ninty-nine years) or for a certain number of lives (with a new "life" beginning with the death of the copyholder and the assumption of the holding by an heir). Fines were paid between lives, with one year's rent the usual fine. When a lease was renewed, two years' rent was charged (Kerridge 1969, pp. 38–50).

Copyholders' customary rents and fines were similar to market rents in the first century after the Black Death because the terms of copyholds were set to entice peasants to vacant tenements. By the sixteenth century, however, most copyhold rents were well below market levels. Manor lords then had an incentive to abrogate copyhold leases and either rent the land to commercial farmers or farm the land themselves.

Copyholders, unlike the tenants-at-will, did not depend upon clerical courts for protection; instead their tenure was defended from landlords by the manor court and beginning in the sixteenth century by the king's courts. Royal courts developed two doctrines to prevent the eviction of copyholders or the rapid increase of their rents during Henry VIII's reign. Tenants could argue that rent increases or evictions violated customary rights of such long standing that those rights should assume the status of common law rights. Another tenant argument was that of "equity." Equity assumed that a previous lease gave the current copyholder the expectation of the same rights (Gray 1963, pp. 34–49).

Few copyholders had the resources to mount legal appeals in royal courts to protect their customary leases from landlord challenges. Royal judges heard only sixty copyhold-tenure cases during Henry VIII's reign (Gray 1963, pp. 34–49). Landlords were able to circumvent both royal and manorial courts by introducing petitions requesting that Parliament appoint surveyors to ascertain (and, it was hoped, disallow) copyholders' land-tenure claims. Such petitions were routinely approved by Parliament in the second half of the sixteenth and the seventeenth centuries.

Surveyors would check manorial court rolls for evidence that the level of fines had been set at an absolute level at some time in the past. Since copyhold terms had usually been set in accordance with unwritten custom, most manor records did not reveal ascertained fines. Even where ascertained fines were recorded, they often were not clearly linked to copyhold tenements of the moment when ascertainment was being conducted. Surveyors could then rule that copyholders did not enjoy protection from arbitrary increases in fines or from eviction at the expiration of their current leases. Tenants were then offered the "right" to ascertain their copyhold rights in return for payment of a special fine of thirty or forty years' customary rent, a price higher than that for the outright purchase of land (Kerridge 1969, pp. 54–58).[5]

Ascertainment was a disaster for the majority of copyholders subjected to that procedure by their landlords. Most were forced into landlessness (Beier 1985, pp. 14–28). A minority with cash reserves was able to rent newly unencumbered land and become small-scale commercial farmers, often hiring their dispossessed neighbors as farm laborers.[6]

Ascertainment prepared the ground for enclosure in two ways. First, peasant communities were disrupted by the eviction of so many families and by the demise of manorial courts. Peasant communities with shrunken and shattered social networks were less able to resist enclosure than were intact villages of manorial tenants. Second, landlords increased their strength under the weighted voting system for approving enclosure plans when they gained control of lands formerly held by copyholders. Landlords, especially if they had acquired their manor's benefices and with it the clerical tithe holder's usual 10 percent weighted vote, had a plurality but not a majority of the votes on enclosure. If enough copyholders could be evicted, however, the plurality became a majority.[7]

Enclosure was a major and often a fatal setback to the viability of freehold and copyhold peasant farms (Beier 1985, pp. 14–28; Spufford 1974, pp. 121–64; Yelling 1977, pp. 214–32 and passim). The various parliamentary enclosure acts, which provided the templates for each private act or Chancery decree, specified that the manor lord and the holder of the clerical benefice (who, after the Dissolution, were often the same person) received a portion of each tenant's land in return for the elimination of rent, tithe, and labor obligations after enclosure was effected (Tate 1967, pp. 121–27). Thus, after enclosure almost all peasants were left with farms smaller than their former tenant holdings. All manors had good and poor land. In theory, property lines were supposed to be drawn fairly. In fact, the manor lord, benefice holder, and other members of the majority voting bloc that approved enclosure received the choice parcels of land (Johnson 1909, pp. 39–74; Tate 1967, pp. 46–48; Yelling 1977, pp. 1–10 and passim).

Landlords combined the five strategies just discussed—ascertainment, enclosure, and the limiting of royal judges' and the gutting of clerical and manorial courts' jurisdiction over land tenure disputes—to obliterate the institutional bases for determining ancient crown and clerical claims upon manorial resources as well as to undermine tenant rights. Once enclosure was completed, with each landowner's holding marked by fences or hedges, the very ground upon which feudal elites or peasants could challenge the gentry's land rights had been scoured of the farming strips, the commons, and often the very villages that embodied feudal elite and class relations. The clean lines of private property, the landless peasants, the lost villages, the abrogated customs, the county commissions of the peace, and the suppressed clerical and manorial courts all combined to ensure that kings, magnates, clerics, and peasants never would be able to reassert their medieval rights to land or its products.

France

Elite conflict in France had almost the opposite effect on agrarian class relations as it did in England. The multiple elites that regulated and profited from peasant agriculture in pre-Reformation England were reduced to a single gentry class during the sixteenth and seventeenth centuries. French elite struggles multiplied jurisdictions. Overlapping judicial and fiscal bodies emerged to regulate and appropriate French agrarian production in the centuries following the Reformation.

While multiple income and use rights to manorial lands were superseded by private ownership of land in England, royal and provincial agents limited French seigneurs' and tithe collectors' claims on agrarian income. Seigneurs became more and more like the *noblesse de robe* and other royal officials in that their income rights, judicial powers, and status privileges were limited by royal regulations and hemmed in by royal grants of similar perquisites to rival elites.

Old feudal and new judicial authorities, in the course of protecting their income rights in land, prevented noble, bourgeois, and peasant proprietors from making full use of the lands they cultivated, leased, bought, or sold. We can trace the shifts in the relative power of each elite by charting changes in the portion of agrarian production that went to seigneurial dues, tithes, taxes, and rents.

French seigneurs were the biggest losers in the centuries from the Reformation to 1789. Their ancient rights to collect dues in-kind or in cash and an array of fines, and to profit from monopolies, were limited by royal decrees and the rulings of intendants and parlements. The crown, thereby, complemented its national- and provincial-level strategies of turning aristocrats into crown dependents by undermining nobles' autonomous bases of wealth and power on manors. As provincial networks of power were compromised by royal agents and sinecures, manor lords lost the allies necessary to resist royal restrictions on their seigneurial privileges.

French peasants, in the centuries before and after the Black Death, won the right to commute their labor dues into cash in those provinces where elites were riven by conflict or where the crown had achieved dominance over local elites.[8] Peasants in most of the rest of France were able to commute their dues to cash in the centuries after the Reformation as the crown further divided provincial elites.[9]

When seigenurial dues, and many tithes, were frozen at depressed fifteenth-century levels, all the benefits of inflation and of increases in agricultural productivity flowed to those who held use rights to French farmland. Peasants were the initial beneficiaries of seigneurs' inability to increase cash dues. Peasants had a hard time holding onto their land rights over the long term, however. French agriculture was plunged repeatedly into depression by harvest failures, destruction from war, and ruinous surtaxes to pay down royal debts incurred in wartimes (Hoffman 1996, pp. 184–92 and passim). Each agricultural depression forced numerous peasants into bankruptcy. When farmers could not pay their debts, their creditors or others with ready cash bought out the bankrupt peasants' debts and thereby secured their land rights.

Use rights to land passed in time from peasants to bourgeois and some noble creditors. As food prices and agricultural output increased, the use value of land soared in contrast to seigneurial dues, which remained fixed at fifteenth-century levels. Inflation became a key determinant of landlords' and peasants' incomes in subsequent centuries. Population increases and frequent devaluations of the gold and silver content of French coins combined to generate significant inflation. Grain prices rose 2,100 percent from 1500 to 1788 (Baulant 1968, pp. 538–40).[10]

Taxes, of course, did not remain frozen at fifteenth-century levels. Crown revenues far outpaced inflation, increasing 4,584% from 1515 to 1788, more than double the inflation rate.[11] The crown thus captured a growing share of national income.[12] Holders of cultivation rights received all the rest of the benefits of increases in agricultural productivity, as well as profiting from the long-term decline in wages and the dramatic fall in the real costs of seigneurial dues (Hoffman 1996).

Seigneurs suffered declining real incomes to the extent to which they had sold or lost the cultivation or rental rights to their estate lands and therefore collected only or mainly cash dues (Jacquart 1974; Le Roy Ladurie [1977] 1987, pp. 172–75; Morineau 1977, p. 914). Seigneurial dues and rents became ever more distinct.[13] They followed diverging trends.

Different individuals or institutions often collected dues and rents from the same piece of land. Some seigneurs and institutions with seigneurial rights retained control over land and collected rents along with seigneurial dues until the Revolution. More often lords sold cultivation rights or lost them through judicial decrees. Those with ready capital, mainly officials and urban merchants and some peasants, bought cultivation rights and became either commercial farmers or rentiers.

Nobles' incomes and wealth were determined after 1500 primarily by whether they were confined to the declining real dues received by seigneurs or acquired offices whose income and value grew faster than inflation (Fourquin [1970] 1976). Seigneurs who retained control over their demesnes were able to realize significant and growing incomes from their estates. Demesnes, whether rented for cash or sharecropped, became the most lucrative source of landed income for seigneurs, far outstripping dues on the vaster portion of estates farmed by tenants (Bois [1976] 1984, p. 224). Seigneurs who had commuted labor dues to cash before and after the Black Death and converted their demesnes to peasant leaseholds were left with little or no land to sharecrop or rent out at market levels in the sixteenth and subsequent centuries and therefore suffered the greatest declines in their incomes (Canon 1977, pp. 17–18; Fourquin 1976, p. 210).

Seigneurs pursued two contradictory strategies to deal with stagnant dues and declining incomes.[14] One was to sell the array of seigneurial rights to peasants or to bourgeois investors. Seigneurs also appropriated and then resold commons and forests that had been used and controlled by peasant villages. The crown generally was unable to prevent seigneurs from transferring peasant common lands, "waste," and forest lands to new purchasers (Jacquart 1975, pp. 296–97; Meyer 1966, pp. 544–48). Landlords sometimes kept the commons and then rented them out or converted them for sharecropping. Bourgeois purchasers of lands almost always were able to prevent the aristocratic sellers or their heirs from later reasserting seigneurial rights.

Nobles received immediate infusions of cash when they followed this strategy. Peasants who purchased seigneurial rights were then relieved of labor and cash dues and their farms were freed of feudal restrictions that prevented the sale or conveyance of land. Bourgeois investors bought feudal rights more for the status of having a country seat than as an investment.[15] Some bourgeois buyers (and a few nobles) in the Île-de-France did buy feudal rights to clear land of tenants and create commercial farms (Le Roy Ladurie 1975). In most of France, however, new landowners like old seigneurs profited from *metayage* (sharecropping) or from renting out lands for cash, both of which became more lucrative for landowners as population, grain prices, and rents rose in the seventeenth and eighteenth centuries (Fitch 1978, pp. 194–98; Jacquart 1974).[16]

The second strategy pursued by landlords, and by bourgeois buyers of feudal rights, was to reassert and enforce ancient seigneurial rights over peasants and their lands. The most lucrative feudal right in an era of population growth and inflation but fixed rents was the *lods et ventes* (fines received for allowing peasants to sell, transfer, or will their tenements). Landlords rediscovered an array of disused seigneurial rights that they sought to reassert, most notably and profitably the requirement that tenants grind their grain at the lords' mill. Seigneurs also could require that wine be pressed in their mills and bread baked in their ovens. Landlords revived tolls on peasant commerce, fairs, and markets. Lords encroached upon peasant lands to build fish ponds. Lords raised birds and rabbits that fed on their tenants' crops. Seigneurs tried to collect *cens,* a fine tenants paid in recognition of the fealty they owed their lord. Landlords also enforced labor dues where those had not been commuted to cash, gaining free if unmotivated labor for their demesnes. Seigneurs of the seventeenth and eighteenth centuries asserted those ancient seigneurial rights to make money; they were little interested in honorific displays of subservience from their tenants.[17]

Landlords considered several factors in choosing between the two strategies. Only those lords who held offices with enforcement powers over tenants, or who had enough political influence to call upon judges to enforce edits on their estates, were able to pursue the second strategy (Dontenwill 1973, pp. 76–78; Fourquin 1976, pp. 46–54; Neveux 1975). Lesser seigneurs, who lacked such "high power," were forced to adopt the first strategy. Even landlords with high power gained little advantage from enforcing *lods et ventes* or labor dues in the first two centuries after the Black Death. While population still was recovering, peasants could leave their home manors and rent vacant tenements elsewhere rather than pay high fines to transfer farms under the jurisdiction of assertive landlords. Landlords who wanted to increase their income prior to the mid-sixteenth century had to do so by accommodating tenants and selling rights. Only after population recovery made land scarce again did peasants and landlords both gain an interest in fighting over the disposition of estate tenements.

Few landlords pursued a third possible strategy of converting that part of their estates that was free of protected peasant farms into commercial farms that they or their managers worked with wage laborers. French landlords avoided engaging in capitalist agriculture themselves for two reasons. First, profits from sharecropping or renting to peasants almost always were greater in the foreseeable future than what could be realized from commercial farming. That was so because sharecroppers and tenants provided their own working capital, and landlords could avoid the expenses of farm management and labor supervision needed on capitalist farms.[18] Peasants in France (and in virtually every other time and place) were so eager to work their own farms that they were willing to engage in self-exploitation to pay rents that could not be justified from the value of crops produced by peasant labor on rented lands.[19] While capital investment in commercial agriculture paid off in the long term, as I show in the last section of this chapter, neither English nor French landlords could have or did foresee that.

Second, unlike the English gentry, French landlords did not need to fear or to counteract a reassertion of clerical or royal claims on land. The crown remained consistent in its protections of peasant land rights, and the church constant in its tithe demands, throughout the final centuries of the ancien régime.[20] The scope of crown and clerical rights and powers over land stayed the same whether French landlords farmed their estates themselves, rented them to bourgeois or peasant tenants, or adopted sharecropping. English gentry were forced to rent land to commercial farmers, sacrificing short-term returns in order to reduce immediate political threats from rival elites, while French landlords were able to profit from sharecropping and rentals to peasants because they did not face similar challenges from crown or clergy.

Peasant Resistance and the Resolution of Agrarian Class Relations

Peasants repeatedly challenged the demands made upon their labor and agrarian production by various elites. When elites reacted to new threats to their existence and well-being posed by elite conflicts by trying to erect new modes of control over peasant land and labor, peasants responded by taking collective action. Peasants' capacities for resistance were transformed as the structures of elite domination and exploitation changed. The targets of peasant ire shifted in response to changes in the levels and sorts of labor, dues in-kind, cash rents, and taxes demanded of them. This section poses and answers the following two questions: How were peasant capacities for protest affected by the different changes in agrarian class relations in England and France? To what extent were the landed elites of England and France able to devise strategies that blunted peasant resistance without inviting challenges from rival elites? I begin by examining England, then turn to France, and conclude with some comparative observations.

England

English landowners achieved great victories against rival elites and transferred a significant share of agrarian income to themselves from their tenants in the century after the Reformation. However, while the gentry were safe from the feudal claims of rival elites and of their former tenants, they were left with the problem of guarding their now private property in land from peasant challenges.

Peasant protests occurred in several waves in the century between the Henrician Reformation and the Civil War.[21] First, were the protests, most notably the Pilgrimage of Grace of 1536–37, which were directed against the king's claim of supremacy over the church and targeted royal agents, especially tax collectors. The Pilgrimage of Grace was concentrated in Lincolnshire, Yorkshire, Cumberland, and Westmorland. Many lords in those counties gave covert or tacit support to the clerical and peasant rebels. Lords did so because they sought to counter Henry VIII's efforts to break the hegemony of the great noble families and their allies in those counties.[22]

The Pilgrimage of Grace was not about land tenure and did not directly affect agrarian class relations. It was instigated by elites in the course of conflicts with other elites. The Pilgrimage of Grace never expanded beyond the elite issues raised by the Henrician Reformation; it did not develop into a conflict that challenged agrarian class relations. Royal tax collectors were the main targets; peasant protesters boycotted taxes while rent strikes were brief and isolated. The rebellion was crushed by the crown. Its main consequence was to accelerate the crown's campaign to weaken the great lords and set in train the creation of new county elites that were able to severely weaken peasant rights in later decades.

The next waves of agrarian uprisings were reactions to landlord efforts to undermine peasant rights. An intense wave of protests occurred in 1548–52. Peasants were passive over the next quarter century, even in the face of elite rebellions in 1553–54 (led by Wyatt against Queen Mary's marriage to Philip) and in 1569–70 (by northern Earls against Elizabeth I over issues of religion and regional autonomy and privilege). Peasant protests resumed in the 1580s and intensified in subsequent decades to reach a climax in the 1607 Midland Revolt. Isolated protests against landlords continued in the Midlands, especially in Warwickshire until just before the Revolution. The crown in its capacity as a landlord was the main target of peasant protests between 1608 and 1639. Peasants in northern counties protested higher rents on royal manors. Residents of fenlands challenged crown efforts to drain the fens. Cotters and laborers who lived in royal forests opposed crown plans for deforestation and enclosure.[23]

Peasants challenges to the crown were easily crushed and did not alter crown plans. Henry VIII, having shared the bounty of the Dissolution with the majority of lay elites, was able to crush the Pilgrimage of Grace without making any concessions to peasant or clerical rebels. Northern peasants were not able to prevent rent increases on crown manors. Crown deforestation and enclosure plans were only slightly delayed by protesters. Protesters did delay fen drainage, especially in Lincolnshire, by sabotaging ditches, sluices, and sewers (Manning 1975, pp. 146–48). Fenlands protests were most effective in 1640–41, when the crown also was being attacked by elite opponents and was unable to respond to peasant challenges.

Peasants were otherwise relatively quiet during the Revolution and Civil War. Peasants opportunistically engaged in rent strikes against the crown and landlords weakened by warfare. English peasants, unlike their French counterparts during the Frondes and Revolution, did not massively challenge existing land tenure arrangements. Peasants did not play a decisive role in the Civil War (Charlesworth 1983, pp. 39–41; Manning 1975).

The most effective peasant protests were directed against lay landlords in the 1540s and again in the half century from the 1580s through the 1630s. Those protests were responses to landlord usurpations of peasant rights. Each rural protest can be classified in terms of the character of its peasant instigators and the organization of its landlord targets (see table 6.1).[24]

The first wave of protests during the 1540s (cells 1, 2, 3, and 4 in table 6.1) occurred when and where landlords underestimated the strength of peasant communities or peasants accurately recognized divisions among landlords or both. All protests in the 1540s were in opposition to landlord initiatives to raise rents, ascertain copyholds, or enclose lands. The protests in Somerset, Wiltshire, Kent, Hampshire, Rutland, and Suffolk (cell 1) were led by freeholders, joined by copyholders and cotters. The elites of those counties were tightly organized and were able to quickly mobilize repressive force against the rebels of 1549.[25] Yet, despite their organizational advantages and superior armed force, the landlord elites sought to divide the peasant rebels by offering concessions to freeholders. Landlords may have been motivated by the fear that widespread armed conflict could create an opening for royal intervention within their counties. Freeholders did indeed abandon the protests once their land rights and personal liberties had been acknowledged and guaranteed by their landlords.

TABLE 6.1. A Typology of Peasant Protests in England, 1540–1639

	Landlord Targets	
Peasant Participants	Tight County Elites	Disorganized Landlords
Freeholders led well-organized communities	(1) 1549: Somerset, Wiltshire, Kent, Hampshire, Rutland, Suffolk	(2) 1549: Cornwall, Norfolk
Freeholders passive, unified copyholders, cotters, and laborers rebel	(3) 1549: Lincolnshire 1607: Midlands 1603–1639: Durham, Cumberland, Westmorland, Northumberland, Lancashire	(4) 1549: Leicestershire
Disorganized cotters and laborers protest	(5) 1608–1639: Lincolnshire and Yorkshire fenlands; Derby, Stafford, Somerset, and Wiltshire forests	(6) —

Sources: Appleby 1975; Charlesworth 1983; Cornwall 1977; Fletcher 1968; Land 1977; Manning 1974; MacCulloch 1979; Sharp 1980.

Landlords were weakly organized in three other counties in which significant rebellion occurred in 1549—Cornwall and Norfolk (cell 2) and Leicestershire (cell 4). Even though the Leicestershire rebels were mainly copyholders, with weak legal claims to their lands, the disorganized landlords of that county quickly gave in to the rebels' demands in order to diffuse the uprising. Copyholders in Leicestershire were quietly ascertained out of their tenancies in the seventeenth century, once the gentry had organized themselves into a tight elite.

Cornwall and Norfolk were the two counties with the most widespread and violent rebellions of 1549. The magnitude and success of peasant opposition were due to the unusual degree of landlord weakness in those two counties. Cornwall was a duchy belonging by right to the king's eldest son. As a result, the crown held a large portion of Cornish manors. There were no great magnates in Cornwall. The majority of manors not belonging to the crown were held by small gentry. These landlords were unable to build networks of cooperation through the commission of the peace, since county offices were dominated by the royal officials who administered the duchy holdings (Cornwall 1977, pp. 41–47). Norfolk manors were held by large and small landlords who were resident in the county. However, the two great Norfolk magnates, the Howards and Courtneys, had come into conflict with Henry VIII and had lost many of their manors and been removed from county offices, weakening their ability to take a leading role in county affairs (Land 1977, pp. 37–41).

Cornish peasants were well-organized through strong manor courts and were able to quickly mobilize across village lines. On the plurality of manors owned by the crown, bailiffs awaited instructions from the royal court. Other landlords deferred to the crown as well. A delay in instructions prevented an early landlord response in terms of concessions or repression, permitting a peasant army to form and gain wide support. After early setbacks, the crown defeated the rebels at Exeter. The county was pacified with executions of rebel leaders and concessions to freeholders. The crown fortified the local gentry by granting manors to victorious military officers. As the balance of power shifted to local gentry, an effective county government developed, and ascertainments and enclosures were accomplished without any further rebellions (Cornwall 1977, pp. 64–136, 176–206; Wordie 1983, p. 489).

The Norfolk rebellion began in a single village with an episode of hedge destruction led by Robert Kett, hence the name Kett's Rebellion. The Norfolk Commission of the Peace, paralyzed by factionalism and crown purges, was unable to move against Kett and his followers. The rebels, believing that they enjoyed royal support against the gentry's plans to undermine freehold and copyhold rights, continued to mobilize and to escalate their demands. As in Cornwall, initial rebel victories were finally countered by royal forces. Again, leaders were executed and the mass of rebels offered concessions (Cornwall 1977, pp. 137–59, 268–75, 207–225; Fletcher 1968, pp. 64–77; Land 1977). The Norfolk gentry established tight control over county government by the end of the sixteenth century and then were able to move against peasants without provoking later rebellions (Bearman 1993).

Lincolnshire, the final site of rebellion in 1549, was similar to the situation in the six counties in cell 1 in that strong peasant communities confronted tight county elites. However, the Lincolnshire protesters were mainly copyholders. The relatively few freeholders of Lincolnshire remained passive in 1549. The Lincolnshire landlords made few concessions, relying on force to end rent strikes (Thirsk 1957, pp. 47–48, 148). This county's experience in 1549 fits that of other counties in later decades (cell 3) in which landlords confronted well-organized peasant communities, with long-standing customary land rights and institutions of self-government, but with few militant freeholders. Landlords, in those situations, were able to successfully repress rebellion without offering concessions, in contrast to the situations (cell 1) in which freeholders were dealt with through negotiations.

Freeholders were largely absent from the later protests, which spanned the half century from the 1580s until the eve of the 1640 Revolution and peaked with the 1607 Midland Revolt. Those protests were mounted by cotters and laborers and were directed against tight county elites. Thus, we need to explain why freeholders withdrew from agrarian class conflict after 1549, and why poorer peasants challenged tightly organized county elites in the decades before the Revolution.

Freeholders were passive after 1549 because landlords had learned from the rebellions of that decade to respect the interests of the powerful and well-organized freeholders. The landlords of late sixteenth and seventeenth century East Anglia allied with freeholders to undermine manor courts and most enclosures were by agreement with freeholders.[26]

A wave of protests and riots began in the 1580s, culminating in the Midland Revolt of 1607 (cell 3). These protests were concentrated in the Midlands (most strongly in Warwickshire, Leicestershire, and Northamptonshire; there were significant uprisings, especially in 1607, in Lincolnshire, Oxfordshire, Bedfordshire, Derbyshire, and Worchestershire as well) where newly hegemonic gentry county elites attempted to ascertain copyholder rights, to impose restrictions on landless peasants' mobility and residence, and to curtail all peasants' use of commons and forests. Five of the eight rebellious Midland counties were among the counties with the highest rates of enclosure in the sixteenth century.[27] Other riots occurred in Northumberland, where gentry who had escaped magnate domination with the help of the crown, formed a tight county elite, and sought to raise rents on their tenants.

The uprisings of 1607 were easily crushed because the absence of freeholder participation weakened rebel unity, and especially retarded mobilization across villages (Charlesworth 1983, pp. 33–36). The defeat of peasant activism combined with gentry hegemony in the Midlands counties to pave the way for widespread enclosure in the seventeenth century. Twelve times as much land was enclosed in England in the seventeenth century as had been in the sixteenth century (Wordie 1983, p. 502). The enclosures of 1600–1699 were centered on the Midlands and most were by agreement between surviving freeholders and gentry who acted in the confidence that copyholders and landless peasants could not challenge their loss of access to commons, forests, and wastes, and that their enclosure plans would be aided, through the county commissions of the peace, by the tight county elites of which they were a part.

The other areas of peasant protest in the period 1580–1639 were the northern border counties, the fenlands of Lincolnshire and Yorkshire, and the forests of Wiltshire, Somerset, Staffordshire, and Derby (Charlesworth 1983, pp. 36–39). Tenants in the border counties of Northumberland, Durham, Cumberland, Westmorland, and Lancashire lost their special tenant rights and royal protections once their participation in border militias was rendered unnecessary by the 1603 Union of the Crowns of England and Scotland. Landlords quickly moved to make use of ascertainment and rejected customary limits on fines for renewal of leases. Border county tenants were mostly copyholders, with few freeholders. Tightly organized county elites successfully defeated protests and, in the absence of many freeholders, had few concessions to make (Appleby 1975).

The protests in the fenlands and forests (cell 5) were mounted by cotters (tenants with below subsistence holdings) and laborers who depended upon common rights in the fens and forage rights in forests to make ends meet. Landlords in those counties were tightly organized and were aided by the crown, which had large landholdings in the fens and forests and invested along with the gentry in fen drainage and deforestation schemes. Protests were repressed, although acts of sabotage against drainage works continued (Charlesworth 1983, pp. 38–39). Drainage and deforestation were halted as elite unity was undermined in the Revolution and Civil War. The restoration of elite unity at the end of the Civil War allowed drainage and deforestation and the expulsion of cotters and laborers to proceed again.

To sum up: Peasant uprisings were most likely where freeholders were relatively numerous and had a high degree of social organization. Those conditions existed mainly in the part of England classified as old arable, areas with open fields regulated by manor courts under strong landlords (Thirsk 1967).[28] Most of the arable counties however, did not experience significant peasant rebellion. Strong peasants rebelled only when and where their ancient rights were challenged by landlords. Landlords in most of England acted slowly, especially after 1549, using strategies that were based on concessions to, and cooperation with, freeholders.

The Midlands and northern border counties were unusual in that the gentry experienced rapid gains in power at the expense of old magnates and the crown. Having quickly formed tight elites and gaining hegemonic control over the commissions of the peace and other county offices, the gentry of those counties moved precipitously to dispossess their tenants. The gentry miscalculated in the short-run by sparking rebellions that required royal assistance to put down.

Landlords moved slowly and cautiously in challenging peasants' traditional land rights in those counties where the gentry remained disorganized in the seventeenth century. That is why cell 6 (table 6.1) is empty, and cells 2 and 4 do not have entries from after 1549.

Peasant communities became less able to rebel as landlords disrupted settled villages through ascertainment and enclosure and attacked tenants' organizational bases through boycotts of manor courts in alliance with freeholders. Landlords focused their attentions first on the counties (and manors within them) where peasants had been strongest and most privileged. Landlords did so because those were the places where the crown and clerics made their strongest claims against lay landlords. Those counties then became the first sites of tight county elites, which could use their new powers to gain use and income rights on land at the expense of settled copyholder communities. Ironically, cotters and laborers on the outlying wastelands of England—fens and forests—were left as the only peasants with the unity to mount rebellions in the 1600s, because they had been overlooked by the gentry in the sixteenth century.

The rebellions were fortuitous for the gentry in three ways over the long-run. First, military force served to break peasant power in the Midlands. Second, the gentry learned from their experiences and respected freeholders' rights in order to divide peasant communities and blunt future protests. Freeholders took advantage of their status and security of tenure to become small-scale, and sometimes larger, commercial farmers. Commercial farmers became the crucial intermediaries between the gentry and agricultural laborers, managing the former's lands and controlling the latter's labor, and thus ensuring that landowners reaped the lion's share of agricultural profits. Thus, the political limits that forced the gentry to respect freeholders' rights had the inadvertent effect of creating the intermediate stratum crucial for the gentry's subsequent prosperity.

Finally, the gentry saw that landless peasants were as much of a threat as were the copyholders who lost their land rights as a result of ascertainment and enclosure. The gentry sought to gain greater control over cottagers and landless peasants who were the most numerous participants in the agrarian protests of the late sixteenth and early seventeenth century. The gentry made use of the Poor Laws to regulate, through the county commissions of the peace, the residence, employment, and behavior of the plurality of peasants who became dependent upon wage labor rather than their own tenements in the century between the Dissolution and the Revolution. The gentry's dual strategy of concessions toward freeholders and repression of cotters and laborers in response to agrarian protests had consequences for English agrarian class relations. Those consequences are examined in the concluding section of this chapter.

France

The modes and objects of French peasant rebellion were transformed in the century and a half from the end of the Frondes to the Revolution.[29] The great provincewide and regional peasant revolts of the seventeenth century gave way to more localized protests, which produced fewer casualties, after 1700. After the final defeat of the Camisards' rebellion in Languedoc in 1710 (Joutard 1976), the countryside and cities experienced no large-scale uprisings until the 1789 Revolution itself. Fewer peasants and laborers died from internal political violence from 1708 to 1788 than in the previous eighty years. We lack comprehensive national totals, but Lemarchand (1990, p. 33) counts 69 deaths due to protests in Provence from 1596 to 1660, but only 3 deaths from 1661 to 1715. More impressionistic accounts make a similar point.[30]

Peasant protesters changed targets over the course of the seventeenth and eighteenth centuries. Taxes, and the officials who collected state revenues, were the principal targets of peasant violence before 1660. Antitax protests fell off in subsequent decades, becoming almost "non-existent" by 1700 (Lemarchand 1990, p. 33), not surprising since the real revenues of the French crown declined 2 percent from the 1650s to the 1720s after climbing 335 percent in the previous five decades. Antitax protests did not revive in frequency or intensity even when royal tax extractions increased again, rising 85 percent from the 1720s to the 1780s (table 5.4).

Peasants shifted their anger toward grain merchants after 1660. Subsistence riots by hungry peasants and laborers became the dominant mode of protest, especially with the poor harvests of the 1690s. Lemarchand hypothesizes that the rise of grain markets increased the likelihood that grain would be hoarded and shipped through regions suffering from poor harvests. Markets, thus, could reduce local supplies and, more important for provoking protests, create visible and dramatic targets in the form of grain convoys (1990, pp. 33–36).

Subsistence protests remained important during the years of the Revolution, constituting 26 percent of all events tallied by Markoff (1996, p. 218), second only to antiseigneurial actions. Markoff and Vovelle both identify factors that indicate that markets are the strongest predictors of revolutionary violence in the countryside. Markoff finds that "the most consistently strong relationships for all forms of mobilization [during the Revolution] are with city size and road length. The propensity to rural mobilization of the *bailliages* with city size above the median is double (or more) that of those below for every type of event; the impact of road length is almost as marked" (p. 380). Cities and roads are proxies for markets. Markoff argues that markets (brought to the countryside from nearby cities by roads) affected agrarian class relations directly by proletarianizing peasant labor and appropriating peasant land for production geared to urban markets. Markets, thus, encouraged antiseigneurial, subsistence, land, and wage conflicts (pp. 380–82, 399–407).[31]

In the century before the Revolution, peasants began to direct their anger at aggressively demanding seigneurs. Lemarchand finds a rise in antiseigneurial protests in those parts of France where seigneurs were most effective at increasing their demands upon peasants. Throughout France the number of antiseigneurial actions more than tripled from 1690–1720 to 1760–89. Such protests remained half as common as antitax protests in the three decades leading up to the Revolution, yet they are indicators of the anger that erupted in 1789.

The French Revolution in the countryside was above all an antiseigneurial revolution. More than a third (36 percent) of events were directed against seigneurs (Markoff 1996, p. 218). Peasant uprisings, whatever their targets, pushed the National Assembly toward its ultimate legislative abolition of all seigneurial rights without compensation in July 1793. Even the counterrevolutionary uprising in the Vendee led the National Assembly to strengthen its antiseignurial legislation rather than to reduce the new taxes that were the main target of Western protests (Markoff 1996, pp. 428–515).[32]

Taken together, Lemarchand, Vovelle, and Markoff reveal a shift in the eighteenth century from protests against grasping state officials toward actions against resurgent seigneurs and emergent grain merchants, employers of agrarian labor, and capitalist farmers. The protests of the late ancien régime and the actions of the Revolution were, to judge from their locations, responses to the efforts of commercial agents as well as of seigneurs to recast agrarian land-tenure arrangements, rural labor, and the movement of grain for their greater profit. Peasants and laborers who suffered from those changes reacted with protests, strikes, and violence.

Rural protests were not ultimately ineffectual "weapons of the weak."[33] Peasants propelled forward a revolution of enormous consequences. The rural actions that made the Revolution were not multiple repetitions by isolated, though unified, peasant villages. "We simply have to abandon the whole notion of a specifically antiseigneurial openfield area, indeed of an intensely solidary peasantry, bound by intravillage solidarities forged in their intermixed fields, and involved in endless battles with the lord over the boundaries of their collective rights and his individual ones, taking the lead in the French rural struggle" (Markoff 1996, pp. 397–98).[34]

Ancien régime and revolutionary actions were conducted in a dialogue with the targets of protests.[35] Peasants responded to and thereby deepened elite divisions and weaknesses. Protests before and through the Frondes reflected the contradictory claims and overlapping jurisdictions of conflicted elites. Urban and peasant rebels challenged tax collectors because the powers and privileges of their offices were the subject of elite conflict. Popular forces rebelled against the exploding burden of taxes and at the opportunity opened by elite divisions.

The popular Frondes had the unintended effect of forcing competing elites to submit to the jurisdictional arbitration of the crown. Elite conflicts over control of "state" revenues abruptly lessened after the Frondes. Peasants had less room for resistance against state officials, even when taxes resumed their increase in the eighteenth century.

New elite conflicts developed over control of agrarian land and labor. Peasants, during the last century of the ancien régime, were burdened by the demands made by the manipulators of markets in land, labor, and grain. Lemarchand, Vovelle, and Markoff's data show the correlation of markets and protests. Antimarket protests could and did take different forms—subsistence riots directed against grain merchants and grain convoys, labor strikes, panics, land conflicts, and antiseigneurial actions.

Why did seigneurs become the prime target of peasants during the Revolution? They did so because seigneurs and their privileges became the focus of elite conflicts. Brittany and Provence were the earliest sites of peasant mobilization with an antiseigneurial cast in 1789. "Elite politics in . . . [those provinces] were among the most polarized in France, perhaps the most polarized" (Markoff 1996, pp. 358–59). Conflicts among nobles and with the bourgeois of the Third Estate suggested to peasants that antiseigneurial protests might bear fruit. The meetings at which the Cahiers de Doleances were composed gave peasants an unprecedented and unparalleled opportunity to hear the divisions within and between the clerical, noble, and bourgeois estates, divisions that were sharpest over the issue of seigneurial privileges. "It hardly seems surprising, then, that the proportion of insurrections targeting the seigneurial regime now doubled in the spring [of 1789]. The country people were discovering that if they pushed hard there would be at least some support from significant portions of the Third Estate and an important portion of the clergy and they were probably aware of the divided and ineffective capacity of the nobility to defend themselves" (p. 495).

The structure of elite relations and the nature of elite conflicts changed in France over the course of the seventeenth and eighteenth centuries. As relations among elites changed, so did each elite's capacity to control and exploit peasants and to withstand peasant opposition. Peasants were able to read and respond to elite divisions and weaknesses in the short term. The abolition of seigneurial privileges was the fruit of elite weaknesses and peasant initiative during the Revolution. The final section of this chapter deals with the effects of that abolition for French capitalism.

Comparisons

Agrarian conflict in England and France differed in fundamental ways. English landlords managed to divide peasantries, co-opting freeholders while decapitating the leadership of copyholders, cotters, and laborers. Victories on battlefields and in lesser confrontations allowed landlords to proceed with strategies—ascertainment, enclosure, the boycott of manorial courts, and the regulation of labor and residence through the Poor Laws—that further weakened peasant communities and undermined the bases for later agrarian mobilizations. As a result, peasants were largely inactive, never playing an important role, in the Revolution and Civil War. Lay landlords were firmly in control of land and labor from the Henrician Reformation on, providing a secure base for their confrontations with rival elites. The gentry could confront the king and his allies in the Civil War without having to fight their laborers and tenants on a second front. The weakness of peasant rebellions in sixteenth- and seventeenth-century England demonstrates that the gentry had subdued class conflicts in the course of removing rival royal and clerical elites from direct roles in regulating or profiting from agrarian production.

French seigneurs, to review, never gained a monopoly of control over agrarian relations of production. As a result, they were unable to adopt strategies that could have co-opted or defeated rebellious peasants. Seigneurs, at each crucial moment of elite conflict, were hampered by peasant rebellions. Aristocratic Frondeurs were forced to surrender to the king when they were attacked by peasant rebels and bankrupted by rent strikes. The Great Fear and subsequent waves of protests undermined both the king and the nobility in their conflicts with the Third Estate, allowing the National Assembly to abolish the landed income rights of the nobility at the same time the Revolution swept away the offices, rentes, tax farms, and bonds that were the other foundations of aristocratic power and wealth.

Economic Development in England and France

Now that we have traced the courses and outcomes of elite and class conflicts in England and France, we can specify the effects of those conflicts upon agrarian production, and on the distribution of the fruits of agricultural land and labor, in the two countries. The changes in land tenure arrangements overlapped with the agricultural revolution that doubled crop yields throughout much of northwestern Europe from the thirteenth to the eighteenth centuries.

Farmers applied an array of new techniques—improved seeds, new crops and more efficient rotations, better stock breeds and bigger flocks and herds (which produced more manure to further boost crop yields), and investments in drainage and irrigation—in an effort to increase their productivity. Knowledge of and access to improved seeds and new technologies diffused quickly and became known within a few decades to farmers throughout northwestern Europe as each innovation was developed.[36]

The new techniques produced dramatic increases in crop yields, which were unprecedented on such a wide scale in human history.[37] Yields per acre doubled throughout England from ten bushels of wheat per acre in the thirteenth through fifteenth centuries to twenty bushels per acre by the late eighteenth century (Allen 1992, p. 131).[38] Farmers in northeastern France, Ireland, the Netherlands, and Belgium also realized yields of at least twenty bushels per acre by the beginning of the nineteenth century (Allen 1992, p. 131; Hoffman 1996, pp. 132–42, 161).

Knowledge of new crops and rotations, and of techniques to integrate intensified livestock-raising with arable farming, were ubiquitous in England, as they were in northeastern France and the other countries that achieved improvements in crops yields per acre similar to those of England.[39] Most of northwestern Europe diverged from the rest of the world in experiencing a doubling of agricultural productivity over the three centuries from 1500 to 1800.

How can we explain an agricultural revolution that spanned different countries, regions, and soil and field types. Demographic models are not helpful since the post-plague population recovery and the rapid growth of the long sixteenth century coincided with agricultural stagnation in southern and eastern Europe as well as with the agricultural revolution of northwestern Europe.[40] Variations in soil types and in medieval field systems within one or several countries cannot be used to account for a uniform and massive improvement in productivity across an entire subcontinental area.[41] Soil types mattered for both commercial and yeomen farmers in the sense that they selected certain new techniques, and rejected others, to best improve the yields in the particular ecological niches in which they farmed.

Regions within northwestern Europe varied mainly in whether any, some, or many farmers undertook improvements. Yields doubled in those places where farmers invested in improvements; yields stagnated where farmers did not undertake improvements. The questions that need to be answered, and which are not addressed by regional comparisons within England and France are: (1) Why did farmers in much of northwestern Europe invest their labor and capital in new agricultural techniques that doubled outputs while farmers in other parts of Europe where innovations also would have yielded impressive improvements in agricultural productivity, such as Spain and Italy,[42] did not? and (2) Who benefited from the gains in productivity? I answer those questions in the remainder of this chapter.

New techniques were applied within decades of their development wherever European farmers enjoyed secure control over land and had control over their own labor or access to wage labor. Secure land tenure was the first necessary precondition since landholders or leasors would invest in improvements only if they could be sure of reaping a large enough share of the benefits of higher productivity over a long enough period to justify the expenses of new crops, bigger flocks and herds, or better drainage. Only landowners or holders of unrevokable long-term leases had the security to make such long-term plans and investments in improvements.

Motivated workers were the second necessary precondition, since the new techniques were complex enough that they had to be carried out by motivated workers to realize the higher yields that would justify the required investments. Family farmers were ideal and wage laborers adequate. Serfs or tenants performing labor dues did not work at a level sufficient to fulfill the demands of the more complex new techniques.[43]

England

Most manors in most counties in England, in arable and pastoral regions alike, attained both conditions necessary for the agricultural revolution during the century following the Dissolution of the Monasteries. The withdrawal of clerical jurisdiction, the weakening of royal judicial review, and above all the boycotting and demise of manorial courts left both leasors (lords and gentry) and many cultivators (copyholders and freeholders) with unencumbered use of former manor lands.

Allen (1992) demonstrates that freeholders and copyholders (whom he and many historians label yeomen) were the initial innovators and improvers of English agriculture. Allen has produced the most comprehensive assessment of changes in agricultural productivity in England and has correlated changes in yield with soil types, enclosure, and the use of family and wage labor. He finds that "yeomen farmers had accomplished [in the late sixteenth and the seventeenth centuries] all of the advance in wheat yields and half of the advance in barley yields realized by enclosed, capitalist farmers in the nineteenth century" (p. 208). Seventeenth-century yeomen, by almost all measures, were as productive and endowed their farms with as much capital as the owners and commercial leasors of large farms in the subsequent centuries. Allen finds that "the capital provided by tenants was of the same magnitude as that supplied by landlords—about £3–£4 per acre per year" (p. 191). Reanalyzing Arthur Young's data, Allen finds:

> First, capital per acre declined with farm size [i.e., smaller farms were better capitalized than large farms]. Second, when finance is the measure of capital, arable farms were more capital-intensive than pastoral farms. This result is due to the fact that finance includes the advance payment of wages, and arable farms were more labor-intensive than pastoral farms. . . . Third when capital is measured by either capital cost or animal density, pastoral farms used more capital per acre than arable farms. . . . It is remarkable that Young's data contradict his belief that large-scale farmers practiced a more capital-intensive agriculture than small-scale farmers." (p. 195)[44]

Large farms of the eighteenth and nineteenth century were more likely to be undercapitalized than were the yeomen farms of the sixteenth and seventeenth centuries. Yeomen who paid stable rents prior to ascertainment and enclosure were able to self-finance agricultural improvements "as long as agriculture simply reproduced itself. In the eighteenth century, however, enclosure followed by the conversion of arable to pasture and the growth in farm size required the declining number of successful farmers to increase their capital rapidly" (Allen 1992 p. 199).

Landowners who had taken yeomen's farms through ascertainment and enclosure rarely invested the needed new capital themselves. The switch from arable to grass in pasture districts, the adoption of new crop rotations in light arable areas, and the digging of drains on heavy arable lands, all were more likely to be instituted on enclosed lands than where open fields remained. Yet, most of the doubling of yields took place before enclosure and occurred on open as well as enclosed lands. Allen concludes that "on average, open field farms accomplished 86 per cent of the advance realized by enclosed farms. Enclosure played a very small role in the yield increase" (1992, pp. 134–35). The improvements to enclosed lands were made by tenants with long-term leases or by surviving copyholders and freeholders rather than by the landlords whose estates were enclosed and who had provided the political muscle to propel enclosure forward.

Even if enclosure did not significantly increase England's agricultural output, it combined with population growth and increasing food prices under protective tariffs to allow landowners to increase their share of the nation's income in the form of rents. Consumers derived no benefit in the form of lower prices from the doubling of productivity between 1400 and 1800. Instead, food prices rose 15 percent from 1450 to 1550, remained stagnant until 1750, and then rose another 25 to 30 percent from 1750 to 1800, thanks to the concentration of land and to protectionist policies. "The rising real price of food burdened the poor especially since they spent a higher share of their income on food than did the rich" (Allen 1992, p. 284).

"The owners of [agricultural] labour and capital also failed to reap gains." The real rental price of animals and tools, which Allen uses as the best proxy for return on agrarian capital excluding land, "fluctuated within narrow limits" from 1450 to 1825 (1992, p. 285). Real wages for agricultural laborers declined almost 50 percent from 1450 to 1600,[45] then recovered slightly over the next two centuries so that wages in 1825 were still a third lower than in 1450 (p. 286). Thus, the consumers of food, the investors in agricultural improvements, and the leasors and wage laborers who worked the land did not benefit from the agrarian revolution in England.

Wages declined in part because the institutions tight county-elites created to protect their estates from royal and clerical claims and to suppress peasant unrest also controlled landless laborers. The most powerful landowners of each county were able to reduce their wage costs to below market levels by putting to work on their estates laborers whose subsistence was paid through poor rates (taxes used to support the poor).

Legislation passed after the 1549 peasant rebellions emphasized the control aspects of relief. Lay parliamentarians, with the support of Warwick's government, transferred charitable foundations and authority over peasants on relief from parish clerics to the justices of the peace (Kelly 1977, p. 165). These poor laws were part of the general effort by lay landlords to weaken clerical control over, and protection of, peasants. Beginning in 1556, justices of the peace (JPs) gained the right to appoint overseers of the poor in each parish with the power to assess and collect a compulsory poor rate (Emmison 1931, pp. 102–16; Hampson 1934, pp. 1–12; Leonard 1965, pp. 57–58). The level at which poor rates could be assessed was increased periodically by Parliament during the last decades of the sixteenth century, as the number of landless peasants dependent on relief multiplied (Leonard 1965, pp. 67–72). Finally, in 1597, JPs were allowed to assess and distribute the burden of poor taxes countywide. This legislation aided JPs in their efforts to act as a county government and to compel parishes where peasants still held strong land rights, and hence there were few vagabonds, to subsidize the relief costs in parishes where tenant evictions had created a large number of landless peasants (Hampson 1934, pp. 13–16; Leonard 1965, p. 76).

Justices of the peace derived broad authority to regulate and punish vagrants from the thirteen poor laws that Parliament passed between 1495 and 1610. Any "masterless man" (or woman or child) defined as a vagrant could be jailed, forced to labor in a workhouse, fined, or whipped (Beier 1985, pp. 8–13). Justices were given the power to limit peasant mobility in a 1556 law that allowed landless peasants to be returned to their county of origin (Hampson 1934, pp. 1–12). Justices only rarely used their power to transport a vagabond across England to his home county; most often they forced the landless to settle away from parishes dominated by enclosed estates (Beier 1969, pp. 172–73; Slack 1974, pp. 360–79). The poor-law powers that justices inherited from the clergy and that were augmented by Parliament were the basis of their authority to finance the subsistence and to police the mobility of landless peasants within the counties.

Justices of the peace and the overseers whom they appointed made restriction of peasant mobility their primary task (Beier 1985; Willcox 1946, pp. 240–47). Villages and parishes that had been enclosed became "closed," with small populations and no available positions for resident laborers. The poor were confined to "open" villages, preventing their encroachment upon enclosed estates. The division of lands into open and closed areas limited the poor rates for landlords who had enclosed entire parishes and thus had no resident poor. Open villages paid the bulk of the poor rates needed to support landless laborers, who then worked on the estates in closed villages at meager wages (Yelling 1977, pp. 214–32). Countywide poor rates were used by seventeenth-century poor law commissioners to assess parishes composed largely of freeholds in which few peasants had been evicted from the land. Countywide taxation increased the burden for prosperous peasants, while owners of enclosed estates avoided increased assessments, since they were often the powerful county politicians who served as JPs and controlled the assessment process (Hampson 1934, p. 221; Leonard 1965, p. 167).

Laws requiring families to hold a minimum of four acres were enforced in closed villages and disregarded in open areas. Landlords would rent tiny plots of land for cottages to the poor on estates that they held in open areas. Records of meetings by JPs and overseers of the poor reveal frequent grants of permission to landlords to rent cottages with less than the minimum of four acres to their laborers. Further, poor relief was applied toward the rent on such cottages, providing a direct subsidy to landlords. Those landlords who were given permission to erect cottages on small plots and who received the bulk of rent subsidies for their tenants usually were JPs, overseers of the poor, or members of leading gentry families (Barnes 1961, pp. 40–90; Fletcher 1968, p. 157; Oxley 1974, p. 107; Willcox 1946, pp. 256–57).

Poor-relief officials differentiated between the ill, elderly, and children—who were objects of private charity (Beier 1985, pp. 3–13 and passim; Oxley 1974, pp. 51–60, 102–19)—and the able-bodied poor, who were put to work with the use of funds raised by poor rates. In addition to the rent on their cottages, the able-bodied poor at times received cash or food (Oxley 1974, p. 107). Since the subsistence needs of the able-bodied poor were met by relief, employers did not need to pay more than a token wage to those poor whom they employed. Relief, thus, functioned as a subsidy from the mass of ratepayers to the employers of able-bodied poor, who were receiving almost free labor (Oxley 1974, pp. 14–33, 102–19). As a result, employers vied for the right to receive relief workers. The same wealthy and politically well-connected landlords who received cottage rents also got the use of subsidized laborers (Leonard 1965, p. 167; Oxley 1974, p. 107).

While poor rates were a smaller burden upon the mass of farmers who paid the bulk of the tax than were rents or tithes (one estimate places the cost of the poor rate at a fifth of the tithe [Gibbons 1959, pp. 93–95]), they added to the burdens that made small holdings unprofitable in bad economic times and so hastened the decline of small holders. The concentration of poor-relief payments to the laborers of a few landlords in each county provided a powerful incentive for those landowners to make use of subsidized wage labor and increased the profitability of their commercial farms. Concomitantly, subsidized labor provided yet another incentive for landlords to expel tenants from their estates and to enclose, which further swelled the ranks of the landless poor.

Landowners reaped virtually all the gains in agricultural productivity in England from the sixteenth through eighteenth centuries. Rents per acre, controlling for inflation, fell slightly from 1450 to 1550, then quadrupled from 1550 to 1600, the first decades of massive ascertainment and dispossession of peasants. Rents then tripled again from 1600 to 1825 (Allen 1992, p. 286).

Allen argues that enclosure was about the fruits of agricultural innovations already put into practice by yeomen. From the discussion of landlord strategies in the first section of this chapter, we can add that ascertainment, the boycotts of manorial courts, and the attacks on royal and clerical court jurisdictions also were efforts by landlords to reap the benefits of higher productivity generated by yeomen. Recall however, that the gentry devised those strategies primarily to fend off challenges from rival elites.

Allen (1994) shows no awareness of the continuing constraints of elite conflicts and does not directly address the political origins of landowners' strategies. He takes for granted landlords' hegemony over land and labor. Yet, by demonstrating that landlords added virtually nothing to the productivity of English agriculture, Allen forever shatters what he calls "agrarian fundamentalism." Tories and Marxists both are agrarian fundamentalists, sharing the conviction that "enclosures and large farms promoted productivity growth. . . . The Tories believe that large farms and enclosures maintained or increased farm employment while increasing production even more; the result was a rise in both yields and labour productivity.[46] In contrast, the Marxists insist that the new institutions reduced farm employment thereby raising productivity" (p. 4). Allen demonstrates that there "were two agricultural revolutions in English history—the yeomen's and the landlords'" (p. 21). The yeomen's revolution created the productivity gains; the landlords' transferred and concentrated the fruits of the revolutionary increase in productivity.

The two revolutions were made possible by the interactions of elite and class conflicts. The elite conflicts centering on the Henrician Reformation gave yeomen the security of tenure (albeit only temporary) to undertake the investments that doubled agricultural yields. Later elite conflicts consolidated power in gentry hands, allowing the landlords to make their revolution by appropriating land from tenants, and garnering, through ongoing rent increases, the full benefits of the productivity increases for which the yeomen had paid and sweated.

Landlord efforts to capture more of the increased productivity (through enclosure and ascertainment) did not reduce productivity. Here is a key difference between England and France. In England, landlords transferred income from peasants to themselves without lowering productivity (although Allen shows that productivity did not increase further when landlords enclosed). In France the seigneurial reaction undermined the productivity of the French equivalent of yeomen.

France

France's agricultural productivity grew at a much slower rate overall than did England's in the sixteenth through eighteenth centuries. "Labor productivity on French farms gained perhaps 27 percent between 1500 and 1800, [while in] England . . . it almost doubled. . . . By the end of the eighteenth century it took only forty English farmers to feed one hundred people. The French needed nearly sixty" (Hoffman 1996, pp. 136, 139–40).

France's overall dismal performance masks wide variations across time and place. Some regions, such as Normandy, experienced virtually no growth from 1520 to 1785, while output in the west and much of the south actually declined substantially during the seventeenth and eighteenth centuries (Hoffman 1996, p. 130). "In the Paris Basin . . . growth rates [of agricultural productivity] could soar high by early modern standards: 0.3 to 0.4 percent per year in the sixteenth century, 0.3 percent per year or more at their peak in the late eighteenth century" (p. 133). Similar long-term growth rates were achieved from 1550 to 1789 in Lorraine and perhaps other parts of northeastern France. The southeast, which began the sixteenth century with lower yields than the Parisian basin, caught up with the prime farmlands of the north in the eighteenth century by sustaining the highest long-term growth rates of any region in France (p. 130). The yields, and the "total factor productivity" of labor and capital invested in agriculture, in these advanced regions of France were as high as in the most productive counties in England (pp. 140–42).

The wide variations among French regions undercuts models that attempt to explain French agricultural change as the consequence of demographic cycles.[47] Regional differences are important, although not for the reasons given by most scholars of French geography. There is no correlation between ancien régime trends in productivity and soil types. Areas Goldstone (1988, p. 290 map) classifies as possessing similarly good soils variously experienced productivity increases (the Paris basin and

Lorraine), stagnation (Normandy), and absolute decline (the northwest), while a region of poor soils (the southeast) enjoyed the highest long-term rates of productivity increases in all of France.

If demography and soil types do not explain the divergent fates of ancien régime french agriculture, then what factors do? Control over land and labor, and access to capital, markets, and transportation networks mattered in France as much as it did in England. Agricultural markets and transportation networks were centered on Paris because royal policies concentrated population and wealth in the capital and because roads and canals emanated from Paris for strategic reasons. In so doing, royal policies created a center of demand that fostered agricultural innovation and improvement in the Paris basin and in other regions linked to the capital.

The majority of the increase in agricultural productivity during the ancien régime occurred in the expanding ambit of regions that served the growing Paris market. As the urban population grew, so did demand for feed for urban livestock, which in turn stimulated farmers' investment in artificial meadows. Farmers carted feed to Paris and returned with manure, which boosted crop yields. Parisians, as their numbers and wealth grew, demanded more and higher quality grains, vines, and livestock (Gruter 1977). Merchants organized transportation networks that reduced transaction and shipping costs and further boosted the Parisian market for specialized agricultural products. Roads and canals, which emanated from Paris, tied the Parisian basin, Normandy, and the northeast to the capital's market, while further disadvantaging the west and south of France (Hoffman 1996, pp. 170–84).[48]

While Paris stimulated agricultural innovation and investment in certain regions, the French crown, and the vertical absolutism it created, undermined agricultural development in all other respects. Taxes, arbitrary seizures, and looting and confiscations during wartime repeatedly robbed French farmers of cash, livestock, and other forms of agrarian investment capital. Each such instance of expropriation or devastation set back agricultural productivity. "The expropriations of the mid-seventeenth century created starving sharecroppers" out of prosperous peasant "entrepreneurs" (Fitch 1978, pp. 204–205). War, and the state fiscal crises that followed in its wake, "ravaged the rural economy and caused productivity to plummet" (Hoffman 1996, p. 202). Recovery took decades; repeated wars left much of France less productive at the end of the seventeenth century than at the beginning. Some French farming regions were poorer in 1789 than they had been in 1500 (Dontenwill 1973; Fitch 1978; Hoffman 1996; Jacquart 1975).

Perpetual elite conflict, and the overlapping jurisdictions engendered by vertical absolutism, ensured that most farmland in ancien régime France never became private property, with a single owner in full control of the land and its output, as happened in seventeenth-century England. Crown stratagems that divided elites, and ensured tax collectors' access to peasant production, also perpetuated legal rights that became insurmountable barriers for those seeking to enclose their property.

French farmers remained limited in their control over land throughout the entire ancien régime. No single elite enjoyed a monopoly of control over land that would have justified capital investments in improvements that could have produced significant increases in yields. Enclosure in France required the unanimous consent of all landholders in a village. French landlords never were able to win legislation allowing for enclosure by majority vote as in England. Any landholder in a village could, if he had sufficient resources, sue to block enclosure. Enclosures in France were confined to the rare villages where a landlord was willing to pay all the lesser landholders a premium for agreeing to enclosure, or where all the other landholders were too poor to sue to block enclosure (Hoffman 1996, pp. 33–34; Jacquart 1974; Neveux 1975; 1980; Venard 1957, pp. 51–55).

Even where landlords were able to make agreements to swap parcels of land with lesser landholders or to force through enclosures, farm "consolidation failed to boost the yield of grain" (Hoffman 1996, p. 160). "Removing the political obstacles to enclosure would have done little for productivity," since the sorts of large-scale drainage projects made possible by enclosure would have boosted productivity by "under 3 percent" (p. 170).[49]

Growth in farm size did contribute to the overall rise in productivity, adding 1 percent to total output in the Parisian basin, and up to 7 percent in Normandy in the late seventeenth and the eighteenth centuries. "Practically none of the [productivity increase] derived from . . . capital improvements [such as] drainage, buildings, or land reclamation" (Hoffman 1996, p. 149). Most of the advantages of size came from efficiencies of scale in the use of animals and tools and from improved labor productivity. Farmers realized those efficiencies regardless of whether they owned a single large farm or leased a number of smaller and physically divided properties from multiple owners (pp. 143–70).

The Frenchmen who invested capital in agricultural improvements and who fostered agrarian innovation were, for the most part, small commercial and family farmers. The richest regions of ancien régime France, like their English counterparts, experienced a "yeomen's revolution." France differed from England in that French agricultural improvements did not spread to regions further from the capital, and because the yeomen's revolution was not followed by the creation of large-scale capitalist farms until well into the nineteenth century, two hundred years after similar developments in England.

Elite conflict and vertical absolutism caused the advance of French agriculture to remain geographically and socially constricted throughout the ancien régime. French noble and bourgeois landlords, unlike their English counterparts, moved away from the countryside in the eighteenth century, attracted by offices in the national and provincial capitals. Landlords almost universally abandoned commercial farming themselves whenever they decamped for offices or court life in the cities. Commercial farming required constant supervision and so was incompatible with the more lucrative and prestigious pursuit of offices and honors.[50]

Landlords, if they wanted to remain absentee, had to find ways to reduce the amount of supervision needed on their estates. All the strategies adopted by absentee landlords to compensate for their lack of supervision—employing managers, leasing to large and small tenants, and sharecropping—reduced their incomes from land to below the level of rentiers who remained resident on their estates in France or England. Absentee landlords tried to hire managers to manage their estates. Competent estate managers were expensive and hard to find, and all estate managers were open to corruption. Managers' salaries, commissions, and corruption could eat up a substantial share of estate revenues.

TABLE 6.2. Relative Risks and Costs of French Landlords' Strategies

Risk of Default	Supervision Needed		
	Low	Medium	High
High	X	Lease to small tenant farmers	X
Low	Lease to large commercial farmers	Share-cropping	Employ wage labor

Landlords therefore often did without managers or employed less skilled and less expensive clerks to send receipts and reports to the landlords at their urban residences. Landlords then made occasional visits to their estates to collect rents or crop shares and to try to ensure that tenants had not despoiled their farms. When tenants defaulted, disappeared, or damaged property, landlords had to recruit and negotiate with new tenants.

Landlords obviously wanted to minimize such disruptive losses. Landlords also wanted to reduce the risk that harvest failures or tenant bankruptcies might interrupt the income stream they used to support their urban lifestyles. Landlords could best satisfy both imperatives by leasing their estates in large blocks to well-capitalized commercial farmers (see table 6.2).

Large, well-capitalized commercial farmers eliminated almost all supervision costs and risk for absentee landlords. Few tenants however, had enough capital to advance the rent on a large farm and at the same time pay for seed, tool, farm animals, and wage labor while waiting months to receive income from the harvest. Those rare wealthy tenants were prized; landlords charged them lower rents per acre than smaller, less secure tenants. That economically rational decision (Hoffman 1996, pp. 49–69) advantaged large tenants, further concentrating land in the hands of the commercial farmers with the most resources. "For the farmer with the requisite skills and capital . . . nothing blocked the way" to the amalgamation of purchased and leased lands into large, efficient, and profitable commercial farms (p. 149).

Rich tenants were able to pick and choose the land they wanted to rent. Not surprisingly, they chose high quality land along transportation routes to Paris so that they could produce high value crops and sell them in the only market with enough consumer demand to justify the high rents and investments in inputs and improvements made by the commercial farmers.

French agriculture in those privileged regions near Paris, at first glance, appeared to acquire a three-tiered system of cultivation similar to that of England. Landlords leased farms to commercial tenants who then hired wage laborers. English landowners, however, lived on their estates and were able to supervise the commercial farmers to whom they leased their land. English landowners noticed when tenants made improvements and therefore could rapidly incorporate productivity gains into higher rents. French landlords who lived away from their estates for all or most of the year were unable to track changes in the productivity of their land or in their tenants' profitability. As a result, rent increases lagged behind productivity improvements, often by decades. Rents did keep up with inflation, which was easier to track even from afar.[51]

Large tenants took advantage of their attractiveness to absentee landlords who were willing to trade potential income for low levels of supervision and low risks of default. Such tenants demanded, and received, long leases. Lease lengths on large farms increased during the eighteenth century from a few years to a decade or more (Dontenwill 1973, pp. 135–214; Meyer 1966, pp. 544–56, 658–61; Morineau 1977; Neveux 1975, pp. 126–38; Venard 1957, pp. 70–75).

Landlords often were willing to grant exceptionally long leases in return for high entry fines. Well-capitalized tenants were able to accept such leases and thereby placed themselves in the position to profit from rising productivity and inflation over the decades of the lease. Landlords offered long leases for a variety of reasons. Nobles in debt had no choice but to mortgage future income in return for an immediate cash infusion. Clerics and lay officials who controlled but did not own land had a powerful incentive to offer long leases that robbed their institutions and successors of future income in return for entry fines they could pocket.[52]

Where tenants were rich and landlords were absentee, the balance of power shifted.[53] Tenants in some areas of the northeast and northwest were able to assert the right to renew leases at old rents (Hoffman 1996, p. 53, 113–14). Tenants in such areas pocketed the entire gains from improved productivity and inflation, although in much of the northwest there was little increase in productivity to profit from.

Landlords elsewhere in France had to settle for less well-capitalized tenants who rented smaller farms or, in the areas totally outside of the Paris ambit, resort to sharecropping. While contracted rents on small plots and returns from sharecropping were higher than rents received from large tenants, both those strategies had costs that reduced landlords' incomes. Landlords had to provide tools and seeds for the impoverished peasants who made up the bulk of sharecroppers. Landlords did not need to advance small tenants' operating costs. However, small tenants generally had little or no cash left after they had purchased tools, seeds, and a few farm animals. A single bad harvest could plunge small tenants into bankruptcy, leaving them unable to pay their rents. Landlords would not receive any income from that farm until a new tenant could be found for the next year. Landlords could, and did, lose all the income from their land as small tenants defaulted year after year. Landlords also had to provide more supervision, either themselves or through paid agents, for small tenants and sharecroppers than they did for large commercial leasees.

Small tenants and sharecroppers almost never enjoyed a series of good harvests, uninterrupted by war or by tax surcharges, long enough to accumulate sufficient capital to advance into the ranks of middle or large-scale tenants. Often when small tenants made their farms profitable, landlords opportunistically reasserted feudal rights to capture those profits. That strategy of seigneurial reaction sacrificed highly uncertain long-term productivity gains in order to maximize landlords' short-term returns. Such a strategy seemed most sensible to landlords in regions where distance from the Paris market or poor soils created few opportunities for large or small farmers to demonstrate the possible returns from sustained improvements in production and marketing.

A growing fraction of French peasants became landless, or their farms fell below the size needed to fully employ and support a family after meeting taxes and other expenses. Three-fourths of rural French families were unable to support themselves from family farms by 1700. Those families subsisted on wages they earned as artisans or day laborers.[54] Wage laborers rarely worked on commercial farms run by landlords. Since, wage labor had the highest supervision costs of all, absentee landlords almost never established farms that depended on wage labor. Farm laborers usually were employed by prosperous peasant farmers who were present to supervise their labor, or they worked in rural cottage industries. Many families supplemented their wage income with small plots that they leased. Such tenants however, were the ones who were in constant danger of default, and who were unable to invest time or money on improvements.

Thus, absentee landlords' risk and supervision minimizing strategies had the effect of further concentrating capital inputs as well as the entrepreneurial and agricultural know-how of the most successful commercial farmers in a few regions of France. Poorer and less knowledgeable peasant farmers were mired on smaller farms removed from the most profitable urban markets. In that way, modest ecological differences among French regions became widened by the disinvestment of absentee landlords and the selection decisions of the relatively few tenants with the capital to undertake an "agricultural revolution."

The factors that limited a full-fledged agricultural revolution to the regions connected to the Paris market were all products of the vertical absolutism that itself was forged in the elite conflicts of the sixteenth and seventeenth centuries (see figure 6.1).

The crown, as we saw in chapter 4, developed vertical absolutism as a second-best response to the power of multiple elites. Vertical absolutism allowed frequent wars to be financed by taxes that verged on expropriation and by the proceeds of the sale of offices. Vertical absolutism also spawned offices that absorbed a growing share of the agrarian (and urban) surplus, while creating multiple jurisdictions that divided control over land. Landlords became absentee, concentrating their presence and their spending in the capital as they pursued state spoils. Paris became the market for high-profit agricultural goods. The crown also built a relatively efficient transportation network that, for military reasons, centered only on Paris. Thus, the regions within the Parisian ambit achieved the factors necessary for agricultural investment and innovation. The rest of France was plagued by loss of capital from war, taxes, and disinvestment. Landlord absenteeism removed the human capital necessary to establish a system of capitalist exploitation and investment. Instead, landlords were driven by the exigencies of their situation to create tenancy and sharecropping regimes that compounded the other bitter fruits of vertical absolutism, "overdetermine" the underdevelopment[55] of the rest of France. Ancien régime France ultimately differed from England in its elite structure and political regime. French landlords never came to have the unity of interest in controlling land and in regulating wage labor that spurred agrarian capitalism in England.

From Agrarian to Industrial Capitalism

English yeomen, and their small-proprietor equivalents in France, the Netherlands, and elsewhere in northwestern Europe, made an agricultural revolution when they applied technological innovations that produced unprecedented increases in yields. Elites affected agrarian production only once the agricultural revolution was under way, and after it had yielded a majority of its fruits.[56] Elites intervened in agriculture for the

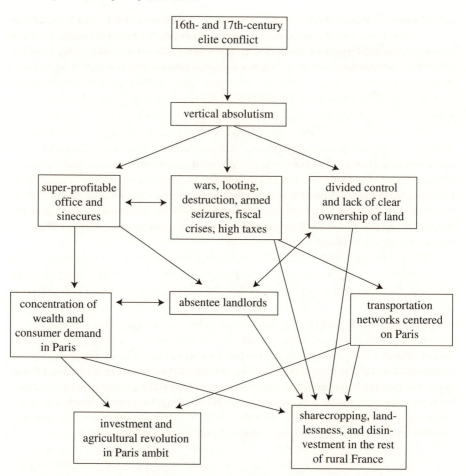

FIGURE 6.1. A Causal Model of Regional Differences in Ancien Régime France.

same reasons they always did: to guard their control over land and its products from rival elites and classes.

Each elite's interests in and capacities for intervention were altered over centuries by the particular trajectories of conflict within their polities. English and French and Dutch, Spanish, and Italian elites each came to possess certain capacities to intervene in the work of peasants and other agriculturalists. In so doing, the elites of each nation shaped modes of production that varied in their productivity and in the ways in which the fruits of land and labor were distributed. Those differences, in turn, shaped the subsequent development of industrial capitalism in each country and in the world as a whole.

Dutch elites were less able to regulate production and to appropriate a surplus from agriculturalists than were the elites of England and France. Thus, the Netherlands can be viewed as a negative case, an indication of how a yeomen's revolution in agriculture would have developed in England or France had it not been interrupted and its fruits appropriated by the elites of those countries.

Dutch commercial farmers, like their English and French counterparts, achieved prosperity for themselves by catering to urban demand for high-margin foodstuffs and industrial crops. Commercial farmers' fortunes rose and fell with the economies of cities and towns. Dutch farmers did well and were able to continue to invest in agricultural improvements, as long as Dutch city-dwellers prospered from international trade and colonialism. When the Dutch lost their colonies and trade networks to the British, urban demand fell off, and Dutch farmers lost income and capital.

Yeomen revolutions in agriculture ultimately depended upon prosperous urban markets. We see that in the rise and fall of agrarian prosperity in the Netherlands, and in how the scope of French agrarian improvement was limited to the regions that fed Paris. Yeomen did not themselves constitute enough of a market to sustain advances in their own agrarian sector, nor could they induce development in manufacturing.

Yeomen may have been sufficient to make an agricultural revolution, but they were only secondary contributors of the capital and of the market demand necessary to propel industrial capitalism. Eric Hobsbawm makes this argument:

> If the cotton industry of 1760 had depended entirely on the actual demand for piece goods then existing, the railways on the actual demand of 1850, the motor industry on that of 1900, none of these industries would have undergone technical revolution. . . . Capitalist production therefore had to find ways of creating its own expanding markets. Except in rare and localized cases this is just what it could not do within a generally feudal framework. . . . Moreover it is not at all clear whether in these early stages social transformation was rapid and vast enough to produce an expansion of demand so swift, or a prospect of further expansion so tempting and certain, to push manufacturers into technical revolution. This is partly so because the creation of the "developed areas" in the seventeenth and early eighteenth centuries were still relatively small and scattered. . . . If there was to be industrial revolution, a number of countries or industries therefore had to operate within a sort of 'forced draught', which fanned the entrepreneurs' cupidity to the point of spontaneous combustion. ([1954] 1965, pp. 43–44)

Hobsbawm identifies three sources of forced draught:(1) "the trade of all countries was largely concentrated in the hands of the most industrially advanced, directly or indirectly," (2) "England in particular generated a large and expanding . . . home market", and (3) "a new colonial system, based mainly on the slave-plantation economy, produced a special 'forced draught' of its own" (1965, p. 44).[57]

All three elements were necessary to sustain the innovation and investment that produced the Industrial Revolution. In the Netherlands, the Golden Age of prosperity did not last long enough to turn Dutch farmers or urban workers into a class of consumers who could become the source of sufficient demand to spur manufacturing. Dutch farmers did become purchasers of finished goods during the Golden Age. But they took third place as customers behind urban Netherlanders and foreign purchasers. When foreign markets were lost to competitors, and urban demand fell, the rural sector was too feeble to sustain significant manufacture in any sector.

French farmers prospered if they had access to Paris. Agricultural investment was justified, and was possible, only for those farmers who served the growing Paris market. Parisian consumer demand, in turn, depended on the absolutist regime's revenues.

French farmers suffered through several great cycles of prosperity and penury. Civil wars and protracted foreign wars, regardless of the outcome, created fiscal crises for the monarchy. Officeholders and investors in state debt suffered declines in income during each fiscal crisis, which, in turn, reduced demand for high-margin agricultural goods, as well as for urban manufacturers. Commercial farmers suffered doubly during such eras: tax increases, seizures, and wartime looting robbed farmers of capital at the same time as reduced demand slowed farmers' ability to save and rebuild their capital.

Yeoman farmers both in the Netherlands and in France were the temporary beneficiaries of prosperity that had been generated in other (colonial or state) sectors. However, the elites that developed the Dutch trading empire and the French state appropriated an ever increasing share of the revenues that accrued to their sectors. As elites in both countries transformed themselves into the functional equivalents of state pensioners (occupying positions Max Weber terms patrimonial), they starved their colonial and commercial institutions of the resources and flexibility needed to compete with the British.

The pool of capital available for rural or urban investments in the Netherlands and France was sapped from two directions in the seventeenth and eighteenth centuries. The narrowing corps of Dutch and French elites who were allowed to invest in state offices and debts funneled their available capital into those opportunities because they yielded far more lucrative returns than any other alternative. As Britain came to control an ever greater fraction of foreign markets, and of the profits from colonialism, French and Dutch farmers and manufacturers suffered from fluctuating and declining demand. Under such circumstances, holders of capital who were locked out of state positions (or privileged elites who could not invest all their capital in state instruments) would not want to gamble on uncertain returns from improving local farms or fostering domestic industries. Instead, French and Dutch capital flowed abroad, including into Britain. Capital became available cheaply to the British state and to British joint stock companies (Carruthers 1996, pp. 53–114 and passim).

British agriculture and industry were fostered by the conjunction of domestic structural relations that funneled capital into productive enterprises and of weaknesses among its rivals that sunk capital into parasitic elite regimes. Foreign weakness allowed Britain to prevail in international military and commercial competition, and to attract capital from throughout Europe.

English agriculture, thus, fostered British industrial capitalism directly and indirectly. English agrarian capitalism freed capital and labor that could be diverted to proto-capitalist home and rural manufacture first and then to large-scale industrial capitalism.[58] Indirectly, English agrarian capitalism acted as a structural bulwark against the waste of capital on political conflict.

English farmers were unique in that the fruits of their agricultural revolution were appropriated by a gentry that did not need to invest in politics to sustain its landholdings. Nor were many opportunities for such political investment left after the English Civil War. Rather than elite conflicts and political opportunities starving investment (as happened in various ways in Renaissance Italy, the Spanish empire, the Netherlands, and ancien régime France), elite structure stabilized at the local level in the Elizabethan era and at the national level after the Civil War.

The English gentry's absolute ownership of land ensured that the profits of agriculture were not appropriated by a parasitic state elite. Nor were the fruits of the agricultural revolution eaten up by population growth, as happened in much of France where secure peasants invested their surplus in extra children who could then be used to generate cash income for the family through wages.[59]

The gentry, with rare exceptions, did not themselves become industrial capitalists. The gentry instead generated and protected an unprecedented surplus against unproductive state elites above and reproductive peasants below. The gentry created an agricultural revolution as an inadvertent by-product of strategies to protect land from rival elites and from peasants. Private property in land, and the related structures of agrarian capitalism and gentry local rule, combined to protect the growing profits of the dominant sector of the early modern English economy from the state and other rival elites, from consumers who continued to pay high food prices, and from the yeomen and agricultural laborers who made the agricultural revolution. The gentry, by highjacking the yeomen's revolution in the course of protecting their own structural positions from above and below, accumulated the capital, proletarianized the labor force, and formed the state best suited for protecting the domestic economy while conquering foreign markets. It was in this way that feudal elite and class conflicts led to an English state and agrarian mode of production that provided the preconditions for Britain's first making of industrial capitalism.

7

Religion and Ideology

R ELIGION IN EARLIER CHAPTERS of the book is addressed primarily in its institutional aspects. Churches were sites of conflict because they were repositories of wealth and power. But churches also were places where people gave allegiance to religious leaders and ideas and, Max Weber believed, as such were crucial to the development of capitalist practices.

By constructing an explanation for the origins of capitalism without recourse to the spiritual motivations of Protestantism, I accomplished what Weber claimed was not possible. I show that medieval and early modern Europeans were rational in that they were aware of their immediate and local interests and capable of identifying allies and enemies in their struggles to maintain and enhance their social positions. At the same time, individuals and groups generally were not able to anticipate either the long-range effects of their strategies or how local events came together to transform the large-scale social structures within which their actions had consequences.

This chapter addresses the objection Weber posed to Marxist, and to other, structural explanations of social action: that people's efforts to reproduce or augment their social positions were motivated and at times transformed by religious interests and ideas. Weber contends that religious innovations—specifically those of Calvinism and theologically equivalent sects—transformed believers' ideal interests, compelling them to adopt new practices that, when applied to secular activities, revolutionized economic and intellectual production and the exercise of authority. That is why Weber rejected the possibility of predicting the sites and trajectories of early capitalist development from an analysis of pre-Reformation social structures.

The causal role of the Protestant ethic in Weber's model is short term. Once people in at least one society begin to engage in rational economic—or political or scientific—action, their neighbors and rivals must do the same in order to protect their material interests. That is why Weber views rational action as an "iron cage."

Weber's careful and specific consignment of the Protestant ethic to the role of a causal trigger mechanism leaves two problems with his thesis still unresolved. First, he cannot explain why some Europeans and not others were attracted to Protestant doctrine. Second, since Weber published *The Protestant Ethic and the Spirit of Capitalism,* several historians have found that early Protestants adopted a diversity of stances toward politics and economics, not all of which were conducive of rational economic action.

Those two problems throw into doubt the validity of Weber's critique of structural explanations for the development of capitalism. This chapter seeks to refute that critique, and to argue for the superiority of a structural model, by showing how the template of social relations developed in the previous chapters can be used to solve the two problems with Weber's thesis by explaining the patterns of religious allegiances and the specific politico-economic doctrines and practices of Protestant and Catholic churches in England and France. That structural template allows us to see the varying practices and beliefs of Protestantism, and of reformed post-Tridentine Catholicism, not as ideological shocks delivered from outside of "traditional" social order, but as ways in which social actors could understand and act upon their changing secular interests while reconciling them with equally real and compelling spiritual needs.

That template also helps us to understand the diverse and incomplete ways in which Europeans moved toward rational action in the early modern era. Historians' recent discoveries of how lightly Europeans bore the "iron cage" of rationality in the sixteenth through eighteenth centuries and even beyond poses a theoretical as well as a historical challenge to Weber's thesis. The politicized and situationally specific nature of rationality, exemplified in the struggles to control magic and to suppress witchcraft, suggests that fragmented elites and classes acting in multilayered social structures exhibit diverse forms of action. Those forms of action are not clarified by Weber's ideal types of rationality and indeed are occluded by the evolutionary schemes of many latter-day Weberians. This chapter demonstrates that the same structural dynamics that set the parameters of religious beliefs and actions also shaped the contrasting histories of elite efforts to control popular religion and magic and produced the different patterns of partial decline of magical beliefs and practices in England and France.

I begin by reviewing previous critiques and revisions of Weber's Protestant ethic thesis. Almost useless for historical analysis are those that submerge the particular effects of the Protestant ethic described by Weber in a broader march toward modernity or nationalism. Highly useful are many of the historically grounded studies that draw connections between believers' social positions and the content of their beliefs.[1] The main sections of this chapter compare the institutional and ideological aspects of the Reformation and Counter-Reformation in England and France. I show that previous analyses are most accurate in their predictions of participants' loyalties, and of the outcomes of those movements in the two countries, when they focus (albeit implicitly or using the language of other theoretical perspectives) upon the structure of elite relations. I find that giving analytic primacy to elite relations also strengthens studies (often couched in class terms) of elite efforts to transform popular beliefs and to curtail the practice of magic. The chapter concludes by recasting rationalization into a not necessarily cumulative set of rationalizations, each championed by elites whose outlooks were limited by their specific historical and structural situations.

Challenges to Weber

Modernization and Rationalism without Calvinism

Talcott Parsons (1937) accompanied his discovery of Weber's work and his presentation of it to an American audience with an effort to reinterpret Weber's arguments to support his "theory of social action." In so doing, Parsons distorted and diluted Weber's concepts of rationality and the Protestant Ethic thesis. For Parsons (see 1966 and 1971 for his last formulations), the Protestant ethic is not necessary; it is merely one of several sufficient causes, which when combined become sufficient to induce modern rational action.

S. N. Eisenstadt, following Parsons, advocates "the search for equivalents of the Protestant ethic in non-Western countries" (1968, p. 17). Eisenstadt's implicit contention—that all people want more material goods and need only to see others making more to be inspired to imitate them—ignores the fact that in the sixteenth century almost all people missed what in retrospect were obvious ways of getting more, and even in subsequent centuries, after some centers of rational capitalism came into existence, most people did not rush to imitate them. Despite his broad references to historical materials, Eisenstadt does not go much beyond the truism that Protestantism or its functional equivalents became "institutionalized" in pluralistic or decentralized societies with "autonomy in the social, cultural, and political orders" (p. 14). As a result, he is unable to explain why some European Protestant countries were transformed while others changed in different or less rapid ways.

Theorists in this tradition try to minimize problems of timing and the forms of change by positing modernization "as a sort of universal social solvent" so that sooner or later "the structures of the relatively non-modernized society have begun to change hands that change has always been in the direction of the structures of the relatively modernized society" (Levy 1966, pp. 742, 744). Marion J. Levy compares "first-comers" and "latecomers" to modernization, arguing that each group of societies enjoys different advantages and encounters varying problems in their passage from one type of society to the other. Levy, like Eisenstadt, however, is certain that the structures of modernized societies will be "disseminated" because most people "have some interest in material improvement, and some of them will always seek to implement that interest if the opportunity seems afforded" (p. 746) and hence will take up modernized ways regardless of the difficulties and social cost of abandoning nonmodern practices.[2]

Charles Tilly flags the limitations of this approach in his critique (1975) of modernization theorists' conceptions of political development. Such models, Tilly writes, draw on an image of "political process which only became prominent in the nineteenth century [namely, steady, orderly evolution]. . . . Such a literature seems unlikely to yield statements about the conditions under which a given political structure [or, I would add, ideological practice] will disintegrate, stagnate, combine with others, or transform itself into a variety which had never been seen before" (p. 615).

James B. Collins, in the latest and most sophisticated version of the modernization position, contends that "Protestantism is only the last intensification of one of the chains of factors leading to rational capitalism. Moreover, its effect now is conceived to be largely negative, in the sense that it removes one of the last institutional obstacles diverting the motivational impetus of Christianity away from economic rationalization" (1980, p. 934).[3]

While Weber intended the Protestant ethic thesis as an explanation only for the initial emergence of the first instances of capitalist practices, Collins takes Protestantism as one of several factors that in combination induce a desire for and inclination toward rationality that can be acted upon where nation-states create the conditions for predictability. Collins's model, however, does not provide a basis for predicting which states will adopt policies most favorable to capitalism. Collins defines capitalism as a practice more than as a set of social relations and therefore is not attentive to the ways in which quite different "capitalist" social relations were formed and transformed within each nation-state.[4]

Catholic Rationality

The universal trend toward rationality posited by modernization theorists finds implicit support, at least for Catholic Western Europe, from some historians of France. Bernard Groethuysen (1968) and Jean Delumeau ([1971] 1977) find that the French Church was able to reinterpret Catholic doctrine to legitimate the business practices of its bourgeois practitioners. These scholars do not confront Weber directly with an alternate theory for the origins of capitalism or rationality. Instead, they claim that religion was irrelevant since capitalism developed in Catholic France as well as in Protestant England, and that capitalists could use either religion to legitimize their behavior.

The corollary of their argument is that clerics' religious interests were not in conflict with lay economic interests. Indeed, Delumeau analyzes the Counter-Reformation as a multifaceted program that used Catholic clerics to convert the French state's enemies abroad and to pacify its unruly subjects at home. In depicting Catholic doctrine and institutions as so malleable, Delumeau slights the real conflicts within the church and between clergy and laity in post-Tridentine France over the right to determine Catholic doctrine as well as to appropriate church assets.

The Decline of Magic

The persistence of superstition and magical practices in the centuries following the Reformation poses a challenge to the theories reviewed in the previous section. Contrary to the claims of modernization theorists, all peoples do not easily assume rational practices. Nor did post-Reformation Protestant ministers and post-Tridentine Catholic clerics have an easy time reeducating the masses to the benefits of rational inquiry and capitalism.

Keith Thomas, in *Religion and the Decline of Magic* (1971), presents a more complex picture of the interaction of magic, religion, and science. Drawing principally on English sources, Thomas demonstrates that until the seventeenth century, religion—Protestant as well as Catholic—was intellectually compatible with magic, and that clerics competed with lay wizards, cunning men, and witches for the custom and allegiance of the populace. "The [Catholic] Church did not deny that supernatural action was possible, but it stressed that it could emanate from only two possible sources: God or the Devil" (p. 255).

Thomas shows how the constant Catholic use of prayer and holy objects to secure everyday ends provided the intellectual base for lay magicians to claim that magical powers were present outside of the church and could be mobilized by cunning men for ends desired by their customers rather than for those rarer ends sanctioned by the Church (pp. 25–50, 253–63). Although the Church of England often, and the Puritans almost always, denied the reality and efficacy of magic whether practiced by priests or by laymen, Protestantism, by intensifying belief in the immanence of the devil, reinforced the idea that magical forces were at large in the world. Indeed, by denying the value of ritual exorcism and instead arguing that faith and works were the only ways to ward off evil, Anglican and Puritan ministers drove fearful laymen to the remaining Catholic priests, and to white witches and those ministers of radical sects who remained eager to practice exorcisms of one variety or another (pp. 469–97).

If the Catholic Church's loss of its virtual monopoly over the practice of magic opened opportunities for rival magicians in the first century after the Reformation, Thomas argues that in the long run Protestant espousal of rationalism and championship of the efficacy of man's works created an intellectual climate that undermined belief in magic. First the Protestant elite of the seventeenth century, and later a growing sector of common people, rejected the possibility of magical power (pp. 641–68).

Thomas's emphasis upon the primacy of intellectual over institutional factors in explaining the decline of magic derives from his finding that in England most people abandoned faith in magic *before* the development of more effective scientific and medical techniques for controlling nature and alleviating suffering. "The change which occurred in the seventeenth century was thus not so much technological as mental. In many different spheres of life [in efforts to control poverty, improve agriculture, reform the state, and above all, in scientific explanation] the period saw the emergence of a new faith in the potentialities of human nature" (p. 661).

The uneven and lengthy rejection of magic challenges Weber's emphasis on the immediate effect of Protestantism in provoking rational thought and action. It also contradicts the assumption of modernization theorists that people change their practices in response to the visible accomplishments of other more technologically advanced sectors. By taking magic seriously as an intellectual enterprise, Thomas is able to expose the "tautological character [of Bronislaw] Malinowski's argument that magic occupies the vacuum left by science" (p. 667). Each system won adherents primarily from the premises it proposed for the relationship between, man, God, and the physical world, and only secondarily from its operative accomplishments. Magic declined, in Thomas's view, because first an elite and then the majority became less and less accepting of its intellectual premises.

Science appealed to some groups sooner than to others, and rejection of magic did not lead all skeptics to advocate state sanctions against the remaining practitioners of magic. Thomas often describes, but does not identify the causes of, variations within England in attitudes toward magic and its practitioners. Specifically, Thomas does not explain the divergences between the intellectual rejection of magic and a willingness to prosecute magicians. Puritans were the first English to deny the possibility of manipulating magical forces in this world, yet were reluctant allies, and at times hostile opponents, of the repeated efforts by officials of the Church of England to prosecute popular magicians, even as Anglicans remained unwilling to totally abandon the practice of magic themselves. Meanwhile, equally well-educated ministers and lay members of radical sects embraced magic even as they tried to differentiate their practices from those of Catholics or private wizards. Nor does Thomas account for the concentration of English attacks on witches in the 1580s and 1590s and the brief period 1645–47 (pp. 256–61, 449–51).

Class and Rationality

Continental studies of magic, in contrast to Thomas, focus their attention on social differences between wizards and their supporters on one hand and inquisitors and skeptics on the other. Emblematic of this approach is Carlo Ginzburg in his essay, "High and Low" (1976). He argues that in the Catholic Church throughout the medieval and Renaissance periods Saint Paul's admonition against moral pride, *noli altum sapere,* "had been interpreted as directed against the intellectual curiosity of heretics about matters of religion . . . as the standard authority against any attempt to overcome the boundaries of human intellect . . . that is, 'do not seek to know high things'" (p. 30).

Ginzburg contends that the religious and secular elites of Europe condemned religious heresy, political subversion, and freethinking science as equally serious challenges to the mutually supporting authority of church and state, both of which were supported by "the time-honoured image of the cosmos" (1976, p. 33). Witchcraft and science were attacked by elites because of "the possibility of drawing subversive analogies from the 'new science' [and from popular systems of magic] to religious and political matters" (p. 35). Ginzburg suggests that individual atheists and leaders of radical political movements also were aware of the subversive potential of science and magic.

Ginzburg's suggestive essay finds support in the work of several French scholars.[5] Robert Muchembled (1978; 1979; 1981) studies witch trials in France and the Low Countries. He argues that both lay seigneurs and clerics associated sorcery with popular challenges against the absolutist state and the Catholic Church. Witches were identified at moments when peasants mobilized to resist royal taxes and conscription demands for war. Such popular mobilization, and therefore witch prosecutions, were most common in areas where seigneurs exploited peasants most intensely (and therefore peasants had no surplus margin to pay the added taxes) and where clerics were poor and with low prestige (and thus most likely to call in outside inquisitors to bolster their positions). Witch trials were furthered as well by divided peasant communities (divisions that were the result of increasing state tax and seigneurial rent demands). The tiny minority of well-off peasants feared the black magic of the mass of poorer peasants and aided the inquisitors by offering the names of uppity poor peasants as witches.[6]

Ginzberg, Muchembled, and others' view of rationalization as a ruling-class project is shared by Delumeau and Groethuysen in their portraits of Catholicism as a rational, procapitalist religion. Both schools of thought give primacy to the desires of a capitalist class or a state elite to augment its power by controlling the thoughts and behaviors of subordinate groups. However, all these scholars exaggerate the ease with which, and the extent to which, ruling groups reached a consensus on their beliefs and therefore overstate the degree to which elites altered popular religion.

Structural Position and Political Theology

The most valuable work on the political and economic consequences of the Reformation acknowledges that Protestants' varying political stances were determined by the particular structural conditions under which people sought to practice reformed religion. Michael Walzer (1965) challenges Weber by noting that early Puritans saw revolutionary political action as an essential part of the religious calling.

Walzer presents the economic effect of Puritanism as contingent upon the particular mix of victories and defeats it sustained in seventeenth-century England. He contends that the Puritans were powerful enough to undermine traditional practices, psychologically preparing people for self-sacrifice and systematic effort. Yet, Puritan discipline and anxiety "led to a fearful demand for economic restriction (and political control) rather than to entrepreneurial activity as Weber described it" (1965, p. 304). Puritans' noncapitalist economic vision was not realized because they were unable to maintain state power after the Civil War. Nevertheless, the Puritans, by defeating medieval privileges, created a climate for a new confident liberalism. "This, then, is the relation of Puritanism to the liberal world: it is one perhaps of historical preparation, but not at all of theoretical contribution" (p. 303). However, Walzer is unable to identify a set of political or institutional factors that could account for the combination of Puritans' psychological successes and political failures.

Mary Fulbrook (1983) tracks Walzer's critique of Weber in her contention that the effects of Protestant beliefs upon economic practices were mediated by political conflicts between believers and state officials. Her characterization of Protestantism is in sharp contrast, however, to Walzer's assumption that all Puritans were revolutionaries. Fulbrook contends that English Puritanism and German Pietism, both "precisionist" variants of Protestantism, did not have a necessary effect on economic practices since there is no inherently economic ideology in their doctrines. She views both as autonomous religious movements, drawing adherents from various classes for mainly religious reasons. Puritans and Pietists were drawn into politics only when, and to the extent that, their institutional freedoms were challenged by the state.

Fulbrook believes that the different political doctrines of English Puritanism, and of Pietism in Prussia and in Württemberg, were contingent upon the particular institutional relations between church and state in the three locations. Fulbrook thereby identifies an institutional basis for religious conflict. However, Fulbrook does not show how the particular precisionist content of Puritanism and Pietism mattered in the struggles to control church offices. As a result, she is unable to explain why church-state conflicts in England and Protestant Germany had different structural consequences from religious struggles in Catholic Germany or France.

An implicit answer to the shortcomings in Walzer and Fulbrook's critiques of Weber is contained in Christopher Hill's study (1972) of Protestant ideologies in England during the century and a half from the Henrician Reformation to the Restoration. Hill challenges Weber's and Walzer's single-minded interpretations of Puritan politics by noting that Protestantism gave rise to a libertarian communist, as well as to a politically repressive and anally compulsive capitalist, ideology. Hill contends that the ultimate political stance of Puritanism was formed in response to conflicts experienced in the early years of each sect. However, while Fulbrook emphasizes conflict between precisionist sects and the state, Hill highlights struggles among numerous Protestant denominations with different bases of support within the monarchy and Church of England, among the gentry, or from "the common people," especially artisans and laborers.

Hill contends that religious conflicts were resolved not at the level of ideas but in each group's capacities to enforce its vision against rival prescriptions for political and economic action. The bourgeoisie's victory in the Civil War made Puritanism the model for action in actually existing English society while radical sects lost resonance as they became merely utopian dreams. Hill's various protestantisms compete ultimately as visions of different classes' hegemony. The institutional bases of each sect in churches, as opposed to their bases in class power, are given little weight by Hill in the competition for adherents.

The Structural Bases of Reformation

Walzer, Fulbrook, and especially Hill offer the most compelling critiques of Weber by showing that the economic stance and effect of Protestantism is contingent upon constellations of class and state forces. However, there is an element of tautology in all three works. Walzer argues that Puritanism sought to have a revolutionary political effect but in the end furthered a capitalism not initially favored by any Puritan. Fulbrook contends that precisionist Protestants had neither a political nor an economic agenda, yet in England were forced by circumstances to oppose absolutism in ways that furthered a liberal state and therefore capitalism. However, neither Walzer nor Fulbrook entertains the possibility that had people elsewhere in Catholic Europe adopted Puritan or precisionist beliefs they might have set in train chains of contingent events that would have independently produced liberal states and capitalism in other countries during the seventeenth century. Similarly, Hill does not speculate on what effect a conflict between classes armed with proto-capitalist and proto-communist ideologies would have had upon states and relations of production elsewhere in Europe.

The preceding paragraph would be unfair as a critique of Walzer's, Fulbrook's, and Hill's books as historical studies. But since I am concerned here with the strength of their challenge to Weber, it is vital to identify their limitations in that regard. While all three authors make important contributions by showing that the relationship between Protestantism and capitalism is structurally contingent in ways not recognized by Weber, a full critique of Weber requires more. Such a critique must explain why certain Europeans and not others embraced Protestant ideologies that were contingently necessary causes of capitalist development, or at least had the effect of allowing emergent classes and elites to articulate their interests in opposition to their rivals.

Robert Wuthnow (1989) is the only contemporary scholar working in this area who recognizes the full burden of proof upon challengers to Weber's Protestant ethic thesis. He self-consciously attempts to offer a structuralist alternative to Weber. Wuthnow argues that city dwellers were the most receptive to religious reform for three reasons: First, the high church officials residing in cities provoked lay resentment by their conspicuous consumption and social distance from parishioners. In contrast, rural clerics were poorer and closer to peasants than their urban counterparts. Second, the Catholic Church's inability to meet the needs of the expanding population of urban poor in the fifteenth and sixteenth centuries exposed the church's misappropriation of funds for clerical luxury rather than charity, undermining one of the principal justifications for clerical property holdings and tithes. Again, Wuthnow claims that clerics were better able to aid the presumably still small numbers of rural poor in the first century after the Reformation and clerical luxury was not visible to most rural poor people. Third, urbanites were able to give direction to the resentments created by the first two factors because their higher rates of literacy and access to publications and preachers made them aware of theological debates (Wuthnow 1989, pp. 38–45).

Wuthnow rightly notes that the residents of many cities and towns in France and Eastern Europe initially were quite receptive to Protestantism, while in England Protestantism gained a significant following only after Henry VIII pressed Parliament to approve an "institutional reformation" (1989, pp. 71–102). Wuthnow concludes that receptivity to Protestant ideas was not sufficient for the triumph of the Reformation; in addition, Protestant towns needed support from a state with relative autonomy from the pro-church "landowning upper stratum" (pp. 46–48).

According to Wuthnow, Henry VIII could attack clerical autonomy and support institutional reformation because he was not financially dependent upon or politically subordinate to landlords. Instead, the crown was able to enlist a Parliament "dominated by a coalition of cloth merchants, burgesses, and royal officials who were closely allied with the crown to approve the Reformation" (p. 78). Wuthnow believes Reformation failed in France because the crown was fiscally and politically subordinate to landowners who remained loyal to the Catholic Church, in part because "they, rather than the king, were the prime beneficiaries of the Concordat of 1516," which transferred control of clerical offices from the pope to the French crown (p. 102).

Wuthnow, by giving emphasis to landlords' interests in and capacities to deflect urban Protestants' attacks on Catholic clerics, does better than any previous sociologist in explaining the national patterns of religious loyalty in early modern Europe. Wuthnow's model is incomplete, however, in two ways. First, his depiction of the aims and abilities of landlords and kings in England and France is not always historically accurate. He discounts English landlords' support for the Henrician Reformation and overlooks the decisive role that elite played in shaping the institutional and ideological Reformation in England. He misses the ways in which the Concordat of 1516 combined with other factors to transfer control of the French church from landlords to the crown during the sixteenth century, even as the Wars of Religion and the extent of Protestant power were still unsettled.

A second, and more serious shortcoming is Wuthnow's sole concern with explaining whether a country became officially Protestant or Catholic. As Walzer, Fulbrook, Hill, and the others suggest, both Protestant and Catholic attitudes toward and effects upon economic and political action varied across time and place, and were contingent. Such contingencies cannot be explained through the single variable of state autonomy from landlords highlighted by Wuthnow.

Elites, Clerical Autonomy, and Religious Reform

Chapter 2 presents clerics as a full-fledged elite in both England and France, with an autonomous institutional mechanism for extracting resources from peasants and for regulating manorial land rights. Chapters 4 and 6 show how the differing structures of elite relations within which the clergies of England and France were situated set in train distinct causal sequences that yielded the particular class and state structures of the two nations. The remainder of this chapter draws upon the relevant discussion of those chapters in order to explain how the shifting structural positions of clerics and of their supporters shaped the patterns of religious allegiances and the specific politico-economic doctrines of Protestants and Catholics in both countries. I pay special attention to highlighting the varying abilities of my elite conflict model, as compared with the theories of religious change outlined earlier in this chapter, to explain the timing and choice of targets for elite campaigns to alter popular beliefs and to understand the particular successes and failures of such efforts by adherents of some doctrines to force others' conformity to their church's beliefs and practices.

Clerics of the medieval Catholic Church made mutually reinforcing institutional and ideological claims. Catholic clergy used their acknowledged abilities to intervene with God on behalf of the laity in this world and in the next to claim tithes and other rights to feudal production. At the same time, clerics' ritual competence was certified by appointment to church offices which, in turn, were identified by their rights to clerical tithes in a particular locality. In theory, the Catholic Church was a self-sustaining body. New clerics were appointed, and their spiritual powers confirmed, by the existing corps of clerics. Superiors chose candidates for lesser church offices. Church doctrine, as enunciated by the popes and repeated by clerics throughout the English and French Catholic Churches, assumed a perfect identity between the institutional and spiritual powers of the church and its officers.

In fact, the existing corps of the Catholic Churches of England and France were forced to share control over clerical appointments and revenues with the monarchs and aristocrats of their nations. The extent to which kings and aristocrats were able to appropriate clerical offices and incomes affected their capacities to claim magico-religious authority as well. English and French kings used their institutional positions as heads of their nations' Catholic Churches to endow their secular offices with magical powers, allowing them to become *rois thaumaturges*. Kings in both countries preempted the clergy's magical claims by healing the sick, using the ritual objects of their secular rule much as priests used the sacraments to minister to their subjects' temporal needs (Bloch 1973; Thomas 1971, pp. 194–204).

Lesser English nobles, lacking control over institutional sites within the church, were unable to make magical claims. However, many French aristocrats and corporate bodies of urban notables were able to appropriate spiritual, as well as economic and political, resources from the church. French nobles attached the clerical assets and priestly services under their control to the lay religious confraternities that they headed. Thus, French aristocrats often were able to situate themselves as mediators between the clergy and laity, directing the church's magical powers toward spiritual and temporal ends of their own choosing. Although few French nobles were able to make personal claims to magical powers comparable to those of the king, lay confraternities became the sites, and their aristocratic heads the objects, of popular appeals for magico-religious intervention in this, and the next, life (Bordeaux 1969, pp. 66–68; Bossy 1970; Hoffman 1984).

Pre-Reformation Catholic clerics encountered a different sort of challenge from popular magicians. Based on records of witch trials, Catholic priests, or at least their superiors in the Inquisitional and other judicial offices of the English and French Churches, were threatened by few competitors in the centuries before the Reformation. Since popular magicians and their believers left no written records, historians never will be able to determine the extent to which such practices existed before the Reformation, either absolutely or in comparison to the far more intensively persecuted, and therefore more extensively documented, unofficial magic of the post-Reformation era. What matters for this study is the contrast between the relative lack of concern by English and French clerical, royal, and aristocratic practitioners of magic over challenges from popular rivals before the Reformation compared with the more intensive, if inconsistent and not entirely successful efforts, to eliminate unofficial magic after the Reformation.

Institutional and Ideological Reformations

The Reformation combined institutional and ideological challenges to the Catholic clergy's monopolistic claims to church offices and assets and to their ability to comprehend and manipulate divine power. Martin Luther's and John Calvin's critiques of Catholicism differed from previous lay efforts to usurp clerical privileges in that they denied any individual's or institution's right to monopolize magico-religious power and knowledge. Instead, they argued that all people could have unmediated access to God's grace. Luther and Calvin further denied that such grace could be used to generate magical powers in this world, thereby undermining the claims of both Catholic priests and their royal and aristocratic interlopers.

Kings, aristocrats, and lesser laymen received Luther's and Calvin's ideas in the context of their capacities to use and appropriate the resources of the Catholic Church. Those capacities, in turn, were determined by the pre-Reformation structure of relations among the crown, aristocracy, and clergy in England and France. The causal sequence I propose here differs from Fulbrook's (1983) argument in that she leaves unexplained the acceptance of "precisionist" religion in parts of Western Europe and contends that at a later historical moment the political meaning of those Protestantisms were determined by state actions. In fact, both religious affiliations and the political content of such affiliations were determined at the same historical moment for the ruling elites of sixteenth- and seventeenth-century England and France.

The minimal Reformation position, shared by all Protestants in England, France, and elsewhere in Europe, was a rejection of papal supremacy and support for state or local congregational control of clerical offices. Stated thus, the great majority of landowners in England were Protestants, while in France Protestantism never commanded the support of more than a minority of the French nobility.

Protestantism received a different reception in England than in France. Contrary to Wuthnow, landlords did not generally oppose Protestantism in England, as well as in France. Instead, in England landlords were Henry VIII's most vital allies in his Reformation. They, rather than the small and politically weak urban elite, were the administrators of most of the nationalized clerical properties and provided the margin of support for Reformation laws in the more powerful House of Lords. Most vitally, the great lay magnates deployed the independent armies that they still controlled in the first half of the sixteenth century to suppress rather than to assist the pro-Catholic rebellions that followed the Dissolution of the Monasteries (Davies 1968, pp. 54–76; Fletcher 1968, pp. 21–47; Harrison 1981; James 1970, pp. 3–78; Smith 1984, pp. 18–35).

The critical difference between England and France was not in the degree of royal autonomy from nobles that, contrary to Wuthnow, was low in both countries. It was the overall elite structure: In England the clergy's high level of autonomy from the lay landlord elite made it a common target of crown and manor lords. In France, the clergy's strong links to aristocrats led most lay landlords, including Protestant aristocrats, to support clerical resistance to royal demands for revenues, provided they had appointed those clerics (Blet 1959; Parker 1978, pp. 22–23). Indeed, sixteenth-century French monarchs succeeded in appropriating church properties only in those localities where clerics previously had avoided aristocratic domination (Cloulas 1958).

The ideological content of English Protestantism was determined by the compromised way in which a non-Catholic Church of England became established. Henry VIII's sale of clerical properties and tithe rights, to build support for his Reformation and to finance foreign wars, divided the institutional powers and resources of the formerly autonomous English Church between the gentry and the crown. His successors tried and failed to recapture former clerical properties under the guise of revitalizing the national church. Hill (1963) shows how such crown challenges gave gentry owners of clerical estates an interest in supporting the more radical Puritan variants of Protestantism that denied kings and bishops, as well as popes, any special religious authority.

Puritan economic doctrine—which sought to guard private property and enterprise against the twin threats of royal appropriation and popular leveling—cannot be separated from Puritan political opposition to royal attempts to control ministries and to dictate religious practices. Walzer's notion that Puritanism began as a political movement and affected economic action only after the Civil War ignores the ways in which religious legitimacy, state power, and property rights were all at stake in the struggle to control clerical institutions. If the Stuart kings had succeeded in their efforts to control appointments to church offices, the monarchy would have been able to regulate both gentry religious practices and their ownership of former clerical lands and income rights. Similarly, Fulbrook ignores how Puritan economics, politics, and theology were forged together in the struggle against the efforts of Henry VIII and his successors to achieve royal supremacy over a Church of England. Puritans were forced to adopt a stance in opposition to royal claims at the outset of the Reformation because the clerical assets and ideological powers needed to practice religion still were allocated through political means.

Protestantism held a different meaning in France, where Catholic and Protestant nobles who already controlled clerical revenues and offices had reason to preserve the formal autonomy of the clerics under their control from royal appropriation. Most French aristocrats rejected institutional challenges, whether of royal or Protestant origins, to church offices that they dominated and used for their own ends. Indeed, the causal relation between the failures of the institutional and ideological aspects of Reformation in France is shown by examining the negative cases: the areas where Protestantism (as a collective opposition to the French Catholic Church rather than just the personal choice of an isolated noble family) gained the strongest aristocratic support. Those areas were the same ones where the crown had successfully appropriated clerical properties in the absence of aristocratic control over church offices (Cloulas 1958).

At first glance, the initial concentration of Protestantism in those areas of France with the strongest crown control of the clergy and autonomy from the aristocracy seems to support Wuthnow's thesis that Protestants needed aid from an autonomous crown to protect their religious reforms from Catholic clerics and their aristocratic allies. However, the dynamic of elite conflict over religion was more complex than Wuthnow describes. By one estimate, half of the French nobility was Protestant in 1560 (Parker 1980, p. 96). For some of those aristocrats, Protestantism was, among other things, a basis for claiming control over the clerical offices in their areas that had been lost to the crown. For many French Huguenots, however, religious reform initially was a personal choice, one that they expected to impose upon ministers in their locales by virtue of long-standing aristocratic claims to particular clerical offices. Such claims required Protestant nobles to respect their Catholic counterparts' control over other clerical offices and to reject crown intervention into local religious decisions (Parker 1978, pp. 21–25 and passim).

Sixteenth-century French monarchs adopted strategies to take advantage of religious differences among Catholic and Protestant nobles and urban officials. The crown accepted payments from Protestants to recognize their control over clerical offices previously controlled by Catholics. The crown thereby gained new revenues and provoked conflict among previously cohesive blocs of provincial nobles in provinces where religious divisions existed.

The opportunities offered by the crown succeeded in tempting many Protestant nobles to abandon the common front of mutual respect for aristocratic control of clerical offices against the demands of crown and the national hierarchy of the French Catholic Church. Protestant nobles, and their coreligionists who held ancient urban offices (the *corps de ville*), were increasingly successful in the mid-sixteenth century at gaining royal support for their claims to control religious offices, both in areas where the crown previously had appointed clerics and in some regions and towns where Catholic aristocrats and officeholders had exercised de facto authority over the clergy (Parker 1980, pp. 96–150; 1978).

The crown's strategy was disrupted by the Catholic Ligue, which was formed to prevent further expansion of Protestant power and to retake areas under Protestant control, and which sparked the Wars of Religion in the later part of the sixteenth century. The Ligue undercut the degree of control over the Catholic Church that the crown had obtained with the 1516 Concordat with the pope. Bishops fearful of losing properties to Protestants in concert with the crown turned to the Ligue for protection (Hoffman 1984, pp. 7–44; Tait 1977). The crown, thus, lost authority over the church in the majority of France that remained Catholic. Contrary to Wuthnow's supposition, Protestants as well as Catholics rediscovered in the last decades of the sixteenth century, and confirmed in the seventeenth century, that they could better protect their interests by amalgamating into parties, under the protection of provincial magnates, than by seeking to compete with rivals for crown protection.

French Huguenots, in their ideology and in the fusion of their political and economic interests, resembled a feudal faction seeking a monopoly of privilege in their local strongholds rather than a sect seeking freedom from state sanctions. The Huguenots' mentality was epitomized in the 1598 Edict of Nantes. The edict put Huguenots on the defensive; they devoted their energies in the seventeenth century to protecting their corporate privileges in the Protestant regions recognized in the edict and respected severe limitations on Protestant practice in the rest of France. Protestant nobles, in accepting the terms of the Edict of Nantes, aped their Catholic counterparts in their efforts to keep lesser strata out of local and provincial office. Huguenots consigned themselves to permanent minority status as their leaders sought to protect their particular local privileges through an antiroyal alliance with Catholic elites. Huguenots thereby foreclosed the possibility of proselytizing throughout France or of reviving the alliance of landlords and middle classes that had allowed Protestants to build a national political base in the sixteenth century (Parker 1978, pp. 16–21).[7]

The structure of elite relations began to change at the end of the sixteenth century, altering the context within which French nobles conceived of their religious interests. The crown's ability to use venality, patronage, and the settlement of the Wars of Religion to limit the autonomy of provincial blocs led the majority of nobles to eschew Protestantism as a basis for challenging the monarch. Most French nobles had reverted to the Catholic Church by the 1610s, and (at least temporarily) employed clientage to the crown rather than political or religious opposition as the main way of gathering revenues from clerical and lay offices. Control of bishoprics passed from the great noble families to clients of the crown, mostly *noblesse de robe,* in the decades leading up to the Frondes (Bergin 1992).

Rationality and Structure

The initial decision by members of various English and French elites to become Protestant or to remain Catholic did not have the immediate social-psychological consequences described by Weber. Elite structures for the control of clerical authority and property did not directly determine attitudes toward rationality. As Walzer, Fulbrook, and Hill suggest, the stances of Protestants (and of Catholics) toward monarchs, subordinate classes, and others, and their pursuit of ends by "rational" means, were partial and contingent results of struggles for power and religious freedom. The remainder of this chapter addresses the outstanding form of "nonrational" behavior against which some early modern Europeans actively mobilized—witchcraft and the practice of magic.

Magic and Witchcraft Prosecutions

Europeans of the sixteenth and seventeenth centuries argued over the boundaries between legitimate religion and illegitimate witchcraft, over where science and magic

TABLE 7.1. Sorcery Trials in Northeast France, 1351–1790

	Years							
	1351–1400	1401–1450	1451–1500	1501–1550	1551–1600	1601–1650	1651–1700	1701–1790
Number of sorcery accusations	2	7	11	23	68	110	67	6

Source: Muchembled 1979.

fit into such schemas, and how best to confront witches. As Thomas (1971) points out, most early modern English saw the critical boundary as the one between white supernatural forces deriving from God and the black forces of the devil and his minions. Robert Mandrou (1968, pp. 75–94) notes a similar distinction in French writings on magic and witchcraft.

Only in the late sixteenth century in England, and well into the seventeenth century in France, did even the most educated people begin to believe that many witches might be impostors rather than instruments of the devil. It took until the late seventeenth century for English and French intellectuals to entertain the possibility that all magicians and witches might be frauds. How intellectuals and their social inferiors came to such conclusions, and why episodic and localized campaigns against witches occurred in the two countries before then, are questions that an adequate theory of rationalization must address.

A difficulty with broad theories of rationalization (Weber, modernization, or, in a different vein, Thomas), or of witch trials as class war (Ginzberg, Mandrou, Muchembled, Delumeau), is that they lack the specificity to account for the relatively few and localized episodes of witch trials in the two countries or for differences in the timing of campaigns against witches across Europe. The fifteenth and early sixteenth centuries was the peak period of witchcraft trials in Spain and the northern regions of Italy. "Official zeal for exterminating witches had largely evaporated in Spain and Italy before it had even begun to appear in certain other lands," such as England and France, while witch trials in Hungary, Poland, and Sweden intensified only after 1650 (Scarie 1987, pp. 20–22).

In France, there were few witchcraft trials before 1500 or after 1670. For example, Muchembled's survey (1979, p. 131) of the number of sorcery trials in what is now the Département du Nord and a small portion of Belgium indicates a dramatic rise following the Reformation, peaking in the late sixteenth and seventeenth centuries (see table 7.1).

In England, witchcraft was a crime only in the years 1542–47 and 1563–1735, with almost all the prosecutions between 1580 and 1647 (Thomas 1971, pp. 449–51; Macfarlane 1970, p. 28). In this later period there may have been as many as one thousand executions, although three hundred seems a more probable estimate. Prosecutions were geographically concentrated in Essex and a few other counties in England (Larner 1984, pp. 71–72; Macfarlane 1970, p. 62), just as most French witch trials were confined to particular villages and towns (Mandrou 1968; Muchembled 1987).

The numbers of trials and executions in England and France were slight compared with the far greater blood baths in the witch panics and inquisitions in Switzerland, Austria, and Germany from 1561 to 1670. At the height of witch accusations and executions, only 15 percent of English defendants in witchcraft trials were executed, compared with 49 percent in Muchembled's data for the Département du Nord, and over 90 percent in German-speaking regions of Europe (Scarie 1987, p. 30).[8]

Religious Interests and Magical Power

Elite attitudes toward magic were bound up in the wider web of interests surrounding religious offices and properties. This is not to claim that elites determined their views of magic after calculating their political interests. In any case such calculations often were confounded by the ideological confusion of the age: the proliferation of religious sects, competition among magical practitioners, and growing skepticism about man's capacity to mobilize supernatural forces in this world combined with optimism about the possibility of discovering and manipulating the forces of nature. People attempted to make order out of confusion by evaluating the character of magical claimants along with the content of their assertions. In other words, people of the Renaissance decided what to believe in part by settling upon whom to believe.

Spiritual allegiance to priests, ministers, and magicians had political and economic, as well as spiritual, consequences. As a result, lay people tended to trust magical practitioners whom they were able to control (or who were subordinated to the same authority as they were) and to fear magicians who were immune from their power. People who found that all claimants of magical power were beyond their influence, or were allied with their enemies, tended to become skeptical of the very possibility of mobilizing supernatural forces in this world through the use of magic.

This hypothesis of affinities between institutional interests and belief in, fear of, and skepticism toward magicians and toward the very possibility of magic can be tested against other models as an explanation of the differences in the targets and achievements of antimagic campaigns in England and France. To the hierarchy of the Church of England and to its royal guardians, all other magicians were challengers to the Anglicans' self-proclaimed monopoly on access to divine power. The Anglican denunciations of rival magicians paralleled similar dictums by their sixteenth-century contemporaries in the French Catholic Church.

The stances of the official churches of the two nations toward magic varied in two significant ways: First, the French Catholic Church took the lead, in the seventeenth century, in educating laymen to its realization that most unofficial magicians were frauds rather than genuine instruments of the devil, while in England Anglican ministers were the last elite to doubt the ubiquity of white and black magic in this world. Second, French clerics enjoyed strong support from the crown and lay elites in their antimagic campaigns while in England the gentry successfully attempted to undermine Anglican prosecutions of witches in almost all instances, while only rarely instigating its own trials of witches in secular courts. These differences in the sources of intellectual leadership for skepticism toward magic (clerical in France, lay in England) and in lay support for clerical attacks on magic (strong in France, negative in England), affected the differences in the post-Reformation practice of magic: French

Catholic priests were the prime purveyors of magical solutions to quotidian problems, while in England commercial wizards filled most of the demand for such services. In England the political uses of magic were successfully suppressed by the end of the Civil War even as commercial wizards continued to be left alone by state and church, while in France state and church battled with limited success against both political and commercial uses of magic through the end of the ancien régime.

England

In England, only the bishops and ministers of the Church of England, joined at the end of the sixteenth century by their royal sponsors, sought to restore a unified hierarchy of religious authority in the nation. From their perspective, rival ministers and practitioners of magic were at best misguided but more probably were instruments of the devil. The Anglican dream of reestablishing a monopoly of religious power required challenging the spiritual as well as the institutional legitimacy of their rivals and proving the unique correctness of their own divine authority. That dual task appeared more righteous and urgent when the enemies of Anglicanism were viewed as instruments of the devil (Cross 1977). However, the Church of England's capacity to suppress rival practitioners of magic—whether Catholic, dissenter, or commercial wizard—was severely limited by a series of post-Reformation parliamentary statutes and by rulings of lay judges that restricted the jurisdiction of ecclesiastical courts (Houlbrook 1976; 1979, pp. 7–20, 214–60 and passim).

The Anglican hierarchy was the only English elite with a clear and unchanging opposition to popular magic during the entire period from the Henrician Reformation through the Civil War. In contrast, the other three elites—crown, magnates, and gentry—in time shifted their views toward magic, and magnates and gentry suffered from internal splits within counties. Such divisions prevented those elites from acting upon their opposition to magic through much of this period. Gentry interests in tolerating or suppressing popular religion and magic were shaped by their stance toward pluralism, which responded, in turn, to crown policies toward gentry control over clerical properties. Gentry capacities to act upon their interests increased as crown and magnate capacities declined.

Crown tolerance of elite pluralism and popular religious dissent underwent a transformation toward the end of Elizabeth I's reign. After the Reformation, Henry VIII, Edward VI, and their advisers tolerated religious dissent (except for movements in support of the deposed Catholic clergy, which they crushed [Fletcher 1968, pp. 21–47; Harrison 1981]) as a way of weakening clerical autonomy. That policy was reversed during Mary's brief reign; however, her purges were directed against Protestants in general and not focused on magicians (Smith 1984, pp. 80–82). Through the last two decades of the sixteenth century, "with the clergy only dubiously protestant, the political subordination of the church [of England] had still been a matter of concern to the government," and so the crown was still supportive of gentry claims to authority over clerical offices and properties (Hill 1963, p. 33). Thus, through the end of the sixteenth century, gentry could still entertain the desire of suppressing popular religious and magical movements without having to fear that they would provide an opening for a crown-Anglican alliance to enforce orthodoxy on them as well.

The crown solidified control over the Anglican clergy by the end of Elizabeth I's reign. As a result, crown policy began a shift, which accelerated under James I and intensified during Charles I's reign, to one of aiding Anglican attempts to reclaim church authority. The fusion of crown and clerical interests in opposition to dissent at the end of the sixteenth century affected gentry attitudes toward popular religion and magic. Before that moment, the gentry could oppose popular magic and radical sects without having to fear crown support for an attack by the Church of England on their religious autonomy. Once Elizabeth I shifted her policy to ally with the episcopacy, the gentry's prime religious interest became the protection of their dissent, even if that meant tolerance for lower-class magic and religion. As the gentry consolidated power in the counties during the reigns of James I and Charles I, Puritans for the most part became "more confident in the ability of wealth to prevail in a system of free competition, and were prepared to accept congregational Independency as the price of alliance with the sectaries" (Hill 1963, p. 345).

The Anglican episcopate and the surviving Catholic priesthood made strong though conflicting claims to magical power; this predisposed dissenters, who already distrusted both groups, to skepticism toward all magical claims. Many dissenters went further and denied Anglican and crown assertions to any form of divine power (Hill 1963, pp. 39–45; Bossy 1975, pp. 52, 278–80; Fulbrook 1983, pp. 102–29). Such "rationalism" among elite dissenters was reinforced in turn by fear of the consequences that would follow from a successful Anglican assertion of a monopoly upon the legitimate use of magic.

The dissenters' rejection of magic in toto did not lead them, for the most part, to replace the Church of England's campaigns against popular magic with independent efforts to suppress witches and magicians. The institutional pluralism that dissenting ministers and their sponsors demanded to secure their own positions was linked of necessity to tolerance for the dissenting beliefs of other ministers and of common preachers and wizards. The institutional location of dissenting ministers and their lay sponsors predisposed them to oppose Anglican efforts to enforce orthodoxy against any targets.

How, then, can we explain the two waves of prosecutions of witches in England, which were mounted by laymen and heard in courts dominated by the gentry? Those prosecutions were concentrated in two periods, the 1580s and 1590s and 1645–47 (Thomas 1971, pp. 449–51; Macfarlane 1970, p. 28). While there were trials and at least one execution in every English county, Essex stands out as having the greatest concentration of executions in both periods. In the earlier period, Kent also had an above average number of executions. In the later period, Norfolk and Suffolk joined Essex as centers of the antiwitchcraft campaign (Macfarlane 1970, pp. 61–63; Thomas 1971, pp. 450–52). The two periods, though in different ways, were unusual conjunctures when the gentry (at least in the counties with the greatest numbers of witch trials) possessed both the interest and the capacity to attack popular magic.

Table 7.2 offers a summary of the interests and capacities of the four principal English elites in each period from the Henrician Reformation to the end of the Civil War. The crown's interest switched from opposition to support of the Church of England's continuing desire to suppress dissent. However, at no point did either of those two elites possess the capacity to carry forward such interests, either alone or

TABLE 7.2. Elite Interests and Capacities for the Suppression of Magic, 1536–1648

	Year							
	1536 Henrician Reformation	1547 Reign of Edward I	1553 Reign of Mary I	1558 Reign of Elizabeth I	1603 Reign of James I	1623 Reign of Charles I	1640	1648 Revolution/ Civil War
Crown								
Interest	–	–	–	– . . +	+	+		+
Capacity	–	–	–	–	–	–		–
Church of England								
Interest	+	+	+	+	+	+		+
Capacity	–	–	–	–	–	–		–
Magnates								
Interest	+ / –	+ / –	+ / –	+ / –	+ / –	+ / –		+ / –
Capacity	B	B	B	–	–	–		–
Gentry								
Interest	+ / –	+ / –	+ / –	+ / –	–	–		+ / –
Capacity	–	–	–	+ / – Essex Kent	+ / –	+		+ Essex Norfolk Suffolk

Notes:

For interests:

   + Elite has interest in suppressing magic.

   – Elite is not interested in suppressing magic.

   + / – Elite is divided over whether to suppress magic.

   – . . + Crown's interest shifts from – to + in this period.

For capacities:

   + Elite has the capacity to suppress magic.

   – Elite does not have the capacity to suppress magic.

   B Elite's capacity to suppress magic is blocked by the crown.

   + / – Elite has the capacity to suppress magic in certain counties but not others.

in concert. The Church of England's independent judicial apparatus had been crippled by the joint efforts of the crown and lay county elites in the first decades after the Reformation. Thus, the enforcement of religious orthodoxy depended upon the cooperation of magnates and gentry.

During most of the period from the Henrician Reformation to 1600, the gentry, regardless of their interests, lacked the organizational capacity to mount campaigns to suppress popular religion. The machinery of county government remained in the hands of magnates—some of whom were still Catholic in practice or sympathy, and who did not see popular challenges to Puritan gentry authority as threats to their own interests (Stone 1965, pp. 257–70, 725–45).

The stalemate of forces within the counties in the years between 1536 and 1558 is reflected in table 7.2 by showing a mix of attitudes (denoted by the + and – for both magnates and gentry). Lay landlords were divided among Catholic, Puritan, and Anglican allegiances. In no county was there sufficient denominational unity among magnate and gentry to overcome the objections of elite members of minority sects to concerted efforts to impose orthodoxy. Where Catholic or Puritan magnates were followed by gentry in attempting to impose those faiths in a county, the crown intervened against what it regarded as threats to royal supremacy over the church (Stone 1965, pp. 257–70, 725–45). In contrast to the French pattern, the English crown allowed pluralism but not local attempts to establish minority religious monopolies. While the crown and gentry of the pre-Elizabethan era lacked the capacities to enforce their faiths, they did have the institutional means to veto efforts by rivals to enforce orthodoxies of which they disapproved.

Where the crown had removed magnates from power, counties often suffered from political vacuums for decades, as the crown sought to prevent the formation of new autonomous political forces. By the time the gentry achieved political hegemony in most counties, the crown's shifting policy toward the Anglican Church had ended gentry interest in turning its new local power against popular religious dissent and magical practices. Essex and Kent were the only counties in which the gentry coalesced into "tight" blocs[9] before the shift in crown attitudes toward the church and thus in gentry attitudes toward pluralism. Thus, only in those two counties did the gentry achieve the capacity to take unilateral action against popular magic while they still possessed an interest in so doing.

The second wave of witch trials, in the same counties in 1645–47, occurred when elite interests and capacities again coincided. The Civil War fractured the gentry political blocs in most counties. Only in those counties where factional divisions were resolved did the gentry regain the capacity to pursue lower-class religious enemies. Only after Charles I had been decisively defeated in 1645, did the gentry find an interest in turning on their antiroyalist allies among the lower classes. Once the threat from above had been removed, gentry launched attacks below, attempting to purge radical elements in the New Model Army, attacking other radical political forces and sponsoring witch trials to counter popular assertions of access to magico-religious power (Hill 1972).

The conjuncture, in 1645–47, of the royalists' imminent defeat and the heightened radical threat created a renewed gentry interest in limiting pluralism to attack popular magic. Only in Essex, Suffolk, and Norfolk did the gentry recreate unified county governments with the capacity to mount witch trials in time to meet the gentry's momentary political interest (Hunt 1983; MacCulloch 1977). After the decisive gentry victory over both royalist and radical forces, popular magic no longer represented a political threat. Apolitical wizards were tolerated because the absence of viable radical political movements emptied magic of its millennial content, reducing it to a quotidian service for the superstitious. The gentry no longer had an interest in pursuing witches.

France

Catholic skepticism toward magic had first been enunciated at the Council of Trent in 1564 when impostor sorcerers were distinguished from true practitioners of black magic. In the early seventeenth century, lay judges of the Paris Parlement began to punish impostor sorcerers as a category of criminal separate from, if as dangerous and as deserving of execution as, real witches (Mandrou 1968, pp. 313–63). Despite those conceptual advances, neither lay nor clerical judges possessed the institutional capacities to pursue many witches or to educate the populace to the difference between rare witches who actually had made pacts with the devil and the more common fraudulent witches. As noted above, Catholic clerics' institutional and spiritual powers were still under challenge from the crown, aristocrats, and corporate bodies in the early sixteenth century. No French elite was willing to allow another the authority to regulate magical power, since each elite continued to assert its control over spiritual forces and clerical offices.

As clerics were incorporated within the absolutist state, and the scramble for clerical assets was resolved by their distribution within provincial and then national hierarchies, the French Catholic Church gained institutional resources and cooperation from lay elites and judicial officers to carry out the post-Tridentine attack upon real and false witches and a reform of popular practices. The causal primacy of institutional over ideological factors in the initiation of antimagic campaigns is demonstrated by the geographic location as well as the timing (beginning more than a century after the Council of Trent) of reform efforts by the Catholic hierarchy. Tridentine reforms were most successfully carried out in those provinces where bishops were appointed by royal governors who exercised control over lesser nobles and over lay courts, especially the parlements, and who enjoyed the support of the crown (Delumeau [1971] 1977; Dent 1975; Mauzaize 1978).

Once all French elites, Protestant and Catholic, were incorporated within the absolutist state, the exercise of magical power no longer was a criterion for, or a reflection of, the distribution of clerical assets. Magic ceased to be a basis for elite competition. Aristocrats and urban elites, both Catholic and Protestant, abandoned their claims to magical powers in the late sixteenth and the seventeenth centuries and acquiesced in the suppression of such practices within confraternities and during holidays under their control. Reformist bishops and clerics took over direction of the confraternities in an effort to enforce a catechism that had been formulated at the Council of Trent but was not widely taught in France until the seventeenth century. Lay elites accepted visits from reforming bishops and the growing presence of priests from the new evangelical missions. The number of Jesuits in France rose from one thousand in 1556 to fifteen thousand in 1600. There was a similar growth in other orders—Capucins, Ursalines, Visitandines, Daughters of Charity, Trappists, and Dominicans. By 1700, each diocese in France had at least a few monasteries, often doubling the number of priests in the diocese (Delumeau [1971] 1977, pp. 75–83).[10]

The final defeat in 1653 of the aristocratic Frondes against the crown ushered in more than a century of relative peace among French elites. Elite magic neither advantaged its practitioners in efforts to control clerical assets nor threatened the positions of other elites. Elites perceived magic as a danger only when it was invoked by popular magicians who inspired or directed peasant rebellions (Castan 1979, pp. 175–242). Magic, then, remained a source of danger to the French ruling class without providing a source of power to any elite in that class against another. Under such conditions, provincial lay elites and parish clergy became more receptive to the long-standing position of Catholic intellectuals and Paris Parlement judges that most magicians were frauds rather than true witches in a pact with the devil.

The new skepticism toward witches was reflected in the reception given to the *Traite des superstitions,* which was written by a Parisian doctor of theology, Jean-

Baptiste Thiers. First published in 1679, Thiers's four-volume work elaborated in exhaustive and exhausting detail on the century-old Tridentine distinction between witches employing true black magic and charlatans who preyed on superstition to convince the masses that their fraudulent claims to supernatural power were real.

> One cannot deny that there are magicians or sorcerers . . . without visibly contradicting the canon and civil laws, and the experience of all centuries and without shamelessly rejecting the irrefutable and infallible authority of the Church that so often throws down the thunderbolts of excommunication against them in its sermons.
>
> That there are sorcerers is indisputable; but, if in fact [they] are actually sorcerers is often very doubtful, because often one accuses of being sorcerers those who in effect really are not. (Thiers 1741, 1:132, 137)[11]

Thiers's work evoked a tremendous response from clerics and educated laymen alike. The work and numerous pamphlet-length summaries of its conclusions were printed by bishops for distribution to clerics and educated parishioners. Thiers's work and its imitators, in the last decades of the seventeenth century, justified an intensification of trials against practitioners of magic who were, for the most part, now recognized as frauds rather than as black witches (Mandrou 1968).

Elite skepticism became so strong during the eighteenth century that prosecution of witches largely was abandoned in favor of efforts to stamp out popular religious practices through education and clerical supervision. Prosecutions were employed only during times of peasant rebellions, and then radical witches were usually tried for crimes of sedition rather than for sorcery (Berce 1974; Delumeau [1971] 1977; Joutard 1976). The crucial manual of this period was *Traite de la police,* written in 1722 by Nicolas Delamare, founder of the national police. Delamare explains the need for police to track down charivaris, feasts of fools, displays of skill by wizards, and all other "profane" activities, not to enforce religious orthodoxy, which he trivializes, but to head off political rebellion. Magicians, in Delamare's view, were obvious frauds and therefore their activities were matters for the police rather than for the clergy (1722, book· 1). The abrupt decline in the number of sorcery trials at the end of the seventeenth century (Muchembled 1979, p. 131), and the subsequent rapid growth of the national police force in the eighteenth century, indicate that French elites—lay and clerical—shared Delamare's perspective (Delumeau [1971] 1977, pp. 308–22).

Rationalities and Their Limits

Following Parsons (1937), and in seeming ignorance of recent historical scholarship on early modern Europe, several sociologists have written with an air of finality on the causes of the "rise of the West." Daniel Chirot (1985) describes "the rationalization of law and religion" as a long process, beginning before the Reformation, but aided by Protestantism. Acknowledging that few Europeans in 1500 "thought and behaved like rational bourgeois," Chirot emphasizes that those "who did think in this way . . . [were] able to benefit from the small material advantage accumulated by Europe [and] led a revolutionary change which turned Western Europe into several successful capitalist societies [over the next] four centuries" (p. 190). Collins describes

Protestantism as "only the last intensification of one of the chains of factors leading to rational capitalism" (1980, p. 934).

As models of very long-term developments and of divergences between Europe and Asia, Chirot's and Collins's articles are plausible and to a degree valid.[12] However, the evidence presented in this chapter should make us skeptical of arguments that describe Protestantism as "this way" of thinking, or that place the Reformation in a causal chain ending in "the last intensification [of] rational capitalism." We have seen that Protestantism and Catholicism assumed a variety of meanings in the post-Reformation era. Walzer and Fulbrook argued that Protestantism's political and economic meaning was contingent upon conflicts between bourgeois (and other) believers on one hand and the state on the other. Hill depicts different Protestantisms waiting on the outcomes of class conflict before one became a model for action in a newly capitalist society.

Walzer, Fulbrook, and Hill are insightful in drawing affinities between Protestant doctrines and constellations of political interests. They are less helpful in identifying mechanisms that could account for Protestants' actions to protect their religious and secular interests. As a result, their models cannot be adapted to explain the differing strategies and achievements of English and French Protestants. Wuthnow recognizes the problem of explaining French Protestantism in particular, and more broadly of accounting for the acceptance and rejection of Protestantism across Europe. However, his comparison of relations among the state, aristocrats, and urban bourgeois does not do justice to the post-Reformation histories of England and France, nor can he account for the different understandings English and French Protestants had of their religions.

The power of a structural approach to the Reformation—suggested in the works of Walzer, Fulbrook, Hill, and Wuthnow—is heightened by using the elite conflict model developed in this book. This chapter has shown that differences in the structures of elites can better account for both the decision to become Protestant and the meanings attached to Protestantism in England and France than can analyses of the social groups highlighted in previous studies.

Elite structures, and the elite and class conflicts they engendered, also provided the social contexts within which rational action occurred to a varyingly limited extent in early modern England and France. This chapter addresses rationalism in its most blatant form: the rise of elite skepticism toward magic and efforts by lay and clerical elites to suppress magical practices among nonelites. By the middle of the seventeenth century in England, and the beginning of the eighteenth century in France, elites were convinced both that witches were frauds rather than instruments of the devil and that magic had disappeared as a significant threat to their command of ecclesiastical institutions and the social hierarchies that they headed.

Although elites were successful for the most part in eliminating magico-religious threats to their power, there is ample evidence of continuing popular belief in everyday magic, of demand for commercial wizards in England in the eighteenth and nineteenth—and even the twentieth—century (Obelkevich 1976, pp. 259–312; Thomas 1971, pp. 663–68). In the face of the continued popularity of magic, and the powerful revival of magical practices and pagan rituals in the festivals of the French Revolution (Ozouf 1988), it is difficult to sustain broad theories of rationalization, and indeed in the quotation from Chirot above he does not attempt to do so. However, the ambivalent attitudes of elites toward magic, in the post-Reformation period covered in this chapter, force us to question the existence of a rational Protestant "way" even among an elite.

Elites and to some extent others in England and France became more skeptical toward magicians and their claims in the Renaissance era. The historical analysis in this chapter indicates that elites lost an interest in manipulating supernatural forces themselves as the possibilities of increasing their control over clerical institutions were closed. The timing and manner in which specific elites lost the opportunity to compete for clerical assets varied in the two countries and, as a result, the sequence in which English and French elites rejected magic differed as well. Further, the degree to which lay and clerical skeptics attempted to enforce conformity to their views depended upon their perceptions of threats to their interests from magicians and their followers.

This chapter's comparison of antimagic campaigns in England and France suggests that elites weighed that threat primarily in terms of their control over clerical properties and powers. Such control, in turn, was determined primarily by the structures of relations among elites. Those structures also determined who had the capacity to persecute witches and thereby selected the timing, the geographic and social locations, the targets (black witches or charlatans), and the strategies (countermagic, witch trials, or education) employed by elites to eliminate the dangers that uncontrolled magic appeared to pose to their social worlds.

Early modern Europeans were rational about their this- and otherworldly spiritual interests in the same way they were rational about their economic and political interests. Elites and others were able to determine their immediate and local interests and were capable of identifying which allies—temporal and spiritual—and which magical or "rational" modes of action would help them to sustain their positions against their enemies. Europeans approached the Weberian ideal type of rationality only when, and to the extent to which, their social situations created opportunities for and interests in such thoughts and actions. We have seen, in this and the previous chapters, that such rational ideologies and strategies developed in response to the unanticipated structural changes that were engendered by elite and class conflicts.

Elite conflicts consolidated states and classes and narrowed local variations in elite interests and capacities. Elites came to share similar "rational" orientations to the extent that they merged into unified classes, inhabiting nation-states within a consolidating transnational capitalist economy. Elite conflicts propelled structural change that in turn altered the contexts within which all social actors understood and pursued their material and spiritual interests.

8

Conclusion

CAPITALISM AND NATION-STATES were not created by visionaries or by grand strategists or by obsessive-compulsive Protestants. Elites and nonelites alike were rational in that they were aware of their own interests, they knew when they were endangered by enemies, they could accurately assess each party's relative capacities, and they could chose allies in their struggles based on cold-blooded political considerations rather than sentiment or tradition. The new social relations and political institutions of early modern Europe developed step-by-step as cautious elites sought to preserve the privileges and powers they already enjoyed. The few elites whose series of mostly defensive maneuvers produced enormous and unanticipated changes in their societies never intended to create new social relations or new modes of production. They truly were capitalists in spite of themselves.

Most European elites found it easy to reproduce their social positions throughout the medieval era. Wars, famines, and demographic crises may have killed elite individuals and families but their positions as rulers, magnates, seigneurs, clerics, or bourgeois endured and were inherited by old members or new entrants into existing elites. Individual and familial mobility had virtually no effect upon social structure in medieval Europe. Studies of medieval stratification and demography can give us insights into the character of everyday life and illuminate the bases of social reproduction. We need to look elsewhere to find the causes of social transformation.[1]

Cities, and the social groups and ways of life that developed in medieval "city air," did not foster the economic and political institutions that came to dominate Europe and then the world. Most cities developed under, and remained dependent upon, royal or noble charters. Cities supplied luxuries to rural nobles and clerics and were forced to share their wealth with their sponsor-protectors. Northern Italian cities were unusual because they were contested by various great powers and so not dominated by a single ruler. Cities in that region won genuine autonomy and eventually sovereignty, creating a new type of European polity.

Elite conflict took a new turn in northern Italy as aristocratic rivals "reached down" to find allies in their battles with one another and with great powers seeking to reestablish their rule over city-states. Single elites eventually established hegemony over most of the city-states. Those emergent ruling elites, such as the Medici-led "new men" of Florence, were limited by the concessions they made to nonelite allies (principally the guildsmen) during their ascent to power. Those concessions, combined with the small scale of consumer markets in the economically backward and poor Europe of the Renaissance, confined Italian agriculture and manufacturing to high-margin luxury goods. Italian elites maximized their political security and economic prosperity by refeudalizing the lands, offices, bonds, and markets that they controlled. Renaissance city-states did not become the capitals of transnational empires, nor did they become the progenitors of agrarian or industrial capitalism.

Western Europe beyond northern Italy was destabilized by conflict among multiple elites in the aftermath of the Reformation. The Reformation was the crucial turning point in European history, though not for the reasons that Weber posits in *The Protestant Ethic and the Spirit of Capitalism.* Protestantism did not evoke a single set of psychological or ideological imperatives and therefore did not in itself spark new orientations and new modes of action. The Reformation, instead, disrupted existing structures of elite and class relations and raised doubts about old belief systems by opening opportunities for competition. Elites challenged one another for control over clerical properties and powers, while Europeans from all strata were presented with an array of choices about whom and what to believe.

Early modern Europeans responded to competition with fear much more than they did with opportunism. Elites almost always were reactionary, seeking to preserve their land rights, judicial powers, and offices. Nonelites also became active in response to changes that threatened their livelihoods and communities. While nonelites may have expressed radical or utopian aims, they acted cautiously, challenging ruling-class privileges only when elites seemed to be divided or preoccupied with challenges from rival elites at home or abroad.[2]

Elite divisions did not necessarily culminate in capitalist relations of production or nation-states, as the trajectories of the northern Italian city-states should make plain. I posit in the Introduction that power gained from elite conflict is transitory unless embedded within the relations of production. Our study of Italian city-states, Spain, the Netherlands, France, and England supports that initial hypothesis and suggests a corollary as well: The strategies successful elites adopted to fend off immediate threats from rival elites and from nonelites determined the long-term consequences that conflict had upon relations of production.

No one could anticipate or control the ultimate effects of their actions, if only because the chains of conflict and structural change were so long in their duration. The English and Dutch transformations were relatively fast. The sequence of conflict in England that began with the Henrician Reformation and was resolved during the Civil War, and the period during which Dutch elites rebelled against Spanish rule and consolidated their domestic hegemony, each lasted a little less than a century. While Henry VIII, English gentry, and the oligarchies of each Dutch city made plans and achieved goals, none of those groups could foresee the consequences of their actions upon themselves or their heirs decades and centuries later. No one anticipated the economic effects of their politically motivated actions.

Dutch elite conflict created a rigid structure of social relations that allowed Dutch merchants to conquer and colonize parts of the Americas and Asia that were "empty" of rivals. Elite unity and social calm in eighteenth-century Holland ensured that Dutch social structure would not change in response to geopolitical and economic challenges from the British. Each enduring Dutch elite became so entrenched in its institutional positions that it was able to block reforms, even as it became ever more apparent in the course of the eighteenth century that the vaunted Dutch system was no match in international trade or domestic manufacture for the rising British.

English gentry created a system of agrarian relations of production that we recognize in retrospect as capitalist. The gentry attacked peasant land rights and created an army of wage laborers to gain tactical advantages in their struggles against crown and clergy. The gentry had no idea that the new system of production would be more lucrative than the old. Indeed, yeomen and commercial tenants, not gentry, came up with almost all the innovations and investments that improved agricultural productivity. Landowners, however, reaped almost all the benefits of the cultivators' efforts and foresight because county elites had gained ironclad control over land as they reacted to the dangers and opportunities created by elite conflict when feudal structure was riven by the Henrician Reformation.

Spain and France fall in the middle, temporally, of the five cases considered. The period from the Wars of Religion sparked by the Reformation in France to the Napoleonic resolution of the Revolution spanned three centuries, as did the era during which local elites were absorbed within an Iberian, and then a European and American Habsburg empire. Italian conflicts, beginning with the struggles for independence opened by great power rivalries and ending with the institutionalization of patrician power in each of the major city-states, lasted five hundred years, the longest of the cases examined in these chapters.

The possibilities for economic transformation were foreclosed early in both the Italian and Spanish sequences of elite conflict. The lengthy Renaissance Italian conflicts had limited effects upon economic institutions because patricians had to make so many concessions to guildsmen at the outset and never were able to challenge guild privileges without opening their own hegemonies to challenge. Spain's economy was so little transformed because the ruling elite acquired its Iberian and European empires without disturbing the existing systems through which local elites appropriated resources. Each local elite was strengthened in its control over land and labor when it was absorbed within the Habsburg empire. Spain's conquest of the Americas had profound effects upon the Indians living there and upon the Africans and Europeans brought there, while having little effect upon the polity and economy of Spain itself.

France was the most fluid and complex case of all. Feudal conflict among multiple elites gave way to competition among inhabitants of an expanding organization that became the royal state. Unlike in the Habsburg empire where elites and classes were incorporated unchanged into a conquering polity, French elites were brought piecemeal into a state as they assumed new offices and received concessions. French offices and privileges varied over time. Each new set of officials assumed a somewhat different set of obligations and benefits than did previous cohorts of entrants into similar positions. Most crucially, the very act of bringing new officials and contract holders into the French state had the effect of transforming all previously existing positions in a way that was not true of the parcellized Habsburg empire. French officials were unable to protect all their privileges and powers from new cohorts and from rival elites in the way that elites and guildsmen guarded their rights in perpetuity in Renaissance Florence. Nor could French officials prevent the creation of new offices or the recruitment of additional holders of existing offices as Dutch oligarchs and their families managed to do through the seventeenth and eighteenth centuries with their contracts of correspondence.

Relations among elites in ancien régime France were so fluid because few elites were able to ground their royal offices and sinecures at the point of production. Agrarian and manufacturing relations of production were not as fossilized in eighteenth-century France as they were in Medician Florence. However few elites were able to control land or extract significant revenues from peasants, or to profit from manufacture, commerce, or financial speculation without relying upon the powers they received from state offices or from privileges granted by the crown. Elites' access to income and their control over the means of production were challenged as their offices and privileges were altered by the development of the state.

The French Revolution had such a profound effect upon elite and class relations precisely because ancien régime elites had lost their capacities to directly appropriate surpluses from agrarian or industrial production. Most French elites were reduced, by the eighteenth century, to jostling for a share of the revenues that all elites collectively appropriated through a state. Once the state was challenged by peasants, sanscoulottes, and bourgeois in the Revolution, old elites were unable to sustain or recreate organizations of surplus extraction on their own. Those elites lost their eliteness.

The French Revolution, in destroying some elites and advancing others as a new state was created, had a dramatic effect upon class relations, though not as profound as the dramatic transition to agrarian capitalism in England during the century from the Henrician Reformation to the Civil War. Our comparison of England and France demonstrates the complexity of the relationship of structure and agency. The most fluid structure (France) did not necessarily produce the greatest transformation. England's simpler structure and clearer lines of elite and class conflict yielded the greatest transformation of the entire era examined in this book.

The story of social change in early modern Europe is one of discontinuities between intentions and effects. Actors almost always intended to be conservative, to merely preserve or perhaps to augment their existing positions. Action usually had little effect. Plans went unfulfilled. Rivals were able to blunt most challenges to their positions. Elites and nonelites only rarely achieved the specific and short-term gains they intended. More rarely, actors set in motion the long chains of contingent elite and class conflict that transformed social structure and produced new and unanticipated forms of production.

Elite conflict is the bright thread of agency that propelled structural changes in all situations. The causal primacy of elite conflict allows us to draw some broad sociological conclusions about social change that transcend the specific, though profound, transformation that is the subject of this book. I conclude with generalizations about the study of social change in four areas: (1) nonelite agency and revolutions, (2) geopolitics and the world system, (3) ideology and culture, and (4) the social spaces for agency.

Nonelite Agency and Revolutions

Elite conflict encourages nonelite mobilization and decisively shapes the structural effects of revolutionary mass action. Nonelites, like elites, are not suicidal and try to read social structures and conflicts to determine when and where mobilization can be effective. Nonelites, like elites, may misread social structure, seeing broad openings in unusual local conditions. All actors, elite and nonelite, often fail to see how the interweaving of elite and class conflicts in complex social structures can yield unintended and unwanted (or occasionally unanticipated though wonderful) consequences.

Nonelites are best able to sustain their struggle and achieve their aims when they find an elite in a strong structural position with which they can ally. When an elite ally was weak (as were the clergy following the Henrician Reformation), then the rebellions by their nonelite allies were intense but isolated and therefore easily defeated (as was the Pilgrimage of Grace in England in 1536) or the rebellions were poorly organized and therefore ineffective even if broad-based (as in the cases of various of the *popolo* uprisings in Renaissance Italy).

Elites were effective allies and helped to sustain mass action as long as the elite allied with popular forces remained unified and was able to command resources over an extended period. The English and French Revolutions were instances where elites (gentry and bourgeois) both were threatened with extinction and had the resources to mobilize nonelite forces and so sustain revolutionary conflict over years. The Ciompi and the Frondes were instances where elites felt themselves under threat, yet in mobilizing popular forces undermined their capacities to remain unified and to marshal resources for a revolutionary challenge; thus the Ciompi and the Frondeurs became disunified and were suppressed by reconstituted multielite alliances.

The overthrow or transformation of the state is not necessarily the primary object or result of revolutions. All the English conflicts examined in chapter 4 are about the local control of organizations of domination and extraction. The two revolutions (of 1640 and 1689), though not the Reformation, did result in changes of rulers but had virtually no effect on the structure of national government that had been determined by previous elite conflicts. The English elite transformation with the greatest immediate and long-term effects on the national constitution was the Henrician Reformation, which overthrew the parallel national administration of the church, an entity not contained in the definitions of the state offered by any sociologist of revolution.

The Florentine Ciompi, the Medici takeover, the French Frondes, and the 1789 Revolution (in the ambitions of both aristocrats and bourgeois) were concerned with gaining improved positions within the existing state for the revolutionaries. The 1789 Revolution overthrew the old state inadvertently, only because of the particular compounding of elite and popular actions.[3]

The long-term consequences of revolutions are even more distant from the ideal notion of state transformation than are the initial plans and events of each revolutionary moment. Each revolution mattered in the long term to the extent to which elites and nonelites were able to disable or absorb the statelike mechanisms of domination and expropriation controlled by defeated elites. The Ciompi briefly, and the Medici takeover permanently, transferred mechanisms of taxation, borrowing, and military mobilization from one elite to another. These were cases of Pareto-like circulations of elites without affecting the overall form in which nonelites were ruled and exploited by the combined organizational capacities of elites.

Only the first of the English conflicts, the Henrician Reformation, seriously and permanently affected the structure of elite rule. The English conflicts of 1640 and 1689 (the ones actually labeled as revolutions) merely ratified the changes in elite and class relations set in train by the Reformation. The French Revolution is unusual among pre-twentieth-century revolutions, in that it initiated transformations of elite and class relations in the course of overthrowing state regimes.

The French Revolution differs from all the other early modern revolutions (and is the one discussed in this book that is closest to Charles Tilly's ideal type [1978]) because it attacked the first regime in which all elite organizations were incorporated within or regulated by national states. Revolutions matter structurally only when they extinguish, amalgamate, or destroy elite capacities that may reside within states but that historically have been found more often within statelike and other elite organizations not included in most definitions of revolutionary targets.

The comparative study of revolutions will stagnate (and it will continue to misinterpret the structural import of recent historical studies of specific revolutions) as long as the Marxist strawman of revolution as class war is challenged only by state-centered theorists who counter by viewing five hundred plus years of European history as a struggle between state and civil society and revolutions as victories or setbacks for one side and the other. Ruling classes and "state elites" must be examined more finely, in terms of multiple elites and their organizations (which may be states or statelike). Then we can answer comparative questions such as: How do elites depend upon states or statelike mechanisms to extract resources and to dominate nonelites? and What interest do elites have in the preservation, modification, or overthrow of states or statelike forms? Answers to these questions provide the essential groundwork for analyzing the ultimate effects of revolutions. We also will be able to determine whether the current weakening of nation-states will once again direct revolutionaries toward nonstate targets.

Finally, the focus on elite and class structures allows one to account for the unanticipated effects of revolution. Karl Marx himself does that in his *Eighteenth Brumaire of Louis Napoleon,* with its careful tracing of alliances and conflicts among multiple class fractions that he identifies at various points through their elitelike control of organizations, as well as their specific relations of production. The interweaving of elite and nonelite conflicts is what makes a revolutionary era different from previous elite conflict. It also is why revolutionary eras are so confusing to those who live through them as well as to scholars trying to reconstruct historical events and their meanings.

Geopolitics and the World System

Interstate military conflicts and international economic exchanges had narrowly limited effects upon elite and class relations within the societies of early modern Europe. Northern Italian cities were more influenced by external forces than were any of the other societies we examined in this book. Yet, even in Italy, foreign actors played a highly specific role in structural change that was narrowly focused in time. Great power rivalries allowed the cities to become autonomous and then independent. Continental and regional conflicts prevented oligarchies from consolidating power within each city-state for several crucial centuries during which rival factions reached down for allies. The "new men," who made fortunes in the expanding and shifting world economy, gained entry into old and new elite positions in their city-states during those centuries of factional conflict.

Elite and class relations became fixed in each city as soon as a single oligarchy consolidated power. Once factional conflict was resolved within a city-state, great power rivalries ceased to affect elite and class relations within that polity. New men no longer were able to translate economic position in the world economy into elite position at home. Indeed, city-states ruled by oligarchies became impediments to the economic ventures of new men, forcing them to transfer their capital and often their political allegiance elsewhere to pursue opportunities in the world economy.

Class relations and the organization of production remained unchanged within each city-state in the absence of factional conflict, even when a city gained or lost control over European markets. The Medici maintained hegemony over Florence, and guilds retained their privileges, even as they lost dominance over the markets for wool and silk and as control over papal and other trans-European banking fell to rivals. The Genoese polity similarly was unaffected by that city-state's rise to and fall from financial eminence in Europe. Venetian elite and class relations did not change as that city became a regional power and then lost military position to the Ottomans.

Dutch structural change under foreign influence parallels the experiences of Italian city-states. Dutch elite relations, like those in northern Italy, were formed in the struggle against foreign rule. Once the Dutch Republic, like the Italian city-states, was freed from foreign domination, social relations became rigid. The structure of relations among Dutch elites, their political institutions, and the organization of agrarian and manufacturing production all remained fixed as the Dutch rose to dominate European and world commerce in the seventeenth century and then lost that leading position to the British in the next century.

Dutch and Italian elites gained organizational advantages in the pursuit of foreign markets as the legacy of their struggle against foreign rule. Dutch and Italian oligarchies could not adapt to subsequent changes in international economic and military competition without undermining their domestic hegemonies. Not surprisingly, the individuals and families that made up each oligarchy never risked their local elite positions for the promise of greater wealth, geopolitical power, or prestige abroad.

Geopolitics and the world system did not affect the survival of established European elites. Such external factors did affect the financial rewards that each elite derived from its control of an organization of surplus extraction within a city-state, nation, or empire. The organizational capabilities that Italian and Dutch elites brought to international commerce and production yielded great rewards at certain historical moments and relatively smaller rewards at later moments as geopolitical conditions and the structure of the world economy changed.

Spanish social structure became more rigid as it incorporated new polities into its empire. Opportunities for elite or class agency in conquered European territories themselves became immobilized as they were absorbed by the Habsburgs. The part of the Netherlands that managed to break free of the Habsburgs was transformed in the process of its struggle for independence. Spanish elites were agents of transformation only when they invaded and conquered the Americas, which was outside and then at the periphery of the world system.

France and England developed distinct varieties of agrarian capitalism before they assumed major roles in international commerce. Merchants engaged in foreign commerce were bit players in French elite conflicts during the ancien régime and in the years of the Revolution. English merchants were somewhat more important to the outcome of the Civil War, helping to mobilize London radicals and harness them to the parliamentary cause. However, the "colonial-interloper merchants" who were most important to the Civil War in London were the most marginal of all English merchants in the scale and consequence of their international commerce. Their key role in the Civil War stemmed from their particular geographic, temporal, and structural position in the chain of events that roiled the British polity in the 1640s. The colonial-interloper merchants won, for their troubles, a new British foreign policy under the commonwealth and continuing under the restored monarchy, which mobilized state power to give them growing and eventually dominant positions in the world economy.

The elite and class conflicts of the 1640s transformed the organizational assets that British merchants brought to their pursuit of market position and geopolitical power in the world system. As a result, colonial-interloper merchants were transformed from marginal actors, in a polity and economy that were marginal to the world system, into the dominant actors in an expanding portion of the world economy. The colonial-interlopers were not seeking world hegemony when they involved themselves in the Revolution and Civil War. They were seeking just to preserve their existing trade from challenges by the crown, chartered merchants, and foreign competitors. Conflict internal to England determined the shares each elite and class would receive from domestic production and from foreign trade and colonialism in the coming centuries.

England and France emerged from their revolutions with fundamentally different social structures that had the effect of making England a far more adept international competitor in the eighteenth and nineteenth centuries than was France (or was the Dutch Republic, Spain, or any other European power). Yet, Britain's advantages, like those of the Dutch Republic, Spain, and the Italian city-states in earlier eras, were forged through domestic conflicts. The contours and dynamics of the world system determined how long the particular structures of each competitor would remain advantageous and produced a different reward for each polity, elite, and family involved directly or indirectly in the world economy. The world system mattered greatly, though in more sharply defined ways than Immanuel Wallerstein and his followers would claim.

Conversely, Western European elite conflicts had a profound effect upon vast parts of the rest of the world. The Americas, Ireland and other weak parts of Europe, Asia, and eventually Africa all were transformed in certain ways because particular elites emerged from the conflicts of each European power with interests and capacities that they brought to bear in their struggles to dominate the peoples and lands of the rest of the world. The colonial-interloper merchants affected the Civil War mainly because of their domestic rather than international positions; however, once they had been rewarded for their role in the Civil War with a new foreign policy they were positioned to profoundly transform British America and then other parts of the world. The one-way nature of the causal relationship between European elites and the world economy is demonstrated most profoundly in the case of Spain. Spanish conquerors exterminated Indian societies, introduced slavery and other forms of forced labor, and remade the ecologies and economies of Latin America. Yet, social relations within Spain were hardly affected by the conquest or the subsequent loss of that American empire.

Just as eliteness is marked by the strategic advantage that elites have over non-elites in initiating conflict, so too does "coreness" in the world system ensure that elites in core polities are able to loot, despoil, and subjugate the lands and peoples of the rest of the world without undermining their own elite positions at home. Italian, Spanish, and Dutch elites lost their coreness while preserving their eliteness. Each newly rising power's participation in the world economy had unanticipated effects upon the structure and dynamics of the world system itself. Among the consequences were openings of opportunities for even newer elites to seize core positions at the expense of previous dominant players. However, once an old-core elite lost much of the rewards it had reaped abroad it remained insulated from domestic challenge. Elites in declining core polities lost their positions as a result of domestic elite and class conflicts that were removed temporally and causally from the shifting dynamics of the world economy.[4]

War, similarly, had a specific and limited effect upon European states and upon the fortunes of the elites vying for political power. Foreign military ventures influenced the occurrence and outcomes of revolutions and of lesser elite and class conflicts, though more narrowly and specifically than in Theda Skocpol and Charles Tilly's models.[5] Elites disagree over whether their nation should fight a war, because elites differ in the benefits they derive from a war and in the share of military costs they will have to shoulder. The monarch or "state elite" was not always the militarist. Kings Charles I (of England) and Louis XVI (of France) were less eager to mount wars against their foreign enemies than were the most radical members of the Parliament and National Assembly.

Each elite in Renaissance Florence and in the Dutch Republic pursued its own foreign policy, forming alliances and promising their city-state's participation in wars, often on the opposite side from that suggested by a rival elite. Elites throughout Spain's European and American empires came to hold and to pursue differing military objectives that contributed mightily to the eventual struggle for independence in Spanish America. Florentine and English elites developed foreign policies to protect their trade and religious interests. Louis XVI and the National Assembly each saw war as a way to mobilize domestic and foreign forces against their opponents.

Wars can strengthen or weaken various elites in addition to the monarch or "state elite." Florentine expenses for wars, which were placed by the ruling elite upon rival elites outside the state, precipitated the oligarchic coup in 1378 and brought the new men into alliance with the Medici in the 1430s. Charles I was forced to recall Parliament, which organized opposition to his reign, to pay for war in Ireland. The Habsburgs were fatally weakened by the costs of wars designed to consolidate and expand their empire.

Conversely, provincial war weakened the Frondeurs and gave relative advantage to the crown. The National Assembly successfully used foreign wars that it instigated to mobilize financial and human resources against domestic enemies and to build the revolutionary state. Foreign war was vital in consolidating the French revolutionary regime and in securing long-term power for the elites served by the new state.

Wars, unlike shifts in the world system, have direct effects upon domestic elites. The effects of war depend upon the specific structure of elite relations and upon the nature of each elite's organization of fiscal appropriation. Broad generalizations about wars' effects upon the formation and development of states or upon the origins and especially upon the outcomes of revolutions and other conflicts are belied by the variety of causal sequences that developed in the cases compared in this book.

Ideology and Culture

Sociologists continue to debate the extent to which people act rationally to maximize their preferred goods or are motivated by cultural norms that produce habitual behaviors. Max Weber and Karl Marx both believed (while highlighting different causes) that localized and traditional cultural preferences were extinguished progressively by the penetration of capitalism into ever more social situations. Marx's and Weber's faith in, though not their abhorrence of, the ultimate and total triumph of capitalist social relations and instrumentally rational action over all traditional forms of behavior and all precapitalist social relations today is proclaimed by rational choice theorists.[6]

We have seen in each chapter of this book that social actors usually were able to maximize their interests by using culturally derived norms of perception and behavior. People in all those times and places were able to fall back on tradition and habit because there were so few opportunities to take effective action that could improve or transform one's social situation. Tradition and culture were and are effective "toolkits" (Swidler 1986) because most of the time people can do no more than maintain alliances with those who share their interests to preserve their existing positions.

The normal stagnancy of societies makes it difficult to distinguish the roles of rational choice and cultural habit in motivating individual and group decisions. When we look at the rare moments when social actors actually could improve their social and material circumstances, we find that they needed to combine instrumentally rational action with culturally derived understandings to be effective. We have seen that medieval and Renaissance Italians, Spanish elites in Europe and the Americas, Dutch, French and English all were instrumentally rational enough to weigh the short-term returns from different courses of action, and they almost always were unencumbered enough by habit and culture to choose the maximizing course.[7]

Elites and classes could not rely upon rational calculation alone to form the alliances they needed to take advantage of opportunities for effective action. Such opportunities arose suddenly and unpredictably as well as infrequently. The opportunity to take effective action or to mount a sufficient defense would have been lost before any actor could determine the material interests of each potential ally. Since the ultimate outcome of such transformative conflicts were unpredictable, each actor could not know if what seemed to be common interests at that moment would diverge in the whole course of conflict, leading an early ally to defect from the coalition as circumstances changed.

Culture and ideology were faster and more reliable than rational calculation alone for finding allies and sustaining communities of interest. The Guelfs and Ghibellines of medieval Italy sustained alliances across cities and over time by pledging loyalty to one another and to either the pope or the emperor. Those who joined such alliances did not abandon rational calculation for habitual loyalty to an ideology. Rather, those cross-polity alliances allowed members to signal one another that they were willing to tie their individual, familial, clan, party, or governmental futures to the fortunes of the whole alliance. Futures were linked together by far more than shared culture or ideological professions of loyalty. Alliance members, both within and across polities, married one another's scions, pooled their capital in joint business ventures, installed one another's protégées in offices, and went into battle together, forcing themselves to depend on their allies for their very lives.

Each elite in the Guelf or Ghibelline alliance recognized that it needed allies, within its own city-state as well as beyond, to counter the initiatives of real and potential elite and class enemies. It was dangerous in medieval Italy, as it is in almost any time and place, to be without sufficient allies. Families moved together into fortified compounds with towers to protect themselves from other clans, intermarrying and pooling their labor and assets to ensure that the clan would remain united in moments of crisis. Clans united into parties that formed grand alliances and took control of cities and larger political units. Elites at each stage of amalgamation reached up, down, and sideways for allies. Allies beckoned one another with the Guelf and Ghibelline ideologies. Once medieval Italians were locked in the embrace of alliance, they formed familial, business, and political joint ventures to ensure that no one in the coalition would ever break free and betray the cause.

Elites in every society in early modern Europe created structures for grounding alliances on ideological and institutional moorings that paralleled the systems perfected in Renaissance Italy. Religion became the main basis for alliance building across families, towns, and regions after the Reformation. Protestantism and Catholicism, and finer denominational and doctrinal differences, became the ideological bases for creating mutualities of interests in the Dutch Republic, France, and Britain. When Dutch converts to Protestantism kept their faith in the face of the Spanish Inquisition, they were signaling to one another their willingness to invest all in the struggle for religious freedom and political independence. Dutch Protestants built communities of interests by concentrating themselves geographically in the northern Netherlands, and by submitting to new political authorities with the power to raise taxes to pay for the military needed to defend against Spanish attacks. Local religious solidarity was built upon previous cooperation in building dikes and irrigation systems in the countryside and in joint business investments in the towns. Protestants further strengthened their unity through intermarriage, by continuing to pool their capital in joint ventures and by investing in state bonds that would be repaid only as long as the Protestants remained united and were able to defeat the Spanish.

Unity forged in the struggle for religious and political freedom created institutional links among elite families that endured for centuries after independence was won. Joint-stock companies and contracts of correspondence ensured that each family could maximize its interests only within the confines of existing kin networks, investment firms, and political institutions. Religious, civil, and class culture were expressed through the practice of building and sustaining social alliances.

Ideology and interest are indistinguishable in analysis once they become insep-
arable in an elite's practice. That is so for the Dutch oligarchies, and it also is true for
Protestants and Ligue Catholics in seventeenth-century France, for Catholics and
various Protestant sects in England in the century after the Henrician Reformation,
and for parties during the revolutionary eras in both England and France. As in Italy
and the Netherlands, French and English elite families intermarried with their coreligionists and political allies. Families invested their political and financial capital in
religious offices, tying their heirs' future security to the establishment of their de-
nomination's religious liberty. Allies in the French Frondes, the English Civil War, and
the 1789 Revolution were confident of one another's loyalties, in large part because
they already shared ties of patronage to religious offices.

Alliances endured during civil wars, revolutions, and other times of mortal danger because they were built upon a foundation of interests that were expressed in
cultural terms and upon shared ideological tenets that were lived when coreligionists
and factional and party members joined together in marriage, business and politics as
well as in prayer, ritual and pledges of faith. Culture and ideology, did not substitute
for, nor did they merely reflect interests. They were programs for building common
interests strong enough to prevent allies from betraying one another and strong enough
to compel allies to invest their human and material assets in the cause.

The Social Spaces for Agency

Individuals are rational maximizers. They do want to preserve and, if possible, better
their circumstances. Humans, as social animals, are limited in their ability to find and
follow a rational path by the complexity of the web of social relations within which
they live. Complexity makes it difficult to see how one can maximize one's interests.
Complexity also limits the opportunities for improving one's social situation.

Nonelites, as we have seen throughout this book, have much narrower and far less
frequent opportunities for effective agency than do elites. Elite agency was severely cir-
cumscribed in feudal Europe before the Reformation. Possibilities for effective agency
widened with the Reformation, although they remained highly specific and depended
upon creating networks of allies that often included nonelites as well as elites.

Once elites took action, they set in train sequences of contingent change that no
one could anticipate or plan for. The social resources that elites took from one era
were of limited value during and after periods of immense and unexpected social
change. Ideological and cultural resources always were useful for holding allies but
often were not helpful for charting a strategic course through a revolution.[8]

The transition from feudalism to capitalism is an important subject for study because so much of present-day social reality was forged in that great transformation. We
can never understand our own possibilities for effecting change, nor can we identify
the optimal sites and moments for social action, without knowing how fundamental
change occurred in the past. We must acknowledge that elites in early modern Europe,
and throughout the capitalist world today, almost always are adept at preserving the
social institutions needed to guard their interests. Change began when elite conflicts
intensified. Fundamental transformation occurred when nonelites were able to ally

with elite factions and win concessions that created long-standing rights for the winning combatants.

Today, we still are contending with the institutions that Florentine patricians, Dutch oligarchs, Spanish conquistadors, and French and British landlords, merchants, and bureaucrats created to preserve the privileges that they won in elite conflict. We understand our own social reality and the possibilities for remaking our world when we comprehend the processes through which elites and classes struggled to overcome old and to form new constraints, making themselves and us still capitalists in spite of ourselves.

Notes

1. Marx, Weber, and Durkheim also considered the implications of the transformation for freedom, democracy, and solidarity. This book is concerned only with explaining European social change. I do not join the first sociologists in an effort to draw moral lessons from history, although I do draw political lessons from my model in chapter 8.

2. Darnton (1991) provides a valuable overview of recent studies of the history of reading. Peter Weiss in *Marat/Sade* and Michel Foucault through the trajectory of his oeuvre both, in different ways, show the subversiveness of pornography and the obscenity of power.

3. For Foucault, and for the many scholars whom he inspired, the transformation of social control, and the resistance engendered by the new disciplinary projects, should be the driving themes of new historical narratives that can counter materialist histories. Readers will find Foucaultian concerns largely absent from this book. I bypass many opportunities to engage questions of cultural and symbolic structures. I examine social actors' experiences with power and resistance only insofar as they were manifested in overt action. In this book I do not take up the Foucaultian project of narrating peoples' subjective engagements with, and resistance against, families, communities, states, and civil society. I believe those issues are important and worthy of deep debate. The task for this book, however, is to see how much of historical change can be explained with the structural model of elite conflict that I develop in the next section of this chapter. I regard the refinement of structural theories of social change as a necessary complement to the different intellectual task of constructing multiple narratives of how social change is perceived and experienced.

4. Demographic determinists are the exception to this effort to "bring people back in." They argue that demographic cycles and long-term population growth create conditions that of necessity evoke certain human behaviors. Motivations, thus, can be assumed and so ignored.

5. This notion of chains of opportunity comes from Harrison White's book (1970) of that title.

6. Elite capacities can be based upon military power, control or ownership of means of production or exchange, access to the means of salvation, or cultural capital. My theory contends that elites access and deploy any and all capacities through their organizational apparatuses. Thus, I agree with Bourdieu ([1972] 1977), Szelenyi, Szelenyi, and Kovach (1995), and others that cultural capital is a basis of elite control, but I differ with them in that I see cultural

capital as vested in the organizations elites inhabit rather than in elite individuals or their families. Families or individuals may transmit cultural capital outside organizations, but cultural capital can only be deployed to appropriate resources or to dominate others through organizations.

7. This definition of an elite "in itself" and "for itself" parallels the Marxist distinction of classes "in themselves" and "for themselves." However, Marx believes that classes in themselves are destined eventually to become classes for themselves, whereas the elite conflict model I develop here hypothesizes that only elites with the capacity to act for themselves can maintain their autonomy. Elites in themselves will be subordinated to rival elites with greater capacities, lose their autonomy, and be unable to act for themselves in the future. Of course, new elites may emerge, perhaps with many of the same organizational characteristics as the former subordinated elite but with greater capacities for conflict.

8. This discussion builds upon Lukacs's analysis in *History and Class Consciousness* ([1922] 1971).

9. This notion is expressed by Brenner (1982) in terms of "ruling-class self-organization" and by Anderson (1974) as the absolutist state. I explore those arguments and their shortcomings in chapter 4.

10. Readers interested in my overview of the entire literature on transition should read Lachmann 1989.

Chapter 2

1. Again, Weber and his followers examine feudal cities to demonstrate why such centers of "politically-oriented capitalism" and the forms of trade between them could not develop into genuine capitalism absent the Protestant Reformation or some other fundamental transformation of the ideological and psychological basis for action. Those who have advanced the argument that cities and trade can constitute an economic sector external to, and ultimately subversive of, feudalism are Marxists and historians outside of the sociological debates.

2. Bois ([1976] 1984, pp. 263–76) makes a similar argument for France. He shows that in the twelfth and early thirteenth centuries, lordly incomes rose, even as the rate of feudal levy fell, because the increasing peasant population cleared and colonized new lands. Thus the total size of noble estates, and the total number of tenants and total volume of feudal dues, increased even as the levy per tenant and per hectare fell. Once all the vacant land that could easily be cleared using the technology available at the time had been settled, lords sought to compensate by raising rents on existing lands, thereby sparking the demographic crisis. Bois believes that if lords had not sought to raise rents, then the end of colonization would have caused a demographic plateau and slow decline rather than the sudden catastrophe that the Black Death caused. However, since Bois posits as the fundamental law of feudalism the tendency of levies to decline over the long term, and as a corollary a tendency of lords to try to maintain the volume of rents, the demographic collapse was an inevitable outcome of the end of colonization, which, for a time, had maintained lordly incomes.

3. In chapter 6 I point out that French landlords of the seventeenth and eighteenth centuries adopted sharecropping on poorer lands, distant from the lucrative Paris market, while leasing better lands, nearer markets for cash. Such economic calculations were possible only when landlords were secure in their control over land. In England, where control over land was more contested among elites, economic maximization took second place to fending off challenges to lordship or ownership of land.

4. The most extreme example of this tendency to locate the practice of capitalism before the sixteenth century is provided by Macfarlane, who argues that the entire debate over the origins of capitalism is invalid for England, where there was an individualist ideology and there-

fore "a developed market and mobility of labour, land was treated as a commodity and full private ownership was established, there was very considerable geographical and social mobility, a complete distinction between farm and family existed, and rational accounting and the profit motive were widespread" from at least the thirteenth century (1978, p. 195). Macfarlane equates those characteristics with capitalism and concludes that England was as capitalist in Marx and Weber's sense of that word "in 1250 as it was in 1550 or 1750" (ibid.) England, therefore, was uniquely positioned to take advantage of the technological advances and colonial opportunities that emerged in the late eighteenth century.

Macfarlane's work is criticized for its almost total reliance upon "tax records and parish registers [because they] leave so many things out" (Stone 1979, p. 40). Macfarlane fails to understand that before the sixteenth century Englishmen were selling or exchanging villeinage rights to work land and not actual private property. "He totally ignores the close communal control, through the manorial court, of almost every aspect of the use of property [including] so many aspects of personal life that it is difficult to see where in the medieval village the concept of individualism found room to flourish outside the one sphere Macfarlane emphasizes: the power to sell or bequeath property" (Stone 1979, p. 41).

5. Biddick offers an outstanding bibliography of English historians who share her view. Fourquin (1976, pp. 176–85) makes a similar argument for France.

6. The fundamental contributions to this model, cited by Brenner, include Habakkuk 1958, Postan 1966, and Le Roy Ladurie 1966. Cooper (1978) advances this approach in his critique of Brenner's 1976 article.

7. Brenner (1976) reduces Postan and Le Roy Ladurie's discussions of the postplague era to the simple proposition that low population results in "declining rents in general, and labour-services in particular . . . [and ends] the fall of serfdom" (1976, p. 39).

Le Roy Ladurie (1978) contends that Brenner ignores the ways in which his *Paysans de Languedoc* (1966) "incorporates (class structure) by making every effort to bring out social groups (landowners, farmers, agricultural workers and the like) over and above abstract economic categories (ground rent, business profits, wages)" (p. 55). Le Roy Ladurie's complaint is justified; Brenner does ignore the numerous ad hoc discussions of social relations in Le Roy Ladurie's work. In doing so, Brenner is too kind to Le Roy Ladurie, giving his various writings a coherence and elegance that they in fact lack. As a result, Brenner misses the real problem with Le Roy Ladurie: The French historian never is able to identify a consistent set of social structural factors, whose differences over time and across provinces, could explain differences in land tenure arrangements over time and across French provinces.

8. A similar argument on the relationship between inheritance systems and land concentration is made for England by Howell (1975; 1983). See Lachmann 1987, pp. 124–27, for a critique of Howell for ignoring the effects of shifts in class relations and state intervention upon peasant income and land holdings. That critique parallels the one made of Le Roy Ladurie in this chapter.

9. This lag between fourteenth-century demographic cause and seventeenth-century capitalist outcome parallels that in Dobb's work.

10. Goldstone discusses the period 1500–1650, but his model would predict the same outcomes in the 1200–1348 era.

11. Goldstone sees enclosure as the only measure of landlord strength. In this he is reacting to the simplistic Marxist view of English capitalist development formulated by Tawney (1912). In fact, as I discuss in chapter 6, English landlords relied more on other techniques such as ascertainment and restriction of clerical and manorial courts to evict tenants from their holdings (Kerridge 1969, pp. 33–50; Hill 1963, pp. 84–92; Lachmann 1987, pp. 102–14; for examples of peasants dispossessed by such methods see Spufford 1974 and Finch 1956). By ignoring the principal institutional sites of agrarian class conflict, Goldstone is able to argue

that the period 1500–1650 "was not a period of either decisive progress in England or marked divergence between England and France" (1988, p. 302).

12. Fenoaltea's discussion applies only to that portion of a manor's land under direct peasant cultivation. His model does not address, it does not even acknowledge, the fraction of a manor's arable held by the lord as demesne.

13. Fenoaltea does not address why the "costs" of establishing manorial social relations were paid by peasants in some regions and not in others. He does not recognize that landlords may have incurred such costs as well, and he does not weigh such transaction costs against the potentially far greater costs of a peasant surrender to landlord demands.

14. I address Fox's argument (1971) in chapters 3 and 6. He argues that there were two Frances in the medieval and later eras; one with access to seas and rivers for easy transport and therefore early market development, the other isolated in areas with limited land transport. I point out the extent to which urban markets and transport networks affected agrarian production in France, England, and Italy.

15. Fenoaltea's work is symptomatic of the disrespect with which the self-proclaimed school of rational choice theorists treats the historical record. Despite repeated if steadily weaker claims to radical political purpose, these scholars mimic the worst tendencies among "bourgeois" neoclassical economists to abstract the "choices" of real economic actors from the contested and shifting context of social relations within which decisions are made. Even Levi (1988), who displays a real acquaintance with the history she attempts to explain, makes a set of assumptions that obscure much of the context within which rulers exercised agency and provoked responses. Her work, and this approach, are discussed in more detail in chapter 4.

16. For a general approach to peasant stratification see Shanin 1972. Political and economic inequality among peasants in the feudal era is discussed for England in Chibnall 1965; DuBoulay 1966; Dyer 1980; Harvey 1965; Hatcher 1970; Hilton 1975; and Howell 1983. For France, the one outstanding study of this era is Bois 1984, but see also Laurent 1972.

17. I use the province as the unit of analysis for two reasons. First, it is the level of generalization at which many French historians work. Although many French studies are of villages, there are too few to make comprehensive comparisons across the country at that most basic level. Second, as I show below and in subsequent chapters, elites were organized at the province level and elites affected agrarian social relations at that level and at the level of the nation.

18. Several provinces are not included in table 2.1 and map 2.1 because published sources do not analyze the state of agrarian class relations in these centuries.

19. To be fair to Goldstone, he never attempts to apply his discussion of soil types to this early period. He is mainly concerned with the later backwardness of southern and western France in the eighteenth century. However, in the preplague era, the poor-soil regions of France appear to be among those moving furthest from classic feudal social relations.

20. The discussion in this and subsequent paragraphs is based on two sources in addition to those cited in the text. Lot and Fawtier 1957 is an edited collection of articles discussing the institutions of France in the eleventh through fourteenth centuries. Major 1980, pp. 1–204, examines the estates of French provinces and independent entities in what later became France in the twelfth through fifteenth centuries. Together, these two sources provide enough evidence to classify the elite structures of all the provinces included in table 2.1.

21. The discussion in this section draws upon chapter 3 of Lachmann 1987. For a fuller discussion readers are referred to that work, which contains an extensive bibliography.

22. Kosminsky and Dyer note that some villeins were larger landholders and had greater household incomes than some freeholders, although in general most freeholders were better off than most villeins.

TABLE N.24. Manor Size and Land Ratios in 1279

	Demesne-Villein Ratio	Freehold-Villein Ratio
Small manors (under 500 acres)	56:44	48:52
Medium manors (500–1,000 acres)	49:51	40:60
Large manors (over 1,000 acres)	33:67	31:69

23. Most famuli occupied this position while waiting to inherit tenements from their elders. Famuli were not under long-term obligations to provide labor on the demense and could abandon that position upon inheriting land of their own (Postan 1954).

24. Kosminsky (1956) provides the most comprehensive look at preplague English social structure through his analysis of the Hundred Rolls of 1279, the only national land survey between the Domesday Book and the Black Death. Kosminsky (p. 101) compares the ratio of land held as demesne to that in villein tenements, and the ratio of freehold lands to villein lands in six counties: Cambridgeshire, Bedfordshire, Buckinghamshire, Huntingdonshire, Oxfordshire, and Warwickshire. He compares the ratios by size of manor (see table N.24).

The differences in land allocation by size of manor and the residual differences among counties after controlling for manor size cam be explained by the historical development of manors. Manors had been granted by English kings to lay and clerical lords in return for the fulfillment of military obligations in the century after 1066. Manor lords, in turn, granted submanors to vassals in return for their services in meeting the military obligations to the king (Pollack and Maitland 1968, pp. 252–53). Submanors, depending on the circumstances of their establishment, received the right to enforce some villein obligations through their own manorial courts. The weaker such rights, the more difficulty manor lords had in bonding villeins to the manor, and therefore the lesser the portion of the submanor's land devoted to villein tenures. Many of the small manors were originally submanors with weak manorial courts and therefore with lower ratios of villeins and villein holdings (Kerridge 1969, pp. 19–23).

The demise of military tenures in the twelfth century removed the ties of service between lords of manors and submanors. Some former military vassals became independent manor lords in their own right. Smaller vassals became freeholders without the rights of lordship. Additionally, many manor lords retained freeholds on their former submanors or granted those holdings to other vassals. After the ties of military service dissolved, manor lords, submanor lords, and peasant freeholders together held a relatively constant quarter of all manor lands as freeholds (Pollack and Maitland 1968, pp. 276–78, 600–601). Residual differences in land allocation ratios among counties and individual manors in 1279 were artifacts of defunct chains of military tenure and subtenure. Counties with smaller portions of villein lands had been more extensively subtenanted, leaving weaker manorial courts on both the small and medium-sized manors (Kosminsky 1956, pp. 119–26).

25. Razi (1981, pp. 17–27) points out that few tenements actually were abandoned after the Black Death. Even when an entire nuclear family was killed by the plague, their holdings were inherited by more distant relatives. Razi goes on to argue that inheritance among distant relatives strengthened peasant communities against the postplague seigneurial reaction (pp. 27–36). Hoyle (1990, pp. 6–12) looks at similar evidence to reach a different conclusion: that landlords' eagerness to find heirs for vacant lands made both landlords and peasants unconcerned and therefore careless about how future inheritance rights were written into leases, with decisive

consequences for copyholder rights in the sixteenth century when population rose and the advantage returned to landlords. In other words, Hoyle believes that peasants were protected by low population, not by community solidarity or legal guarantees in the first century after the plague, and were undone by high population and the carelessness of their ancestors in reading and writing leases in the sixteenth century. This argument is similar to that made by Cooper (1978, pp. 38–40). The question of how postplague copyhold leases affected agrarian class relations in the sixteenth and seventeenth centuries is taken up in chapter 6. The remainder of this section addresses the competing views of postplague class consciousness: Razi's of peasant awareness and unified opposition to landlords in contrast to Hoyle's contention that all classes were relatively inattentive to legal language since the postplague labor shortage dictated the immediate conditions of land tenure (and those of the future as well, since Hoyle believes all actors thought the future would be as the present, a surprising assumption of medieval mentalities since the landlord and peasant creators of copyhold leases had experienced an unprecedented demographic collapse that changed so much else in their social world.)

26. Goldstone (1988) emphasizes the post-1650 period in his discussion of regional differences; the logic of his argument suggests geographic contrasts should emerge in the postplague era as well.

27. Abel's index for wheat prices shows a decline from 100 in 1301–50 to 70 in 1391–1400.

28. Martin (1983) argues that the peasant revolt of 1381, while having little immediate effect, had the long-term effect of strengthening peasant communities enough to allow tenants to win freedom from labor dues in the fifteenth century. Martin argues that the fifteenth-century royal state was able to preserve lords' landholdings but not their feudal control over peasant labor. Martin's work is important in identifying peasant solidarity and revolt as necessary conditions for peasant freedom. In so doing, Martin makes a major advance on the demographic determinists who assume that changes in the ratio of land to labor automatically gave peasants enough of an advantage to win freedom from labor dues.

Martin also furthers our understanding by highlighting the delayed, uneven, and contingent nature of the transition from feudal labor dues to peasant leaseholds and the eventual dispossession of many tenants in the sixteenth and subsequent centuries. Unfortunately, Martin's state-landlord dualism is too simple to explain why land tenure relations were transformed in the specific ways that they were following the Black Death and then in the sixteenth and subsequent centuries.

29. Marx develops the concept of the Asiatic mode of production in his *Contribution to the Critique of Political Economy* ([1859] 1970), *Capital* (1867–94] 1967) and the *Grundrisse* (1857–58] 1973) and makes reference to it elsewhere in his work. The concept was popularized by Wittfogel (1957).

30. Japan is an exceptional case. It is regarded, almost unanimously, by historians and social scientists as a feudal society that made a transition to capitalism, perhaps after that of England, but well before most of the rest of the world. Japan has been used to support various Marxist (Anderson 1974), world system (Moulder 1977), or Weberian (Eisenstadt 1996, Ikegami 1995, Collins 1997) models. I hope to address this important case in a later work.

31. The debate in the *Journal of Peasant Studies* over Harbans Mukhia's article "Was There Feudalism in Indian History?" (1981) is revealing. The various contributors to a special issue edited by T. J. Byres and Mukhia (1985) all agree that the notion of an Asiatic mode of production is not helpful for understanding any region of India. The articles taken together offer important understandings of the range of agrarian modes of production in the different parts of India over centuries of history. However, the articles all bog down when the authors attempt to develop a model of modes of production, or to articulate modes of production, that

could explain a particular slice of Indian history. Readers are treated to a series of critical exegeses of Marxian concepts but never learn what factors propel change.

32. Eisenstadt (1996) and Collins (1997) fall into this trap in different ways, as do Hall (1988) and Baechler (1988). Weber himself, in *The Religion of China* ([1916] 1964) and *The Religion of India* ([1916–17] 1958), allowed for more contingency as he traced the two-way causality between social structure and religious world view. Ikegami (1995) is closest to Weber in the subtlety with which she traces the interaction between conflict and cultural change. Ikegami does not draw theoretical conclusions from her historical work and so offers only implicit suggestions for how to examine Japan in comparison with Europe or other Asian societies.

Chapter 3

1. Holton (1986) is helpful in identifying some of the differences in Pirenne and Weber's writings on medieval cities. However, Holton regards their approaches as basically the same and does not identify the very different roles Pirenne and Weber assign to city dwellers in their models of the origins of capitalism.

2. While Braudel and Wallerstein's theoretical perspectives have much in common, Wallerstein is more exacting in his definition of capitalism than is Braudel. For Wallerstein, a trading city is not truly capitalist, or at the core of a capitalist world system, unless it plays a more active role in shaping the forms of production and exploitation in peripheral regions than did Renaissance Italian and Low Country cities. Further, Wallerstein, and Abu-Lughod (1989), who deals with the period 1250–1350, allow for the possibility of multiple cores in a world system, unlike Braudel's single world capital. Therefore, my critique in this chapter of Braudel does not directly address Wallerstein's arguments. I address the limits of Wallerstein's world system model in the course of building my argument in chapters 4–6.

3. Cohen (1980) makes a similar argument, contending that Renaissance Roman Catholics, especially those of the Italian city-states, exhibited the capitalist spirit in their pursuit of profit, regardless of the ways in which wealth was spent. Holton (1983) criticizes Cohen for conflating rational technique, which the Renaissance Italians did practice, with rational economic action, which was substantially absent in Florence and the other city-states.

4. Of course the question of which disjunctures are crucial are the basis for my differences with Marx and Weber and of the debates between and among Marxists and Weberians.

5. Abu-Lughod (1989) reminds us that European merchants, however they are classified, were pikers compared with the traders of the Middle East and Asia. Her valuable synthetic work identifies Western European cities as the nodes in just one of eight subsystems in world trade during the thirteenth century. She points out that the "Fall of the East" preceded the "Rise of the West." Abu-Lughod's work cannot tell us why the units she identifies as the leading urban centers of the thirteenth century—the fair towns of Champagne, the textile and commercial towns of Flanders, and the great cities of northern Italy—failed along with Islamic and Asian cities to sustain economic leadership.

6. Wallerstein's useful discussions of the causal interaction between world system position and internal politics in peripheral regions is not readily adaptable to the problem of shifts in core leadership. In this respect, Wallerstein's model of the rise of England and France to core positions in the sixteenth through eighteenth centuries, presented in *The Modern World System*, vols. 1–3 (1974–89), runs into difficulties similar to those of Braudel's discussion (1979) of the Renaissance.

7. Weber first sought to explain Renaissance businessmen's loss of competitive advantage in his dissertation on the history of the medieval trading companies (1889), by comparing those business organizations with the enterprises established by capitalists in Protestant Germany and

especially in England. In *Economy and Society,* Weber defines politically oriented capitalism as an orientation to profit opportunities obtained through political domination, predatory activity, and extraordinary transactions with political bodies ([1921] 1978, pp. 164–66, 193–201; see also 1961, pp. 246–47). In contrast, economically oriented capitalism is the "orientation to the profit possibilities in continuous buying and selling on the market . . . or it may be orientation to the profit possibilities in continuous production of goods in enterprises with capital accounting" (1978, p. 164).

Economically oriented capitalism also encompasses profit "in the execution of the continuous financial operations of political bodies" (Weber 1978, p. 165). Investments in state bonds, or profits from continuing trade and industries reliant upon state protection, require the legal protection of a stable bureaucratized state. As such, these investments became prevalent only after the rationality induced by Puritanism bureaucratized states. Before the Reformation, profit from "political activities was everywhere the product of the competition of states with one another for power, and of the corresponding competition for capital which moved freely between them" (1978, p. 165).

8. Weber saw the Reformation and the development of a Protestant ethic as necessary preconditions for the bureaucratic state, to which they are temporally and causally prior, as well as for capitalism. I directly address that contention of Weber's in chapter 6. To address the issues raised in this chapter it is necessary only to determine the relationship between forms of economic action on one hand and structures of social relations, most notably political institutions, on the other hand.

Collins dismisses Protestantism not just from the study of the Renaissance but also from Weber's, and his, full model of capitalist development. In "Weber's Last Theory of Capitalism" Collins (1980, p. 934) contends that in Weber's *General Economic History* "Protestantism is only the last intensification of one of the chains of factors leading to rational capitalism." As a result, Collins sees the Italian Renaissance cities as sites of capitalist development, especially after the fourteenth-century popular rebellions "which replaced the charismatic law of the older patrician class with the universalistic and 'rationally instituted' law upon which so much of the institutional development of law was to depend" (p. 939).

Collins, in this part of his argument, follows Weber's view that the occidental city contributed to rationality by freeing urban dwellers from feudal constraints. For Weber, urban freedom was comprised of two elements. The first was liberty from the restrictions and obligations imposed upon subjects by feudal lords. "The urban citizenry . . . usurped the right to dissolve the bonds of seigneurial domination; this was the great—in fact, the *revolutionary*—innovation which differentiated the medieval Occidental cities from all others" (Weber 1978, p. 1239). Burghers were able to claim that freedom because, with the decentralization of military and political power in feudal Europe (as opposed to the unified political power of Imperial China), urban corps could pay for their own armed forces to challenge or at least scare off the armies of kings (pp. 1239, 1260–62; Weber 1961, pp. 237–38).

The second element of occidental urban freedom was the absence of "the magical, totemic, ancestral and caste props of the clan organization which in Asia impeded confraternization into a city corporation" (Weber 1978, p. 1243; see also 1961, p. 238). In Weber's view pre-Reformation Christianity fostered rationality in the sense that it allowed European burghers to form political alliances with others who shared their economic situation, rather than being divided along clan lines. Thus Christianity gave medieval European bourgeois the desire, while the feudal basis of military organization provided the means, to realize interest derived neither from a magical conception of kin nor from the noble concept of status honor.

According to Collins (1980, p. 940), the decline of Italian city-states relative to England is due more to the advantage that nation states enjoyed in the competition of the world market than to the added capitalist fervor induced by the Protestant ethic. Collins believes that to be

Weber's last word in the *General Economic History*. I see that as Collins's own model, not Weber's, and I evaluate it as such at the end of this chapter.

Collins's recognition of the role of nation-states in the transformation of European economic action in the sixteenth and subsequent centuries is a far more sophisticated Weber-inspired view of history than the arguments of Hall (1985) and Chirot (1985), who take just the broad historical elements of Weber's argument presented in just this endnote as the basis for contending that all the necessary conditions for Europe's special development were present by the early medieval period. Hall and Chirot ride high above the sorts of historical "details" that are the subject matter of this book. Therefore, the evidence and arguments I develop here cannot be used to evaluate their arguments except insofar as their confident determinism is subverted by demonstrations of the highly contingent and contested nature of structural change in subsequent centuries.

9. I discuss the limits to Weber's terminology as a tool for understanding state formation in chapter 4.

10. Kreidte (1983; see also Kreidte, Medick, and Schlumbohm 1981) offers an analysis of the decline of urban manufacture using a logic comparable to Tilly's. Kreidte argues that city-states were bested by rural-based capitalists who used the vast hinterlands of nation-states to draw upon large and cheap labor forces of peasants looking for by-employment. Rural manufacture undercut expensive guild manufacture. Although guild producers were more highly skilled, that advantage mattered only for luxury production, a sector that was eclipsed as the overall economy of Europe expanded in the sixteenth century. Kreidte's description begs the question of why nation states rather than networks of city-states gained control of such rural manufacture. Many of the earlier entrepreneurs of rural proto-industry were city-state merchants. The explanation for why those merchants turned to nation-states for protection in the sixteenth century (yet had thrived as citizens of city-states before then) is bound up in the overall decline of city states as the dominant political powers of Europe—a development not explainable through the proto-industrialization rubric.

11. Of course, a similar argument could be made for an intensive study of Venice, Genoa, or Antwerp instead of Florence. Ideally, I would have steeped myself in the history of all four cities before writing this chapter. Limits of time, and of space in relation to the overall plan of this book, led me to concentrate on one city. I do attempt, largely in a few extended endnotes, to show how and why other Italian city-states often followed the Florentine pattern and to highlight the conditions that accounted for those cities' divergences from Florence's path. I concentrate my comparisons on Venice, which, among the major cities, was the most distinct from the Florentine archetype. Students of those other cities will best be able to judge whether the conclusions of this chapter do justice or violence to the histories of Genoa, Venice, and Antwerp. I hope historian critics will distinguish between those of my omissions and errors that are merely annoying and those that require qualification of the broader conclusions of this chapter and the book as a whole.

12. The limits of capitalism in Amsterdam are addressed in chapter 5 instead of in this chapter. Amsterdam of the sixteenth and seventeenth centuries is more aptly compared with its rivals—the nation-states of England, France, and Spain, rather than to the Renaissance city-states of this chapter.

13. Russell (1972) divides thirteenth-century Europe and the Near East into twenty-two regions. Each region was characterized by a hierarchy of cities that were centered around a lead city that profited from its commercial and political dominance of lesser cities and their hinterlands. Regions differed in the extent to which they were urbanized and hence in the degree to which the lead city interacted with and prospered from its region.

Skinner (1977) focuses on the relation between cities and networks of periodic markets to gauge the influence of urban centers upon rural production and social relation. For Rozman

(1976) "premodern societies can be classified according to seven stages of development . . . [that] signify a sequential pattern of growing complexity in commercial and administrative interactions among settlements (p. 282).

Two recent, and outstanding, works on the development of European cities (Hohenberg and Lees 1985; Bairoch 1988) compare degree of urbanization and number and level of cities in various regions of Europe, and over time, as measures of urban wealth and power over hinterlands.

14. The third, and most dramatic, phase of European urban growth occurred in the nineteenth and first half of the twentieth century (Bairoch 1988, p. 216).

15. The figures for urbanization in this paragraph are rough averages of the estimates presented in Bairoch 1988 (p. 179) and De Vries 1984 (pp. 30, 36). De Vries counts as urban only residents of cities with populations greater than ten thousand; for Bairoch the cut-off is five thousand. Both those measures differ from Russell's count of the top ten towns as a percentage of the region's population. Because the three measures differ, I am presenting ratios rather than percentages for the latter two dates.

For De Vries, exact percentages for urbanization in each "territory" can be calculated by dividing the total urban populations he gives on page 30 with his total populations on page 36. (When discussing northern Italy, I am combining the data for what De Vries calls northern and central Italy.) Those regional percentages yield almost exactly the same ratios to De Vries' European-wide average as does taking the middle of the ranges provided by Bairoch. Cities are attributed to countries by Bairoch and De Vries on the basis of twentieth-century borders. Of course, borders differed and many of these countries did not exist in 1500 or 1700.

16. I limit myself to Christian Europe in order to avoid the need to discuss cities that were linked to empires and trading systems largely based outside Europe, such as the Ottoman Empire and Muslim Spain.

17. Cordoba, and in the second period Granada, are special cases. They became large cities while part of a Muslim world largely sited outside of Europe. Both Cordoba and Granada underwent drastic and fairly rapid population declines after their "reconquest" by Christian Spaniards. Cordoba had a peak population of perhaps ninety thousand just before the collapse of the caliphate in 1031. After its reconquest in 1236, the city gradually lost its role as the commercial and political center of Islamic Spain. The population fell to between forty thousand and sixty thousand by 1300, finally stabilizing at thirty thousand in 1500. Cordoba's removal from the Islamic world was a boon for the city of Granada, which gained political and commercial control over the remains of Islamic Granada after 1236. Granada rose to thirty thousand in 1300 and reached a peak of perhaps ninty thousand in the fifteenth century. After its reconquest in 1492 it fell rapidly. While still registering as a major city of seventy thousand in 1500, Granada's population was down to thirty-five thousand in 1700 (Russell 1972, pp. 181–84; Chandler 1987, pp. 129–31). Since both cities gained prominence as part of an Islamic world not under consideration here, and lost population along with political and commercial significance following their reincorporation into Christian Spain, I do not give them further consideration in this chapter.

18. Table 3.2 also excludes the "reconquered" cities of Cordoba and Granada.

19. Palermo, the capital of a sometime independent Sicily, enjoyed "a rapid increase in population" during the sixteenth century "for which there seems no very good reason" (Russell 1972, p. 55). Russell is not alone in expressing bewilderment at the enormous population of the capital of a minor political unit with relatively little industry and commerce. No historical demographer offers any explanation for the growth of that city. Whatever the causes, Palermo's growth did not add to the positions of Venice, Florence, or the other city-states in sixteenth-century Europe.

20. The dates in this and the previous paragraph are from Abu-Lughod (1989, pp. 51–134) and Braudel (1982, pp. 96–174), who offers the best chronology of shifts in economic centrality among European cities.

21. Population figures provide a good measure for the rise and fall of the Champagne fair towns as centers of European industry and commerce. No clear data exist for Bar-sur-aube and Lagny, but for the other two fair towns, Provins and Troyes, which also were the co-capitals of independent Champagne, the data are clear. In the first half of the thirteenth century, both cities peaked at a population of around twenty thousand, placing them among the fifty largest cities in Christian Europe. (One source, based on the number of churches in Provins, suggests a peak of thirty thousand in the thirteenth century). With the subordination of Champagne to France, and those two cities' loss of capital status, growth halted. Troyes stagnated at a population of twenty thousand for the next several centuries, while Provins declined drastically to three thousand inhabitants in 1361 (all data from Chandler 1987, pp. 160, 167).

22. The arguments in this and the following three paragraphs are based upon the historical analyses presented by Friedrichs (1981) and Mauro (1990).

23. The schism between the papacy and the German emperors is explored in detail in Partner 1972 (chap. 4).

24. The remainder of this chapter, up to the conclusion, focuses upon Florence. As I noted above, limits of time and space preclude more than a cursory comparison with other Italian cities.

25. White (1992, pp. 262–65) describes "reaching down (for getting action)" as efforts to organize actors lower down in a hierarchy in order to create new openings for agency by their superiors, actions that the superiors could not take without organizing their inferiors.

26. The "muda system" of Venice, which became hegemonic within that city-state by the 1330s and lasted two centuries, was in crucial aspects the mirror image of the entrepreneurial system that emerged in Florence. The Venetian state controlled all merchant galleys and set routes, sailing dates, and cargo rates (McNeil 1974, pp. 60–64). Any Venetian citizen could rent space on a galley, making it impossible for a merchant or a syndicate to dominate a trade route or corner the market on a commodity. As a result, all Venetian merchants were dependent for their economic prosperity on the military fortunes of their city-state. Under the protection and control of their state, Venetians had neither need nor opportunity to establish independent ties to foreign merchants or political powers that might have sustained Venetian merchants, as it did Florentines, after the collapse of their state's military power in the Aegean.

McNeil draws a similar contrast between Venice and Genoa. "The persistent weakness of the commune of Genoa was, perversely, a strength: private groups had to organize on a more enduring basis and with larger resources to carry through everyday activities, such as the construction of a new ship. From this it proved feasible to organize entire fleets as private ventures: and a privately organized fleet that happened to capture valuable territory could transform itself into a territorial sovereign" for the sole benefit of its merchant shareholders (1974, p. 58). Yet, while Genoese commerce was more privatized than the Venetian muda system, it too was dependent for its success on military power. Genoa's economic gains over Venice followed the Genoese victories in its 1350–55 and 1378–81 wars with Venice (Lane 1973, pp. 174–96; Epstein 1996, pp. 230–42).

Genoese merchants, like Venetian merchants, concentrated their commerce on routes and ports under their military control. Before the rise of militarily more powerful nation-states, Venetian and Genoese merchants profited from their cities' military prowess. After city-states were eclipsed by larger military powers, Venetian and Genoese merchants lacked any bases for entree into the economies and polities of nation-states. Florentines then gained a commercial advantage over their Venetian and Genoese rivals, only to suffer from different rigidities in their system in later centuries.

27. Historians continue to debate whether popes favored Florentine bankers for their superior financial skills or for their slavish loyalty to papal positions in international affairs. Perhaps the way to resolve this debate is to ask why Venetian, Genoese, or other Italian bankers did not, or could not, bring themselves and their cities to adopt the foreign policies demanded by popes. The answer to that question is that devotion to papal desires would have required abandoning the push for Mediterranean hegemony, which in turn would have meant the loss of at least some of the trade routes that the Venetians and Genoese found far more lucrative than papal tax farms. Because the Florentines had no Mediterranean trade routes to lose in supporting the papacy, the bankers had little difficulty in persuading other Florentine elites to adopt a propapal line. Indeed, when antipapal factions gained control of the Florentine government, the papacy then withdrew financial concessions to Florentine bankers, or the bankers were forced to leave the city and conduct their business from elsewhere. The financial loss was not made up elsewhere, leading to the inevitable fall of antipapal governments, and a return to propapal policies in Florence (Trexler 1974 offers a case study of this process in Florence; Partner [1965, 1968, 1972] has compiled the most comprehensive history of Florentine-papal relations). In contrast, propapal forces in Genoa and Venice continually were hobbled by the great wealth that citizens of those two cities received from trade routes secured against the wishes of the papacy. Lane (1973) describes repeated occasions when the Venetians defied papal edicts to trade, negotiate, and ally with the pope's current enemies.

28. The old Venetian aristocracy eventually was undermined by the high cost of the War of Chioggia against Genoa and Hungary from 1378 to 1381. Forced purchases of state bonds during the war totalled 107 percent of assessments, which Lane estimates as 25 to 30 percent of the actual value of property. The value of bonds crashed from 92 1/2 percent of par in 1375 to 18 percent in 1381 when the state suspended interest payments. The forced purchases fell most heavily on land-owning aristocrats who had to sell property to meet their obligations, leading to a collapse of real estate values paralleling the depression in bond prices. Nonaristocrats with unassessed commercial wealth (much of it abroad) escaped most taxes and were relatively uneffected by the bond and real estate crashes. State finances were revived with the admission of new families to the aristocracy in the 1380s. Once the Venetian state had been stabilized fiscally and militarily, government and the aristocracy were once again closed to new entrants and remained closed throughout the fifteenth century (Lane 1973, pp. 196–201, 252–54).

29. I find Brucker (1977) and Najemy (1982) most useful in understanding the period of flux from the end of aristocratic hegemony in the 1250s to the final establishment of oligarchic rule in 1400. My argument, in this and the following section, is based upon those two works, Hyde 1973, Trexler 1980, Martines 1979, and the other more narrowly focused works that I cite along with these five works as sources in my references for specific claims.

30. Brown (1982, pp. 148–76) takes issue with Becker, contending that gabelles and duties, ultimately paid by mostly urban consumers, rather than land taxes were the main source of "rural" payments to the commune. However, Brown's study concentrates on the fifteenth and sixteenth centuries, an era when the Medici and their allies were reestablishing themselves as an aristocracy and acquiring rural estates. It does not contradict Becker's argument, that urban patricians of the period 1283–1400 used state power to impoverish old aristocrats, to find that two centuries later commune tax policy was changed again to favor the new patrician aspiring-aristocratic purchasers of rural estates.

31. This statement, of course, applies only to lay lords, not to clerical lords whose fiefs were held only by virtue of their church offices.

32. Martines (1979, pp. 111–16) traces the use of exile in Florentine politics. Edgerton (1985) shows the power of effigies of shame (*pittura infamante*) to compel traitors and criminals to reach an accommodation with the communal government, a power that was derived from the commune's capacity to confer status and identity upon its citizens. The extension of such

sanctions to nobles in the latter half of the thirteenth century (Waley 1969, pp. 214–18) is a sign of the subordination of aristocrats to the commune.

33. I discuss this point further, and cite the sources for this claim, later in this chapter under "The Economic Limits of the Florentine Polity."

34. My analysis of these five episodes is based upon the accounts in Brucker 1962 and 1977, pp. 39–44.

35. In 1301 Charles of Valois and his troops entered Florence to put propapal Black Guelfs in power, massacring many White Guelfs and exiling the rest. Charles moved on to Sicily, where his troops were defeated. With the elimination of Charles as a military force in Tuscany, the White Guelfs regained control of the Signoria, exiling in turn their Black Guelf enemies (Holmes 1986, pp. 163–85). In 1313 King Robert of Naples engineered his selection as Signore for five years in lieu of the elected Signoria. Robert, however, lacked the military power to enforce his edicts and those of his minions over the communal government and never established effective control over Florence. In 1326, in reponse to the military threat mounted by the Lucchese despot, Castracani, the Signoria invited Robert's son Charles of Calabria to be dictator for ten years. In 1328 both Castracani and Charles died, and elective government resumed in Florence.

36. Florence never held direct elections to the Signoria. Instead, corporate groups (the Signoria of the moment, the Guelf party, and the guilds) nominated citizens for "scrutiny." A committee then voted to approve or to veto each nominee. Those nominees who passed muster with the scrutiny committee had their names placed in bags. Every six months a new Signoria would be chosen by drawing names from the scrutiny bag. After serving, a citizens would not be eligible for drawing for the next two years. Najemy (1982) traces the shifts in the relative weight given to members of each corporate group in nominating and scrutinizing candidates for the Signoria. In essence, the struggles between patricians and guildsmen during the fourteenth century were over the extent to which nonpatrician guildsmen and members of lower guilds would be eligible for nomination and to serve on the scrutiny committee. During most of the 1300s, guilds played little or no role in the scrutiny. Only during 1343–48 and 1378–82 did the guilds come close to dominating scrutinies. Finally, in 1382, the patricians developed a way to limit guild participation in the scrutiny to a nominal level without making guildsmen aware of their exclusion. The patricians allowed virtually open nominations for scrutinies and then, in the scrutiny committee that they dominated, moved to exclude most guildsmen. Since the scrutiny's results were secret, guildsmen did not learn for years, until all the names in the scrutiny bags had been drawn, that most of them had been excluded from service on the Signoria. This system continued into the era of Medici hegemony.

37. The account in this and the following seven paragraphs is based upon Najemy 1982, pp. 166–262 and Brucker 1962, pp. 183–396.

38. They are joined in this consensus by many other scholars of Florence, notably Mohlo (1968), Becker (1968b), Trexler (1980), and Najemy (1982). Brucker (1977) reiterates this point. Padgett and Ansell (1993, pp. 1295–96) and Martines (1963, pp. 18–84) trace the ways in which patricians disciplined any of their number who sought to recruit political allies from below.

39. Term limits in the contemporary United States have a similar effect, leaving power in the hands of executive branch officials, lobbyists, and others who finance elections.

40. The profound consequences of the guilds' continuing control over the manufacturing sector of the Florentine economy are discussed in the next section of this chapter.

41. This is in great contrast to the Venetian aristocracy's ability, noted above, to limit the wealth of citizens without titles.

42. Membership in the inner circle of power did provide the opportunity to use inside information to make windfall profits speculating in *monte* debt. However, such information also

was available to the temporary occupants of high offices who were not oligarchs and thus quickly spread among patricians. Often the keys needed to predict and manipulate the market in *monte* debt came from advance knowledge of foreign diplomatic and military events, rather than internal Florentine politics. Such external information became available first to partners in international banks, such as the Medici, rather than oligarchs tied into local networks. Large cash reserves were needed for any successful market manipulations, however, and such reserves were held mainly by banking and cloth tycoons. (Molho 1971 provides the best discussion of the *monte* in the decades leading up to the Medici seizure of power. Goldthwaite [1987, p. 27] discusses Medici manipulations of the Monte prior to 1434).

43. In 1447 Pope Eugenius IV, who had turned from a friend into an enemy of Florence, died and was replaced by the pro-Medici Nicholas V. The Medici retained a continuing influence, and often control, over the papacy for two centuries. Medici power in Rome culminated in the election of family members Giovanni as Pope Leo X in 1513 and of Giulio as Pope Clement VII in 1523 (Hale 1977).

44. Hale (1977, pp. 76–126) and Stephens (1983) offer clear summaries of the history of the period discussed in this paragraph and in the following two endnotes. Trexler (1980, pp. 462–553) discusses the extent of popular mobilization against the Medici and in the non-Medici governments of this period.

45. In 1494, Medici concessions to an invading French army sparked popular resistance, culminating in an uprising when Piero (son of Lorenzo) de Medici brought his own armed gang to threaten the Signoria. Oligarchic factionalism revived as the Medici were exiled and their closest allies excluded from government. Factionalism opened the way for popular mobilization, culminating in the de facto rule of Savonarola, whose religious fanaticism led to his execution in 1498. The constitutional revisions sponsored by Savonarola only temporarily allowed for nonpatrician involvement in government until the non-Medici oligarchs reunited and manipulated the councils of government to regain power. This oligarchy coaleced under the leadership of Soderini.

Medician rule was interrupted once more in 1527 when an imperial-led alliance defeated the papacy's French allies and sacked Rome. Again, a temporarily widened democracy was subverted by non-Medici oligarchs.

46. The Medici regained power when the French, weakened by heavy military losses, withdrew from Italy in 1512, leaving a vacuum filled by an alliance of Spain, Venice, and the papacy, in which Cardinal Giovanni de' Medici (soon to be Pope Leo X) was the leading figure.

The republican interlude of 1527–30 was cut short by a renewed alliance between Medici Pope Clement VII and Emperor Charles V. By 1530, Charles was the undisputed military power in Italy and was able to force Florence to accept a permanent end to the republic and its replacement by a heriditary Medici dukedom.

47. Guilds had been crucial to the patricians' efforts to take power from aristocrats in other Italian cities and therefore retained control over production in those city-states as well. Genoese, Milanese, and other guilds prevented the establishment of rural and nonguild cloth manufacture in those states until the late seventeenth or eighteenth centuries (Belfanti 1993, pp. 255–60). Venice, again, was exceptional. Since the unified elite governing an independent Venetian Republic had been able to avoid factional strife, that elite did not need to make concessions to guildsmen in return for political aid. As a result, Venetian guilds were less able than those in other Italian cities to prevent wage cuts or to block the establishment of rural industries (Lane 1973, pp. 104–9, 312–21); Belfanti (1993) identifies the mountain valleys of Brescia and Bergamo, under Venetian rule since the 1400s, as major centers of Italian rural proto-industry (pp. 260–64).

48. Zeitlin and Ratcliff (1988) find a similar unity among landlords and industrial and finance capitalists in Chile during the 1960s, a unity created and sustained by intermarriage among a core of capitalist families that through pyramiding, joint ventures, and interlocking

directorships owned and controlled a plurality of the largest banks, corporations, and estates in the nation. Zeitlin concludes, "the dominant agrarian and capitalist elements have been internally related, if not 'fused,' in so complex a pattern that neither of them possesses a specific autonomy or distinctive social identity" (pp. 181–82).

49. The Milanese silk industry also benefited from an expansion of Lombard mulberry cultivation in the fifteenth and sixteenth centuries (Dowd 1961, p. 155).

50. Cipolla's picture (1952) of an absolute decline in the Italian silk industry is challenged by Goodman (1981), who finds that "output during the seventeenth century was relatively stable" (p. 423). However, stable production, especially in an era of falling prices, is in fact decline. Goodman's image of stability is contradicted by his careful description of how Florentine silk manufacturing firms were unable to generate the capital to pay for the purchase of raw silk from Tuscan farms. As a result, the newly ennobled patrician owners of silk-producing estates (along with bankers and merchants who often were the same individuals or from the same families as the estate owners) became the senior partners in most silk firms (Goodman 1981, pp. 424–35). The main profit in the luxury silk industry became realized at the point of cultivation in the seventeenth century, rather than at the point of production or sale, as had been true in previous centuries.

51. Similar guild support for a single ruling family that shut out merchants from political power prevented changes in work rules in seventeenth century Milan and its Lombard *contado* (Dowd 1961). Belfanti (1993) shows that guilds were critical enough to ruling elites in other Italian cities (with the exception of Venice noted above) to block rural manufacture. Italian sites of proto-industry were "enclaves of institutional particularism" (p. 259); that is, micro-states with unified elites under papal protection, or with semi-autonomous ties to other, larger political entities. Often guilds were weak or absent in such predominately rural political units. The rulers of micro states had enough papal or royal backing to challenge such guilds as existed in their polities, and the promise of tax revenues from new rural industries outweighed any losses from the slight urban commerce that existed in those out-of-the-way places.

52. Of course these industries were eclipsed by British cotton textiles, the first mass-production industry in world history, in the later half of the eighteenth century.

53. Once again, Florentine businessmen adopted strategies that were more profitable in the long term because they were excluded from the most lucrative short-term investment opportunities. Thirteenth-century Florentines had been kept from the most profitable trade routes, because of the relative military weakness of their city-state, and ended up in the wool trade and in a position to become papal bankers. Those seventeenth-century Florentines who had not been able to invest all their capital in politically advantaged businesses or in the old silk trade were left with the liquid assets and the freedom of movement to make what seemed to be second-best choices to invest in proto-industry, which then overtook the old cloth industries in scale and profitability.

54. I discuss the reasons for this concentration of wealth, and of types of investment, among seventeenth-century Florentines below.

55. I discuss the other great Italian contribution to rational economic technique, the invention of marketable government bonds, when I examine the *monte* in the following section.

56. Florentine borrowers were charged from 7 to 15 percent on domestic loans.

57. The return on wool and silk is calculated from de Roover 1963, pp. 61, 69. De Roover (1963) gives the 1441 investment in two wool shops and one silk shop as 14,981 florins excluding goodwill, and profits from those businesses as 29,498 florins over the sixteen years from 1435 to 1451. I calculate the return by averaging the total profit over the sixteen years and dividing it by the 1441 capital investment.

58. Lopez and Miskimin (1962, p. 424) give the number of Medici bank employees in 1469 as sixty, compared with eighty-five for the Peruzzi in 1336 and fifty-five for the Acciaivoli in 1341.

59. Papal banking in particular became less profitable in the fifteenth and sixteenth centuries as clerical tithe revenues increasingly were appropriated by national churches and monarchs rather than by popes and their direct appointees. I discuss the "nationalization" of churches in chapter 4. At this point it is important to note that as popes lost control of tithes, papal bankers lost the benefits of collecting and holding tithe monies on behalf of the papacy.

60. A similar fate befell the Medici's profitable alum business. "Alum was third only to salt and silver as one of the most sought-after products of the age. It was used in the glass and leather industries and, more important still, it was essential in textile manufacture both to cleanse the wool and to fix the dye in cloth. And it was in short supply. The only source of any importance in Europe was on papal territory, . . . and from 1466 the Medici bank had controlled its output and sale as papal concessionaires" (Hale 1977, p. 65). The Medici sold alum throughout Western Europe through its banking and textile network. They and the papacy sought to increase their profits by excluding alum from Turkish mines and from small mines in Catholic lands from the Western European market. The Medici abruptly lost their papal concession in 1476, however, when Sixtus IV awarded it to the Pazzi and later to non-Florentines (deRoover 1963, pp. 152–64; Goldthwaite 1987, p. 28). There is no evidence that the Medici took any interest in expanding the volume of production in the papal alum mines or in making the process of production more efficient.

61. Leo died in 1521 and, following the brief pontificate of Adrian VI, the Medici resumed power in Rome with Giovanni di Bicci de' Medici's reign from 1523 to 1534 as Pope Clement VII.

62. Bankers in Venice confined themselves mainly to accepting deposits of coins from merchants and then "making payments on behalf of [their] clients" at home and abroad. Such Venetian "giro-banks" rarely made loans. The banks were closely regulated by the Venetian state and in 1587 were replaced by a state-owned bank. Both private and public banks were used by the Venetian state to finance wars through issuance of inflationary bank credits. Banking did not become a source of private fortunes in Venice (Lane 1973, pp. 147, 327–31 and passim). Genoese banks rose and fell along with the local commercial firms to which they loaned almost all their capital. "Neither Rome nor Genoa became banking leaders in the [twelfth or thirteenth] centuries (Lopez 1979, p. 10 and passim).

63. Genoa established a stable oligarchic republic by 1528, which meant that the bankers who made fortunes after 1557 already were part of the ruling elite. Genoese politics were not destablized by factional divisions or reaching down during either the decades of banking wealth or the period when Genoa was superseded by Dutch bankers (Martines 1979, pp. 66–72, 94–102, 130–32).

64. The Venetian *montes,* which began in 1262, were created to meet war expenses. During periods of war, and especially following wars which it lost, Venice often was unable to pay interest on debt and *Monte* share prices plunged. *Monte* share prices dropped from 92 percent of par value in 1375 to 18 percent of par in 1381 when interest payments were suspended following Venice's loss of the War of Chioggia. Many wealthy families were forced to sell shares and land to meet expenses, causing a crash in land values as well that financially destroyed many of the Venetian elite.

The financial catastrophe of 1381 was instructive for the surviving rich families of Venice, and for new recruits into the largely unified economic and political elite of the city. The 130 to 150 families that dominated the Great Council and higher bodies of government and that made up the bulk of taxpayers with high assessed wealth and hence the bulk of forced loan obligations (Lane 1973, pp. 95–98, 151–52) redoubled their efforts to raise consumption taxes on urban consumers and on the mainland territories under Venetian control and to reduce military expenses by adopting a less aggressive foreign policy. Those efforts were only partially successful in the fifteenth century as Venice continued to face foreign military threats. However, as

Venice became a relatively unthreatened regional power in the sixteenth century, the *monte* became an annuity for its aristocratic shareholders. (Lane 1973, pp. 65, 150, 184–85, 196–97, 238, 325–26, 402, 425–27 discusses the *monte.*)

The Venetian aristocracy's interest in guarding its income from the *monte,* even at the cost of surrendering opportunities (however uncertain) of foreign conquest, parallels the Florentine patricians' transfer of capital from active to passive investments. For the Venetian aristocracy, control over their polity and preventing political devolution was far less problematic than for the shifting elites of Florence; however, the Florentines found it easier minimize costly foreign wars than did the Venetians. Ultimately, both military and political stability were necessary for turning *montes* into stable income supports of the idle rich in Venice and Florence.

65. In late sixteenth-century Venice, "the more than 200,000 ducats paid out in salaries annually to 700–1,000 [out of a total of 2,500–3,000] nobles was a substantial contribution by taxpayers to the income of that class." Non-noble "citizens-by-birth," of whom there were 4,000 male adults in 1575 held lower-level state jobs, paying 50 to 200 ducats per annum as opposed to the 100 to 500 ducats for noble offices (and higher for the most important officials. On top of official salaries was "in either case the collection of fines or gratuities" and shadier sources of extra-legal incomes from offices (Lane 1973, p. 324 and passim.; see also Mousnier 1970, pp. 390–99).

66. Mohlo (1971, chap. 3) argues that heavy taxes and commodity price controls sapped the economy of the *contado,* retarding its recovery from the Black Death of 1348. Brown (1982) argues that Florence did not exploit the *contado;* nevertheless, her data and descriptions of tax policies concur with Becker and Mohlo's findings.

67. Jones (1966; 1968), Emigh (1996; 1997); Litchfield (1986), McArdle (1978), Dowd (1961), Diaz (1978), McNeill (1974), Woolf (1968), and Aymard (1982) all share this view. The discussion in this and the subsequent nine paragraphs is based on these authors' discussion of Italian agriculture.

68. Historians of Italy have yet to mine the archives to produce the sorts of detailed studies of peasant stratification we have for England and France. As a result, this discussion of peasant land tenure arrangements must remain somewhat vague, lacking the quantitative specificity of the analysis of class formation in chapter 6.

69. Chapter 6 examines similar problems of supervision facing absentee landlords in England and France.

70. Woolf (1968) presents Venice as a partial exception to this shift. He argues that tax assessments continued to favor urban over rural property owners, and urban consumers still were subsidized at the expense of rural peasants and landlords, in the sixteenth and seventeenth centuries. Venice may be exceptional in this respect because of the unusual unity and continuity of its ruling aristocracy. Even as the wealthiest aristocrats turned away from trade and invested in less risky and less profitable rural estates, the ruling elite as a whole continued to subsidize the city and its trade and military ventures partly at the expense of its landowning members. Nevertheless, Venetian aristocrats invested in land as enthusiastically as their Tuscan and Lombard counterparts (Burke 1974, pp. 106–8).

71. For Tilly and like-minded scholars, the demise of city-states as important geopolitical entities begins and ends with the consolidation of feudal lords, once loosely dispersed in great but weak empires, into centralized nation-states. Even poor agrarian nation-states were better able to appropriate coercive resources than the rich but tiny city-states. When and where the stalemate among empires and aristocracies ended, and rival feudal elites were incorporated within states, cities lost their comparative advantage and were subjugated by bigger states, or if they retained their independence were locked out of commerce within the newly consolidated states and so lost their commercial privileges. As I noted at the outset of this chapter, Tilly's model begs the question of why rural aristocrats were incorporated into states ruled by monarchs

instead of into expanding city-states or urban leagues ruled by bourgeois oligarchies. The answer to that question, given in our analysis of Florence, is that devolution and reaching down created political structures that precluded expansive efforts to dominate rural regions far from each city.

Braudel, who rightly rejects Weber's view of pre-Reformation capitalists as not capable of fully rational economic action, is unable to explain why Italian merchants did not always pursue economically oriented capitalism. Our focus upon elite conflict and its structural consequences allows us in this chapter to explain the behavior of Florentine capitalists and offers a framework for analyzing the timing and dimensions of the successes and failures of capitalists in the parade of leading cities described by Braudel.

Chapter 4

1. This debate began in the pages of *Science and Society.* The original contributions to that debate and some later contributions are reprinted in Hilton 1978.

2. Chapter 7 directly addresses Weber's Protestant ethic thesis and proposes a different social psychological model that better fits the mass of historical evidence at odds with Weber's arguments.

3. Poulantzas (1975, pp, 157–67) echoes Marx and Engels's relative autonomy model. Unlike Marx and Engels, Poulantzas does not even attempt to explain how feudal class struggle might have altered the capacities of the contending aristocratic, bourgeois, and peasant classes. He merely asserts that a bourgeois class gained economic power in England, without identifying a mechanism, or even describing a process, that could account for the greater penetration of capitalist production and exchange in seventeenth-century England as compared with France in the same era. Since Poulantzas sees state structure as merely the reflection of class forces in civil society, he does not analyze what effect the actions of the "relatively autonomous" English and French state elites had upon class relations. He relies upon the outcomes of the English Civil War and the French Frondes to divine the class character of the two states and then presumes that the state form reflects the balance of classes in civil society. That sequence of inferences substitutes assumptions of affinity for the analysis of cause and effect and is untested by the empirical reality of states and classes in concrete societies.

4. Thomas Ertman's *Birth of the Leviathan* (1997) offers an important qualification to Tilly's and Mann's models. Ertman distinguishes between two aspects of states: their "political regimes" (i.e., whether the state is absolutist or constitutional) and the "character of state infrastructure" (i.e., whether state offices are patrimonial or bureaucratic). Ertman, following Otto Hintze ([1902–6] 1975), points to the strength of representative institutions as the key explanatory variable in determining absolutist or constitutional outcomes. Bicameral legislatures with geographically based constituencies were better able to defy monarchs than were tri-cameral, estate-based legislatures that monarchs had an easier time dominating through divide-and-conquer strategies.

Ertman pays special attention to the timing of state formation. Paralleling the distinction between "first-comers" and "late-comers" from modernization theory (Levy 1972), he distinguishes between the first states to become involved in geopolitical competition and those that became continental belligerents after 1450. Ertman argues that the first military competitors had to create venal and other patrimonial offices to mobilize the resources needed to fight wars. Monarchs, after 1450, had access to larger corps of jurists, trained at newly founded and expanded universities, who could staff bureaucracies and so did not need to surrender state offices to venal aristocrats. Ertman's model is more complex that Tilly's or Mann's, and it becomes more complex still when he tries to explain the anomalous cases of England, Hungary, and Poland. He reintroduces a discussion of parliaments, arguing that those three countries had especially strong legislative bodies, which in England transformed a patrimonial monarchy into a less corrupt bureaucratic state under gentry control. The Hungarian and Polish legislatures acted to safeguard aristocrats' control over patrimonial offices against reforming kings. Ertman, like Michael Mann (1980) and Perry Anderson (1974), ends up treating seventeenth-century England as almost a "black box" into which go strong kings and rebellious Parliaments and out of which come weak kings and limited bureaucratic government. I show in this chapter that we can examine England in comparison with France by tracing out chains of contingent elite and class conflicts. We do not have to settle for correlations of factors that leave the key moments of transformation unexamined and unexplained.

Similarly, Bruce Porter (1994) and Brian Downing (1992) correlate wars with changes in the characteristics of states without really specifying how military conflicts set off or altered contingent chains of conflict. Thus, Porter makes the important observation that internal (i.e., civil) wars affect states differently than do international wars. Downing points out that foreign conquests could generate wealth for militaristic states, so that wars did not necessarily require domestic mobilizations and political transformations. Both authors, despite their theoretical contributions and despite their nuanced typologies of wars and war finances, abstract the actual wars from domestic politics. Neither author acknowledges that kings might want or need to challenge domestic elites, even in the absence of war-induced fiscal crises. Even Porter, who after all discusses civil wars, examines them mainly for their effects on the fiscal and military capacities of states, not for the ways in which they transformed the structure of political alliances and conflicts.

5. Derek Sayer (1992) argues that the precocious political centralization of England, in which a powerful king shared governance with a relatively open national ruling class based in Parliament, "molded a civil society in which capitalist political economy was possible" (p. 1411). Sayer is careful to conclude, "I have not argued here that state formation was the cause of capitalism, in England or anywhere else. . . . Nor have I attended overmuch to the proximate causes of economic take-off. My concern has been with the multiple ways in which . . . English state formation . . . molded a civil society in which capitalist economy was possible" (pp. 1410–11).

The aspects of the English state highlighted by Sayer existed for centuries before the advent of agrarian capitalism. In ignoring proximate causes, Sayer is unable to specify the causal relationship between the English state and capitalism and contents himself with the broad conclusion that the state had something to do with "the novel emergence of 'the individual' . . . endowed with private rights and public representation. It is such individuals who are agents of capitalist economy" (pp. 1398–99).

Sayer's formulation leaves each link in the causal chain vague and untestable. He does not address the conflicts that gave rise to a particular state form or how that state form limited and determined political and economic rights. (That latter task is begun in Corrigan and Sayer 1985, in which the authors are more open to the contingent and contradictory effects of political conflicts and state forms than Sayer has become in this recent dogmatic pronouncement.)

6. Many historians subscribe, at least implicitly, to one of the three perspectives, although they define the actors and their interests in somewhat different terms from the theories examined here. Thus, Christopher Hill (1963), the most prominent exponent of the class analysis model for England does not discuss a general bourgeois class interest. Instead he describes how purchasers of former monastic properties came to share an interest in protecting their property rights against crown attempts to reappropriate church lands and tithes. A similar inability to identify bourgeois and aristocratic classes with opposing interests means that few English historians have accepted or elaborated Dobb's (1947) rendition of the relative autonomy model. The main thrust of English scholarship, including many of the sources used here, resembles the state-centered approach. However, the argument, initially expounded by Trevor-Roper (1965)

and Stone (1970), rejects the historical and theoretical sweep of Tilly and Mann for a focus on the particular characteristics of "Renaissance states." The historical school led by Russell (1971) and Hunt (1983) rejects all theoretical generalizations in favor of viewing the Civil War as an amalgam of particularistic localized disputes, tied by a Puritan ideology that championed parochial self-interest, though not bourgeois acquisitiveness. Russell and Hunt argue that Puritanism delegitimized royal government without creating or articulating a new group interest. As a result, the antistate coalition that won the Civil War disbanded once a new state was able to maintain order without antagonizing Puritans.

Historians are divided in their assessments of the salience of class categories for understanding seventeenth-century French politics. The view of the absolutist state as an instrument of the aristocracy is expressed more often by historians of the Revolution, notably Lefebvre (1967) and Robin (1970), than by scholars of the sixteenth or seventeenth centuries. Most Marxist studies of French absolutism adopt the relative autonomy perspective; in addition to Porchnev (1963) and Lublinskaya (1968), key studies include Mandrou (1965) and Morrill (1978). Non-Marxist French historians have also worked mainly within a state-centered approach, for example, Goubert (1969–73), Major (1980), and Mousnier (1984). However, these historians reject any sort of class analysis and deny the existence of a unified state elite. Instead, they analyze the state as an amalgam of "orders" competing for prestige and power. Several scholars have sought to bring class back into the analysis of the French state in order to explain the difficulties state officials encountered, and often failed to surmount, in their efforts to control and exploit civil society. (See Castan 1974 and Asher 1960 for outstanding examples of this tendency.)

7. Fulbrook (1983) develops this case as a contrast to England.

8. See chapter 3, n. 25 for White's (1992) definition of reaching down.

9. The crown's ordinary revenues—the income from royal lands held prior to the Reformation, customs revenues (which Parliament voted for each new king for life and which kings generally could not increase without further parliamentary approval), and wardships and other feudal dues—was all spent on the ordinary expenses of the royal household and government. Thus, war expenses were met entirely with extraordinary revenues.

10. The Pilgrimage of Grace is discussed by Fletcher (1968, pp. 21–23), Davies (1968), and Harrison (1981).

11. Savine (1909, p. 77) calculates the "net income" from monastic lands (i.e., the gross income minus costs of administering the estates at £135,000. Thus, the potential sale value may have been £2.7 million rather than £3.2 million. Estate documents and historical studies are unclear, as probably were buyers and sellers of sixteenth-century estates themselves, on whether the price should be based on the gross or net income of estates. Habakkuk (1958) shows, however, that prices rose to an average of thirty years' rent by the 1560s, which makes it likely that the higher gross value could have been obtained in honest sales.

12. Dietz's study of government finance (1964), and Braddick's compilation and analysis of primary and secondary fiscal sources (1994), show that the monies from the rental and sale of former monastic lands and from sales of monastic treasures once they arrived in the jewel house were not held in reserve to meet later expenses. Thus, royal revenues in the prewar years (1535–39) and the monastic treasures, most of which were seized before 1539, must have been spent or given away almost immediately by Henry VIII.

13. I base this claim upon the following calculations: Net income from monastic lands was £135,000 a year. The crown had seized virtually all those lands by 1539. If the crown received full net rental income for the eight years from 1539 to 1547, it would have received £1,080,000, an amount only £234,500 short of the total received from rents *and sales* of monastic lands from 1535 to 1547. We can assume that the crown could have cut its extraordinary spending by 8 percent to meet the shortfall, or borrowed that much, especially if financiers did

not have the opportunity to invest cash in monastic lands that would not have to have been put up for sale if the crown could have realized the full potential rental income from them.

14. Dietz makes a similar point. He concludes that for a war with inconsequential results, "Henry had squandered his resources. He left his son a debt, . . . a debased currency, [and] depleted estates" (1964, p. 158).

15. It would seem difficult to explain war making under a rational choice rubric. The best effort to do so is Margaret Levi's (1988). She does not argue that war making paid for nations as a whole by winning colonies and markets. Instead, she contends that war making shifted resources from subjects to kings because the idea of the nation (i.e., of national identity and patriotism) was forged by war, and as a corollary war presented the crown as the guardian of national interest, convincing subjects to pay taxes for the support of war. Levi goes further and offers the specific proposition that as the cost of war increases there is an increase in rulers' abilities to convince subjects to contribute to war costs. Levi does not make clear why expensive wars should create a stronger sense of patriotism, especially if the wars are fought abroad away from the sight of the paying subjects. Levi compares England and France and argues that the English kings' weaker bargaining power with respect to the nobles forced them to make concessions that strengthened the state's capacity to convince or force subjects to pay taxes. French kings were stronger and had to do less bargaining, but therefore they also won less voluntary support for taxes and had higher "agency" (i.e., collection) costs. (The core of Levi's argument is on pp. 95–121.)

There are two significant problems with Levi's analysis. First, she merely asserts without offering any evidence that expensive wars prompted greater eagerness to pay taxes. Second, she presents expensive wars leading to greater patriotism leading to higher tax collections leading to greater capacities to fight wars leading to more wars and even higher military expenses as a progressive and uninterrupted cyclical process of state development, at least in England and France. However, as this chapter demonstrates, wars and the resulting fiscal demands upon kings and subjects had widely differing consequences depending upon the specific configuration of elite and class relations at each historical moment. The 1539–47 war permanently weakened English kings; wars destroyed monarchies in England in 1640–49 and during the French Revolution. War undermined elite opponents of the French crown in the 1648–53 Frondes. In all those instances, kings could have been motivated to make war by domestic or foreign calculations. Wars quickly produced unintended consequences in all those instances, making it impossible for kings or scholarly observers to predict that war always was rational for self-aggrandizing rulers.

16. The implications of the clergy's loss of authority over land tenure, and of the eventual achievement by lay landlords of a monopoly of legal control over land rights, for agrarian class relations is discussed in chapter 6. Here it is sufficient to point out that any revival of clerical autonomy and authority would have meant a loss of lay power, creating an interest on the part of lay landlords in preserving royal supremacy over the Church of England against Catholic challenges.

17. Given-Wilson (1987, pp. 55–68 and passim.) provides the best description of the membership and power of the magnates in pre-Reformation England.

18. Bearman is exemplary at highlighting the unique characteristics of Norfolk and thereby explaining the extent to which his analysis of one county is applicable to other counties. Less systematic studies of other counties (Barnes 1961, Chalklin 1965, Everitt 1966, Cliffe 1969, Fletcher 1975, Forster 1973, James 1974, MacCulloch 1977, Morrill 1974) lend support to the general outlines of Bearman's model, as do synthetic studies (such as Dibble 1965; Clark 1977; Everitt 1969; Fletcher 1983), suggesting that he has identified the essence of political change in English counties from Elizabeth I to Charles I.

19. Fulbrook 1983 reaches a similar conclusion in her comparison of England with Prussia and Württemberg.

20. Tawney (1954), Hill (1963), Stone (1970), and Dobb (1947) present merchants as capitalist and opposed to absolutism. Hill (1972) comes closer to Anderson's view (1974) that merchants may have begun as creatures of the monarch but became a distinct class, with interests opposed to the crown, by the time of the English Revolution. Brenner (1993, pp. 638–44) offers a summary and critique of this position as well as references to the key works of this line of argument.

21. The revisionists, most notably Conrad Russell, John Morrill, and Anthony Fletcher (again, see Brenner 1993, pp. 644–47 for a critical summary and bibliography of this perspective), are almost postmodern in the delight they take in highlighting the confusion, complex shifting alliances, and supposed failures of localized actors to sustain national coalitions in seventeenth-century Britain. They argue that because the Revolution had many meanings, it had no meaning, and because people had various reasons to choose sides in the Civil War, that conflict is beyond our understanding.

In a related vein, Jack Goldstone (1991) describes the political conflicts of the 1640s (and indeed most revolutions) as a spasm provoked by a too-rapidly multiplying population lashing out at its rulers in an unreasoned, and ultimately inconsequential, protest against declining opportunities and increasingly narrow personal or class prospects.

22. Stone (1965, pp. 199–270) discusses the demilitarization of the English ruling class and the concurrent creation of a system of military financing dependent upon taxes voted by Parliament rather than armed men mobilized by magnates.

23. I explore the effects of those elite conflicts upon agrarian class relations in *From Manor to Market: Structural Change in England, 1536–1640* (Madison: University of Wisconsin Press, 1987), pp. 100–141.

24. See my discussion of Bearman's findings earlier in this chapter.

25. See table 2.3 for a summary of the elite structures of French provinces before the Reformation, and for the sources upon which this paragraph's conclusions are based.

26. Merchants and manufacturers had the resources to buy urban posts, but rarely could they compete with the landed aristocracy for the more expensive offices at the provincial level (Beik 1985, pp. 3–55; Dewald 1980, pp. 69–112; Harding 1978; Wood 1980, pp. 95–98).

27. See Major (1966; 1980). Major argues that the establishment of the *paulette* was decisive in weakening magnate power and creating a new dynamic of conflict between the crown and venal officials. However, evidence presented by Bonney (1981) and Parker (1983) indicates that even during the sixteenth century the crown protected venal claims on offices as a way of undermining magnates. As a result, the *paulette* accelerated but did not initiate the shift in the terrain of elite conflict.

28. Beik (1985, pp. 98–116), Bonney (1978, pp. 237–50), Kettering (1986), and Mousnier (1970, pp. 179–99) all explain how the crown created networks of clients centered on governors, intendants, or unofficial brokers with varying ties and loyalties toward the crown. Harding (1978, pp. 191–99) discusses how the crown used temporary intendants for similar purposes beginning in the 1560s.

29. This point is made by Dewald (1980, pp. 69–112); Parker (1980, pp. 56–95); Tait (1977, pp. 1–20); and Kettering (1978, pp. 13–50).

30. My analysis of French vertical absolutism in the century leading up to the Frondes in comparison with the development of English horizontal absolutism in the same century provides only limited support for the three theoretical perspectives presented earlier in this chapter. Anderson's description of absolutism as the "displacement of politico-legal coercion upwards towards a militarized summit" (1974, p. 19) is fairly accurate for France. There, a growing share of the surplus was extracted through taxes rather than rents, and even non-office-holding landlords became increasingly dependent upon royal edicts and parlementaire decisions to raise peasant rents and to bring land under their direct control (Dewald 1980, pp. 162–201). Most

manorial and magnates' feudal courts fell into disuse by the sixteenth century. Instead, lords and peasants took their disputes to provincial parlements or requested reviews by governors, intendants, or their aides. Anderson's approach is less helpful for understanding England, where the state's development was shaped by the singular opportunity to appropriate clerical property and authority. The English Reformation had the unintended effect of reinforcing landlords' abilities to appropriate the bulk of peasant payments and to regulate agrarian production themselves (albeit through Commissions of the Peace organized on the county level rather than by virtue of seigneurial authority on the manor).

The emphasis given by Marx, Engels, Dobb, Porchnev, and Lublinskaya to the bourgeoisie as purchasers of state offices and as counterweights to the nobility receives less support from my analysis of the situation. Nobles in both countries and untitled English landlords, more than urban merchants, were the principal buyers of state offices in France and of the former clerical properties in England. A more persuasive case can be made that English and French monarchs, by stimulating markets in land and in offices, helped develop bourgeois interests, rather than the reverse causality that Engels posited. Monarchs in both countries expanded the ranks of the bourgeoisie by granting monopolies in trade and manufacture (Brenner 1993; Stone 1970, pp. 85–86; Parker 1983, pp. 73–81). However, many monopolists were nobles, and others sought to marry into noble families. Merchants in both countries were as likely to ally with aristocrats to protect their comparable privileges as with the monarchs whose fiscal demands threatened to appropriate or to reassign the profits from previously granted commercial concessions.

Finally, Tilly's and Mann's emphasis on the expanding military and fiscal capacities of the states misses the crucial contrasts in the two cases. The English crown grew wealthy by receiving and spending a windfall from the Dissolution of the Monasteries. Yet it was unable to build a bureaucracy capable of collecting taxes without the cooperation of Parliament and the gentry tax collectors. English monarchs gained security by disarming the armies of rival magnates. In contrast, sixteenth-century French kings did not achieve military hegemony against domestic rivals. Although the French "state" did increase revenues dramatically in the sixteenth century, most of the funds were collected and retained by venal officials whose interests often opposed those of the crown. Similarly, Ertman's (1997) contrast of patrimonial and bureaucratic regimes and strong bicameral and weak tricameral legislatures ignores crucial aspects of the English and French polities. The clergy and the Reformation are ignored in his work (Gorski in his 1998 review of Ertman makes a similar point). As a result, Ertman is forced to assume that the English Parliament always was strong and so cannot explain why it gained the interest or capacity to challenge the crown. He also misses the sources of crown political (as opposed to fiscal and organizational) weakness *within* venal institutions in France and so is unable to predict the crown's shifting capacities internally and abroad.

The problems faced by theorists from the three perspectives in describing English and French absolutism stem from their failures to give sufficient causal weight to conflict among elites and to the divergent fates of clerics in the two countries. Elite relations created the opening for the Reformation in England and foreclosed it in France. The ability of English monarchs to build a horizontal absolutism derived from the weakness of the clergy, not from the crown's previous capacities, either absolutely or in comparison with the aristocracy.

31. Chapter 6 is devoted to a more extensive comparison of elite structures and agrarian class relations in England and France. There, I am concerned with the implications of structural differences for capitalist development; here I draw out the implications for politics and state formation.

32. Skocpol (1979) does not examine how different locations in the state generated cleavages in the dominant class. Instead, she argues (p. 59) that the crown faced a unitary dominant class, although one based "in both older institutional forms, such as seigneurial rights and proprietary offices, and the new absolutist functions, mainly those related to the state's capacity to

promote the military success and to tax the economic expansion of the country (insofar as the tax revenues came from the nonprivileged)."

33. Kettering 1986, pp. 28–32, describes instances of patron shopping.

34. See table 5.4 and the accompanying discussion in the next chapter for the evidence supporting these comparisons.

35. I discuss the interaction of royal fiscal demands and peasant economics in chapter 6.

36. At the time of the first lease in 1726, more than one-third of the CGF were common- ers and less than one-half were nobles. By the last lease before the Revolution in 1786 only one-tenth were commoners and two-thirds were noble. This shift was due primarily to poorer commoners dropping from the CGF (see Durand 1971, pp. 282–362).

37. See Hoffman 1996; Fourquin 1976; Jacquart 1974; Peret 1976; Dontenwill 1973; Bastier 1975. I discuss this issue more fully in chapter 6.

38. For a useful summary of the debate between Marxist and revisionist historians of the French Revolution, see McLennan 1981, pp. 175–205.

39. This section addresses the elite conflicts that gave rise to the Revolution and exam- ines the ways in which the French state was transformed through the revolutionary years. I ex- amine the dynamics of peasant uprisings, and the consequences of elite and class conflicts upon agrarian class relations, in chapter 6.

40. On the consolidation of state finances see Dessert 1984 and Matthews 1958. Matthews and Bosher (1970) discuss the rise in state revenues, income from offices, and the fiscal crisis of the 1770s and after.

41. There is a long and ongoing debate over the class character of the "Third Estate" in the National Assembly and throughout France. While bourgeois could buy offices that gave them aristocratic status, and both aristocratic and bourgeois landlords pursued similar strate- gies of leasing unencumbered lands to commercial farmers while trying to extract greater feu- dal dues from peasants in a "seigneurial reaction," there were clear divisions between elites, even if members of those elites were ambiguously feudal and capitalist at the same time. Fi- nanciers, who derived revenues from their sole access to the great amounts of capital needed by the crown and their control over the administration of state debt and tax collection, were a different elite, inhabiting a different organizational apparatus than did the provincial office- holding elites. The aristocratic reaction of 1787–89 was an attack by the latter elite on the for- mer; the legislation of the Third Estate in the National Assembly was a response that favored the former elite at the expense of the latter. The National Assembly's legislation on feudal dues and landownership favored those who primarily held land as property over those who retained ancient dues rights by virtue of their old aristocratic titles—again the former elite over the lat- ter. Soboul is clear on those fundamental distinctions of interest, although he anachronistically expresses them in class rather than elite terms. The most useful recent discussions of these is- sues are contained in Comninel 1987 (pp. 179–207) and Wallerstein 1989 (3:57–112), which provides a penetrating review of debates on this issue.

42. This is the key insight offered by Comninel (1987, pp. 203–5).

43. The events and political alliances of those years are analyzed in Soboul 1974, pp. 255–449.

Chapter 5

1. Of course, England, France and Spain (and Sweden and Russia too) benefited from "in- ternal colonialism." At this point, I am concerned with colonialism outside of Europe.

2. These questions parallel and follow up on the central questions of chapter 3. In that chapter I ask why did the great cities of medieval and Renaissance Europe not become the cen- ters of subsequent capitalist development and political amalgamation and why were city-state

elites overwhelmed in the sixteenth and subsequent centuries by rival rural elites that were able to consolidate vast rural territories and to dominate the cities in their midst?

The questions posed in this chapter substitute empire for city-states. Imperial decline was primarily economic, while that of the city-states was politically derived. The city-state elites, as I point out in chapter 3, retained a high degree of economic autonomy and indeed centrality in the European economy in the centuries after they were subordinated politically to nation-states. Spain's subordination was economic rather than political. Most elements of the Habsburg empire gained independence or autonomy without directly affecting the polity of the Spanish metropole. Only the Netherlands (for a brief time) gained economic hegemony over its former master.

My questions also are similar to the problem posed by Immanuel Wallerstein in *The Modern World System* (vol. 1, 1974). Wallerstein asks, "How did Spain come to play such a central role" in the developing transatlantic trade of the sixteenth century, and why couldn't Spain parlay that role into imperial domination of the emerging European world system?" (1974, p. 165 and passim).

3. S. N. Eisenstadt's *The Political Systems of Empires* (1963) is the beginning, and often the end, of most sociologists' readings on empires. Eisenstadt's approach differs from that taken in this chapter in several ways. First, Eisenstadt is concerned with differentiating empires (including the Spanish empire) as an ideal type from other types of political systems. Thus, Eisenstadt minimizes variations among empires and fails to offer a blueprint, or even an extended example, for how sociologists might go about constructing explanations for the particular developments of each empire. This chapter's discussion of Spain is devoted to the task of identifying the particular complex of elite and class relations that made the Spanish empire and that explain the demise of that imperium. I use Spain and the Netherlands to draw conclusions about the limits of capitalist class formation in the metropoles of empires in early modern Europe. I do not generalize those conclusions to empires in all eras as does Eisenstadt.

Second, Eisenstadt believes that the rulers of empires have a high degree of freedom in crafting an imperial social order that solves the "problems of allocation, regulation, and integration" that arise with "the differentiation and . . . various free-floating resources created" (p. 95) by the formation of empires. This chapter, by contrast, identifies the severe limits of elite agency within the Spanish empire.

Third, Eisenstadt devotes only a few pages (1963, pp. 333–40) to an analysis of "total change" (i.e., the destruction of empires). He sees imperial decline as a combination of "inherent structural reasons [and] accidental reasons" (p. 338). What Eisenstadt means by structure in this context is quite different from the way I use that term. For Eisenstadt, structure is the relatively unchanging social relations and cultural orientations of the subject populations of the empire. The ruler and his inner circle exist seemingly above and beyond Eisenstadt's structure. Eisenstadt contends that rulers can remain in power as long as their demands for resources and obedience respect the structural realities of the subject populations. If the ruler makes demands that are "continuously incompatible" with social structure, actions that reveal that the ruling elites "became alienated from the existing social institutions" (p. 336), then the rulers' "traditional legitimation" is weakened (p. 337). Eisenstadt does not explain why rulers would make sudden changes in the means and ends of their rule, except insofar as rulers come under "foreign," or "universalistic" (i.e., modern) influences (p. 335). Thus, the dynamic for change in *The Political Systems of Empires* is external to all empires. Here I find an internal dynamic—conflict among multiple elites within the empire—to explain the decline of the Spanish and Dutch empires.

4. Here I offer a similar plea to that made in chapter 3 concerning my brief comparisons of Venice and Genoa with Florence. I hope historian critics will distinguish between those of my omissions and errors concerning the histories of Spain and the Netherlands that are merely

annoying and those that require revision of the broader conclusions of this chapter and the book as a whole.

5. See Table 5.4 for the specific data on government revenues.

6. Castile, unlike some of the French provinces analyzed in chapter 2, never was dominated by a single magnate. Grandees were hegemonic in some parts of Castile. Taken as a whole, the Castilian polity is closest to the pattern of "feudal system without magnate" characteristic of medieval Normandy and some of the central French provinces, except during the Civil War when Castile fit the pattern of magnate struggle.

7. The discussion of Castile in this and the following two paragraphs is based on Bush 1967, pp. 44–62; Lynch 1991, pp. 1–94; Payne 1973, pp. 31–169 and passim; and Phillips 1979.

8. The Aragonese Cortes is the outstanding example of aristocratic assertion. It was the most powerful legislative counterweight to a monarchy in Europe until the English Parliament made its own broad claims in 1640.

Perry Anderson is more apt in his description of Spain as a collection of "autarchic patrimonies" (1974, p. 71 and pp. 60–14 passim) melded into an empire through the strategic marriages and inheritances of Ferdinand and Isabella and their successors than is Wallerstein in his emphasis on the absence of political feudalism in Castile.

9. Galicia was the exception to this pattern. There, the church retained its property. The church held 52% of Galician land in the eighteenth century compared with 18% in the rest of Spain (Dupla 1985, p. 95). The strong Galician clergy was an effective counterweight to the great lords. As a result, the crown was able to mobilize an alliance of clergy, urban bourgeois, and peasants, unique in Iberia, to disarm and politically weaken the great lords. The crown realized little benefit from that alliance. Indeed, in the eighteenth century, the crown held a smaller share of the land in Galicia than in any other region of Spain (10% in Galicia compared with 30.6% in the rest of Spain [p. 95]).

The hidalgos and clergy were the main beneficiaries of the demise of the great lords in Galicia. The clergy, of course, held an outsized share of land. Eventually, however, the hidalgos received a growing share of the agrarian surplus because they held *foros* (the right to farm land in return for rents that can never be increased) and *subforos* (a part of a farm held as a *foro*, which is subleased for rents that can be increased by the holder of the *foro*) on a majority of clerical lands, entitling them to manage or rent out those lands in return for fixed payments, rendered increasingly nominal by inflation, to the clerical "owners" of the land (Dupla 1985, pp. 44–126).

The pattern in Galicia is revealing of the balance of elite and class power in Spain. The crown, by allying with the church instead of the great nobles during the fifteenth-century incorporation of Galicia into the monarchy, was able to shape elite relations in Galicia and so determine the unusual Galician agrarian class structure. However, the crown never was able to disrupt the resulting clerical-hidalgo alliance and therefore was unable to weaken Galician autonomy or to extract anything but nominal taxes from that province. From the point of view of the crown, Galicia had to be as lightly ruled and therefore was as unprofitable as all the other non-Castilian provinces of Spain that were dominated by great nobles.

10. Thompson 1976, p. 288, comes up with a somewhat higher share from taxes but concurs that the Church contributed more than the Americas to the royal budget by 1621.

11. The crown was able to subordinate the clergy because they were part of a transnational elite headed by the papacy. The Cortes would not have offered the clergy protection from the papal-crown alliance mainly because the aristocracy ultimately was the greatest political beneficiary of the clergy's decline.

12. The fate of the Castilian Cortes is discussed by Thompson (1982; 1984).

13. The discussion of Spanish colonialism in the Americas in this and the next four paragraphs is based on Davis 1973; Lynch 1992, pp. 229–347; and TePaske and Klein 1981.

14. The crown's receipts in pesos are given by Flynn (1982, p. 142). Flynn's figures for total exports of American treasure have been revised upward for the post-1580 period by Lynch (1992, p. 283) to take into account the rise of unofficial shipments of bullion beginning in 1581. The figure for 1656–60 is from Lynch (1992, pp. 270, 283).

The silver pesos used to count American treasure were worth 272 maravedis, yielding a conversion of .725 into ducats worth 375 maravedis. Figures for total royal income are taken from table 5.5. Based on those figures I get American treasure receipts as 6% of royal revenues for 1621–40, compared with Kamen's (1991, p. 218) 10.7% cited earlier in this section. Kamen gets a higher percentage because he is dividing into Castilian revenues only, not total royal receipts.

15. International trade and foreign markets became spurs to domestic development only when and where capital and labor were free to be redeployed in industries geared toward international demand. Labor and capital became free as byproducts of agrarian transformations of the sort only England underwent before the eighteenth century. Spain, thus, is the counterexample to Eric Hobsbawm's argument in his "The Crisis of the Seventeenth Century" (1965). Hobsbawm correctly notes that sixteenth-century manufacture was limited until the seventeenth-century crisis consolidated control over world markets first in Dutch and then in British hands, creating the critical mass of demand needed for industrial production. Spain with its empire and its American colonies had a level of demand to support some industries in the sixteenth century. Yet, without the structures of capital and production of the Netherlands and Britain, Spain was unable to take advantage of its colonies' demand. Instead, the centers of industry in the Habsburg empire were in Italy and the Low Countries. The political weakness of the Spanish empire is reflected in imperial Castile's continuing economic subordination to its political dependencies. The Spanish experience demonstrates that Hobsbawm's market concentration, while one of the necessary preconditions for industrialization, was not in itself sufficient.

16. The *almojarifazgo* taxed the value of exports leaving Spain for the Americas at 15%, and goods shipped from America to Spain at 17.5%. Some goods were taxed at a higher rate. Transatlantic shippers also had to pay the *averia*, a tax on goods in official fleets that was supposed to pay for the crown's costs in providing military protection to merchant fleets. The tax in fact was used to meet general naval costs as well as the direct costs of Atlantic military escorts. That tax was placed at 6% of value in 1602–30, then rose to 31% in 1631 as both the Dutch military threat and the Spanish crown's fiscal crisis intensified (Lynch 1992, pp. 234–41). The two taxes together came to also 50% of the value of goods, an enormous incentive to avoid Spanish ports and official fleets.

17. The totals include revenues from Iberia and the Americas. Revenues from the Holy Roman Empire, including the northern (Dutch) and southern Netherlands, which were actually remitted to the monarch, are counted in the totals up to the end of the seventeenth century. Eighteenth-century revenues do not include those territories. Spain was able to get little from those lands once they challenged Habsburg control during the War of Spanish Succession. Any revenues from those territories were permanently lost when the Spanish monarch renounced his claims on the southern Netherlands, Italy, and Germany in favor of the Austrian Habsburgs in the 1713 treaties that settled the war. Table 5.1 controls for devaluations, but only partly for inflation, by converting the silver content of Spanish ducats into British pounds.

18. The Soviet Union in its final decade may be the next instance of such absolute imperial fiscal decline.

19. These percentages are calculated from the data in table 5.4.

20. The discussion of the course of the Spanish-Dutch conflict in this and the next two paragraphs is based on Israel (1995). For a general discussion of Spain's wars and military burdens see Lynch (1991, 1992, and 1989); Payne (1973); Thompson (1976); and Kamen (1969 and 1991).

21. Arrighi's work is a major extension of world systems theory. He sees Wallerstein as carrying out Marx's direction to "take leave for a time of [the] noisy sphere [of circulation], where every thing takes place on the surface and in view of all men, and follow [the possessor of money and the possessor of labor-power] into the hidden abode of production. . . . [Here] . . . we shall at last force the secret of profit making" (*Capital,* vol. 1, quoted in Arrighi 1994, p. 25).

Arrighi, inspired by Fernand Braudel, takes on a different, though complementary task. "Follow the possessor of money into another hidden abode, . . . which is one floor above, rather than one floor below the marketplace. Here, the possessor of money meets the possessor, not of labor-power, but of political power. And here, promised Braudel, we shall force the secret of making those large and regular profits that has enabled capitalism to prosper and expand 'endlessly' over the last five to six hundred years, before and after its ventures into the hidden abodes of production" (Arrighi 1994, p. 25).

22. Dutch merchants who were blocked from the most lucrative concessions in the Republic and its empire because of their weak political positions were forced to invest in emerging industries abroad. This parallels the movement of Florentine capital, blocked from Medici-controlled offices, bonds, and titles, into proto-industries abroad.

23. The Netherlands territories controlled first by the Burgundian bishops and then the Habsburgs comprised both the southern Netherlands, which today are Belgium and Luxembourg, and the northern Netherlands, which became the Dutch Republic (officially the United Provinces) of the sixteenth through eighteenth centuries and the present-day Netherlands. (For a discussion of terminology see Israel 1995, p. v.)

24. The absence of feudalism in the northern Netherlands made the commercialization of Dutch agriculture a less momentous development than it became in England. The rapid rise in Dutch land rents in the sixteenth and the first half of the seventeenth century did not transfer wealth from a dispossessed peasantry to a newly powerful gentry as happened in England. Instead, peasants along with urban investors and aristocrats were the joint beneficiaries of the rising income from and increasing value of farmland. Dutch farms could not provide enough food to supply the growing urban population of Holland in the Golden Age. Cheap grain was imported from the Baltics, while Dutch farmers concentrated on dairy products, vegetables, and industrial crops. Rents and farm incomes rose with the growing demand by Dutch townspeople (whose wages outstripped those of all other European workers) for better foods. (This discussion of Dutch agriculture is based upon De Vries 1974; van Houtte 1977; and van der Wee 1993, pp. 47–68.)

Winners in the process of land consolidation varied across the United Provinces. In Holland, most farmland not held by peasants came under the ownership of noble and bourgeois landowners based in the cities. The concentration of land "in the hands of distant lords engendered a purely business-like relationship between the rural population and the seigneur," who viewed land as just another investment (De Vries 1974, p. 39). During the Golden Age, the richest peasants (along with urban merchants) were able to accumulate larger farms, buying land from financially pressed aristocrats and marginal peasants. Urban capitalists also were the main investors in, and therefore the principal owners of, new lands created by large-scale and expensive drainage projects (pp. 192–202). Property transfers consolidated land holdings throughout the Netherlands, although the shares held by bourgeois, nobles, and peasants varied among Dutch provinces. Peasant holdings were closer to a normal distribution in Friesland than in Holland and Utrecht in the sixteenth century (pp. 49–73). Peasant polarization increased in the late sixteenth and seventeenth centuries in all Dutch provinces (De Vries 1974; Israel 1995, pp. 332–37).

Urban investors in land and peasants were the joint beneficiaries of the high prices paid by urban consumers of Dutch agricultural products. Profits were invested in agricultural improvements. Those heavy expenditures on drainage and other improvement projects turned out to be poor long-term investments since commodity prices and land rents and values slumped from the 1680s on. However, they provided a permanent basis for high value-added agriculture and rural prosperity that lasted through the weak Dutch urban economy of the eighteenth century.

Dutch agriculture transferred wealth primarily from urban consumers to all landowners in the sixteenth and the first half of the seventeenth centuries. The overassessment of land relative to urban wealth for the Verponding tax on the rental value of all property transferred wealth from landowners to bondholders thereafter. Great landowners accumulated wealth in commerce and industry and parked some of their money in land. Land did not define an elite in the Netherlands as it did in England. Class polarization and the consolidation of wealth in the agrarian sector were overshadowed, as they were largely determined, by the greater concentration of wealth and power in the urban commercial sector of the northern Netherlands. However, the relative wealth of the Dutch following their fall from the pinnacle of the European economy at the end of the seventeenth century is explained in large part by the investment in "Dutch husbandry" during the Golden Age.

25. Urban Groningen had its "own sovereign administration. From of old, the city had much power over the countryside owning the market staple rights, . . . and its attempts to maintain or extend its power frequently clashed with the rural representatives" (T'Hart 1993, pp. 75–76). Because the city had its own autonomous administration, the Groningen urban elite was invulnerable to efforts by the rural aristocracy to foster factionalism or mobilize guildsmen.

26. The ruling elite of Amsterdam came to dominate the government of Holland, and to a varying extent that of the United Provinces as well, in the fifteenth through eighteenth centuries. Thus, I refer, in the rest of this section, to that overlapping and hegemonic ruling group as the Amsterdam-Holland oligarchy.

27. Conflicts between Remonstrants (less orthodox Protestants) and Counter-Remonstrants (rigid Calvinists) erupted in the first decades of the seventeenth century (Israel 1995, pp. 421–505). By that time, however, the membership of each town's and province's ruling oligarchy had been fixed. Contenders for national power and popular forces both were animated by the religious conflicts of the early seventeenth century. But popular forces were unable to topple town governments, and the national divisions reinforced each town and provincial elite's determination to preserve its own power in autonomous governments that were less vulnerable to national political forces, undercutting the formation of a cohesive national elite and of a powerful national state.

28. Amsterdam and Rotterdam each had a navy, and Hoorn and Enkhuizen, the main towns of the "Northern Quarter" of Holland, had a third. These three Holland admiralties never were united. In addition, Zeeland and Friesland each had their own admiralty (T'Hart 1993, pp. 39–43).

29. This discussion of the control of Dutch military forces is based on T'Hart 1993, Israel 1995, and Geyl 1958.

30. The organization and receipts of the Dutch fiscal system are presented in T'Hart 1993 and Israel 1995.

31. Amsterdam and its allies reduced the size of their armed forces to prevent the resumption of full-scale war against France after the Twelve Years' Truce ended in 1621 (T'Hart 1993, pp. 46–47). Amsterdam by this decision insured the permanent division of northern and southern Netherlands and guaranteed Holland and Amsterdam a high degree of autonomy from the stadtholder, whose national government was permanently stunted. Amsterdam later blocked the stadtholder's plans to recapture the southern Netherlands from France after France's withdrawal from Dutch territory in 1674.

Amsterdam led the Republic into war against Britain in 1652–54 to gain access for Holland merchants in Spanish and other markets Britain wished to monopolize; again in the 1655–60

Anglo-Spanish War to win control over Spanish trade and American colonies for Amsterdam and for WIC; and in the Second Anglo-Dutch War of 1665–67 for access to Africa and to protect VOC and WIC colonies. Amsterdam provoked the 1672–74 war with Britain and France through commercial aggression and secret alliances (negotiated by Amsterdam diplomats often without informing the other provinces or Republic officials). That Third Anglo-Dutch War was ended on terms favorable to Amsterdam in part at the expense of other towns and provinces that wished to fight on for their own interests. (These wars and the Dutch political coalitions that favored or opposed them are analyzed in Israel 1995.)

32. Holland paid interest on its debt from 1542 to the end of the Republic with only a single, brief suspension in 1581 (Israel 1995).

33. Of course efforts to override the contracts of correspondence would have precipitated a revolutionary confrontation between the stadtholder and the regents just as similar royal efforts to attack elite privileges en masse led to the Frondes and the 1789 Revolution in France, to the 1640 and Glorious Revolutions in England, and to the various coups and countercoups, the civil wars, and the Ciompi in Florence.

The outcomes of such revolutionary confrontations reveal the relative power of each elite and class in the particular structural setting of those times and places. So it was when Stadtholder William IV took advantage of popular pro-Orangist uprisings in 1747–51 to purge officials, especially tax farmers. William V continued this process, creating a court nobility like those of other European monarchies. The stadtholders and Orangists, despite their successes in the other Dutch provinces, made no headway in dislodging the regent elites of Holland. There the regent oligarchy retained full power even through the French invasion of 1794–95 (Israel 1995, pp. 1079–1121).

34. Unfortunately, available data do not allow a direct comparison of Dutch with British and French revenues. The data for the Netherlands are of military expenditures, which in every European country of that era almost always were greater than state revenues. The Netherlands maintained naval parity with the British and protected itself from French, Spanish, or German conquest by running up its combined Republic and provincial debt, as noted above, from under 10 million guilders in 1620 to over 150 million by 1650 (Adams 1994b, p. 340). All the other European powers also took on debt to pay for their war expenditures. Yet, such an extension in debt, and the military machine for which it paid, clearly was more easily sustained by the Dutch polity and economy of that century than by its rivals. Interest on Dutch debt fell from 8 to 4 percent over the first half of the seventeenth century (T'Hart 1993, p. 163), well below the rate paid by the British, not to mention the often bankrupt French or Spanish monarchs.

35. Julia Adams (1994a) highlights the important addition of familial constraints. She shows that business holdings and political offices were managed to further the prestige, wealth, and power of familial dynasties rather than just of the family patriarch who controlled those assets in his generation. Adams shows how familial considerations, and the contracts of correspondence that protected the collective interests of the lineages of the regent elite, first mobilized Dutch resources for foreign conquest and commercial domination and then immobilized assets as mobility from below was blocked even as regents became rentiers, investing their efforts and wealth in preserving familial standing locally at the expense of Dutch maneuverability in international commerce and European power politics.

Adams notes parallels to the Medician system in Florence and finds strong similarities for England and France (and much of Europe) as well. It would take another book to determine the extent to which familial considerations opened or narrowed the strategic possibilities that I am able to explain here in terms of the dynamics of elite and class conflicts and the structural relations created by those two dynamics. In sum, I agree with Adams that familial dynamics are more than a structural overdetermination of elite and class forces, but I am not able to specify when and where the dynamics of family and patriarchy must be studied to explain social outcomes.

Chapter 6

1. Hirst 1975 is the best source on this political interaction. Hughes 1987 offers a good summary of recent work on Stuart politics. See also Russell 1979, pp. 17–22 and passim.

2. My summary of the process and history of enclosures is based upon Allen 1992, pp. 25–36; Tate 1967; Wordie 1983; and Yelling 1977.

3. Parliamentary restrictions on clerical courts first were passed during Edward VI's minority when magnates and lesser lay lords backed Warwick's coup against Somerset. Lay lords installed Warwick as lord protector with the express purpose of gaining crown approval for legislation strengthening their control of land against peasants. The laws restricting clerical courts were part of that package (Cornwall 1977; Land 1977).

While Edward's minority, like any monarch's minority, was a time of unusual crown weakness, the events of 1549 had enduring consequences because lay landlords' unity on questions of peasant tenure and the crown's inability to undermine or overcome that unity continued through all the Tudor and Stuart monarchies and beyond.

4. The minority of peasants with fixed-term or "at-will" were concentrated on former monastic manors. Monasteries had been more reluctant than lay lord to compete for tenants after the Black Death by offering tenancies without labor dues (which, as I show in chapter 2, became copyhold tenancies). Thus, much land on monastic estates remained vacant until population recovery created a demand for farms with high rents or labor dues. Monastic manors then were able to lease lands for fixed terms and at will. The tenants on those manors suffered the further disadvantage of lacking a strong manor court around which they could organize resistance to seigneurial demands. Manors courts had not met, and thus had weakened or fallen into disuse, where monastic manor lords had refused to lease vacant tenements as copyholds. The terms of fixed or at-will tenancies were set directly between monastic manor lords and peasants, circumventing and undermining the manor court.

When such monastic manors were bought by laymen after the Dissolution of the Monasteries, the new lords could easily raise rents or expel tenants since the leaseholders lacked the strong legal protections of robust manors courts that blocked other landlords from summarily evicting tenants or unilaterally changing the terms of leases (Kerridge 1969). The former monastic manors were the main sites of quick and drastic evictions and enclosures following the Reformation. Spufford (1974, pp. 58–93), Howell (1983, pp. 58–77, 147–97), and Finch (1956, pp. 38–76) provide examples of this process.

5. Another strategy was available to landlords who either lacked the political strength to win petitions of ascertainment or whose copyholders had strong enough legal claims to survive ascertainment. Landlords in those cases tried to win support from freeholders for a boycott of the manor court.

Freeholders had reason to boycott manor courts in the sixteenth and subsequent centuries. Recall that freeholders allied with villeins in manor courts after the Black Death to force landlords to eliminate labor dues and to reduce cash dues. Villeins gained the ability to move from their old positions into more advantageous copyhold tenancies. Freeholders won the opportunity to expand their farms by leasing lands without incurring additional labor obligations to the lord.

Freeholders faced a different calculus in the sixteenth and subsequent centuries. Common law enhanced freeholders' security of land tenure. Under manor custom, landlords were able to increase freehold dues to a limited extent, but under common law freehold rents became fixed at existing rates, which were made increasingly nominal by inflation. Further, common law gave freeholders unlimited rights to sell their lands or to leave lands to heirs without paying a fine. Finally, since population density was increasing in the sixteenth century, in contrast to the century after the Black Death, the only way freeholders could lease new lands was if landlords expelled copyhold tenants.

Freeholders therefore had reasons to join landlords in a boycott of the manor court. Once landlords had made concessions to freeholders, won those tenants' support, and divided the peasant community, the landlords were able to appeal to the county commission of the peace for the common law right not to renew copyhold leases. The end result (except for the greater concessions to freeholders) was the same as ascertainment, with the copyholders losing their land rights and the landlord gaining full control of the former tenements (Kerridge 1969, pp. 33–35, 65–93).

6. A minority of copyholders also held small parcels of freehold land that they retained even after ascertainment. However, the loss of copyhold usually reduced those peasant families' holdings to below subsistence. Eventually, those families either sold their freehold lands or used them as a core of a commercial farm. Of course, if the landlord wanted to covert his holdings into pasture, or to create a large commercial farm, then the former copyholders and small free-holders were unable to rent enough land to become commercially viable and were bankrupted or forced to sell out in short order.

Spufford (1974, pp. 58–93) offers a clear example of how ascertainment affected peasant landholdings.

7. Landlords eager to amass the votes needed to force through an enclosure thus had a reason to evict even those copyholders willing and able to pay market prices for their tenements.

8. See chapter 2. Table 2.3 presents a summary of the relationship between elite structure and class relations across French provinces.

9. The fraction of land on which in-kind and labor dues had been commuted to cash varied widely in France, ranging across provinces from 33 to 90 percent by 1789. There were even wider variations, from no commutations to all cash rents, among villages within a single province (Jones 1988, pp. 48–49). French historians, in both synthetic overviews and in local studies, agree, however, that the vast majority of French tenants paid cash dues by the sixteenth century, while labor and in-kind dues provided a negligible share of seigneurial income after 1600 (Jacquart 1974; Le Roy Ladurie [1977] 1987; Neveux 1975; 1980; Venard 1957).

10. Unfortunately, we do not have wholesale or retail price indices for ancien régime France. Baulant's price series for grain in Paris is the only series that is consistently measured for three centuries. It is an accurate measure of the single most important item of consumption for most French families in those centuries and thus is the best signpost to contrast changes in rents, wages, and government revenues.

11. Hoffman (1994, pp. 238–39) finds that crown revenues increased from 9,000,000 livres in 1515 to an annual average of 421,520,000 livres in the 1780s. Controlling for inflation and devaluations, as in chapter 5, yields a real increase of 964 percent. If we control grain prices to account for devaluations, we get an inflation rate for grain of 468 percent. Under these adjustments, crown revenues still increased at more than double the rate of grain prices.

12. In the Île-de-France, the province in which landlords received the highest incomes per acre (and part of the region with the richest land and greatest peasant output in France), the share of peasants' production that went to royal taxes doubled from 6 percent in 1600–20 to 12 percent by 1789, while seigneurial levies declined from 32 to 20 percent of peasants' agrarian output (Dupaquier and Jacquart 1973, pp. 172–77).

13. Seigneurial dues refer to the bundle of payments in-kind and in cash and other obligations that peasants and other cultivators owed to the overlord of the territory on which their farms were located. Seigneurial dues could be sold or otherwise alienated and peasants could end up paying different types of dues to a variety of individuals and institutions.

Seigneurial dues were "passive income rights." Marx and Marxists traditionally refer to them as "feudal rents." Both terms express the notion that while seigneurs or their agents needed to be active in collecting the dues they were owed, seigneurs were able to collect their dues without having to play any role in planning or carrying out agricultural production. In other words, seigneurs received dues because of their political power over land and peasants, rather than because of any economic activity.

Dues can be differentiated legally and conceptually from rents. Rents were the profits gained from leasing the right to cultivate land. Rents were active income in the sense that the holders of cultivation rights needed to farm the land themselves or make sharecropping or lease arrangements to ensure that the land was farmed. The level of rents ultimately depended upon the leasor's ability to improve the land and its yields or to make it possible for the leasee or sharecropper to do so.

14. The discussion of landlord estate strategies in this and the next two paragraphs is based on Dontenwill 1973; Fitch 1978, pp 181–87; Le Roy Ladurie [1977] 1987; Neveux 1975; Varine 1979; Venard 1957; and Wood 1980, pp. 141–55.

15. Bourgeois land buyers probably also were seeking, like Renaissance Florentine patricians and new men (Emigh 1997, p. 436), to diversify their investments to reduce risk. Early modern Europeans did not publish investment newsletters; however, we can see from their practices that they, like present-day investors, were willing to accept reduced returns on some of their investments in return for reduced risk.

16. Dontenwill (1973, p. 160) calculates that grain prices doubled while cash rents for farmland quadrupled from 1630 to 1665.

17. See Markoff (1996, pp. 16–64) for an analysis of seigneurial obligations and their perceptions by peasants, bourgeois, and nobles on the eve of the Revolution.

18. Hoffman (1996, pp. 35–69) specifies the conditions under which sharecropping and renting were the most profitable and least risky strategies. He notes that absentee landlords, who became the norm in the seventeenth century, found it especially difficult to find managers who could be trusted to supervise commercial farms. Emigh (1997) finds similar reasons for the shift to sharecropping in fifteenth-century Tuscany.

19. Peasant self-exploitation leads to the inefficient application of extra labor to land, which encourages larger family size and causes the excessive subdivision of land, a process Geertz (1963) labels "agricultural involution." Twentieth-century Americans' willingness to give up corporate jobs for the dream of owning their own business, despite the high rate of failure and low returns from most small businesses, is another form of self-exploitation, one that corporate downsizers take advantage of, just as French landowners profited from peasant self-exploitation three hundred years ago.

Hoffman (1996, pp. 51–52) argues that peasants wanted to farm some land themselves if only as a hedge against times when wages declined and food prices rose. Such a hedging strategy justified, in Hoffman's view, rents that would be uneconomical on a commercial basis.

20. Le Roy Ladurie [1977] 1987, p. 66; Neveux 1975, pp. 134–38; and Canon 1977 discuss crown interventions in landlord-peasant disputes. For a case study of crown intervention in agrarian class struggle see Loirette 1975.

21. Charlesworth (1983) has compiled a comprehensive atlas of rural protests from 1548 on. For the Pilgrimage of Grace and the other protests that occurred before 1548, I make use of Davies 1968 and Fletcher 1968, pp. 21–47. These sources, along with specific analyses of individual rebellions in particular counties (which I cite in the test) are the bases for the discussion in this section.

22. Davies (1968) offers the best analysis of the Pilgrimage of Grace. He carefully shows why economic hardships cannot explain the location or timing of these uprisings and documents the role of clerics and lords in encouraging peasant actions against the crown.

23. I confine my discussion to England. As in the rest of this chapter, I ignore developments in Wales, Scotland, and Ireland.

24. The sources for the discussion in the remainder of this section are given in the sources for table 6.1.

25. I define tight county elites and explain their emergence in chapter 4.

26. See Charlesworth 1983, pp. 8–16, 29–31; Wordie 1983; and Yelling 1977.

27. Lincolnshire and Derbyshire had some enclosure, and the parishes that had been enclosed in those counties were the centers of revolt. Worchestershire had experienced almost no enclosure; the revolt there was a reaction to ascertainments and evictions. (Charlesworth 1983, pp. 16–21, 31–36, summarizes the causes of the peasant uprisings. Wordie 1983, p. 493, provides the data on rates of enclosure.)

28. Somers (1993) is the newest and most sophisticated proponent of the argument that arable and pastoral regions generated different polities. She contrasts the open field arable regions, where the gentry achieved political hegemony and used their power to control peasant land and labor, with the pastoral counties of irregular fields where weak landlords had to share power with peasants organized through unified villages. Somers is concerned with explaining the development of a political culture that fostered both political and social welfare notions of citizenship. She finds that such a culture did not develop as well in the open field regions where the gentry controlled politics and shaped the economy on the county level as it did in the irregular field pastoral regions where notions of the village community, which were forged in struggles with landlords, were transformed into citizenship claims in the eighteenth and nineteenth centuries. Peasants and landless laborers in the arable regions looked to politics and the law with fear and resignation. In the pastoral regions, in which rural industries were concentrated, peasants and the growing number of industrial workers defended old village rights and presented new working-class demands in the context of their collective participation in village and other political institutions.

Somers, in contrast to Goldstone and other scholars of his ilk, is able to identify mechanisms that can account for the timing and the scope of different actors' capacities to realize their interests. She does so by tracing the historical development of political institutions and cultures, rather than merely assuming an automatic relationship between demographic cycles and agrarian systems of production as mediated by soil types. Somers's work, though concerned with the emergence of class politics and democratic institutions, and focused on the eighteenth through twentieth centuries, is compatible with the model I advance here. Somers and I both approach politics and economics in institutional terms, explaining relations of power and forms of production as outcomes of historically contingent chains of events rather than as mere maximizations of individual or group interests at discrete moments of time.

29. France is too vast, and its peasants were too rebellious, to allow construction of a single source like Charlesworth's (1983) historical geography of English protests over several centuries. The discussion in this section is based on the only three comprehensive and systematic quantitative analyses of ancien régime and revolutionary protests. Lemarchand has constructed a data set of violent protests from 1661 to 1789. He presents the results of that study in a single (1990) article. (I am grateful to Markoff 1996 for making me aware of that article.)

Lemarchand offers only a few, though crucial, quantitative results. Lemarchand, despite his published brevity, offers an important systematic corrective to Charles Tilly's vast yet impressionistic writings on French contention. Tilly's thesis, which informs most sociological discussions of early modern France, that the state replaced landlords as the principal object of peasant protests in the centuries from the Reformation to the Revolution, is directly contradicted by Lemarchand. Tilly's thesis also is undermined by the other two quantitative studies: Vovelle 1993 and Markoff 1996. Vovelle offers a geography of various forms of revolutionary actions, which he correlates with measures of development, population density, family size, literacy, and agrarian class relations. Markoff has constructed a comprehensive data set of protests during the Revolution that he correlates with his analysis of the Cahiers de Doleances of all three estates as well as social measures of markets, state power, and seigneurial reaction.

Vovelle and Markoff both concur with Lemarchand, and contradict Tilly, in finding that antiseigneurial and subsistence protests against landlords, grain merchants, and their agents, not tax protests against state officials, remained the most common forms and targets of protests during the revolutionary years, just as Lemarchand shows they became in the decades before 1789.

30. Tilly (1986) points to a lessening of violence and deaths in ancien régime contention. Collins (1988, pp. 194–213) finds tax protests of the post-Fronde era involved mainly withholding of taxes, not attacks on officials. Royal troops responded by seizing crops and livestock rather than killing protesters. Beik (1985) finds a diminution of violence by provincial elites, crown, peasants, and urban residents after the Frondes. Bernard (1964) traces major post-Fronde rebellions and finds a decline in scope and violence after 1675.

31. Vovelle's data (1993, pp. 297–344) point to a similar conclusion. He finds strong correlations between density of post offices, population density, and urbanization (all three of which he considers proxies for markets) with revolutionary action. Vovelle concludes that markets, whether in capitalist or seigneurial reactionary guises, provoked revolutionary action.

32. Markoff finds that antitax protests were concentrated in the west. "The Revolution rather drastically shifted the tax burden away from some places onto others; the regions losing out, [which had been the most privileged provinces under the ancien régime], one is hardly surprised to learn, became the center of the western counterrevolution" (1996, p. 350).

33. Scott (1976; 1985) of course denies that the protests he chronicles are ineffective. However, he devotes almost all of his efforts to documenting the cultural bases of protests without specifying the effects of such protests on social relations.

34. Markoff's conclusion here is at odds with Brenner's class analysis and with regional ecological models that present ideal-type peasant communities as regional realities.

35. This is the main conclusion and the great insight of Markoff's wonderful book.

36. White (1962, pp. 39–78) presents a chronology of the invention of new agricultural techniques in Europe. Allen (1992, pp. 107–49) and Hoffman (1996, pp. 165–66, 202) both caution that the vast majority of the increases in yields were due to the early, relatively low capital innovations, while the more expensive capital improvements, such as drainage and irrigation improvements and enclosures, yielded at most a fifth of the total increases in yields.

37. Allen (1992, pp. 131–33) notes that farmers in Norfolk, some French and Flemish producers, and the entire Nile basin already realized twenty bushels per acre in the thirteenth century (and for the Nile "probably also in antiquity)" (p. 133). Those exceptions are explained by extraordinarily lush land farmed intensively with unusually high levels of labor. Indeed, the Norfolk, French, and Flemish yields declined after the Black Death with the switch to less intensive farming by depleted labor forces.

38. Yields for the other crops doubled as well. "Barley and bean yields were similar to wheat yields; oats produced 15 bushels per acre" (Allen 1992, p. 131), and "corn yields approximately doubled" as well (p. 208).

39. See Hoffman 1996 for France, Allen 1992 for England, and De Vries 1974 for the Netherlands on the diffusion and adoption of new agricultural techniques.

40. I review the demographic determinist models and their critics, most notably Robert Brenner, in chapter 2.

41. Readers may be surprised that this chapter has not given more emphasis to regional differences within the two countries. A number of scholars continue to emphasize differences between arable and pastoral regions in England. Thirsk (1967; 1984) and Goldstone (1988) are the ones most often cited by sociologists. Baker and Butlin (1973) and Allen (1992), who distinguishes "three natural districts"—heavy arable, light arable, and pasture—offer nuanced analyses in contrast to the simpler and less accurate dualism presented by Thirsk and Goldstone.

Thirsk and Goldstone argue that feudal land tenure arrangements and the later development of capitalism or lack thereof were products of efforts to maximize output and profits from varying types of soils in the context of demographic cycles. I summarize and critique Jack Goldstone's analysis of regional ecology (1988) in chapter 2. It is important to note at this point that Goldstone is selective in the transformations he recognizes, and therefore he is unable to explain why the gentry and large commercial farmers got rich, while so many peasants were dispossessed and impoverished in the sixteenth and subsequent centuries, even though the new agricultural techniques raised productivity on farms large and small (Allen 1992, pp. 191–231).

42. Certainly, some soils were better than others. However, all of Europe has been able to boost yields far beyond medieval levels. In 1997, British and French cereals yields, at 101.9 and 101.1 bushels per acre, respectively, have equalized at ten times the medieval level. British and French equality in yields in itself refutes Goldstone's contention (1988) that only part of France had the natural endowments that allowed all of England to advance. Other countries in Europe, which never invested as much in agricultural improvements as Britain and France, still have been able to boost yields far beyond medieval levels: in Italy to 69.6 bushels per acre, and in Spain and Poland to 42.0 and 43.4 bushels per acre, respectively (1997 yields are calculated from the "Cereals, Rice Milled Equivalent, Metric Tons Produced" divided by "Hectares Planted" from the Food and Agriculture Organization Statistical Databases [http://www.fao.org]).

All European soils, thus, were capable of producing far above the standard medieval level of 10 bushels per acre. The question remains, Why did northwestern Europeans use available early modern technologies to move ahead, while other Europeans did not?

43. Wallerstein (1983) makes this point on a theoretical level. For analyses and case studies of the organization and productivity of labor in the agrarian sector see, for England: Howell 1975, 1983; Kussmal 1981; Spufford 1974; Thirsk 1957; Wrightson and Levine 1979; and Yelling 1977. Neveux 1975 provides an overview for France, while Bois [1976] 1984; Dontenwill 1973; Gruter 1977; Leon 1966 (see especially the chapters by Sabatier and Guichard); Peret 1976; and Venard 1957, pp. 63–68 and passim, offer an array of case studies that reveal the constraints on agricultural investment, innovation, and improvement in France.

De Vries (1974) still offers the best summary of Dutch agriculture. He finds that investment in improvements were made by family farmers who owned their farms or had secure leases and who worked the land with their own labor and with limited wage labor.

Italy and Spain offer negative examples. Recall that there was little investment in and improvement of farms in Renaissance Italy, with Lombardy as the exceptional case because in that city-state commercial farmers were able to win de facto permanent leases on clerical lands at fixed rents. Such permanent tenure justified investments in irrigation and new crops (mainly silk). In Spain the persistence of feudal land control and labor dues also prevented much investment in improvements (Davis 1973, pp. 143–56; Dupla 1985, pp. 44–126; Kamen 1980, pp. 226–59; Lynch 1992, pp. 1–16; Vilar 1962).

44. Arthur Young's mistaken belief (see *A Six Month's Tour Through the North of England* [London, 1771]) is shared by most historians and sociologists, Marxist and non-Marxist alike, who have written on the origins of English agrarian capitalism. That is why Allen (1992) is such an important book, and why I need to present his findings in some detail.

45. Demographic determinists also can predict the timing and magnitude of the decline in wages, since the sharpest decline was during a period of rapid population increase, and the slow recovery began when population growth slowed dramatically. The demographic model cannot explain why the lower labor cost of producing food did not benefit either consumers or the commercial leasors who invested capital in land improvements and who employed wage labor. Only models that trace the location and uses of power can explain why all the benefit went to the landowners who had the political leverage to control land, rents, and tariffs, and to regulate laborers' mobility and residence.

46. Thirsk (1967; 1984) and Goldstone (1988) also share the Tory view, albeit with the caveat that employment increased only in arable areas, while in pastoral regions former agricultural laborers became tradesmen.

47. This parallels the problem with the demographic determinist models noted above: that continentwide demographic cycles cannot be invoked to explain changes in agriculture that occurred in one part of the continent and not others. Robert Brenner makes that point most ably, although his countermodel is inadequate for the reasons I discuss specifically in chapter 2 and more generally throughout this book.

48. The absolutist monarchy's politico-military policies combined with merchants' organizations and the pull of the Paris market to reorder French transportation networks. Proximity to Paris or to merchant networks trumped access to waterways. The boundaries of Fox's "other France" (1971) shifted as state and merchant activities pulled some regions into the French core, while leaving other regions that once had used waterways to build commercial networks centered on provincial towns as isolated backwaters.

Hechter and Brustein (1980) draw a more sophisticated map of three regional modes of production. They argue however, that each region's social structure was set in the twelfth century. They contend that states formed in the feudal regions because the nobilities in those regions were able to extract larger surpluses than could the landlords in sedentary pastoral and petty commodity regions. Hechter and Brustein's theory is essentialist; it analyzes state formation (or capitalist development) as effects created by a fixed complex of causes. Their model falls short because it fails to take account of the ways in which the agricultural regimes of each region were altered over the centuries by elite and class conflicts. Capitalist development and state formation are processes, not outcomes. They cannot be predicted from starting sets of causes observed centuries earlier. That is why the most developed French regions in the eighteenth century were not all the regions with the most ample natural endowments or the most advanced social structures in the medieval era.

49. On this point, Hoffman's findings for France echo those of Allen for England.

50. The discussion of landlord strategies in this and the next ten paragraphs is based on Hoffman 1996; Le Roy Ladurie 1975; [1977] 1987; Venard 1957; Jacquart 1974; Neveux 1975; Dontenwill 1973; Gruter 1977; Meyer 1966; Mireaux 1958; Peret 1976; Saint-Jacob 1960; Vovelle and Roche 1965; Wood 1980.

51. Le Roy Ladurie [1977] 1987; Neveux 1975; Morineau 1977; Dontenwill 1973; and Peret 1976 give varying figures for rent increases, which reflect the particular locales they studied. They all agree however, that rents increased to take account of inflation at each lease renewal, while productivity increases were not always reflected in new leases. Hoffman (1996) is more confident that landlords were able to track productivity improvements, which he argues were reflected in the rising market rate for land rentals on short-term leases of one or two years in their locales. No matter how alert landlords were to productivity improvements, they surrendered such gains for the length of a tenant's lease. The tenants who were most likely to achieve improvements were the big tenants who could demand long leases and so postpone having to share their productivity gains with landlords.

52. English clerics engaged in the same self-dealing at the expense of their institutions. Such corruption was eliminated when clerical lands seized in the Reformation were sold to lay owners. The absence of such expropriations and sales in France allowed clerical corruption to continue until the Revolution.

53. This pattern is similar to that of the English peasant rebellions examined earlier in this chapter. Where the gentry remained disorganized in the seventeenth century, which was in part due to the absenteeism or elimination of magnates, landlords were limited in their abilities to raise rents or to challenge peasants' traditional land rights. Similarly, in France, wealthy peasant and commercial farmers (the equivalent of freeholders and secure copyholders) were

able to assert *droit de marche* (the right of occupancy at traditional rents) or to practice *mauvais gré* (collective actions against rent-raising landlords or new tenants seeking to bid for farms) where they confronted disorganized and absentee landlords. Rents stagnated at traditional levels in those regions of France and England where strong peasants and weak landlords faced off.

54. "The most careful examination of the issue . . . suggests that it would more likely take 10 hectares (or nearly 25 acres) to support a family, feed livestock, and pay all the necessary taxes, even on the fertile soil of the Paris Basin" (Hoffman 1996, p. 36). Hoffman (1996, p. 40) and Jacquart (1974, pp. 165–66) both conclude that three-fourths of families depended on wage labor for the majority of their incomes. Neveux (1980), Dupaquier and Jacquart (1973), Sabatier (1966), and Guichard (1966) find that from two-thirds to over 90 percent of families in the regions they study became dependent on wage labor by the eighteenth century.

55. Althusser and Balibar ([1968] 1970, p. 106) make this point on an abstract theoretical level. "It is only in the specific unity of the complex structure of the whole that we can think the concept of these so-called backwardnesses, forwardnesses, survivals and unevennesses of development which co-exist in the structure of the real historical present." I read them to mean that any particular development of capitalism or of the state or of any other social phenomenon can be understood only if it is examined as the product of ongoing social struggles that define and remake whole social structures in a never-ending process of historical change.

56. The adoption of Industrial Revolution machines, fertilizers, pesticides, and seeds created a second great increase in agricultural yields while drastically reducing the need for labor inputs in the late nineteenth and the twentieth centuries. That second agricultural revolution is beyond the scope of this book.

57. Immanuel Wallerstein's study of the world system (1974–89) builds upon Hobsbawm's basic insight and is especially concerned with understanding the dynamic of the third source of demand and its impact upon the development of capitalism in its core as well as within the entire world system.

58. Allen (1992, pp. 211–62) traces the absolute decline in agricultural employment in the seventeenth and eighteenth centuries, even as total output increased. Allen demonstrates that landowners received the entire benefit of improved productivity. Food prices did not decline and wages did not rise. Allen argues (pp. 263–80) that agrarian profits were wasted because landowners spent them on luxuries and invested in agricultural improvements, especially the conversion to pasturage, which did not yield returns justifying such heavy expenditures. Carruthers (1996) shows, however, that landowners' profits also were invested in state debts and in shares of joint-stock companies that indirectly lowered the costs of capital for entrepreneurs who built productive industries, as well as supporting military campaigns, to win foreign markets for those industries.

59. Allen (1992, pp. 303–311) projects that if the gentry had not appropriated the yeomen's land rights, then agricultural wages would have risen by 67 to 100 percent in the eighteenth century. However, if wages had risen this much, or if yeomen had had more land under their control, then farmers and laborers would have been able to consume most of the fruits of the agricultural revolution. Howell (1975; 1983) shows that yeomen with private property in land restricted their fertility so that the land could be passed undivided onto a single heir, while cash accumulations would pass to a second heir (as dowry or investment in a trade or profession for a second son). In parts of England where peasants had more access to land, albeit on a less secure basis, fertility rates were higher, as was true in France and elsewhere in Europe. In Britain, higher fertility was confined to the landless, whose growing numbers kept them at close to subsistence wages. The gentry's defeat of the yeomen and control over the landless aided the "primitive accumulation" necessary for later industrial capitalism.

Chapter 7

1. Weber never offers an explanation for why particular social groups chose to remain Catholic or to join one or another Protestant church, although in *Ancient Judaism, The Religion of China,* and *The Religion of India,* Weber does formulate structural explanations for group differences in religious loyalties.

2. My argument parts most fundamentally from the modernization perspective in that I doubt, and believe I have demonstrated, that the opportunity for agency in the direction of modernization or any other direction of change is rarely afforded. Levy, Eisenstadt, Parsons, and their intellectual followers operate on the principal that where there is a will there is a way, and they see a will to modernize and therefore modernization in most of the world.

3. I offer a critique of Collins's argument in chapter 3.

4. Rosemary Hopcroft (1997) presents a different causality. She argues that "rationalist religions typically received popular support in regions characterized by individual property rights in land and little communal control over agriculture" (p. 158). Experiences of being responsible for one's own fate in agriculture, Hopcroft argues, predisposed and prepared farmers for the asceticism and rationality of Protestantism. Hopcroft's work has the merit of placing religious change in the context of broader changes in agrarian social relations. Unfortunately, Hopcroft does not address variations within Protestantism and Catholicism, nor does she explain how people used their new religious worldviews to understand their social interests and to decide upon plans of action.

5. Other studies that link magic with popular radicalism and find a class interest in the repression of sorcery include Delumeau [1971] 1977, pp. 161–74; Joutard 1976, pp. 59–90; Julia 1974; and Mandrou 1968.

6. Nachman Ben-Yehuda (1980) follows Ginzburg and Muchembled in seeing witch trials as proxies for deep social conflicts but differs from them in describing the trials as manifestations of "social anxiety" rather than class conflict. Ben-Yehuda argues that the main persecutors of witches were Catholic inquisitors who were reacting to the weakening of church authority and saw the campaign against witches as a way to advance their specific institutional interests rather than a general class interest. The inquisitors were supported by a populace that was anxious over the breakdown of a communal medieval order. Peasants angered at violations of traditional customs turned on single women, whose sexual freedom and employment as wage laborers made them symbols of the challenge to a family-based village order and easy targets for denunciation as witches. Similarly, Alan Macfarlane (1970) sees witches as violators of traditional standards of charity, hospitality, and social dignity within peasant communities rather than as representatives of popular class interests. Both Ben-Yehuda and Macfarlane can be read as a critique of modernization theory, since both hypothesize that modernity provokes an anxiety that is expressed in renewed belief in magic and a willingness to fight witches through traditional social mechanisms rather than disdaining such nonrational beliefs as would be predicted by theories of rationalization.

7. The Huguenot's strategy of institutionalizing Protestantism through the defense of local privilege is the inverse of what Wuthnow's model, which sees monarchs as the necessary protectors of Protestants from Catholic landlords, would predict.

8. Eastern European execution rates were comparable to those of France, while Geneva's was similar to England's. Of course, these data do not reflect those people who were accused of witchcraft but never formally tried. From the limited documentation available it appears that such pre-indictment dismissals were more common in England than on the Continent and quite rare in German-speaking areas, suggesting that the real execution rate is even lower than 15 percent for England, and perhaps even higher than the formal data indicate for German-speaking Europe. France, again, falls somewhere in the middle of these two extremes.

9. Gentry achieved "tight" political hegemony within a county when: (1) there was a jump in the portion of manors controlled by gentry rather than by king, clergy, and magnates; (2) the dominant magnate or magnates no longer were capable of using armed force or patronage to intimidate lesser landholders and bring them within a magnate-led political machine; and (3) total membership of the county commission of the peace increased and shifted to a majority with local, as opposed to national or mixed, orientations.

Control over manors in most counties had shifted to the gentry by the second half of the sixteenth century (Stone 1984, pp. 181–210). Essex and Kent stand out in terms of the second and third criteria. Those two counties, along with Norfolk and Suffolk, were among the first in which Elizabeth I successfully eliminated magnate power. In Norfolk and Suffolk, however, the gentry did not form a cohesive bloc until the early 1600s, while in Essex and Kent locally based gentry, with little connection to the royal court, came to dominate the county commissions of the peace in the 1560s and 1570s. (For Essex, see Hunt 1983; Chalkin 1965; Clark 1977; for Kent, Everitt 1969; for Norfolk and Suffolk, MacCulloch 1977 offers the best analysis on the sixteenth-century disarray and seventeenth-century cohesion of gentry in those two counties. See Fletcher 1983 for a survey of gentry political organization across English counties. For an earlier discussion of gentry tightness see Lachmann 1987, pp. 84–100, 128–34).

10. The sources for the summaries, in this and the subsequent three paragraphs, of lay elite attitudes toward reforms in the Catholic Church, and of clerical efforts to transform lay religious beliefs and practices are: Julia 1973; Delumeau [1971] 1977, pp. 65–83, 256–92; Hoffman 1984, pp. 71–97 and passim; Dhotel 1967; Perouas 1964, pp. 222–86; Ferte 1962, pp. 201–369; Schaer 1966, pp. 134–80; Croix 1981, pp. 1155–1246.

11. The translation is my own.

12. The difficulties with seeing capitalism as a general European phenomenon that predated the Reformation in significant aspects are addressed in chapter 2.

Chapter 8

1. Ronald Burt makes a similar point in *Structural Holes* (1992) when he argues that social actors are defined by their structural positions in networks rather than by their attributes. "The problem is that the connection between attributes and social changes across populations and over time. How frequently the connection changes and how much it changes is an empirical question. The point is that the connection isn't causal. It is a correlation . . . idiosyncratic to when and where observations are recorded for analysis" (p. 189).

Burt goes on to advocate, "The escape from attributes requires conceptual and research tools to look past the player attributes associated with significant structural forms to see the forms themselves. The result is stronger, more cumulative theory and research. The structural hole argument [which Burt develops in his book] is illustrative" (p. 193). I would argue that the elite conflict theory presented in this book is another way of escaping from the inappropriate focus on attributes.

2. Charles Kurzman (1996) argues that participants in social movements often perceive possibilities for revolutionary change that in fact were not there based on a Tocquevillean analysis of structural opportunities. He gives the Iranian Revolution of 1979 as an example and contends that in such cases the revolutionaries achieve success because so many people act on their perceptions. I found, in the revolutionary situations examined in this book, that nonelites did not need to determine the strength of "the state" as long as they could ally with elites. The structure examined here for early modern Europe, and which Kurzman and others would do well to examine in Iran and other contemporary cases, is the totality of elite relations, not merely the state.

3. Twentieth-century revolutions (the Russian, Chinese, Nicaraguan, anticolonial, and 1980s Eastern European) differ from those in previous centuries in that they were initiated with

the express goal of overthrowing and replacing states. Yet they too were fought by alliances of elites and nonelites and their outcomes were shaped by the dual effects of elite and class struggles.

4. This is the weakness of the world system model developed by Wallerstein and his followers. They do not recognize that core social structures can generate and sustain barriers to external influences upon domestic elite and class relations that are independent of, and that can survive, shifts in the dynamic of the world system itself. Wallerstein does recognize that peripheral countries lack such structural insulation from external dynamics. Whether the same is true of semiperipheral countries, and whether core countries have become less insulated in the twentieth century, or will become less insulated in the next century, are open questions that neither this book nor the oeuvre of existing world systems scholarship have yet resolved.

5. Skocpol (1979) sees foreign wars as generally destabilizing of old regimes. For Tilly (1978, 1990, 1993), wars have the long-term effect of strengthening states against civil society, while leading to the demise of nations and regimes unable to keep up in the continually escalating scale of human, financial, and technological resources needed to compete in European (and later worldwide) military confrontations.

6. Capitalism is celebrated in pseudo-academic publications and in the popular media through simplistic proclamations of "the end of history" and assertions that all nations, organizations, and individuals must subject themselves to the dictates of world markets that ultimately will produce the greatest material bounty for the greatest number.

7. The Spanish effort to subdue the Protestant Netherlands, even though the costs far exceeded any foreseeable material gains, stands as the clearest instance of ideology trumping rational calculation of any of the historical cases we have examined.

8. This truth is reflected in Arthur Stinchcombe's contention (1965) that sociologists should limit themselves to explaining revolutionary situations rather than revolutionary outcomes since many variables determine who wins power in the end. For that reason, outcomes are highly contingent, and so unpredictable, while revolutionary situations are more common and flow from identifiable causes.

References

Aalbers, J. 1977. "Holland's Financial Problems (1713–1733) and the Wars against Louis XIV." Pp. 79–93 in *Britain and the Netherlands,* vol 6, edited by A. C. Duke and C. A. Tamse. The Hague: Martinus Nijhoff.

Abel, Wilhelm. 1980. *Agricultural Fluctuations in Europe from the Thirteenth to the Twentieth Centuries.* New York: Methuen.

Abulafia, David. 1981. "Southern Italy and the Florentine Economy." *Economic History Review* 34, no. 3:377–88.

Abu-Lughod, Janet L. 1989. *Before European Hegemony: The World System, A.D. 1250–1350.* New York: Oxford.

Adams, Julia. 1994a. "The Familial State: Elite Family Practices and State-Making in the Early Modern Netherlands. *Theory and Society* 23:505–39.

Adams, Julia. 1994b. "Trading States, Trading Places: The Role of Patrimonialism in Early Modern Dutch Development." *Comparative Studies in Society and History* 36:319–55.

Adams, Julia. 1996. "Principals and Agents, Colonialists and Company Men: The Decay of Colonial Control in the Dutch East Indies." *American Sociological Review* 61:12–28.

Allen, Robert C. 1992. *Enclosure and the Yeoman: The Agricultural Development of the South Midlands, 1450–1850.* Oxford: Clarendon.

Althusser, Louis, and Etienne Balibar. [1968] 1970. *Reading Capital.* London: New Left Books.

Anderson, Perry. 1974. *Lineages of the Absolutist State.* London: Verso.

Appleby, Andrew. 1975. "Agrarian Capitalism or Seigneurial Reaction? The Northwest of England, 1500–1700." *American Historical Review* 20.3:574–94.

Arrighi, Giovanni. 1994. *The Long Twentieth Century: Money, Power, and the Origins of Our Times.* London: Verso.

Asher, Eugene. 1960. *The Resistance of the Maritime Classes: The Survival of Feudalism in the France of Colbert.* Berkeley and Los Angeles: University of California Press.

Aston, Trevor, ed. 1965. *Crisis in Europe, 1560–1660.* London: Routledge and Kegan Paul.

Aymard, Maurice. 1982. "From Feudalism to Capitalism in Italy: The Case That Doesn't Fit." *Review* 6.2:131–208.

Babeau, Albert. 1894. *La Province sous l'ancien régime.* 2 vols. Paris: Fermin Didot.

Baechler, Jean. 1988. "The Origins of Modernity: Caste and Feudality (India, Europe, and Japan)." Pp. 39–65 in *Europe and the Rise of Capitalism,* edited by Jean Beachler et al. Oxford: Blackwell.

Bairoch, Paul. 1988. *Cities and Economic Development.* Chicago: University of Chicago Press.

Baker, Alan, and Robin Butlin. 1973. *Studies of Field Systems in the British Isles.* Cambridge: Cambridge University Press.

Barnes, Thomas. 1961. *Somerset.* Cambridge: Harvard University Press.

Bastier, Jean. 1975. *La Féodalité au siècle des lumières dans la région de Toulouse (1730–1790).* Paris: Bibliothèque Nationale.

Baulant, Micheline. 1968. "Le Prix des grains à Paris de 1431 à 1788. *Annales E.S.C.* 23.3: 520–40.

Baxter, Douglas Clark. 1976. *Servants of the Sword: French Intendants of the Army, 1630–70.* Urbana: University of Illinois Press.

Bean, J. M. W. 1991. "Landlords." Pp. 526–86 in *The Agrarian History of England and Wales.* Vol. 3, *1348–1500,* edited by Edward Miller. Cambridge: Cambridge University Press.

Bearman, Peter. 1993. *Relations into Rhetorics: Local Elite Social Structure in Norfolk, England, 1540–1640.* New Brunswick: Rutgers University Press.

Beaulieu, Eugene-Pierre. 1903. *Les Gabelles sous Louis XIV.* Paris: Berger-Laurault.

Becker, Marvin B. 1959. "Some Economic Implications of the Conflict between Church and State in 'Trecento' Florence." *Medieval Studies* 21:1–16.

Becker, Marvin B. 1966. "Economic Change and the Emerging Florentine Territorial State." *Studies in the Renaissance* 13:7–39.

Becker, Marvin B. 1967. *Florence in Transition.* Vol. 1. Baltimore: Johns Hopkins University Press.

Becker, Marvin B. 1968a. *Florence in Transition.* Vol. 2. Baltimore: Johns Hopkins University Press.

Becker, Marvin B. 1968b. "The Florentine Territorial State and Civic Humanism in the Early Renaissance." Pp. 109–39 in Rubenstein 1968.

Behrens, Betty. 1963. "Nobles, Privileges, and Taxes in France at the End of the Ancien Regime." *Economic History Review,* 2d ser., 15:451–75.

Beier, A. L. 1969. "Studies in Poverty and Poor Relief in Warwickshire, 1540–1680." Ph.D. diss., Princeton University.

Beier, A. L. 1985. *Masterless Men: The Vagrancy Problem in England, 1560–1640.* London: Methuen.

Beik, William. 1985. *Absolutism and Society in Seventeenth-Century France: State Power and Provincial Aristocracy in Languedoc.* Cambridge: Cambridge University press.

Belfanti, Carlo Mareo. 1993. "Rural Manufactures and Rural Proto-Industries in the 'Italy of the Cities' from the Sixteenth through the Eighteenth Century." *Continuity and Change* 18.2:253–80.

Ben-Yehuda, Nachman. 1980. "The European Witch Craze of the 14th to 17th Centuries: A Sociological Perspective." *American Journal of Sociology* 86:1–31.

Berce, Yves-Marie. 1974. *Croquants et nu-pieds: Les Soulèvements paysans en France, du XVIe au XIXe siècle.* Paris: Gallimard.

Bergier, Jean-François. 1979. "From the Fifteenth Century in Italy to the Sixteenth Century in Germany: A New Banking Concept?" Pp. 105–29 in *The Dawn of Modern Banking,* edited by Center for Medieval and Renaissance Studies, UCLA. New Haven: Yale University Press.

Bergin, J. A. 1982. "The Decline and Fall of the House of Guise as an Ecclesiastical Dynasty." *The Historical Journal* 25:781–803.

Bergin, J. A. 1992. "Richelieu and His Bishops? Ministerial Power and Episcopal Patronage under Louis XIII." Pp. 175–202 in *Richelieu and His Age,* edited by Bergin and Laurence Bockliss. Oxford: Clarendon.

Berktay, Halil. 1987. "The Feudalism Debate: The Turkish End: Is 'Tax-vs.-Rent' Necessarily the Production and Sign of a Modal Difference?" *Journal of Peasant Studies* 14.3:291–333.

Bernard, Leon. 1964. "French Society and Popular Uprisings under Louis XIV." *French Historical Studies* 3:454–74.

Berner, Samuel. 1971. "Florentine Society in the Late Sixteenth and Early Seventeenth Centuries." *Studies in the Renaissance* 18:203–46.

Biddick, Kathleen. 1987. "Missing Links: Taxable Wealth, Markets, and Stratification among Medieval Peasants." *Journal of Interdisciplinary History* 18.2:277–98.

Blanchard, I. S. W. 1971. *The Duchy of Lancaster's Estates in Derbyshire, 1485–1540.* Derby: Derbyshire Archaeological Society.

Blet, Pierre. 1959. *Le Clergé de France et la monarchie.* 2 vols. Rome: Université Gregorienne.

Blet, Pierre. 1972. *Les Assemblées du clergé et Louis XIV de 1670 à 1693.* Rome: Université Gregorienne.

Bloch, Marc. 1973. *The Royal Touch: Sacred Monarchy and Scrofula in England and France.* London: Routledge and Kegan Paul.

Blockmans, W. P. 1978. "A Typology of Representative Institutions in Late Medieval Europe." *Journal of Medieval History* 4:189–215.

Bois, Guy. [1976] 1984. *The Crisis of Feudalism: Economy and Society in Eastern Normandy c. 1300–1550.* Cambridge: Cambridge University Press.

Bonney, Richard. 1978. *Political Change under Richelieu and Mazarin, 1624–1661.* Oxford: Oxford University Press.

Bonney, Richard. 1981. *The King's Debts: Finance and Politics in France, 1589–1661.* Oxford: Oxford University Press.

Bordeaux, Michèle. 1969. *Aspects économiques de la vie de l'église aux XIVe et XVe siècles.* Paris: Librarie Generale de Droit et de Jurisprudence.

Bordes, Maurice. 1960. "Les Intendants de Louis XV." *Revue Historique* 223:45–62.

Bordes, Maurice. 1972. *L'Administration provinciale et municipale en France au 18ème siècle.* Paris: Société d'Édition d'Enseignment Supérieur.

Bosher, J. F. 1970. *French Finances, 1770–1795: From Business to Bureaucracy.* Cambridge: Cambridge University Press.

Bossy, John. 1970. "The Counter-Reformation and the People of Catholic Europe." *Past and Present* 47:51–70.

Bossy, John. 1975. *The English Catholic Community, 1570–1850.* London: Darnton, Longman and Todd.

Bourdieu, Pierre. [1972] 1977. *Outline of a Theory of Practice.* New York: Cambridge University Press.

Braddick, M. J. 1994. *Parliamentary Taxation in Seventeenth-Century England: Local Administration and Response.* Woodbridge: Royal Historical Society.

Braudel, Fernand. [1966] 1972. *The Mediterranean and the Mediterranean World in the Age of Philip II.* 2 vols. New York: Harper & Row.

Braudel, Fernand. 1977. *Afterthoughts on Material Civilization and Capitalism.* Baltimore: Johns Hopkins University Press.

Braudel, Fernand. [1979] 1982. *Civilization and Capitalism, 15th–18th Century.* Vol. 2, *The Wheels of Commerce.* London: Collins.

Braudel, Fernand. [1979] 1984. *Civilization and Capitalism, 15th–18th Century.* Vol. 3, *The Perspective of the World.* New York: Harper & Row.

Braudel, Fernand, and Frank Spooner. 1967. "Prices in Europe from 1450 to 1750." Pp. 378–459 in *The Cambridge Economic History of Europe.* Vol. 4, *The Economy of Expanding Europe in the Sixteenth and Seventeenth Centuries,* edited by E. E. Rich and C. H. Wilson. Cambridge: Cambridge University Press.

Brenner, Robert. 1976. "Agrarian Class Structure and Economic Development in Pre-Industrial Europe." *Past and Present* 70:30–75.

Brenner, Robert. 1982. "The Agrarian Roots of European Capitalism." *Past and Present* 97: 16–113.

Brenner, Robert. 1993. *Merchants and Revolution: Commercial Change, Political Conflict, and London's Overseas Traders, 1550–1653*. Princeton: Princeton University Press.

Brown, Judith. 1982. *In the Shadow of Florence: Provincial Society in Renaissance Pescia*. New York: Oxford University Press.

Brucker, Gene. 1962. *Florentine Politics and Society, 1343–1378*. Princeton: Princeton University Press.

Brucker, Gene. 1969. *Renaissance Florence*. New York: John Wiley.

Brucker, Gene. 1977. *The Civic World of Early Renaissance Florence*. Princeton: Princeton University Press.

Buisseret, David. 1968. *Sully and the Growth of Centralized Government in France, 1598–1610*. London: Eyre and Spottiswoode.

Bullard, Melissa Meriam. 1980. *Filippo Strozzi and the Medici*. Cambridge: Cambridge University Press.

Burke, Peter. 1972. *Culture and Society in Renaissance Italy, 1420–1540*. New York: Scribner's.

Burke, Peter. 1974. *Venice and Amsterdam: A Study of Seventeenth-Century Elites*. London: Temple Smith.

Burke, Peter. 1986. *The Historical Anthropology of Early Modern Italy: Essays on Perception and Communication*. New York: Cambridge University Press.

Burt, Ronald S. 1992. *Structural Holes: The Social Structure of Competition*. Cambridge: Harvard University Press.

Bush, M. L. 1967. *Renaissance, Reformation, and the Outer World*. London: Blandford.

Bush, M. L. 1983. *Noble Privilege*. New York: Holmes and Meier.

Butters, H. C. 1985. *Governors and Government in Early Sixteenth-Century Florence, 1502–1519*. Oxford: Clarendon.

Byres. T. J., and Harbans Mukhia. 1985. "Feudalism and Non-European Societies." Special issue of *The Journal of Peasant Studies* 12, no. 2–3.

Canon, Marie-Thérèse. 1977. *La Société en France à la fin du moyen âge*. Paris: Presses Universitaires de France.

Carrière, Victor. 1936. *Les Epreuves de l'église de France au XVIIe siècle*. Paris: Letouzey.

Carruthers, Bruce. 1996. *City of Capital: Politics and Markets in the English Financial Revolution*. Princeton: Princeton University Press.

Castan, Yves. 1974. *Honnêteté et relations sociale en Languedoc, 1715–1780*. Paris: Plon.

Castan, Yves. 1979. *Magie et sorcellerie a l'époque moderne*. Paris: Albin Michel.

Chalkin, C. W. 1965. *Seventeenth-Century Kent*. London: Longman.

Chandler, Tertius. 1987. *Four Thousand Years of Urban Growth*. Lewiston, N.Y.: Edwin Mellen.

Charlesworth, Andrew. 1983. *An Atlas of Rural Protest in Britain, 1548–1900*. Philadelphia: University of Pennsylvania Press.

Chaussinand-Nogaret, Guy. 1970. *Les Financiers de Languedoc au 18e siècle*. Paris: SEVPEN.

Chibnall, A. C. 1965. *Sherington*. Cambridge: Cambridge University Press.

Chirot, Daniel. 1985. "The Rise of the West." *American Sociological Review* 50:181–95.

Cipolla, Carlo M. 1947. "Une Crise ignorée: Comment s'est perdue la propriété ecclésiastique dans l'italie du nord entre le XIe et le XVIe siècle." *Annales E.S.C.* 2:317–27.

Cipolla, Carlo M. 1952. "The Economic Decline of Italy: The Case of a Fully Matured Economy." *Economic History Review* 2:178–87.

Cipolla, Carlo M. 1965. *Guns and Sails in the Early Phase of European Expansion, 1400–1700*. London: Collins.

Cipolla, Carlo M. 1974. "L'échec italien." Pp. 7–9 in *Transition du féodalisme à la société industrielle: L'Échec de l'Italie de la Renaissance et des Pays-Bas du XVIIe siècle*, edited by Paul M. Hochenberg and Frederick Krantz. Montreal: Centre Interuniversitaire d'Etudes Européennes.

Cipolla, Carlo M. 1982. *The Monetary Policy of Fourteenth-Century Florence*. Berkeley and Los Angeles: University of California Press.

Clark, Peter. 1977. *English Provincial Life*. Sussex: Harvester.

Cliffe, John Trevor. 1969. *The Yorkshire Gentry from the Reformation to the Civil War*. London: Athlone.

Cloulas, Ivan. 1958. "Les Aliénations de temporel ecclésiastique sous Charles IX et Henry III (1563–1587)." *Revue d'histore de l'église de France* 44:5–56.

Cochrane, Eric. 1965. "The End of the Renaissance in Florence." *Bibliotheque d'Humanisme et Renaissance* 27:7–29.

Cohen, Jere. 1980. "Rational Capitalism in Renaissance Italy." *American Journal of Sociology* 85:1340–54.

Cohn, Samuel Kline. 1980. *The Laboring Classes in Renaissance Florence*. New York: Academic Press.

Collins, James B. 1988. *Fiscal Limits of Absolutism*. Berkeley and Los Angeles: University of California Press.

Collins, Randall. 1980. "Weber's Last Theory of Capitalism: A Systemization." *American Sociological Review* 45:925–42.

Collins, Randall. 1986. *Weberian Sociological Theory*. Cambridge: Cambridge University Press.

Collins, Randall. 1997. "An Asian Route to Capitalism: Religious Economy and the Origins of Self-Transforming Growth in Japan." *American Sociological Review* 62:843–65.

Comninel, George C. 1987. *Rethinking the French Revolution: Marxism and the Revisionist Challenge*. London: Verso.

Cooper, J. P. 1967. "The Social Distribution of Land and Men in England, 1436–1700." *Economic History Review*, 2d ser., 20.3:419–40.

Cooper. J. P. 1978. "In Search of Agrarian Capitalism." *Past and Present* 80:20–65.

Cornwall, Julian. 1977. *The Revolt of the Peasantry, 1549*. London: Routledge and Kegan Paul.

Corrigan, Philip, and Derek Sayer. 1985. *The Great Arch: English State Formation as Cultural Revolution*. Oxford: Blackwell.

Croix, Alain. 1981. *La Bretagne aux 16ème et 17ème siècles*. Paris: Maloine.

Cross, Claire. 1977. "Churchmen and the Royal Supremacy." Pp. 15–34 in *Church and Society in England: Henry VIII to James I*, edited by Felicity Heal and Rosemary O'Day. Hamden, Conn.: Archon.

Darnton, Robert. 1991. "History of Reading." Pp. 140–67 in *New Perspectives on Historical Writing*, edited by Peter Burke. University Park: Pennsylvania State University Press.

Davies, C. S. L. 1968. "The Pilgrimage of Grace Reconsidered." in *Past and Present*, no. 41.

Davis, Ralph. 1973. *The Rise of the Atlantic Economies*. London: Weidenfield and Nicholson.

Delamare, Nicolas. 1722. *Traité de la police*. 2 vols. Paris: Michel Brunet.

De la Ronciere, Charles. 1968. "Indirect Taxes or 'Gabelles' at Florence in the Fourteenth Century: The Evolution of Tariffs and Problems of Collection." Pp. 140–92 in Rubinstein 1968.

Delumeau, Jean. [1971] 1977. *Catholicism between Luther and Voltaire*. London: Burns and Oates.

Dent, Cynthia. 1975. "Changes in the Episcopal Structure of the Church of France in the Seventeenth Century as an Aspect of Bourbon State-Building." *Bulletin of the Institute of Historical Research* 48:214–29.

Dent, Julian. 1967. "An Aspect of the Crisis of the Seventeenth Century: The Collapse of the Financial Administration of the French Monarchy (1653–61). *Economic History Review*, 2d ser., 20:241–56.

De Roover, Raymond. 1963. *The Rise and Decline of the Medici Bank, 1397–1494.* New York: Norton.

Dessert, Daniel. 1984. *Argent, pouvoir et société au Grand Siècle.* Paris: Fayard.

De Vries, Jan. 1974. *The Dutch Rural Economy in the Golden Age, 1500–1700.* New Haven: Yale University Press.

De Vries, Jan. 1984. *European Urbanization, 1500–1800.* Cambridge: Harvard University Press.

Dewald, Jonathan. 1980. *The Formation of a Provincial Nobility: The Magistrates of the Parlement of Rouen, 1499–1610.* Princeton: Princeton University Press.

Dhotel, Jean-Claude. 1967. *Les Origins du catéchisme moderne.* Paris: Aubier.

Diaz, Furio. 1978. "Recent Studies on Medician Tuscany." *Journal of Italian History* 1, no. 1: 95–110.

Dibble, Vernon K. 1965. "The Organization of Traditional Authority: English County Government, 1558 to 1640." Pp. 879–909 in *Handbook of Organizations,* edited by James G. March. Chicago: Rand McNally.

Dietz, Frederick. 1964. *English Public Finance, 1558–1641.* London: Frank Cass.

Dobb, Maurice. 1947. *Studies in the Development of Capitalism.* New York: International Publishers.

Dontenwill, Serge. 1973. *Une Seigeneurie sous l'ancien régime: L'Etole en Bionnais de 16ème au 18ème siècle (1575–1778).* Roanne: Horvath.

Dowd, Douglas. 1961. "The Economic Expansion of Lombardy, 1300–1500: A Study in Political Stimuli to Economic Change." *Journal of Economic History* 21.2:143–60.

Downing, Brian. 1992. *The Military Revolution and Political Change.* Princeton: Princeton University Press.

DuBoulay, F. R. H. 1965. "Who Were Farming the English Demesne at the End of the Middle Ages?" *Economic History Review,* 2d ser., 17.3:443–55.

DuBoulay, F. R. H. 1966. *The Lordship of Canterbury.* London: Nelson.

DuBoulay, F. R. H. 1970. *An Age of Ambition: English Society in the Late Middle Ages.* London: Nelson.

Duby, Georges. 1978. *Atlas historique Larousse.* Paris: Librarie Larousse.

Dupâquier, Jacques. 1979. *La Population française aux XVIIe et XVIIIe siècles.* Paris: Presses Universitaires de France.

Dupâquier, Jacques, and Jean Jacquart. 1973. "Les Rapports sociaux dans les campagnes françaises au 18e siècle: Quelques examples." Pp. 167–79 in *Ordres et Classes,* edited by Daniel Roche. Paris: Mouton.

Dupla, Tomas. 1985. "State Intervention in Agriculture: Capitalist Accumulation and Class Struggle in Franco's Spain." Ph.D. diss., University of Wisconsin, Madison.

Durand, Yves. 1971. *Les fermiers généraux au XVIIIe siècle.* Paris: PUF.

Dyer, Christopher. 1980. *Lords and Peasants in a Changing Society: The Estates of the Bishopric of Worchester, 680–1540.* Cambridge: Cambridge University Press.

Edgerton, Samuel Y., Jr. 1985. *Pictures and Punishment: Art and Criminal Prosecution during the Florentine Renaissance.* Ithaca: Cornell University Press.

Eisenstadt, S. N. 1963. *The Political Systems of Empires: The Rise and Fall of Historical Bureaucratic Societies.* New York: Free Press.

Eisenstadt, S. N. 1968. "Introduction." Pp. ix–lvi in *Max Weber on Charisma and Institution Building.* Chicago: University of Chicago Press.

Eisenstadt, S. N. 1996. *Japanese Civilization: A Comparative View.* Chicago: University of Chicago Press.

Eisenstein, Elizabeth L. 1969. "The Advent of Printing and the Problem of the Renaissance." In *Past and Present,* 45:19–89.

Emigh, Rebecca Jean. 1996. "Loans and Livestock: Comparing Landlords' and Tenants' Declarations from the Catasto of 1427." *Journal of European Economic History* 25.3:705–23.

Emigh, Rebecca Jean. 1997. "The Spread of Sharecropping in Tuscany: The Political Economy of Transaction Costs." *American Sociological Review* 62:423–42.

Emmanuelli, François-Xavier. 1981. *Un Mythe de l'absolutisme bourgonien: L'Intendance, du milieu du 17ème siecle à la fin du 18ème siècle.* Aix: Université de Provence.

Emmison, F. G. 1931. "Poor Relief Accounts of Two Rural Parishes in Bedfordshire, 1563–1598." *Economic History Review* 3.1:102–10.

Engels, Frederick. [1884] 1972. *The Origin of the Family, Private Property, and the State.* New York International Publishers.

Epstein. S. R. 1991. "Cities, Regions, and the Late Medieval Crisis: Sicily and Tuscany Compared." *Past and Present,* no. 130:3–5.

Epstein, Steven A. 1996. *Genoa and the Genoese, 958–1528.* Chapel Hill: University of North Carolina Press.

Ertman, Thomas. 1997. *Birth of the Leviathan: Building States and Regimes in Medieval and Early Modern Europe.* Cambridge: Cambridge University Press.

Everitt, Alan. 1966. *The Community of Kent and the Great Rebellion.* Leicester: Leicester University Press.

Everitt, Alan. 1969. *Change in the Provinces.* Leicester University, Department of English Local History Occasional Paper, 2d ser., no. 1. Leicester: Leicester University Press.

Farmer, David L. 1991. "Prices and Wages, 1350–1500," Pp. 431–525 in *The Agrarian History of England and Wales.* vol. 3, *1348–1500,* edited by Edward Miller. Cambridge: Cambridge University Press.

Fenoaltea, Stefano. 1988. "Transaction Costs, Whig History, and the Common Fields." *Politics and Society* 16.2–3:171–240.

Ferté, Jeanne. 1962. *La Vie religieuse dans les campagnes parisiennes, 1622–1695.* Paris: Vrin.

Finch, Mary. 1956. *The Wealth of Five Northamptonshire Families, 1540–1640.* Northampton: Northamptonshire Record Society.

Fitch, Nancy. 1978. "The Demographic and Economic Effects of Seventeenth Century Wars: The Case of Bourbonnais, France." *Review* 2.2:181–206.

Fletcher, Anthony. 1968. *Tudor Rebellions.* London: Longman.

Fletcher, Anthony. 1975. *A County Community in Peace and War: Sussex, 1600–1660.* London: Longmans.

Fletcher, Anthony. 1983. "National and Local Awareness in the County Communities." Pp. 151–74 in *Before the English Civil War,* edited by Howard Tomlinger. London: Macmillan.

Fliche, Augustin. 1957. "L'État Toulousian." Pp. 71–99 in Lot and Fawtier 1957.

Flynn, Dennis O. 1982. "Fiscal Crisis and the Decline of Spain (Castille)." *Journal of Economic History* 42.1:139–47.

Forster, G. C. F. 1973. *The East Riding Justices of the Peace in the Seventeenth Century.* East Yorkshire Historical Society, no. 30.

Fourquin, Guy. [1970] 1976. *Lordship and Feudalism in the Middle Ages.* London: George Allen and Unwin.

Fox, Edward Whiting. 1971. *History in Geographic Perspective: The Other France.* New York: Norton.

Fréville, Henri. 1953. *L'Intendance de Bretagne (1689–1790).* Rennes: Plihon.

Friedrichs, Christopher R. 1981. "The Swiss and German City-States. Pp. 109–42 in *The City-State in Five Cultures,* edited by Robert Griffeth and Carol G. Thomas. Santa Barbara Calif.: ABC-Clio.

Fryde, E. B., and M. M. Fryde. 1965. "Public Credit, with Special Reference to North-Western Europe." Pp. 430–553 in *The Cambridge Economic History of Europe,* Vol. 3, *Economic*

Organization and Policies in the Middle Ages, edited by M. M. Postan, E. E. Rich, and Edward Miller. Cambridge: Cambridge University Press.

Fryde, E. B., and M. M. Fryde. 1991. "Peasant Rebellion and Peasant Discontents," Pp. 744–819 in *The Agrarian History of England and Wales.* Vol. 3, *1348–1500,* edited by Edward Miller. Cambridge: Cambridge University Press.

Fulbrook, Mary. 1983. *Piety and Politics.* Cambridge: Cambridge University Press.

Gascon, Richard. 1971. *Grand Commerce et vie urbaine au 16ème Siècle: Lyon et ses marchands.* Paris: SEVPEN.

Geertz, Clifford. 1963. *Agrarian Involution: The Processes of Ecological Change in Indonesia.* Berkeley and Los Angeles: University of California Press.

Geyl, Pieter. 1958. *The Revolt of the Netherlands (1559–1609).* New York: Barnes and Noble.

Gibbons, Jane. 1959. "Chiddingstone Early Poor Law Accounts." *Archaeologia Cantiana* 73: 193–95.

Ginzberg. Carlo. 1976. "High and Low." *Past and Present* 73:28–41.

Giordanengo, Gérard. 1988. *Le Droit féodal dans les pays de droite écrite: L'Exemple de la Provence et du Dauphiné, XIIe–début XIVe siècle.* Rome: École Française de Rome.

Given, James. 1990. *State and Society in Medieval Europe: Gwynedd and Languedoc under Outside Rule.* Ithaca: Cornell University Press.

Given-Wilson, Chris. 1987. *The English Nobility in the Late Middle Ages: The Fourteenth Century Political Community.* London: Routledge and Kegan Paul.

Gleason, John Howes. 1969. *The Justices of Peace in England, 1558–1640.* Oxford: Clarendon Press.

Goldstone, Jack. 1988. "Regional Ecology and Agrarian Development in England and France." *Politics and Society* 16.2–3:287–334.

Goldstone, Jack. 1991. *Revolution and Rebellion in the Early Modern World.* Berkeley: University of California Press.

Goldthwaite, Richard A. 1968. *Private Wealth in Renaissance Florence: A Study of Four Families.* Princeton: Princeton University Press.

Goldthwaite, Richard A. 1980. *The Building of Renaissance Florence: An Economic and Social History.* Baltimore: Johns Hopkins University Press.

Goldthwaite, Richard A. 1987. "The Medici Bank and the World of Florentine Capitalism." *Past and Present* 114:3–31.

Goodman, Jordan. 1981. "Financing Pre-Modern European Industry: An Example from Florence, 1580–1660." *Journal of European Economic History* 10:415–35.

Gorski, Philip. 1998. "Review of Thomas Ertman's *Birth of the Leviathan.*" *Contemporary Sociology* 27.2:186–88.

Goubert, Pierre. 1969–73. *L'Ancien Régime.* 2 vols. Paris: A. Colin.

Gray, Charles Montgomery. 1963. *Copyhold, Equity, and the Common Law.* Cambridge: Harvard University Press.

Groethuysen, Bernard. 1968. *The Bourgeois: Catholicism vs. Capitalism in Eighteenth-Century France.* New York: Holt, Rinehart and Winston.

Gruder, Vivian R. 1968. *The Royal Provincial Intendants.* Ithaca: Cornell University Press.

Gruter, Edouard. 1977. *La Naissance d'un grand vignoble.* Lyon: Presses Universitaires de Lyon.

Guéry, Louis. 1981. *Mouchamps: Histoire d'une paroisse vendeenne.* Fontenay-le-Compte: Luissaud.

Guichard, Pierre. 1966. "D'une société repliée a une société ouverte: l'évolution socio-économique de la région d'andance, de la fin du 17e siècle, a la révolution." Pp. 141–218 in Pierre Leon, ed. *Structures Économiques et Problèmes Sociaux du Monde Rural dans la France du Sud-est.* Paris: CNRS.

Habakkuk, H. J. 1958. "The Market for Monastic Property, 1539–1603." *Economic History Review* 10.3:362–80.

Hale, J. R. 1977. *Florence and the Medici.* New York: Thames and Hudson.

Hall, John A. 1985. *Powers and Liberties.* Oxford: Blackwell.

Hall, John A. 1988. "States and Societies: The Miracle in Comparative Perspective." Pp. 20–38 in *Europe and the Rise of Capitalism,* edited by Jean Beachler et al. Oxford: Blackwell.

Hamilton, Earl J. 1969. "The Political Economy of France in the Time of John Law." *History of Political Economy* 1:123–49.

Hampson, E. M. 1934. *The Treatment of Poverty in Cambridgeshire, 1597–1834.* Cambridge: Cambridge University Press.

Harding, Robert R. 1978. *Anatomy of a Power Elite: The Provincial Governors of Early Modern France.* New Haven: Yale University Press.

Harrison, Scott M. 1981. *The Pilgrimage of Grace in the Lake Counties, 1536–7.* London: Royal Historical Society.

Harsin, Paul 1970. "La Finance et l'état jusqu'au systeme de Law (1660–1726)." Pp. 267–321 in *Histoire économique et sociale de la France,* vol. 2, *Desderniers temp de l'âge seigneurral aux préludes de l'âge industriel (1660–1789),* edited by Ernest Labrousse et al. Paris: PUF.

Harvey, P. D. A. 1965. *A Medieval Oxfordshire Village: Cuxham, 1240 to 1400.* Oxford: Oxford University Press.

Hatcher, John. 1970. *Rural Economy and Society in the Duchy of Cornwall, 1300–1500.* Cambridge: Cambridge University Press.

Hayden, J. Michael. 1974. *France and the Estates General of 1614.* Cambridge: Cambridge University Press.

Heal, Felicity. 1976. "Clerical Tax Collection under the Tudors." Pp. 97–122 in *Continuity and Change,* edited by Rosemary O'Day and Felicity Heal. Leicester: Leicester University Press.

Heal, Felicity. 1977. "Economic Problems of the Clergy." Pp. 99–118 in *Church and Society in England: Henry VIII to James I,* edited by Heal and Rosemary O'Day. Hamden, Conn.: Archon.

Hechter, Michael, and William Brustein. 1980. "Regional Modes of Production and Patterns of State Formation in Europe." *American Journal of Sociology* 85:1061–94.

Heers, Jacques. [1974] 1977. *Family Clans in the Middle Ages: A Study of Political and Social Structures in Urban Areas.* Amsterdam: North Holland Publishing.

Herlihy, David. 1957. "Treasure Hoards in the Italian Economy, 960–1139." *Economic History Review* 10:1–14.

Herlihy, David. 1961. "Church Property on the European Continent, 701–1200." *Speculum* 36: 81–105.

Herlihy, David. 1967. *Medieval and Renaissance Pistoia: The Social History of an Italian Town, 1200–1430.* New Haven: Yale University Press.

Hill, Christopher. 1963. *Economic Problems of the Church.* Oxford: Oxford University Press.

Hill, Christopher. 1972. *The World Turned Upside Down.* London: Penguin.

Hilton, Rodney. 1947. *The Economic Development of Some Leicestershire Estates in the Fourteenth and Fifteenth Centuries.* London: Oxford University Press.

Hilton, Rodney, 1975. *The English Peasantry in the Later Middle Ages.* Oxford: Clarendon Press.

Hilton, Rodney, ed. [1976] 1978. *The Transition From Feudalism to Capitalism.* London: Verso.

Hintze, Otto. [1902–6] 1975. *The Historical Essays of Otto Hintze,* edited by Felix Gilbert. New York: Oxford University Press.

Hirst, Derek. 1975. *The Representative of the People? Voters and Voting in England under the Early Stuarts.* New York: Cambridge University Press.

Hobsbawm, Eric. [1954] 1965. "The Crisis of the Seventeenth Century." Pp. 5–58 in *Crisis in Europe, 1560–1660,* edited by Trevor Aston. London: Routledge and Kegan Paul.

Hoffman, Philip T. 1984. *Church and Community in the Diocese of Lyon, 1500–1789.* New Haven: Yale University Press.

Hoffman, Philip T. 1994. "Early Modern France, 1450–1700." Pp. 226–52 in *Fiscal Crises, Liberty, and Representative Government, 1450–1789,* edited by Hoffman and Kathryn Norberg. Stanford: Stanford University Press.

Hoffman, Philip T. 1996. *Growth in a Traditional Society: The French Countryside, 1450–1815.* Princeton: Princeton University Press.

Hohenberg, Paul M., and Lynn Hollen Lees. 1985. *The Making of Urban Europe, 1000–1950.* Cambridge: Harvard University Press.

Holmes, George. 1986. *Florence, Rome, and the Origins of the Renaissance.* Oxford: Clarendon.

Holton, R. J. 1983. "Max Weber, 'Rational Capitalism,' and Reniassance Italy: A Critique of Cohen." *American Journal of Sociology* 89:166–87.

Holton, R. J. 1986. *Cities, Capitalism, and Civilization.* London: Allen and Unwin.

Hopcroft, Rosemary. 1997. "Rural Organization and Receptivity to Protestantism in Sixteenth-Century Europe." *Journal for the Scientific Study of Religion* 36.2:158–81.

Hoshino, Hidetoshi. 1983. "The Rise of the Florentine Woolen Industry in the Fourteenth Century." Pp. 184–204 in *Cloth and Clothing in Medieval Europe,* edited by N. B. Harte and K. G. Ponting. London: Heinemann.

Houlbrooke, Ralph. 1976. "The Decline of Ecclesiastical Jurisdiction under the Tudors." Pp. 239–57 in *Continuity and Change,* edited by Rosemary O'Day and Felicity Heal. Leicester: Leicester University Press.

Houlbrooke, Ralph. 1979. *Church Courts and the People during the English Reformation, 1520–1570.* Oxford: Oxford University Press.

Housley, Norman. 1982. The Italian Crusades: *The Papal-Angevin Alliance and the Crusades against Christian Lay Powers, 1254–1343.* Oxford: Clarenden.

Howell, Cicely. 1975. "The Economic and Social Conditions of the Peasantry in South East Leicestershire, A.D. 1300–1700." *Journal of Peasant Studies* 2.4:468–82.

Howell, Cicely. 1983. *Land, Family, and Inheritance in Transition: Kibworth Harcourt, 1280–1700.* Cambridge: Cambridge University Press.

Hoyle, R. W. 1990. "Tenure and the Land Market in Early Modern England; or, A Late Contribution to the Brenner Debate." *Economic History Review,* 2d ser., 43.1:1–20.

Hughes, Ann. 1987. Pp. 87–113 in *Politics, Society and Civil War in Warwickshire, 1620–1660.* Cambridge: Cambridge University Press.

Hunt, William. 1983. *The Puritan Moment.* Cambridge: Harvard University Press.

Hurt, John J. 1976. "Les Offices au Parlement de Bretagne sous le règne de Louis XIV: Aspects financiers." *Revue d'historie moderne et contemporaine* 23:3–31.

Hyde, J. K. 1973. *Society and Politics in Medieval Italy: The Evolution of Civil Life, 1000–1350.* London: Macmillan.

Ikegami, Eiko. 1995. *The Taming of the Samurai: Honorific Individualism and the Making of Modern Japan.* Cambridge: Harvard University Press.

Israel, Jonathan. 1989. *Dutch Primacy in World Trade, 1585–1740.* Oxford: Clarendon Press.

Israel, Jonathan. 1995. *The Dutch Republic: Its Rise, Greatness, and Fall, 1477–1806.* Oxford: Clarendon.

Jacquart, Jean. 1974. "French Agriculture in the Seventeenth Century." Pp. 165–84 in *Essays in European Economic History 1500–1800,* edited by Peter Earle. Oxford: Oxford University Press.

Jacquart, Jean. 1975. "Immobilisme et catastrophes, 1560–1690." Pp. 175–353 in *Histoire de la France rurale.* Vol. 2, *1340–1789,* edited by Emmanuel Le Roy Ladurie. Paris: Seuil.

James, M. E. 1970. "Obediance and Dissent in Henrician England: The Lincolnshire Rebellion of 1536." *Past and Present,* 48:3–78.

James, M. E. 1974. *Family, Lineage, and Civil Society: A Study of Society, Politics, and Mentality in the Durham Region, 1500–1640.* Oxford: Oxford University Press.

Johnson, Arthur H. 1909. *The Disappearance of the Small Landowner.* Oxford: Clarendon.

Jones, P. J. 1965. "Communes and Despots: The City State in Late-Medieval Italy." *Transactions of the Royal Historical Society,* 5th ser., 15:71–95.

Jones, P. J. 1966. "Medieval Agrarian Society in Its Prime: Italy." Pp. 340–430 in *The Cambridge Economic History of Europe,* vol. 1, edited by M. M. Postan. Cambridge: Cambridge University Press.

Jones, P. J. 1968. "From Manor to Mezzadria: A Tuscan Case-Study in the Medieval Origins of Modern Agrarian Society." Pp. 193–239 in Rubinstein 1968.

Jones, P. M. 1988. *The Peasantry in the French Revolution.* New York: Cambridge University Press.

Joutard, Philippe. 1976. *Les Camisards.* Paris: Gallimard.

Julia, Dominique. 1973. "La Reforme posttridentine en France d'après les procès-verbaux de visites pastorales: Ordre et résistances." Pp. 311–415 in *La Società religiousa nell'età moderna.* Naples: Guida Editori.

Julia, Dominique. 1974. "La Religion: Histoire religieuse." Pp. 137–67 in *Faire d'histoire, nouvelles approaches.* Paris: Gallimard.

Kaeuper, Richard W. 1988. *War, Justice, and Public Order: England and France in the Later Middle Ages.* Oxford: Clarenden.

Kamen, Henry. 1969. *The War of Spanish Succession in Spain, 1700–1715.* Bloomington: Indiana University Press.

Kamen, Henry. 1978. "The Decline of Spain: A Historical Myth." *Past and Present,* 81:24–50.

Kamen, Henry. 1980. *Spain in the Later Seventeenth Century, 1665–1700.* London: Longman.

Kamen, Henry. 1991. *Spain 1469–1714: A Society of Conflict.* London: Longman.

Kelly, J. Thomas. 1977. *Thorns on the Tudor Rose.* Jackson: Mississippi University Press.

Kent, Dale. 1978. *The Rise of the Medici: Faction in Florence 1426–1434.* Oxford: Oxford University Press.

Kerridge, Eric. 1969. *Agrarian Problems of the Sixteenth Century.* London: Allen and Unwin.

Kettering, Sharon. 1978. *Judicial Politics and Urban Revolt in Seventeenth-Century France: The Parlement of Aix, 1629–1659.* Princeton: Princeton University Press.

Kettering, Sharon. 1982. "The Causes of the Judicial Frondes." *Canadian Journal of History* 17:275–306.

Kettering, Sharon. 1986. *Patrons, Brokers, and Clients in Seventeenth-Century France.* New York: Oxford University Press.

Kosminsky, E. A. 1956. *Studies in the Agrarian History of England in the Thirteenth Century.* Oxford: Basil Blackwell.

Kriedte, Peter. 1983. *Peasants, Landlords and Merchant Capitalists: Europe and the World Economy, 1500–1800.* Cambridge: Cambridge University Press.

Kriedte, P., Medick, H., Schlumbohm, J. 1981. *Industrialization before Industrialization.* Cambridge: Cambridge University Press.

Kurzman, Charles. 1996. "Structural Opportunity and Perceived Opportunity in Social Movement Theory: The Iranian Revolution of 1979." *American Sociological Review* 61:153–70.

Kussmal, Ann. 1981. *Servants in Husbandry in Early Modern England.* New York: Cambridge University Press.

Lachmann, Richard. 1987. *From Manor to Market: Structural Change in England, 1536–1640.* Madison: University of Wisconsin Press.

Lachmann, Richard. 1989. "Origins of Capitalism in Western Europe: Economic and Political Aspects." *Annual Review of Sociology* 15: 47–72.

Land, Stephen K. 1977. *Kett's Rebellion: The Norfolk Rising of 1549.* Ipswich: Rowman and Littlefield.

Lane, Frederic C. 1958. "Economic Consequences of Organized Violence." *Journal of Economic History* 18:401–17.

Lane, Frederic C. 1973. *Venice, a Maritime Republic.* Baltimore: Johns Hopkins University Press.

Lane, Frederic C. 1979. *Profits from Power.* Albany: SUNY Press.

Larner, Christina. 1984. *Witchcraft and Religion.* Oxford: Basil Blackwell.

Larner, John. 1980. *Italy in the Age of Dante and Petrarch, 1216–1380.* London: Longman.

Laurent, Jeanne. 1972. *Un Monde rural en Bretangne au 15e siècle: La Quevaise.* Paris: SEVPEN.

Lefebvre, Georges. [1932] 1973. *The Great Fear of 1789.* New York: Vintage.

Lefebvre, Georges. [1947] 1967. *The Coming of the French Revolution.* Princeton: Princeton University Press.

Lemarchand, Guy. 1990. "Troubles populaires au XVIIIe siècle et conscience de classe: Une Préface à la Révolution française." *Annales historiques de la Révolution française* 279:32–48.

Léon, Pierre. 1966. *Structures Économiques et Problèmes Sociaux du Monde Rural dans la France du Sud-est.* Paris: CNRS.

Léon, Pierre. 1970. "L'Elan industriel et commercial." Pp. 499–528 in *Histoire économique et sociale de la France.* Vol. 2, *Des derniers temps de l'âge seigneurial aux préludes de l'âge industriel (1660–1789),* edited by E. Labrousse et al. Paris: Presses Universitaires de France.

Leonard, E. M. 1965. *The Early History of English Poor Relief.* London: Frank Cass.

Le Roy Ladurie, Emmanuel. 1966. *Les Paysans de Languedoc.* Paris.

Le Roy Ladurie, Emmanuel. 1975. "Un 'Modèle septentrional': Les Campagnes parisiennes (XVIe–XVIIe siècles)." *Annales: E.S.C.* 30.6:1397–413.

Le Roy Ladurie, Emmanuel. [1977] 1987. *The French Peasantry, 1450–1660.* Aldershot, England: Scolar.

Le Roy Ladurie, Emmanuel, ed. 1978. "A Reply to Professor Brenner." *Past and Present* 97: 55–59.

Levi, Margaret. 1988. *Of Rule and Revenue.* Berkeley and Los Angeles: University of California Press.

Levy, Marion J. Jr. 1966. *Modernization and the Structure of Societies.* Princeton: Princeton University Press.

Levy, Marion J. Jr. 1972. *Modernization: Latecomers and Survivors.* New York: Basic.

Litchfield, R. Burr. 1986. *Emergence of a Bureaucracy: The Florentine Patricians, 1530–1790.* Princeton: Princeton University Press.

Loirette, Francois. 1975. "The Defense of the Allodium in Seventeenth-Century Agenais:" An Episode in Local Resistance to Encroaching Royal Power." Pp. 180–97 in *State and Society in Seventeenth-Century France,* edited by Raymond F. Kierstead. New York: Franklin Watts.

Lopez, Robert S. 1979. "The Dawn of Medieval Banking." Pp. 1–23 in *The Dawn of Modern Banking,* edited by Center for Medieval and Renaissance Studies, UCLA. New Haven: Yale University Press.

Lopez, Robert S., and Harry Miskimin. 1962. "The Economic Depression of the Renaissance." *Economic History Review,* 2d ser., 14:408–26.

Lot, Ferdinand, and Robert Fawtier, eds. 1957. *Histoire des institutions françaises au moyen âge.* Vol. 1, *Institutions seigneuriales.* Paris: Presses Universitaires de France.

Lublinskaya, A. D. 1968. *French Absolutism: The Crucial Phase, 1620–1629.* Cambridge: Cambridge University Press.

Lukacs, George. [1922] 1971. *History and Class Consciousness: Studies in Marxist Dialectics.* Cambridge: MIT Press.

Luthy, Herbert. 1959. *La Banque protestante en France de la révocation de l'édit de Nantes à la Révolution.* 2 vols. Paris: SEVPEN.

Luzzatto, Gino. 1961. *An Economic History of Italy.* London: Routledge and Kegan Paul.

Lynch, John. 1989. *Bourbon Spain, 1700–1808.* Oxford: Blackwell.

Lynch, John. 1991. *Spain 1516–1598: From Nation State to World Empire.* Oxford: Blackwell.

Lynch, John. 1992. *The Hispanic World in Crisis and Change, 1598–1700.* Oxford: Blackwell.

MacCulloch, Diarmaid. 1977. *Power, Privilege and the Country Community: Politics in Elizabethan Suffolk.* Ph.D. diss., Cambridge University.

MacCulloch, Diarmaid. 1979. "Kett's Rebellion in Context." *Past and Present* 184:36–59.

Macfarlane, Alan. 1970. *Witchcraft in Tudor and Stuart England.* New York: Harper & Row.

Macfarlane, Alan. 1978. *The Origins of English Individualism.* New York: Cambridge University Press.

Major, J. Russell. 1964. "The Crown and the Aristocracy in Renaissance France." *American Historical Review* 69:631–45.

Major, J. Russell. 1966. "Henry IV and Guyenne: A Study Concerning Origins of French Absolutism." *French Historical Studies* 4:363–383.

Major, J. Russell. 1980. *Representative Government in Early Modern France.* New Haven: Yale University Press.

Mandrou, Robert. 1965. *Classes et luttes des classes en France au debut du XVIIe siècle.* Messina: Anna.

Mandrou, Robert. 1968. *Magistrats et sorciers en France au XVIIe siecle: Une analyse de psychologie historique.* Paris: Plon.

Mandrou, Robert. 1979. *From Humanism to Science, 1480 to 1700.* Hassocks, England: Harvester Press.

Mandrou, Robert. 1980. *Magistrats et sorciers en France au XVIIe siècle: Une Analyse de psychologie historique.* Paris: Seuil.

Mann, Michael. 1980. "State and Society, 1130–1815: An Analysis of English State Finances." Pp. 165–208 in *Political Power and Social Theory,* vol. 1, edited by Maurice Zeitlin. Greenwich, Conn.: JAI Press.

Mann, Michael. 1986. *The Sources of Social Power.* Vol. 1. Cambridge: Cambridge University Press.

Manning, Brian. 1975. "The Peasantry and the English Revolution. *Journal of Peasant Studies* 2.2:133–58.

Manning, Roger B. 1974. "Patterns of Violence in Early Tudor Enclosure Riots." *Albion* 6.2: 120–33.

Marion, Marcel. 1974. *Les Impôts directs sous l'ancien régime.* Geneva: Slatkine.

Markoff, John. 1996. *The Abolition of Feudalism: Peasants, Lords, and Legislators in the French Revolution.* University Park: Pennsylvania State University Press.

Martin, John E. 1983. *Feudalism to Capitalism: Peasant and Landlord in English Agrarian Development.* London: Macmillan.

Martines, Lauro. 1963. *The Social World of the Florentine Humanists, 1390–1460.* Princeton: Princeton University Press.

Martines, Lauro. 1979. *Power and Imagination: City-States in Renaissance Italy.* New York: Vintage.

Marx, Karl. [1846] 1970. *The German Ideology.* New York: International Publishers.

Marx, Karl. [1852] 1963. *The Eighteenth Brumaire of Louis Bonaparte.* New York. International Publishers.

Marx, Karl. [1857–58] 1973. *Grundrisse.* New York: International Publishers.

Marx, Karl. [1859] 1970. *A Contribution to the Critique of Political Economy.* New York: International Publishers.

Marx, Karl. [1867–94] 1967. *Capital,* vols. 1–3. New York: International Publishers.

Matthews, George Tennyson. 1958. *The Royal General Farms in Eighteenth-Century France.* New York: Columbia University Press.

Mauro, Frederic. 1990. "Merchant Communities, 1350–1750." Pp. 255–86 in *The Rise of Merchant Empires: Long-Distance Trade in the Early Modern World, 1350–1750,* edited by James D. Tracy. Cambridge: Cambridge University Press.

Mauzaize, Jean. 1978. *Le Rôle et l'action des Capucins de la Province de Paris dans la France religieuse du 17e siècle.* Lille: Université de Lille III.

Mazzaoui, Maureen Fennell. 1981. *The Italian Cotton Industry in the Later Middle Ages, 1100–1600.* Cambridge: Cambridge University Press.

Mazzei, Rita. 1979. "The Decline of the City Economies of Central and Northern Italy in the Seventeenth Century." *Journal of Italian History* 2.2:197–208.

McArdle, Frank. 1978. *Altopascio: A Study in Tuscan Rural Society, 1587–1784.* Cambridge: Cambridge University Press.

McLennan, Gregor. 1981. *Marxism and the Methodologies of History.* London: Verso.

McNeil, William H. 1974. *Venice: The Hinge of Europe, 1081–1797.* Chicago: University of Chicago Press.

Meyer, Jean. 1966. *La Noblesse bretonne au 18e siècle.* Paris: SEVPEN.

Mireaux, Emile. 1958. *Une Province française au temps du grand roi: La Brie.* Paris: Hachette.

Mohlo, Anthony. 1968. "The Florentine Oligarchy and the *Balìe* of the Late Trecento." *Speculum* 43:23–51.

Mohlo, Anthony. 1971. *Florentine Public Finances in the Early Renaissance, 1400–1433.* Cambridge: Harvard University Press.

Moir, Esther. 1969. *The Justice of the Peace.* Hammondsworth: Penguin.

Moote, A. Lloyd. 1971. *The Revolt of the Judges: The Parlement of Paris and the Fronde, 1643–1652.* Princeton: Princeton University Press.

Morineau, Michel. 1977. "La Conjuncture ou les cernes de la croissance." In *Histoire économique et sociale de la France,* vol. 1, pt. 2, edited Fernand Braudel et al. Paris: PUF.

Morrill, J. S. 1974. *Cheshire 1630–1660: County Government and Society during the English Revolution.* Oxford: Oxford University Press.

Morrill, J. S. 1978. "French Absolutism as Limited Monarchy." *Historical Journal* 21:961–72.

Morrill, John. 1993. *The Nature of the English Revolution.* London: Longman.

Moulder, Frances V. 1977. *Japan, China, and the Modern World Economy: Toward a Reinterpretation of East Asian Development, ca. 1600 to ca. 1918.* Cambridge: Cambridge University Press.

Mousnier, Roland. 1959. "Recherches sur les syndicats d'officiers pendant la Fronde: Tresoriers generaux de France et élus dans la révolution." *XVIIème siècle* 42–43:76–117.

Mousnier, Roland. 1970. *La Plume, la faucille et le marteau: Institutions et sociète en France.* Paris: Presses Universitaires de France.

Mousnier, Roland. 1979. *The Institutions of France under the Absolute Monarchy, 1598–1789.* Vol. 1. Chicago: University of Chicago Press.

Mousnier, Roland. 1984. *The Institutions of France under Absolute Monarchy, 1598–1789.* Vol. 2. Chicago: University of Chicago Press.

Muchembled, Robert. 1978. *Culture populaire et culture des élites dans la France moderne.* Paris: Flammarion.

Muchembled, Robert. 1979. *La Sorcière au village.* Paris: Gallimard.

Muchembled, Robert. 1981. *Les Derniers Bûchers: Un Village de Flandre et ses sorcières sous Louis XIV.* Paris: Ramsay.

Muchembled, Robert. 1987. *Sorcières: Justice et société aux 16e et 17e siècles.* Paris: Éditions Imago.

Mukhia, Harbans. 1981. "Was There Feudalism in Indian History?" *Journal of Peasant Studies* 8:273–310.

Muto, Giovanni. 1995. "The Spanish System: Centre and Periphery." Pp. 231–59 in *Economic Systems and State Finance,* edited by Richard Bonney. Oxford: Clarendon.

Nabholz, Hans. 1944. "Medieval Agrarian Society in Transition." Pp. 493–561 in *Cambridge Economic History of Europe,* vol. 1, edited by J. H. Clapham and Eileen Power. Cambridge: Cambridge University Press.

Najemy, John M. 1979. "Guild Republicanism in Trecento Florence: The Successes and Ultimate Failure of Corporate Politics." *American Historical Review* 84.1:53–71.

Najemy, John M. 1982. *Corporatism and Consensus in Florentine Electoral Politics, 1280–1400.* Chapel Hill: University of North Carolina Press.

Neveux, Hugues. 1975. "Déclin et reprise: La Fluctuation biseculaire." Pp. 11–173 in *Histoire de la France rurale.* Vol. 2, *L'âge classique des paysans, 1340–1789,* edited by Emmanuel Le Roy Ladurie. Paris: Seuil.

Neveux, Hugues. 1980. *Vie et declin d'une structure économique: Les grains du Cambresis.* Paris: Ecole des Hautes Etudes en Sciences Sociales.

Obelkevich, James. 1976. *Religion and Rural Society: South Lindsay, 1825–1875.* Oxford: Clarendon Press.

O'Day, Rosemary. 1977. "Ecclesiastical Patronage: Who Controlled the Church?" Pp. 137–55 in *Church and Society in England: Henry VIII to James I,* edited by Felicity Heal and Rosemary O'Day. Hamden, Conn.: Archon.

Oxley, Geoffrey. 1974. *Poor Relief in England and Wales.* Newton Abbot: David and Charles.

Ozouf, Mona. 1988. *Festivals and the French Revolution.* Cambridge: Harvard University Press.

Padgett, John F., and Christopher K. Ansell. 1993. "Robust Action and the Rise of the Medici, 1400–1434. *American Journal of Sociology* 98.6:1259–319.

Parker, David. 1978. "The Huguenots in Seventeenth-Century France." Pp. 11–30 in *Minorities in History,* edited by A. C. Hepburn. London: Edward Arnold.

Parker, David. 1980. *La Rochelle and the French Monarchy: Conflict and Order in Seventeenth-Century France.* London: Royal Historical Society.

Parker, David. 1983. *The Making of French Absolutism.* London: Edward Arnold.

Parsons, Talcott. 1937. *The Structure of Social Action.* New York: McGraw Hill.

Parsons, Talcott. 1966. *Societies: Evolutionary and Comparative Perspectives.* Englewood Cliffs, N.J.: Prentice-Hall.

Parsons, Talcott. 1971. *The System of Modern Societies.* Englewood Cliffs, N.J.: Prentice-Hall.

Partner, Peter. 1965. "Florence and the Papacy, 1300–1375." Pp. 76–121 in *Europe in the Late Middle Ages,* edited by John Rigby Hale et al. Evanston: Northwestern University Press.

Partner, Peter. 1968. "Florence and the Papacy in the Earlier Fifteenth Century." Pp. 381–402 in Rubinstein 1968.

Partner, Peter. 1972. *The Lands of St. Peter.* London: Methuen.

Payne, Stanley G. 1973. *A History of Spain and Portugal.* 2 vols. Madison: University of Wisconsin Press.

Peret, Jacques. 1976. *Seigneurs et seigneuries en Gatine Poitevine.* Poitiers: La Société des Antiquaires de l'Ouest.

Peronnet, Michel C. 1977. *Les Évêques de l'ancienne France.* Lille: Université de Lille.

Pérouas, Louis. 1964. *Le Diocèse de la Rochelle de 1648 à 1724.* Paris: SEVPEN.

Phillips, Carla Rahn. 1979. *Ciudad Real, 1500–1750: Growth, Crisis, and Readjustment in the Spanish Economy.* Cambridge: Harvard University Press.

Phytillis, Jacques. 1965. "Une Commission extraordinaire du Conseil du Roi: La Commission des Postes et Messageries et le Contentieux des Messageries." Pp. 1–153 in *Question administratives dans la France du XVIIIe siècle.* Paris: PUF.

Pirenne, Henri. 1925. *Medieval Cities: Their Origins and the Revival of Trade.* Princeton: Princeton University Press.

Pollack, Frederick, and Frederic Maitland. 1968. *The History of English Law before the Time of Edward I.* Cambridge: Cambridge University Press.

Porchnev, Boris. 1963. *Les Soulèvements populaires en France de 1623 à 1648.* Paris: Flammarion.

Porter, Bruce. 1994. *War and the Rise of the State: The Military Foundations of Modern Politics.* New York: Free Press.

Postan, M. M. 1954. "The *Famulus.*" *Economic History Review,* supp. no. 2.

Postan, M. M. 1966. "Medieval Agrarian Society in Its Prime: England." Pp. 548–632 in *The Cambridge Economic History of Europe,* 2d ed., vol. 1, edited by M. M. Postan. Cambridge: Cambridge University Press.

Postan, M. M. 1972. *The Medieval Economy and Society.* Harmondsworth: Penguin.

Poulantzas, Nicos. 1975. *Political Power and Social Classes.* London: Verso.

Prestwich, Michael. 1979. "Italian Merchants in Late Thirteenth- and Early Fourteenth-Century England." Pp. 77–104 in *The Dawn of Modern Banking,* edited by Michael Prestwich. New Haven: Yale University Press.

Previté-Orton, C. W. 1964. "The Italian Cities till c.1200." Pp. 208–41 in *The Cambridge Medieval History,* vol. 5, edited by J. R. Tanner et al. Cambridge: Cambridge University Press.

Pullan, Brian. 1972. *A History of Early Renaissance Italy: From the Mid-Thirteenth to the Mid-Fifteenth Century.* New York: St. Martin's.

Putnam, Bertha Haven. 1908. *The Enforcement of the Statute of Laborers during the First Decade after the Black Death, 1349–1359.* Columbia University Studies in History, Economics, and Public Law. New York: Columbia University Press.

Raftis, J. Ambrose. 1957. *The Estates of Ramsey Abbey.* Studies and Texts no. 3. Toronto: Pontifical Institute of Medieval Studies.

Raftis, J. Ambrose. 1964. *Tenure and Mobility.* Studies and Texts no. 8. Toronto: Pontifical Institute of Medieval Studies.

Razi, Zvi. 1981. "Family, Land, and the Village Community in Later Medieval England." *Past and Present,* 93:3–36.

Reeves, Eileen. 1997. *Painting the Heavens: Art and Science in the Age of Galileoq.* Princeton: Princeton University Press.

Renouard, Yves. 1941. *Les Relations des papes d'Avignon et des compagnies commerciales et bancaires de 1316 à 1378.* Paris: Boccard.

Renouard, Yves. 1949. *Les Hommes d'affaires italiens du Moyen Âge.* Paris: Colin.

Robin, Regine. 1970. *La Société française en 1789: Semur-en-Auxois.* Paris: Plon.

Romano, Ruggiero. 1964. "Encore la crise de 1619–22. *Annales E.S.C.* 19:31–37.

Rozman, Gilbert. 1976. *Urban Networks in Russia 1750–1800 and Premodern Periodization.* Princeton: Princeton University Press.

Rubinstein, Nicolai, ed. 1968. *Florentine Studies: Politics and Society in Renaissance Florence.* Evanston: Northwestern University Press.

Russell, Conrad. 1979. *Parliaments and English Politics, 1621–1629.* Oxford: Clarendon Press.

Russell, Josiah Cox. 1972. *Medieval Regions and Their Cities.* Bloomington: Indiana University Press.

Sabatier, Gérard. 1966. "Une économie et une société en crise: l'emblavès au début du 18eme siecle: 1695–1735." Pp. 331–40 in *Structures Économiques et Problèmes Sociaux du Monde Rural dans la France du Sud-est,* edited by Pierre Léon. Paris: CNRS.

Saint-Jacob, Pierre de. 1960. *Paysans de la Bourgogne du Nord au derniere siècle de l'Ancien Régime.* Paris: Société des Belles Lettres.

Salmon, J. H. M. 1975. *Society in Crisis: France in the Sixteenth Century.* London: Ernest Benn.

Savine, Alexander. 1909. *English Monasteries on the Eve of Dissolution.* Oxford Studies in Social and Legal History, vol. 1. Oxford: Oxford University Press.

Sayer, Derek. 1992. "A Notable Administration: English State Formation and the Rise of Capitalism." *American Journal of Sociology* 97:1382–1415.

Scarie, Geoffrey. 1987. *Witchcraft and Magic in Sixteenth and Seventeenth Century Europe.* Houndmills: Macmillan.

Scarisbrick, J. J. 1960. "Clerical Taxation in England, 1485 to 1547." *Journal of Ecclesiastical History* 11:41–54.

Schaer, Andre. 1966. *Le Clergé paroissial catholique en Haute Alsace sous l'ancien régime, 1648–1789.* Paris: Sirey.

Schevill, Ferdinand. 1961. *Medieval and Renaissance Florence.* New York: Harper & Row.

Schofield, R. S. 1963. "Parliamentary Lay Taxation, 1485–1547." Ph.d. diss., Claire College, Cambridge University.

Scott, James C. 1976. *The Moral Economy of the Peasant: Rebellion and Subsistence in Southeast Asia.* New Haven: Yale University Press.

Scott, James C. 1985. *Weapons of the Weak: Everyday Forms of Peasant Resistance.* New Haven: Yale University Press.

Sella, Domenico. 1974. "The Two Faces of the Lombard Economy in the Seventeenth Century." Pp. 10–14 in *Transition du féodalisme à la sociéte industrielle: L'Échec de l'Italie de la Renaissance et des Pays-Bas du XVIIe siècle,* edited by Paul M. Hochenberg and Frederick Krantz. Montreal: Centre Interuniversitaire d'Etudes Européennes.

Shanin, Teodor. 1972. *The Awkward Class.* Oxford: Clarendon.

Sharp, Buchanan. 1980. *In Contempt of All Authority: Rural Artisans and Riot in the West of England, 1586–1660.* Berkeley and Los Angeles: University of California Press

Shennan, J. H. 1969. *Government and Society in France, 1461–1661.* London: George Allen & Unwin.

Skinner, G. William. 1977. *The City in Late Imperial China.* Palo Alto: Stanford University Press.

Skocpol, Theda. 1979. *States and Social Revolutions: A Comparative Analysis of France, Russia, and China.* Cambridge: Cambridge University Press.

Slack, Paul. 1974. "Vagrants and Vagrancy in England, 1598–1664." *Economic History Review* 27:360–79.

Smith, A. Hassell. 1974. *County and Court: Government and Politics in Norfolk, 1558–1603.* Oxford: Clarendon Press.

Smith, Alan G. R. 1984. *The Emergence of a Nation State: The Commonwealth of England, 1529–1660.* London: Longman.

Soboul, Albert. [1962] 1974. *The French Revolution, 1787–1789.* 2 vols. London: New Left Books.

Somers, Margaret. 1993. "Citizenship and the Place of the Public Sphere: Law, Community, and Political Culture in the Transition to Democracy." *American Sociological Review* 58:587–620.

Sommerville, C. John. 1992. *The Secularization of Early Modern England.* New York: Oxford.

Spini, Giorgio. 1979. "The Medici Principality and the Organization of the States of Europe in the Sixteenth Century." *Journal of Italian History* 2.3:420–47.

Spufford, Margaret. 1974. *Contrasting Communities.* Cambridge: Cambridge University Press.

Stephens, J. N. 1983. *The Fall of the Florentine Republic, 1512–1530.* Oxford: Clarendon Press.

Stinchcombe, Arthur L. 1965. "Social Structure and Organizations" Pp. 142–93 in *Handbook of Organizations,* edited by James G. March. Chicago: Rand McNally.

Stone, Lawrence. 1965. *The Crisis of the Aristocracy.* Oxford: Clarendon Press.

Stone, Lawrence. 1970. "The English Revolution." Pp. 55–108 in *Preconditions of Revolution in Early Modern Europe,* edited by Robert Foster and Jack P. Greene. Baltimore: Johns Hopkins University Press.

Stone, Lawrence. 1979. "Goodbye to Nearly All That." *New York Review of Books* 26:40–41.

Stone, Lawrence, and Jeanne C. Fawtier Stone. 1984. *An Open Elite? 1540–1830.* Oxford: Oxford University Press.

Swales, T. H. 1969. "The Redistribution of Monastic Lands in Norfolk at the Dissolution." *Norfolk Archaeology* 34:14–44.

Swanson, Robert N. 1989. *Church and Society in Late Medieval England.* Oxford: Blackwell.

Sweezy, Paul. [1950] 1976. "A Critique." Pp. 33–56 in Rodney Hilton, ed., *The Transition From Feudalism to Capitalism* (London: Verso).

Swidler, Ann. 1986. "Culture in Action: Symbols and Strategies." *American Sociological Review* 51:273–86.

Szelenyi, Sonia, Ivan Szelenyi, and Imre Kovach. 1995. "The Making of the Hungarian Postcommunist Elite: Circulation in Politics, Reproduction in the Economy." *Theory and Society* 24.5:697–722.

Tackett, Timothy. 1977. *Priest and Parish in Eighteenth-Century France: A Social and Political Study of the Cures in a Diocese of Dauphine.* Princeton: Princeton University Press.

Tackett, Timothy. 1979. "L'Histoire sociale du clerge diocesian dans la France au 18e siècle." *Revue d'historie moderne et contemporaine* 26:198–234.

Tait, Richard. 1977. "The King's Lieutenants in Guyenne, 1580–1610: A Study in the Relations between the Crown and the Great Nobility." Ph.D. diss., Oxford University.

Tate, W. E. 1967. *The English Village Community and the Enclosure Movement.* London: Gollancz.

Tawney, R. H. 1912. *The Agrarian Problem in the Sixteenth Century.* New York: Franklin.

Tawney, R. H. 1954. "The Rise of the Gentry: A Postscript." *Economic History Review* 7.1: 91–97.

Taylor, Mary Margaret. 1950. "The Justices of Assize." Pp. 219–58 in *The English Government at Work, 1327–1336,* vol. 3, edited by James Willard, William Morris, and William Dunham Jr. Cambridge, Mass: Medieval Academy of America.

Temple, Nora. 1966. "The Control and Exploitation of French Towns during the Ancien Régime." *History* 51:21–32.

TePaske, John J., and Herbert S. Klein. 1981. "The Seventeenth-Century Crisis in New Spain: Myth or Reality?" *Past and Present* 90:116–35.

T'Hart, Marjolein C. 1993. *The Making of a Bourgeois State: War, Politics, and Finance during the Dutch Revolt.* Manchester: Manchester University Press.

Thiers, Jean-Baptiste. [1679] 1741. *Traite des superstitions.* 4 volumes. Paris: Compagnie des Libraries.

Thirsk, Joan. 1957. *English Peasant Farming: The Agrarian History of Lincolnshire from Tudor to Recent Times.* London: Rouledge and Kegan Paul.

Thirsk, Joan, ed. 1967. *The Agrarian History of England and Wales IV, 1500–1640.* Cambridge: Cambridge University Press.

Thirsk, Joan, ed. 1984. *The Agrarian History of England and Wales.* Vol. 5, pt. 1, *1640–1750: Regional Farming Systems.* Cambridge: Cambridge University Press.

Thomas, Keith. 1971. *Religion and the Decline of Magic.* New York: Scribner's.

Thompson, I. A. A. 1976. *War and Government in Habsburg Spain, 1560–1620.* London: Athlone Press.

Thompson, I. A. A. 1982. "Crown and Cortes in Castile, 1590–1665." *Parliaments, Estates, and Representation* 2.1:29–45.

Thompson, I. A. A. 1984. "The End of the Cortes of Castile." *Parliaments, Estates, and Representation* 4.2:125–33.

Thompson, I. A. A. 1994. "Castile: Polity, Fiscality, and Fiscal Crisis." Pp. 140–80 in *Fiscal Crises, Liberty, and Representative Government, 1450–1789,* edited by Philip T. Hoffman and Kathryn Norborg. Stanford: Stanford University Press.

Tilly, Charles. 1975. *The Formation of National States in Western Europe.* Princeton: Princeton University Press.

Tilly, Charles. 1978. *From Mobilization to Revolution.* Reading, Mass.: Addison-Wesley.

Tilly, Charles. 1981. *As Sociology Meets History.* New York: Academic Press.

Tilly, Charles. 1985. "War Making and State Making as Organized Crime." Pp. 169–91 in *Bringing the State Back In,* edited by Peter Evans, Theda Skocpol, Dietrich Rucksmeyer. Cambridge: Cambridge University Press.

Tilly, Charles. 1986. *The Contentious French.* Cambridge: Harvard University Press.

Tilly, Charles. 1987. "Cities and States in Europe, 1000–1800." Center for Studies of Social Change, working paper no. 51.

Tilly, Charles. 1990. *Coercion, Capital, and European States, A.D. 990–1990.* Cambridge, Mass: Basil Blackwell.

Tilly, Charles. 1993. *European Revolutions, 1492–1992.* Oxford: Blackwell.

Traugott, Mark. 1995. "Capital Cities and Revolution." *Social Science History* 19.1:147–68.

Treasure, Geoffrey. 1967. *Seventeenth-Century France.* New York: Anchor.

Trevor-Roper, H. R. [1959] 1965. "The General Crisis of the Seventeenth Century." Pp. 59–95 in Aston 1965.

Trexler, Richard C. 1974. *The Spiritual Power: Republican Florence under Interdict.* London: Brill.

Trexler, Richard C. 1980. *Public Life in Renaissance Florence.* New York: Academic.

van der Wee, Herman. 1993. *The Low Countries in the Early Modern World.* Aldershot, England: Variorum.

van Hoboken, W. J. 1960. "The Dutch West India Company: The Political Background of Its Rise and Decline." Pp. 41–61 in *Britain and the Netherlands,* edited by J. S. Bromley and E. H. Kossmann. London: Chatto and Windus.

van Houtte, J. A. 1977. *An Economic History of the Low Countries.* New York: St. Martin's.

Varine, Beatrice. 1979. *Villages de la vallee de l'Ouche aux 17e et 18e siècles.* Roanne: Horvath.

Veenendaal, Jr., Augustus J. 1994. "Fiscal Crises and Constitutional Freedom in the Netherlands." Pp. 96–139 in *Fiscal Crises, Liberty, and Representative Government, 1450–1789,* edited by Philip T. Hoffman and Kathryn Norborg. Stanford: Stanford University Press.

Venard, Marc. 1957. *Bourgeois et paysans au 17e siècle.* Paris: SEVPEN.

Vilar, Pierre. 1962. *La Catalogne dans l'Espagne moderne: Recherches sur les fondements économiques des structures nationales.* 2 vols. Paris: SEVPEN.

Villain, Jean. 1952. *Le Recouvrement des impôts directs sous l'Ancien Régime.* Paris: Marcel Rivière et Cie.

Vovelle, Michel. 1993. *La Découverte de la politique: Géopolitique de la Révolution française.* Paris: Editions de la Découverte.

Vovelle, Michel, and Daniel Roche. 1965. "Bourgeois, Rentiers, and Property Owners: Elements for Defining a Social Category at the End of the Eighteenth Century." Pp. 25–46 in *New Perspectives on the French Revolution,* edited by Jeffrey Kaplow. New York: John Wiley and Sons.

Waley, Daniel. 1969. *The Italian City-Republics*. London: Weidenfield and Nicholson.

Wallerstein, Immanuel. 1974–89. *The Modern World System*. Volumes 1–3. New York: Academic Press.

Walzer, Michael 1965. *Revolution of the Saints*. Cambridge: Harvard University Press.

Weber, Max. 1889. *Zur Geschichte der Hendelsgesellschaften im Mittelalter* (On the history of medieval trading companies). Stuttgart: Enke.

Weber, Max. [1916] 1964. *The Religion of China: Confucianism and Taoism*. New York: Free Press.

Weber, Max. [1916–17] 1958. *The Protestant Ethic and the Spirit of Capitalism*. New York: Scribner's.

Weber, Max. [1916–17] 1958. *The Religion of India: The Sociology of Hinduism and Buddhism*. New York: Free Press.

Weber, Max. [1922] 1978. *Economy and Society*. Edited by Guenther Roth and Claus Wittich. Berkeley and Los Angeles: University of California Press.

Weber, Max. [1923] 1961. *General Economic History*. New York: Collier.

Westrich, Sal Alexander. 1972. *The Ormee of Bordeaux*. Baltimore: Johns Hopkins University Press.

White, Harrison C. 1970. *Chains of Opportunity: System Models of Mobility in Organizations*. Cambridge: Harvard University Press.

White, Harrison C. 1992. *Identity and Control: A Structural Theory of Social Action*. Princeton: Princeton University Press.

White, Lynn, Jr. 1962. *Medieval Technology and Social Change*. London: Oxford University Press.

Wickham, Chris. 1981. *Early Medieval Italy: Central Power and Local Society, 400–1000*. Totowa, N.J.: Barnes and Noble.

Willcox, William. 1946. *Glouchestershire: A Study in Local Government, 1590–1640*. New Haven: Yale University Press.

Wittfogel, Karl August. 1957. *Oriental Despotism: A Comparative Study of Total Power*. New Haven: Yale University Press.

Wood, James B. 1980. *The Nobility of the Election of Bayeux, 1463–1666: Continuity through Change*. Princeton: Princeton University Press.

Woodward, G. W. O. 1966. *The Dissolution of the Monasteries*. London: Blandford.

Woolf, S. J. 1968. "Venice and the Terraferma: Problems of the Change from Commercial to Landed Activity." Pp. 175–200 in *Crisis and Change in the Venetian Economy,* edited by Brian Pullan. London: Methuen.

Wordie, J. R. 1983. "The Chronology of English Enclosure, 1500–1914." *Economic History Review,* 2d ser., 26.4:483–505.

Wrightson, Keith, and David Levine. 1979. *Poverty and Piety in an English Village: Terling, 1525–1700*. New York: Academic Press.

Wrigley, E. A., and R. S. Schofield. 1981. *The Population History of England, 1541–1871*. Cambridge: Harvard University Press.

Wuthnow, Robert. 1985. "State Structures and Ideological Outcomes." *American Sociological Review* 50:799–821.

Wuthnow, Robert. 1989. *Communities of Discourse*. Cambridge: Harvard University Press.

Yelling, J. A. 1977. *Common Field and Enclosure in England, 1450–1850*. New Haven: Archon.

Zeitlin, Maurice, and Richard Earl Ratcliff. 1988. *Landlords and Capitalists: The Dominant Class of Chile*. Princeton: Princeton University Press.

Index